101 Principles for Positive Guidance with Young Children

Creating Responsive Teachers

Katharine C. Kersey
Old Dominion University

Marie L. Masterson
Dominican University

Boston   Columbus   Indianapolis   New York   San Francisco   Upper Saddle River
Amsterdam   Cape Town   Dubai   London   Madrid   Milan   Munich   Paris   Montréal   Toronto
Delhi   Mexico City   São Paulo   Sydney   Hong Kong   Seoul   Singapore   Taipei   Tokyo

Vice President and Editorial Director: Jeffery W. Johnston
Senior Acquisitions Editor: Julie Peters
Editorial Assistant: Andrea Hall
Vice President, Director of Marketing: Margaret Waples
Senior Marketing Manager: Christopher D. Barry
Senior Managing Editor: Pamela D. Bennett
Senior Project Manager: Linda Hillis Bayma
Senior Operations Supervisor: Matt Ottenweller
Senior Art Director: Diane C. Lorenzo
Cover Designer: Jennifer Hart
Cover Art: Emily Setran
Full-Service Project Management: Electronic Publishing Services Inc.
Composition: Jouve
Printer/Binder: Edwards Brothers Malloy
Cover Printer: Edwards Brothers Malloy
Text Font: Times

Photo Credits: Jack.Q/Shutterstock.com, p. xiii; Marie Masterson, pp. xvi, 3, 5, 34, 44, 70, 79, 104, 120, 131, 148, 157, 164, 182, 191, 242, 277, 305; Monkey Business Images/Shutterstock.com, pp. 14, 97, 137; © matka_Wariatka/Fotolia LLC, p. 52; iofoto/Shutterstock.com, p. 73; Losevsky Pavel/Shutterstock.com, p. 92; Anatoliy Samara/Shutterstock.com, p. 198; sonya etchison/Shutterstock.com, p. 212; © darko64/Fotolia LLC, p. 219; ZouZou/Shutterstock.com, p. 226; © Bryan Creely/Fotolia LLC, p. 249; © reflektastudios/ Fotolia LLC, p. 255; rSnapshotPhotos/Shutterstock.com, p. 274; © micromonkey/Fotolia LLC, p. 280.

Credits and acknowledgments for material borrowed from other sources and reproduced, with permission, in this textbook appear on the appropriate page within the text.

Every effort has been made to provide accurate and current Internet information in this book. However, the Internet and information posted on it are constantly changing, so it is inevitable that some of the Internet addresses listed in this textbook will change.

Library of Congress Cataloging-in-Publication Data
Kersey, Katharine C.
    101 principles for positive guidance with young children: creating responsive teachers / Katharine C. Kersey, Old Dominion University, Marie L. Masterson, Dominican University.
        p. cm.
    ISBN-13: 978-0-13-265821-8
    ISBN-10: 0-13-265821-6
    1. Early childhood education—United States. 2. Effective teaching—United States.   I. Masterson, Marie L.
II. Title.   III. Title: One hundred one principles for positive guidance with young children.   IV. Title: One hundred and one principles for positive guidance with young children.
    LB1139.25.K47 2013
    372.21—dc23
                                                                                        2012008791

10 9 8 7 6 5 4 3 2 1

ISBN 10:   0-13-265821-6
ISBN 13: 978-0-13-265821-8

*To all who are making the world a more just
and better place for children*

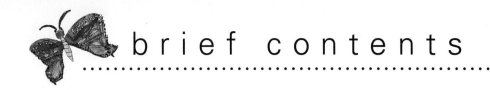

brief contents

contents

chapter 3   Showing Respect

chapter 4   Giving Nurturance

introduction

The Purpose of This Book

The purpose of *101 Principles for Positive Guidance with Young Children: Creating Responsive Teachers* is to address the beliefs, knowledge, skills, and practices of positive, relational behavior guidance and responsive teaching. The 101 principles provide a comprehensive framework to support you in becoming a more responsive teacher, more tuned in to the developmental needs of the children in your care, and more thoughtful and intentional in your interactions with children and families. The principles present effective strategies to build social–emotional competence and nurture a positive classroom community.

The readings, reflections, and activities will help you become more aware of your beliefs about guiding children. The principles encourage insight and self-awareness about the ways your words, actions, and responses influence the responses of children and others with whom you interact. They place an important emphasis on the elements a teacher brings to interactions with children that can influence the nature and direction of the outcome. The result is that children as well as adults learn new ways to connect and become healthy people capable of living with kindness and respect.

The philosophy of relational respect will help you build children's powerhouse tools of authentic connection, enriched language, prosocial skills, and self-regulation. The techniques equip children to become self-directed, consequently requiring less time for you to attend to behavior issues and more time to accomplish the real goal—empowering children with the skills they need to thrive and helping them to take control of their own lives in meaningful and productive ways.

You will develop the beliefs, knowledge, dispositions, and skills to guide children effectively without the use of punitive practices. You will do this by teaching children healthy ways to get along and make choices with results that are satisfying and successful. You will learn to create a safe and caring community where you can maintain positive connections with children, nurture resilience, and empower change.

The 101 principles will help you to:

- Create a positive classroom climate
- Gain effective strategies for behavior redirection
- Provide authentic relational skills for connection and modeling
- Create cooperation without power or coercion
- Diffuse power struggles and confrontation
- Build motivation and self-regulation
- Support healthy decision-making
- Empower choice and autonomy
- Equip children with resilience and independence
- Help children create positive outcomes for themselves and others

Audience for This Book

The text provides explicit training in positive guidance and responsive teaching for schools and organizations that serve children from birth to age 8 in early care and education, pre-K, and early elementary settings. The content and materials integrate practical language, interactive activities, and a learner-centered approach that aligns with professional standards for best practice. All who advocate on behalf of ethical and responsible early childhood practices and support high-quality early experiences for young children will find this to be a useful training and mentoring resource.

Professional Development

101 Principles for Positive Guidance with Young Children introduces a comprehensive approach to professional development for school-based in-service programs. The format provides a standardized training system for mentors and coaches in Quality Rating and Improvement Systems. In addition, it provides a self-contained, collaborative professional development model for directors and teachers in center-based early education and home-based centers. Centers, schools, and individuals will find this to be an effective, appealing, and engaging self-study guide for teachers and early care providers.

 Higher Education

The content, materials, activities, research, and practical applications make this resource an excellent text for behavior guidance and classroom management courses in higher education. It is effective for adult education, alternative certification programs, and alternative delivery (online) and collaborative course designs. The format is useful as a manual for on-site teacher candidate field experiences, practicum placements, and student teacher training seminars in teacher licensure and state certification programs. Trainers, teachers, and mentors will find this training model to be a significant resource in connecting research to practice.

101 Principles for Positive Guidance with Young Children: *Creating Responsive Teachers* supports the following training objectives:

- Establishes a foundational relational framework for responsive practice
- Provides explicit instruction in effective skills for positive behavior redirection
- Presents comprehensive skills to build children's social and emotional competence
- Supports active observation to increase sensitivity and cultural competence

- Introduces the metacognitive processes involved in behavioral guidance decisions
- Integrates meaningful reflection to practice, including sensitive evaluation of teachers' feelings, thoughts, and personal experiences
- Promotes intentional and proactive ways to build and enhance prosocial skills
- Focuses on active and immediate use of strategies to build positive classroom climate
- Introduces materials for ongoing professional learning and growth
- Provides a practical roadmap for teachers to promote optimal school outcomes for all children

Themes and Features

101 Principles for Positive Guidance with Young Children: Creating Responsive Teachers provides research-based solutions for behavior guidance that are built on authentic, respectful relationships with strategies to build prosocial skills needed to achieve school success. The techniques, skills, and strategies are supported individually and collectively by well-established theoretical, educational, psychological, neuroscience, and social research that substantiates the benefit of responsive, positive teacher–child interactions, with particular efficacy for children at risk.

The benefits of positive responsive practices for children are impressive. When responsive, sensitive interactions are consistent in the classroom, social and learning outcomes are higher (Burchinal, Howes, & Pianta, 2008; Haynes, 2008). Children gain positive social and emotional skills and focus more on learning (Barnett, 2008; Downer & Pianta, 2006; Pianta, Howes, Burchinal, Byrant, Clifford, & Early, 2005). Positive interactions increase needed skills for learning such as listening, following directions, self-control, planning, and cooperation (McClelland, Acock, & Morrison, 2006; Pianta

& Hadden, 2008). Positive, caring teachers have influence on all areas of children's development.

Although consistently rated among the most important teaching skills by general as well as special education teachers, classroom management is the area for which classroom teachers report feeling least prepared (Skiba, Michael, & Nardo, 2000). Dealing with behavior issues can be a constant struggle for teachers and causes a great deal of stress (Cornell & Mayer, 2010). Eighty percent of teachers report that problem behavior negatively affects their job (Fox & Smith, 2007). Disruptive behavior continues to be the most pressing challenge in early childhood classrooms (Schultz, Richardson, Barber, & Wilcox, 2011).

Sixty percent of children enter school with the cognitive skills needed to be successful, yet only 40% have the social–emotional skills needed to succeed in kindergarten (Yates, Ostrosky, Cheatham, Fettig, Shaffer, & Milagros Santos, 2008). Over one-third of kindergarten teachers feel their students have difficulty following directions and working independently (Rimm-Kaufman, Pianta, & Cox, 2000; Schulting, Malone, & Dodge, 2005). Teachers report disruptive behavior as a significant reason for leaving the profession (Ingersoll & Smith, 2003). Addressing challenging behavior remains the most often requested training priority for early childhood educators (Hemmeter, 2006).

Teachers often lack effective skills and continue to be frustrated with challenging behaviors (Fox & Smith, 2007; Oliver & Reschly, 2007). "If a teacher cannot effectively manage children's behavior, she is likely to spend a disproportionate amount of time addressing misbehavior, thereby limiting her opportunities to teach" (Pianta & Hadden, 2008, p. 21). Coaching for quality improvement needs to provide explicit goals, a focus on skill building, and development of a formal guide for training. Most quality improvement programs will benefit from a manual or set of materials to guide coaches in daily practice (Smith, Schneider, & Kreader, 2010).

High-quality responsive teaching is a critical factor in school achievement. The quality of teacher–child interactions is essential to children's optimal learning and school adjustment (Mashburn, 2008; Mashburn & Pianta, 2006). Yet quality varies widely and is not correlated with the level of a teacher's training (Haynes, 2008; Horn, Cheng, & Joseph, 2004). The quality of teacher–child interactions can vary significantly, even within one school (Pianta et al., 2005; Pinderhuges, Dodge, Bates, Pettit, & Zelli, 2000; Schultz, 2008).

Most important, children who most need responsive, supportive interactions are least likely to receive them (Haynes, 2009; Schultz, 2008). Reports from the Children's Defense Fund and U.S. Department of Education Office of Civil Rights show that disproportionate discipline of minority students is consistent across state and national sources. "Teacher training in appropriate and culturally competent methods of classroom management is likely then to be the most pressing need in addressing racial disparities in school discipline" (Skiba, Michael, & Nardo, 2000, p. 17).

The strategies provided in this book are recommended for use by the American Academy of Pediatrics in their SCAN Newsletter (2005). The content and the principles also meet the recommendations of National Association for the Education of Young Children's Code of Ethical Conduct (NAEYC, 2010a) and standards of professional practice in early childhood programs (see Table 1). The 101 principles support NAEYC Standard 1: Relationships: The model "promotes positive relationships among all children and adults to encourage each child's sense of individual worth and belonging as part of a community and to foster each child's ability to contribute as a responsible community member" (NAEYC, 2010b).

The principles are supported by more than 30 years of testing in the early childhood teacher preparation, parent education programs, and preschool classrooms at Old Dominion University, a nationally recognized program for effective early childhood teacher training. They serve as the foundation of the Child Study Center laboratory school and the Old Dominion University Director's Institute. The 101 principles for positive guidance are used in Virginia, Illinois, and around the country as a training model for Head Start programs, licensed homecare centers, private and military centers, and technical assistance and training organizations. They are a professional development resource in public, private, and charter schools. They provide the guidance model for Parent Chats, a family behavior support program sponsored

Table 1 Objectives and Standards Addressed in This Text

Positive Strategy Objectives	Professional Standards/Criteria		
	NAEYC Accreditation Criterion for Programs	Council for Exceptional Children (CEC) Standards for Professional Practice	Special Education Early Childhood Specialists in Early Childhood Special Education/Early Intervention (Birth to Eight)
Counter bias and discrimination: Treat all children with equal respect	1.B 1.B.09 1.B.10	Management of Behavior 1, 4 Instructional Responsibilities 5	ACC5K3
Show consistency and ethical behavior	1.B.03	Instructional Responsibilities 2	ACC5S1
Encourage cooperation	1.F.02	—	AEC2S8
Support emotional regulation	1.F.01	—	—
Build self-discipline	1.B.15	—	ACC5S3
Scaffold competence	2.B.04	Instructional Responsibilities 3	ACC1S2 ACC5S2
Engage motivation	1.E.03	—	ACC2S3 AEC2S1
Provide individual-appropriate practices	1.B.07	—	ACC2K6 ACC2S4
Develop engaged learners	2.B.01	—	ACC5S5
Reinforce prosocial skills	1.D.05	—	—
Establish positive relationships between school and home	1.A 7.C.01	—	AEC2S3

by Smart Beginnings in Virginia. They are used as the foundation for community college, 4-year college, and university development and behavior guidance courses, and are promoted by child and family service organizations to support respectful interactions with children.

Data from The Director's Institute, a research partnership between Old Dominion University and licensed childcare centers, revealed changes in underlying attitudes about teacher–child interactions and greater understanding of the need for positive, responsive interaction practices in center classrooms. Over five years, 115 directors representing more than 2,474 teachers showed significant changes in guidance approaches after being trained in the 101 principles. Outcomes from this study showed statistically significant positive changes in attitudes, competencies, and positive guidance practices of participating directors; increased skills and interaction strategies for social, academic, and literacy development for children at risk; increased leadership and training competencies with staff, teachers, and parents; and overall effectiveness of the training, coaching, and group facilitation model.

Additional training with 232 Head Start teachers in an urban setting revealed that effective positive redirection strategies were the most critical and needed skill to address challenging behavior. Three to one, the most frustrating behavior issue reported was related to the need to instill cooperation and compliance. After training in the 101 principles, teachers felt they had gained the necessary competence to successfully affect behavior outcomes through effective positive guidance.

Ongoing research in 34 urban at-risk preschools and in cross-cultural study indicated that training using the 101s materials, reflection activities, and classroom implementation changed teacher and parent attitudes and resulted in better school adjustment and behavior outcomes (Masterson, 2008; Masterson, Kersey, & Myran, 2012; Thanasetkorn, 2009). As a result of training, significant changes were found in the quality of teacher interactions, teacher attitudes,

and children's prosocial responding, including increased positive climate, teacher sensitivity, regard for student perspectives, and behavior management, as measured by the Classroom Assessment Scoring System (CLASS) (Pianta, LaParo, & Hamre, 2009). Trained teachers were more likely to use positive behavior redirection and responsive social–emotional support than those who were not trained.

Teachers using the 101 principles were more likely to spend extra time with children, validate their feelings and experiences, show respect in their interactions, give more important responsibility, connect in more personal conversation, and show responsiveness to children's needs. The trained teachers were more likely to provide physical affirmation and direct focus. In addition, the use of the principles was highly positively correlated with children's prosocial skills, including self-control, compliance, emotional regulation, attention, helping, asking, sharing, and cooperation. Teachers' use of the skills and strategies significantly influenced their belief that children could be cooperative when non-punitive approaches were used.

Features in This Book

101 Principles for Positive Guidance with Young Children is a "take along" text that can be used actively on a daily basis in classroom teaching. The scope and sequence provides an easy-to-use format for instructors, mentors, trainers, teachers, and students. The text, activities, reflections, and applications encourage vital engagement and participation. The unique interactive format gives skills, tips, and strategies to revitalize classroom practices, inspire cooperation, and increase the quality of teacher–child interactions in early childhood classrooms.

Each chapter provides a practical format with explicit strategies to support children's developing social and emotional competence. Real-life descriptions of the classroom make the principles come to life with experiences and challenges you will recognize. The content and materials are

crease engagement for children birth to age 3 as well as children ages 3 to 8. Activities and applications are given throughout each section to mobilize transitions, enhance environments and materials, and extend the principles into action. You will find hundreds of easy-to-implement strategies for promoting learning while enhancing social and emotional competence.

Using the Principles in Your Classroom. Explicit reflection and activation strategies encourage vital implementation of the principles as you learn skills for behavior guidance, apply new knowledge, and transform the quality of interactions in your classroom. Each concise section is designed to be read, used, and applied to create meaningful change. The direct connection between knowledge, reflection, and application is coupled with detailed classroom tips to enhance responsive teaching practice.

aligned with national professional standards and include case studies, role-play, and guided practice. Each section provides explicit language modeling sequences and real-life scenarios for practice and analysis. Adaptations are provided to help you use the suggested activities and to apply the principles to the unique setting and needs of your school community.

Think About It! Each section is designed with in-depth reflection questions to link the concepts presented to active personal engagement and understanding. New material is followed immediately by reflection and application to behavior guidance practices. As soon as a new strategy is presented, you can take action, consider your own experiences, and implement the skills and activities.

Strategies for Children Birth to Age 8. Each chapter provides extended tips and activities to enrich language interactions, incorporate music and movement, promote multimodal learning, and in-

Research on the Run. These helpful sections have been developed to provide an intensive synthesis of facts and resources that support the content of the text. Readers who might otherwise skim over research references can now learn to articulate important research foundations and benefit from the condensed highlight of critical issues. For those who desire further study, Research on the Run sections can act as a catalyst for further growth in understanding of child behavior guidance practices. Professional organizations, web resources, research reports, and institutes are highlighted to provide an innovative guide to further research and professional learning.

Teacher Tips. Communication from teachers who use the principles provides a rich application of the ideas introduced in each chapter. These stories and conversational vignettes show the use of the principles and are designed to inspire ongoing motivation to try new strategies and to illustrate the impact of new practices on children's responses.

Getting Positive Results Using the Principles in Action.   Each chapter provides the opportunity for you to examine what happened that led up to your interactions with children, to describe how you used a principle, and to reflect on how the interaction was resolved. This application, action, and reflection sequence is integrally related to the effective process of responsive behavior guidance.

Study Guide.   Chapter study guides support interactive class discussion, extensions, and activities for those who will use this text in higher education or community college settings. For those who will use the guide for professional development, suggestions are provided for leading training and discussion. Book studies are a common feature in many school districts and early education settings, as they are recognized for the collaborative benefit of learning. The resources provided at the end of each chapter facilitate discussion, organize activities, and promote higher level learning and reflection, as well as activate the use of principles into practice.

Classroom Resources.   Developmental milestones related to each chapter topic, along with the principles (provided in the English and Spanish appendixes) can be used on a daily basis in the classroom and shared with families and colleagues. This book is designed to be used "on the job" in the classroom through application materials, handouts, and activities.

Alignment with Professional Standards.   The principles, text, resources, reflections, and activities of this book align with the NAEYC Early Childhood Standards for Professional Preparation Programs, Council for Exceptional Children (CEC) standards, *Special Education Early Childhood Specialists in Early Childhood Special Education/Early Intervention (Birth to Eight)* (ACC), and the Head

Figure 1   Alignment with Head Start Child Developmental and Early Learning Framework

For classrooms with children ages 3 to 5, *101 Principles for Positive Guidance with Young Children* aligns with the revised Head Start Child Development and Early Learning Framework (Head Start Resource Center, 2010) and directly supports the areas of social and emotional development, approaches to learning, and language development. Throughout the content, strategies, tips, and activities, teachers are presented with enriched teaching strategies to enhance all of the following domains:

- Social & Emotional Development (social relationships, self-concept and self-efficacy, self-regulation, emotional and behavioral health)
- Approaches to Learning (initiative and curiosity, persistence and attentiveness, and cooperation)
- Language Development (receptive and expressive language)
- Literacy Knowledge & Skills (book appreciation, phonological awareness, early writing)
- Creative Arts Expression (music, creative movement and dance, art, and drama)
- Physical Development & Health
- Logic & Reasoning (reasoning and problem solving; symbolic representation)
- Social Studies Knowledge & Skills (family and community, history and events, people and the environment)
- Support for Content Areas (integrated approaches that scaffold learning, social skills, and learning dispositions throughout the day)
- English Language Development (receptive English language, expressive English language, engagement in English literacy activities)

Start Child Developmental and Early Learning Framework. (See Figure 1.)

Using the Study Guide

Whether used as a higher education classroom text, a training manual for professional development and mentoring, or a group and personal study guide, the following structure will help you gain deeper insight about positive behavior guidance and responsive teaching. Each set of prompts will promote active learning while connecting research to practice. Each chapter study guide provides the following scope and sequence.

a. Goal Setting: Set a purpose to relate the content of each chapter to personally identified goals and needs. "What is working well for you? In what areas do you need help or support in improving? How will the strategies presented make a difference?"

b. Questioning and Reflection: Focus on previous experience. "How do the principles presented differ from what you were taught or have used in the past? What part of the reading challenges your thinking or conflicts with current beliefs? How can you use these principles to create the best outcomes for children—and for yourself?"

c. Case Studies: Provide a problem-centered approach that requires learners to examine complex situations and apply strategies to new contexts. "What principle will work to address the issues presented and why? How will the principle change the way you respond? How will the change in you affect the way the child, family, or colleague will respond? How will the use of the principle influence behavior in the long run?"

d. Personal Examples/Group Brainstorming: Promote empathy, collaboration, personal identification, and motivation for change. "What behaviors have you struggled with? How has this issue affected you? How do the principles you have learned provide solutions to these behaviors in your classroom?"

e. Learners as Experts: Share unique perspectives. Respect minority views, realizing that learning and understandings are influenced by background knowledge, culture, and perceptions. As the shared experience of learning continues, the level of consensus and understanding will develop. "How have you used this strategy? What strategy do you think would be most effective in this situation?"

f. Principles in Action: Boost interactive learning. Participants record results on the "Getting Positive Results Using the Principles in Action" sheet and then discuss. "How did the principle work? How did the child or children respond? What did you learn?"

g. Research on the Run: Professional standards promote the use of evidence-based practice. "How does the research affect your perspective? How will the use of the principles in this chapter make a difference to the children and families in your classroom?"

The text and activities can be personalized to the needs of your organization or group. For a 15-week syllabus, divide Chapters 2, 6, 7, 8, and 9 for extended implementation, feedback, and reflection. For a 10-week study, you will want to review one chapter per week. You may assign chapters to be led by teams of students or participants. Relevant questions can be discussed in a large group or assigned to smaller groups. Mentors can discuss chapter goals for learning and application. For individual or small-group study, the workbook format will guide the course of study.

Acknowledgments

The authors wish to thank our families for their love and support. For all of our students who have shared their experiences and lives with us, for the directors and teachers with whom we have worked, we are honored to share this book. For the schools, families, centers, and organizations who have graciously joined in our journey, we thank you for your open doors and for the blessing of your faithfulness to the lives of children. For our trusted colleagues and friends, we are truly grateful. We thank our editor Julie Peters for her guidance and wisdom in helping us launch this project.

We also thank the reviewers for their thoughtful comments and helpful suggestions: Lorraine Breffni, Nova Southeastern University; Mary Ann Costello, Frontier Central School District; Lucia Obregon, Miami Dade College; Margarita Perez, Worcester State University; Annie Rooney French, Kentucky Department of Education; Kara Williams, Oregon Department of Education; and Christian Winterbottom, Florida State University.

New! CourseSmart eTextbook Available

CourseSmart is an exciting new choice for students looking to save money. As an alternative to purchasing the printed textbook, students can purchase an electronic version of the same content. With a CourseSmart eTextbook, students can search the text, make notes online, print out reading assignments that incorporate lecture notes, and bookmark important passages for later review. For more information, or to purchase access to the CourseSmart eTextbook, visit www.coursesmart.com.

References

American Academy of Pediatrics. (2005). Using positive discipline. *SCAN Newsletter,* Suspected Child Abuse and Neglect (SCAN) Program.

Barnett, S. (2008). Preschool education and its lasting effects: Research and policy implications. National Institute for Early Education Research. Retrieved October 28, 2011, from http://nieer.org/resources/research/Preschool LastingEffects.pdf

Burchinal, M., Howes, C., & Pianta, R. (2008). Predicting child outcomes at the end of kindergarten from the quality of pre-kindergarten teacher–child interactions and instruction. *Applied Developmental Science, 12*(3), 140–153.

Cornell, D., & Mayer, M. (2010). Why do school order and safety matter? *Educational Researcher, 39*(1), 7–15.

Downer, J., & Pianta, R. (2006). Academic and cognitive functioning in first grade: Associations with earlier home and child care predictors and with concurrent home and classroom experiences. *School Psychology Review, 35*(1), 11–30.

Fox, L., & Smith, B. (2007). Promoting social, emotional and behavioral outcomes of young children served under IDEA. Retrieved November 5, 2011, from www.nectac.org/ ~pdfs/calls/2007/challengingbehavior/2-smith-619policy brief.pdf

Haynes, M. (2008, June). Building state early learning systems: Lessons and results from NASBE's Early Childhood Education Network. *State Education Standard,* 12–19.

Haynes, M. (2009, March). Promoting quality in preK–grade 3 classrooms: Findings and results from NASBE's Early Childhood Education Network. *Issues in Brief: National Association of State Boards of Education,* 1–15.

Head Start Resource Center. (2010). The Head Start child development and early learning framework: Promoting positive outcomes in early childhood programs serving children 3–5 years old. Retrieved from http://eclkc.ohs .acf.hhs.gov/hslc/ttasystem/teaching/eecd/Assessment/ Child%20Outcomes/HS_Revised_Child_Outcomes_ Framework.pdf

Hemmeter, M. (2006, November). *Research findings and issues for implementation, policy and scaling up: Training & supporting personnel and program wide implementation.* Presented at the Annual Policy Maker's Summit, Center on Evidence-Based Practices: Young Children with Challenging Behavior, Washington, D.C.

Horn, I., Cheng, T., & Joseph, J. (2004). Discipline in the African American community. *Pediatrics, 113,* 1236–1241.

Ingersoll, R. M., & Smith, T. M. (2003). The wrong solution to the teacher shortage. *Educational Leadership, 60*(8), 30–33.

Mashburn, A. (2008). Quality of social and physical environments in preschools and children's development of academic, language, and literacy skills. *Applied Developmental Science, 12,* 113–127.

Mashburn, A., & Pianta, R. (2006). Social relationships and school readiness. *Early Education and Development, 17*(1), 151–176.

Masterson, M. (2008). *The impact of the 101s: A guide to positive discipline training on teacher interaction practices, attitudes, and prosocial skill outcomes in preschool classrooms.* Norfolk, VA: Old Dominion University.

Masterson, M., Kersey, K., & Myran, S. (2012). *Director's institute evaluation report for Tidewater Children's Foundation.* Norfolk, VA: Old Dominion University.

McClelland, M., Acock, A., & Morrison, F. (2006). The impact of kindergarten learning-related social skills on academic trajectories at the end of elementary school. *Early Childhood Research Quarterly, 21,* 471–490.

National Association for the Education of Young Children. (2010a). Code of Ethical Conduct and Statement of Commitment. Retrieved from www.naeyc.org/files/naeyc/file/positions/PSETH05.pdf

National Association for the Education of Young Children. (2010b). Overview of the NAEYC Early Childhood Program Standards. Retrieved from www.naeyc.org/files/academy/file/OverviewStandards.pdf

Oliver, R., & Reschly, D. (2007). Effective classroom management: Teacher preparation and professional development. National Comprehensive Center for Teacher Quality. Retrieved November 5, 2011, from www.tqsource.org/topics/effectiveClassroomManagement.pdf

Pianta, R., & Hadden, S. (2008, June). What we know about the quality of early education settings: Implications for research on teacher preparation and professional development. *The State Education Standard,* 20–27.

Pianta, R., Howes, C., Burchinal, M., Byrant, D., Clifford, R., & Early, C. (2005). Features of pre-kindergarten programs, classrooms, and teachers: Do they predict observed classroom quality and child–teacher interactions? *Applied Developmental Science, 9*(3), 144–159.

Pianta, R., LaParo, K., & Hamre, B. (2009). *Classroom Assessment Scoring System Scoring Manual.* Baltimore, MD: Paul H. Brookes Publishing.

Pinderhuges, E., Dodge, K., & Bates, J. Pettit, G., & Zelli, A. (2000). Discipline responses: Influences of parents' socioeconomic status, ethnicity, beliefs about parenting, stress, and cognitive-emotional processes. *Journal of Family Psychology, 14,* 380–400.

Rimm-Kaufman, S., Pianta, R., & Cox, M. (2000). Teachers' judgments of problems in the transition to kindergarten. *Early Childhood Research Quarterly, 15*(2), 147–166.

Schulting, A., Malone, P., & Dodge, K. (2005). The effect of school-based kindergarten transition policies and practices on child academic outcomes. *Developmental Psychology, 41,* 860–871.

Schultz, B., Richardson, R., Barber, C., & Wilcox, D. (2011). A preschool pilot study of connecting with others: Lessons for teaching social and emotional competence. *Early Childhood Education Journal, 39,* 143–148.

Schultz, T. (2008, June). Tackling PK–3 assessment & accountability challenges: Guidance from the national early childhood accountability task force. *The State Education Standard,* 411. Retrieved June 15, 2008, from www.nasbe.org/index.php/file-repository?func=startdown&id=764

Skiba, R., Michael, R., & Nardo, A. (2000, June). The color of discipline: Sources of racial and gender disproportionality in school punishment. Policy Research Report SRS1. Bloomington: Indiana University, Indiana Education Policy Center.

Smith, S., Schneider, W., & Kreader, J. (2010). Features of professional development and on-site assistance in child care quality rating improvement systems: A survey of state-wide systems. National Center for Children in Poverty. Retrieved from www.nccp.org

Thanasetkorn, P. A. (2009). *The impact of the 101s: A guide to positive discipline teacher interaction practices, teacher adjustment, and academic outcomes in kindergarten classrooms in Bangkok, Thailand.* Norfolk, VA: Old Dominion University.

Yates, T., Ostrosky, M., Cheatham, G., Fettig, A., Shaffer, L., & Milagros Santos, R. (2008). Research synthesis on screening and assessing social–emotional competence. Retrieved November 5, 2011, from http://csefel.vanderbilt.edu/documents/rs_screening_assessment.pdf

Building a Caring Community

This chapter will explore the role and influence of the teacher in creating high-quality interactions and fostering positive relationships with children. The essential framework for learning begins when a child feels valued and respected within meaningful and caring relationships. Whether you work with infants and toddlers or teach children in a preschool or early elementary school setting, your first priority is to help guide them toward a healthy understanding of themselves and to instill confidence in their ability to make positive connections with others.

The strategies in this chapter will help you create a caring community that encourages the gifts and strengths of every child and promotes a sense of belonging and purpose. You will be able to instill in your classroom a fresh spirit of celebration and enjoyment. This responsive classroom climate will influence children's excitement for learning and will enhance their ability to relate well with others. As you create this caring community, you will have a lasting positive influence in the lives of children and their families, both now and in the future.

Chapter Principles

1: Connect Before You Correct

2: Time In

3: Belonging and Significance

4: Love

5: Class Meeting

6: Make a Sacrifice

7: Establish Routines and Traditions

8: Talk About Children Positively to Others

9: Put It in Writing

10: Kiss Your Brain

11: Positive Closure

Chapter Objectives

- As you explore the text and activities in this chapter, you will be able to:
- Implement effective strategies to build a positive classroom climate
- Foster sensitivity and responsiveness to individual, cultural, and language needs

- Establish traditions that encourage belonging, purpose, and responsibility
- Enhance self-esteem and increase emotional competence
- Boost learning and engagement through affirming words, actions, and activities
- Use positive relationships and supportive interactions to create a caring community with young children and families

Creating a Caring Community

The most important influence in the classroom is *you!* Your words and actions, tone, engagement, and modeling establish the quality and nature of the emotional, physical, and social environment of your classroom. Your relationships with children are your strongest asset. How you respond to them will help them decide if they will connect to school as a place of success and belonging, or if they will disconnect because of challenges and difficulties. Your examples of kindness, respect, caring, and consistency set the tone for them.

Interactions with adults have the power to change the way a child feels about himself and others, and to affect the way he interprets experiences. *The way you respond to a child can influence the way the child in turn responds to you.* This concept is foundational to the philosophy and approach of the 101 principles. Your interactions and emotional response affect how a child reacts to you and has a significant role in the way he relates to his peers. What you say and do influences every aspect of children's emotional, social, ethical, and intellectual development! By considering the ways adults influence outcomes, you can gain powerful insight into your role as a teacher.

● THINK ABOUT IT!

If you needed to tell someone something that had embarrassed you, or to ask for help with a situation that meant a lot to you, who would you choose? What qualities would that person possess?

_____

_____

_____

Most people describe this person as loving, trustworthy, non-judgmental, kind, or understanding. These also are the traits that children need to see in adults. They need to know that we love and support them as they are and that they can never lose our love and respect, no matter what they do.

In the classroom, a teacher must guide and support individual children, as well as respond to children within group and peer interactions. In which of these contexts do you find it most difficult to respond with the traits you have listed above? Why do you think this can be a challenge?

_____

_____

_____

Participating in a caring community is foundational to a child's sense of self. At school and at home, children need to feel they belong and are loved. Our responsiveness can ensure satisfying relationships between children as they learn and play together. It is our privilege to show compassion and empathy toward the children in our care. It is our responsibility to demonstrate loving behavior and to teach children to have compassionate regard for themselves and others. Our interactions can transform the classroom into a positive, happy place where children like to come and parents want to contribute.

The Power of Connection

All of us need to be connected to others. Being connected to other people keeps us healthy. Think how we feel when we are disconnected from someone we care about. When we have had a misunderstanding, it weighs on us all day. It consumes our energy as we consider how we can resolve the conflict—whether we can make peace, let it go, or need to address it. We want to feel the relief that comes from reconnecting and to know that everything is going to be OK.

If we don't have close relationships, we become isolated. Being in relationships with others helps us see other points of view and take on other perspectives. As adults, we have control over the people with whom we choose to be connected; it is a conscious choice. Children, however, are totally dependent on adults for these connections. Young children, even infants, will go to great lengths to re-establish a bond when they feel disconnected. We are the lifeline for children who need a safe connection. They depend on us with complete trust to guide and care for them.

Children are born wired to seek this emotional and physical connection. When a baby smiles and coos and his parent responds, the child learns that he matters! When an adult stays present in the child's world—watching, responding, laughing, listening, sharing, and respecting—the child will learn to watch, respond, laugh, listen, share, and be respectful in turn.

Children's early experiences determine their perceptions about themselves and the world. Our sensitive and consistent care protects them from stress and helps them make sense of their new feelings and experiences. When an adult is empathetic and comforting, children will in turn show empathy toward others and learn to nurture their own needs in healthy ways. We will be more effective at guiding behavior when we first have a strong foundation of meaningful relationships in the context of a caring community.

Forming a Sense of Community in the Classroom

To form a sense of community, we want to engage children in positive experiences that support their security and well-being. Whether we work with infants, toddlers, or with children in preschool, kindergarten, or the early elementary years, creating a sense of belonging and safety is a priority. Consider the qualities of a caring teacher and observe the emotional climate of a classroom. As we view these important interactions through the eyes of children, we can better understand what they need from us.

Ms. Garcia's kindergarten class has been studying insects. Earlier, they visited the butterfly garden outside their school and drew pictures in their science journals of their observations. Now the children are pressed together looking at picture books and it is time for a break. Their teacher whispers, "If you can hear me, touch your nose. If you can hear me, touch your ear." The children look up right away. "It's time to put away your notebooks." The children carefully return their folders to the science box. Nate collects the pencils, while Jared puts away the magnifying glasses.

Ms. Garcia sings, "If you're ready to go outside, clap your hands," to the tune of "If You're Happy and You Know It." The children know that this is their cue to line up, so they move right over to the door. Two girls hug each other and smile, while two others go over to the closet to get the bag of balls for the playground. Without needing to give further direction, the children are ready to go out the door with their teacher.

The groundwork prepared by a teacher makes it possible to create smooth transitions in the classroom. Ms. Garcia has been practicing routines throughout the year with her class. She is pleased to see the children sharing and helping each other. They have been taking increasing responsibility for themselves and the classroom.

● **THINK ABOUT IT!**

What does this teacher do to make this classroom community work so effectively?

_____

_____

_____

What are some indications that show the children are engaged in caring about their classroom and each other?

_____

_____

_____

What responsibilities that are part of this classroom routine give the children a sense of significance and belonging?

_____

_____

_____

What qualities described in the previous scenario would help a child feel connected to the teacher and to the other children?

_____

_____

_____

Building Meaningful Connections

There are six principles that will help you focus on creating positive connections with children. These strategies will influence children to engage with you and with each other. These principles will pay off in helping you gain children's confidence and trust.

Principle 1: Connect Before You Correct

Find multiple ways to connect with a child. Get to know him and show him that you care about him before you begin to try to adapt his behavior. Help him to discover his strengths, his uniqueness, and his special gifts by calling attention to them.

There are simple ways to connect that will make children identify with you and feel close to you. The following skills will boost your connection power quickly, and cooperation will be a natural outcome. Building a caring, empathetic relationship will invite a child to respond positively to your guidance. There are many opportunities to do this.

Get to know each child better by showing personal interest. Pay attention to his temperament, needs, and strengths. Make daily authentic connections.

Birth to Age 3

- Spend individual time sharing private conversation with each child. The heart of connecting is helping each child feel special and important to you.

- Give a hug, a gentle pat on the arm, or a special message such as "I love you" in sign language.

- Share special songs or a preferred book that you read each day. Spend time doing activities the child enjoys, such as playing a game or assembling a puzzle. Stay in his world as you watch and listen.

- Sing favorite songs and poems. Peek-a-Boo, Pat-a-Cake, and other finger plays and rhymes are gentle ways to connect.

- Peek into a mirror and exclaim over the special face you see!

- Toddlers love to be helpers. Find projects you can do together, such as sort doll clothes, stack books, roll yarn, or wash dishes. Children will feel connected when they know they are helping you.

Ages 3 to 8

- Ask a child questions about himself and really listen. Children often share more when their hands are busy painting, creating, or helping.

- Have special activities waiting for children in a bag, basket, or envelope that contains materials relating to their unique gifts or interests. A child who loves art can be given paper with various textures and colors to create a collage. Let the child know that you have created this activity just for him.

- Ask a child for advice in solving a problem.

- Invite one child to help another child with a task and connect them through comfortable conversation.

- Sit by a child at lunch and give him your focus as you ask questions.

● **THINK ABOUT IT!**

What are three ways you can connect meaningfully with children in your classroom?

1. _____

2. _____

3. _____

How do you think these specific connections will make a difference in the way children will respond to you later?

_____

_____

_____

- Identify each child's interests, and guide him to books and activities that are meaningful. Use each connection to turn him on to learning and engagement in school.
- Remember that the more you connect, the less you will have to correct.

Investing "time in" is the first step in building a positive relationship with children. *Time in* is when we meet a child's need for undivided attention as we respond to his questions, conversation, and activities. What he wants most is time with us. Our first priority is to make ongoing deposits into his "transaction account." The investment we make increases his sense of value and worth to us. We "make a deposit" that grows when we give him our empathy, mental focus, emotional presence, and physical proximity. Each time we make a personal relational connection with him, he senses how important he is to us. The following principles can be used together to build up and strengthen our relationships with children and build a positive climate in the classroom.

Principle 2: Time In

When you are near a child, give him a gentle touch, a thumbs-up, or a high-five. Think about it. Words don't always covey the message you want to give someone. However, touching is different. Children are less likely to seriously misbehave when they sense a love and respect on the part of an adult who matters to them. What you do is as important as what you say. We need to seize every opportunity to be intentional in showing our personal interest and making sure each child has received individual time and focus from us.

Birth to Age 3

- There are many caring ways to say, "You are special! I am glad you are here!"
- Receive infants and toddlers with focused attention and verbal affirmation for their arrival and through the day as you pick them up or help them.
- When holding, picking up, or transferring responsibility of a young child from one adult to another, pay attention to the child's verbal and physical cues as you talk with him.
- Talk *to* rather than *about* the child.
- Be sure to give every parent a positive welcome. Connect by giving explicit compliments about his or her relationship with the child. "I love the way Jacquie laughs just like you! I can see how much you enjoy each other."
- Provide warm interaction to pre-verbal children with compliments. "I love your sweet smile. I've been waiting for you!" The child will feel and respond to your genuine interest.
- Comment about an object the child has with him. "Is Teddy Bear coming to school with you?" Both the child and parent will experience your presence and focus.
- Be sure to reconnect through special one-on-one "time in" moments throughout the day.

Ages 3 to 8

- Start each day standing by the door. Come in early to finish paperwork and planning. Give all of your attention to children when they first arrive.

- Focus on each parent and child during drop off and pick up. Interact with eye contact, a smile, and welcoming words.
- Greet each child by name; smile and tell him you are glad he came. Help each child feel special to you. "It makes me glad to have you in my classroom." "Your smile makes the day happy for me." "I am so glad you are here." "I missed you yesterday." (These greetings have an exponential impact on children who need extra encouragement or with whom you have been struggling.)
- Give preschool and elementary children a choice of a hug, a high-five, or a handshake. Post pictures of each option (a hug, high-five, or handshake) so that children can point to the one they want when they arrive at the door.
- Spend "time in" with children in appropriate ways, being sure to honor what is culturally appropriate and accepted in your school. You will want to be cautious and make sure you respect children's boundaries. Not all children want to be touched. Often a touch on the shoulder is non-threatening and doesn't feel intrusive to the child. Make sure you are sensitive and honor what the child needs.
- Give a genuine compliment: "Hi Tanisha! How did things go with your brother? He is lucky to have you to read to him [or paint with him]." Help each child feel special and welcomed. "Good morning, Dariah. I've been waiting for you to come. Don't you have a big smile today!" We want family members who come to school to see that we are happy for their child to come and join our day.
- Be sure to provide "time in" throughout the day. Whisper a cheer, touch their shoulder, and let them know you are noticing their effort and contributions.

Imagine how this investment of time will make a difference when children respond to you later in the day. Investing in a positive start to every day with positive interactions is a priority that will help children feel comfortable and secure. Your energy given to "time in" will quickly help them feel accepted and safe.

THINK ABOUT IT!

Describe two specific ways you will build a stronger relationship with a child in your class who needs more positive support. What specific activities or "time in" plans will make this happen?

1. _____

   _____

2. _____

   _____

Principle 3: Belonging and Significance

Remember that everyone needs to feel that he belongs and is significant. Help each child to feel important by giving him important jobs to do and reminding him that if he doesn't do them, they won't get done! Help him feel important by being responsible.

When children are productive and engaged in meaningful tasks, they are less likely to engage in mischief. They need to do something constructive with their energy and focus. Let a child check off others who complete the art or writing projects. In a toddler classroom, a wandering child can pass out cups and set the table. Assign a child of any age to be a greeter at the door in the morning or when guests arrive. Create important responsibilities, such as "feelings helper." The feelings helper takes the tissue box to a child who is crying or sad. Help each child feel important by being responsible, and you will quickly see irresponsible behavior turn around.

Birth to Age 3

- When interacting with infants, use descriptive language to explain what you are doing. For example, "Doesn't that feel better? Ooh, this ointment feels cold. Here is your dry diaper." By using enhanced language interaction, you are highlighting the sequence of their experiences through intimate communication.

- Use children's natural inclination to help and imitate. As soon as children are able to carry their plate or put away their belongings, make responsibility fun and support their contributions. Young toddlers can "help" sweep the floor or wash the table (with water), carry their plate, or pass out needed items. Invite them to help you sort crayons, carry toys, water plants, or feed the fish.

- As soon as children can do things for themselves, support their growing independence. Give assistance only until they can accomplish a job alone. Pair children to help one another in order to build confidence and teamwork.

- Help children be responsible for their own belongings, and ask them to take responsibility for specific jobs in the classroom.

Here are some creative ways to give older children belonging and significance:

Ages 3 to 8

- The Time Keeper is responsible for starting and stopping the timers throughout the day.
- The Book Helper helps the teacher pass out books and helps hold the big books.
- The Door Holder is always second in line.
- The Disk Jockey is responsible for the music in the room.
- The Germ Buster is responsible for squirting soap or hand sanitizer (or passing out towels) before lunch or when needed.
- The Class Cleaner can wipe tables, wash mirrors or walls, and sweep the floor.
- The Guest Greeter gets up to meet guests at the door. This person asks guests their names and introduces them to the teacher and class. (Have a procedure for greeting guests when they come in.)

Think outside the box! There are many creative ways to name jobs. Make sure that every child has a special job to do each day.

What are some jobs you can give to a specific child that will help him invest meaningfully in your room?

_____

_____

_____

What other jobs can you name that will help children feel they can make a significant contribution?

_____

_____

_____

Principle 4: Love

Every child needs an adult who cares and wants to spend time with him. Make an effort to show him how special he is to you.

Consider it an honor when children come to you. Realize that they choose you because they feel that you have something they need. When you really listen and stay emotionally present, they trust that you will be responsive and that you will care. When you make the effort to see life through their eyes, it will pay off in the way they respond to you and to each other.

Take every opportunity to connect with children. With an older child, sit quietly to talk and spend time together. With an infant or toddler, rock or sway together and tell what you love and enjoy about him. With an older child, take a walk together. Let him come with you to deliver a message to another teacher or to the office.

Learning to stay sensitive and aware of children's activities, attention span, emotional experiences, and challenges is part of creating a caring environment. When you see that a child is upset, invite him to step aside with you, gently touch his back or shoulder, and ask him if there is anything you can do to help. Really listen, and reassure him that you are glad he is there. Help him get involved in positive interactions with others or in another activity after you have focused on your time together.

For those who speak another language at home or are just learning English at school, interacting through picture books, games, and activities is especially important. Let two children be "buddies" to double their connection and assist each other. Teach signs or cues that children can use when they need something, so that each child can communicate what is needed. Your sensitivity and support will let them know they can be comfortable coming to you for help.

Here are some ways we can show children of *all ages* that you care:

- Be fully present. Be conscious in your focus.
- Give your full attention. Give eye contact.

- Sit on the floor with young children and really concentrate on their world.

- Listen intently without interrupting.

- Wait patiently. Let children finish their thoughts.

- Resist the urge to change the subject.

- Follow and see where the child will lead in conversation.

- Sometimes not saying anything at all is good.

- Be still in silence. You'll be amazed at the wisdom a child can share.

- Have a secret sign or private word of endearment.

- Tell the child often how much he means to you.

- Protect and nurture your connection every day.

● THINK ABOUT IT!

When are children hardest for you to love? (Do you feel it is when they are disobedient, angry or upset, whiny, or disrespectful?) What do you think children need from you at these times?

_____

_____

_____

 Principle 5: Class Meeting

Take time to gather children together any time you sense the need to connect or address a particular issue. Starting the day off with a meeting is a good way to show that you care. Give them an opportunity to reflect, listen, empathize, and problem-solve. Focus on two-way communication. Listen more than you talk. Teachers and children will learn from each other.

Children do not always arrive at school ready to learn. They may be tired, stressed, or in need of a gentle transition into their "classroom family" through a focused sharing activity. Children may never see each another outside of school, so a class meeting gives them an opportunity to develop understanding and connection to each other. When many cultures are present, this focused time builds respect and empathy for each child's unique experiences.

The purpose of a class meeting is to connect and work together as a group. It may be a scheduled time or an impromptu meeting after lunch or recess. It might be better to have a smaller meeting if several children want or need to talk privately. Sit together on the floor or arrange chairs in a circle to create a feeling of unity, respect, and equality. The purpose is to connect and open communication. Children learn to listen and appreciate other perspectives. This guided time allows them to express their feelings and bond around common understandings, decisions, or compromises.

You can help children share their joys and concerns. They may be happy or excited—or need to talk about what is worrying or bothering them. It helps to keep a "Feelings Jar," where children can place their worries or joys on a slip of paper in a "safe" place. These may be shared at the next meeting. Expressing excitement and sharing frustrations help children lift their burdens, connect to others, and feel more positive about what lies ahead.

Birth to Age 3

- Class meetings are a perfect way to start the day for infants and toddlers. They will sense the consistent comfort and familiar routine.

- Sing a daily greeting song to welcome everyone. Sing or chant a name song that focuses attention on each child. "G is for Georgia, she's sitting next to me . . . "

- Highlight a new sign. Teach young children sign language for frequent needs, such as *drink, eat, potty, please, milk, more,* and *enough.* There are many wonderful books, videos, and websites dedicated to early sign language for infants, toddlers, and school-age children.

- Talk about feelings (emotional experiences). Use puppets or stories to highlight feeling words such as *sad, happy,* or *upset.* "It's sad to leave Mommy. Wave bye bye! It's happy to see our friends. Wave hello!"

- Sing feelings songs that name and describe emotion words. You can make songs to easy tunes. Add verses to "If You're Happy and You Know It." You can vary the speed and pitch of the song as well as the actions to focus on children's feelings and experiences.

- Ask transition questions: "Tell what you had for breakfast. What is one thing you did at home this morning? Who helped you get ready for school?" "What did you do to help someone?" If you are with infants or pre-verbal children, ask questions and "talk through" the routines. They will benefit from your descriptions. You can include what you learned when children were dropped off, or recreate what you know they did: "Who helped you put your socks and shoes on?" (Describe activities in detail!)

- Adapt "open up" questions from the list below to the needs of younger children.

Here are some effective ways to encourage children to "open up" and talk!

Ages 3 to 8

- Ask them to finish feeling sentences: "I like it when; I don't like it when; I was sad when; I was angry when; I don't think it is fair that; I wish that I didn't have to; I am afraid when . . . " "Tell if you are mad, sad, or glad, and give one reason."

- Ask "What would you do if?" questions: "What would you do if you were the king/queen of the world? What would you say if you could talk to the president?

What you would invent if you could solve a problem? Where would you travel if you could take a hot air balloon ride and see the sights from the sky? What character would you be if you could jump into a book for a day?"

- Ask "what is/was" questions: "What is the good news and bad news of the day? What is something you are thinking about today? What was something special that happened to you today? What was the best thing you learned in school yesterday?"

- Ask "far-fetched" questions: "What would you do if it snowed 10 feet and you needed to get out of your house? What would you do if you had to make pancakes for everyone in school? What would you do first every day if you were the (janitor, fireman, doctor, librarian, etc.)?"

- Ask "you" questions: "What jobs do you do at home? What is something you are proud of? What do you want to be when you grow up? What surprised you today? What is something that happened to you since yesterday? What is something helpful you did this morning for someone else?"

- Ask them to finish "when I am" statements: "When I'm a teacher, I will; when I'm a teacher, I will not; when I'm a mom/dad, I will; when I'm a mom/dad, I will not . . . "

When you create authentic conversation and connections, children will listen and will be ready to move forward in the day with positive feelings about themselves and for each other.

Principle 6: Make a Sacrifice

Make sure you have taken care of your personal business before school begins so you can give full attention to the children. Plan to arrive a few minutes earlier to school so that when children need your attention, you aren't entering grades, checking e-mail, taking the lunch count, or texting. During the children's rest or quiet time, settle the children and remain available rather than hurrying off to the computer. Giving extra time to children when they come in and throughout the day is an important way to help children feel they are loved.

Make a commitment to spend more time with children who need extra attention, to create special moments, and to focus on them. You will quickly see the trust blossom and experience a change in the way they will open up to you. Children who feel unconditional love and trust will respond by returning this trust to you.

An important part of creating a learning community is to have adults join in activities. Assistants or volunteers should sit with the children during learning times, showing their own enthusiasm for a story, rubbing the back of a child who needs soothing, and staying "present" in the children's world. Be sure materials are set out ahead of time, and use learning, dancing, singing, and eating times to focus on the children.

Can you think of a specific child you know who needs extra support, love, and encouragement? What activity could you plan to do with this child? What does this child need to hear from you? How can you connect with him in a special way?

_____

_____

What changes could be made to prepare materials or activities ahead of time so that more focus is put on supporting children's positive learning experiences?

_____

_____

Creating a Unique Identity for Your Classroom

The following principle will help you build a strong foundation for identity and caring and will transform the way you see your role in the classroom. Establishing unique routines and traditions for your classroom will boost your influence and engage children in meaningful cooperation. As you build positive relationship connections, you will find many productive ways to link academic training with character and social–emotional support.

🦋 *Principle 7: Establish Routines and Traditions*

Children behave better when they know what they can count on. Establish traditions that they can anticipate and that provide them with fond memories and feelings of belonging and security.

Use every opportunity to create experiences that build a sense of common identity. Create special classroom customs. These can be simple celebrations done each day, such as having children give compliments to a child next to them in a circle or keeping a compliment box. When we establish routines and traditions, children take pride in belonging to the classroom community. These special events and activities help children grow and learn as they feel safe within a nurturing environment.

Creating Unique Traditions in the Classroom

Creating happy expectations for children when they first enter the classroom will set the tone for positive memories. Activities that are age appropriate for younger children may continue to be used to enhance communication in preschool and elementary years. Be creative in application to the children and parents with whom you work. Here are some examples.

Birth to Age 3

- Take photos of babies and pre-verbal children when they are happy and write a note describing the moment to the parents or caregiver.

- Record babies laughing (or toddlers singing) and e-mail the file to the parents or caregiver.

- Prepare calming activities, such as chants, poems, songs, or finger plays to welcome and assist children through transitions.

- Set out baskets of materials, activities, books, or toys ahead of time to make the room inviting.

- Celebrate milestones such as crawling, walking, new words, new skills, and acts of caring. Create a special routine, like adding a flower to a wreath or a chain to a paper chain. Celebrations of kindness and achievement can be as elaborate and as creative as you and your students can design and enjoy together.

Ages 3 to 8

- Use a digital camera daily. Take candid photos of the children when they are working, giving reports, or engaged in academic projects. Post them in the hall to show parents and others what they are doing. This is important for infants and toddlers too.

- Keep a class yearbook to record special events and remember highlights. At the end of the year, give each child a copy. Let them sign each other's books with compliments.

- Establish meaningful "rites of passage." Children may spend a night at school, place flowers on local memorials, participate in a local volunteer service event, or stage an indoor holiday parade.

- At the end of each day, read a chapter from a book as a way to model a love of reading and to entice children to look forward to the next day of being together.

- Ask children to set their own positive goals and check on daily progress: "Did you eat your vegetables and fruits, give a compliment, or exercise today?"

- Snack time should be used for conversation and social interactions. However, when children finish, let them transition into a meaningful activity. They can lead motions and singing together ("YMCA," the color song, etc.). This keeps everyone active and involved.

- Let children bring in flashlights (or you may provide them) for a "reading day." Be creative! There are many possible variations on this theme.

- Have children write a letter to themselves saying what they hope to learn that year or what they want to be like in the future. At the end of the year (or when the child graduates from your school or moves), send the letter home with the child to keep. Younger children can dictate their letter to the teacher.

Creating Traditions That Connect School to the Home

All Ages

- Send books to read at home with an activity for children to do with parents, such as a related song, drawing, puzzle, or craft.

- Send a class "mascot" (such as a stuffed teddy bear) with a backpack, clothing, and writing journal with a child each weekend. The child can (with the help of his parent, if needed) write about what the bear did while he was visiting and have it read to the class on Monday morning.

Ages 3 to 8

- Create special ways to participate in community service activities as a class to help children develop caring and empathy for others. Children can participate in a food drive or collect stuffed animals for a local charity or organization. Helping children and families reach out to others in need will create lasting memories for everyone.

Creating Traditions That Connect Home to the School

Birth to Age 3

- Bring in photos of families and keep them on a bulletin board low enough for the children to look at and talk about.

- Allow young children to keep a laminated family picture in their "cubbie." If they are sad, they may get the photo to hold for comfort. A teacher can point to and name each family member.

- Encourage children to hold a family photo while they are going to sleep at naptime.

- Ask children to bring a familiar comfort item that is soothing to them, such as a blanket or stuffed animal from home. Holding a favorite toy that is comforting and familiar can help ease transitions to naptime or comfort a child who is missing his family.

Ages 3 to 8

- Assemble a class quilt, allowing children to create a square (paint, collage, or drawing) about themselves and their family.

- Have children write notes complimenting other students. Younger children may draw a picture and dictate the message to the teacher. Let the children bring these notes or drawings home so that family members can see how much the children bring pleasure and are good friends to others at school.

- Have children write and illustrate a book about their family. Younger children may dictate words.

- Create a timeline of each child's life, telling what events were important and illustrating with photographs or drawings. These can be displayed in the room or hall.

When children identify with the purposes and traditions of the classroom, they want to come to school, because they feel needed and know they have a purpose. They don't want to miss the experiences that are awaiting them each day. They become eager learners because you have created a caring community.

● **THINK ABOUT IT!**

Review and reflect on your schedule and activities to be sure each child is supported in success and is given a sense of importance to the goals of the classroom. What two changes could you make to make sure every child is included in activities and traditions that will encourage his sense of belonging in your classroom community?

_____

_____

_____

_____

Creating Traditions That Value and Honor Diversity

Helping children accept and honor differences can create good memories and support multicultural understanding. We can never know exactly what someone else is feeling—because "I am not you!" But we can continually support the growth of empathy by creating a culture of kindness.

In early childhood it is important for us to make a point to discuss diversity and feature the heritage of students in our classroom. Invite family members to share customs and traditions. Share values that support understanding. A teacher from a Native American background taught a unit on customs from her culture and had the children make dream catchers. She explained the ways her background taught her to honor nature, the spirit of her Native American culture, and the wisdom and stories of her elders. The class read books that illustrated the struggles of Native American children learning to live within two cultural settings in a changing world.

In response, the children interviewed their own grandparents to ask about memories of stories passed on from generation to generation. They learned about courage and determination, and reflected on valuable lessons about tolerance, integrity, and generosity. Similar units and projects can coincide with Grandparents' Day or national holidays honoring American heroes. These traditions help children to appreciate and value differences in cultures.

Adapting teaching and activities to connect with English language learners and their families will make a big difference to children in the early childhood years. Building cultural bridges opens the academic gate for children to literacy and social success. Provide pictures and objects that demonstrate and illustrate new vocabulary. Make many connections to children's experiences. Be sensitive to how children feel when they are immersed in a new language or cultural environment.

Rather than ignore an issue, talk openly with children in your classroom about cultural, racial, and language differences. Often, in attempts to not draw attention to differences, we ignore many opportunities where we can help children show support and give empathy to one another. Supporting friendship and respect for differences will help children feel they belong and can be successful.

Be sure to provide bilingual translation for materials and have an interpreter present at parent meetings, if necessary. When you send home materials and books, suggest activities that children can do with older siblings who may have a stronger grasp of English. Identify support systems in your local public school district and community that can provide professional development and support for you and your students.

Here are some projects that can be adapted to the ages of the children in your classroom that will help them take on other perspectives:

- At the beginning of the year, ask parents what traditions they would like to have honored while their child is at school or that they would like to come and share with other children. This sharing of culture can become a source of pride to families and a wonderful learning opportunity for the children in your classroom. This communication also serves to connect you in positive ways to families.

- For very young children, including infants and toddlers, have parents contribute songs and lullabies in home languages and play these at nap or rest time. Invite parents to read stories in other languages and tell what they mean in English.

- Let children share songs and traditions from home, or have parents or caregivers come to sing and share songs in a native language.

- Make sure that "heroes" who visit your classroom (people from the community and parents who come to share their career, talent, or hobby) represent many cultures and backgrounds.

- Invite someone with a special ability (exceptionality/disability) to come and share with your class about his or her experiences. Let children ask questions.

- Don't forget that regions of the country differ considerably, so while you study social studies and geography, let children share their experiences. Families frequently move, so you already have experts in your midst.

- Be sure to have a globe or map of the world, and let children stick a "flag" where they, their parents, or grandparents are from. You and they will be amazed by the diversity represented in your classroom.

- Link to a classroom in another location via Internet or visual teleconference and share a lesson or story. Let children reflect afterwards about the differences and similarities they observed.

- Let children in your classroom who speak other languages at home participate in writing activities in their own language and have them translate for the class. This exposure will ignite an early passion for languages and later cross-cultural study.

● THINK ABOUT IT!

How do children feel when they leave home and come into a new group setting for the first time?

_____

_____

If you were the child, what would you want someone to do to help make you feel comfortable and to help you adjust? (Doesn't it make sense to involve them in meaningful activities?)

_____

_____

_____

_____

Using the Power of Positive Affirmation

Words have influence! It matters what words we use because words have the power to change the way a child thinks and feels about himself. Words that may not seem important to a parent or teacher may be the defining moment of a child's life. Here are four ways to communicate your positive regard that make a big difference in the way children feel about themselves and their peers—and you.

Principle 8: Talk About Children Positively to Others

Let children overhear you speaking positively about them—bragging about their good qualities, efforts, and actions—to others.

We want children to know how proud we are of the skills they are learning. The more we say good things, the more children want to do them. Refrain from talking about what a child did wrong; instead, use positive words to tell others what he did that made you proud.

Using positive approaches will increase the quality of your connection to children and parents. Here are some examples that will help you use positive interactions to support caring connections.

- When parents bring children to school, say at least one positive thing about each child as he or she comes and goes. This is as important for parents of infants and toddlers as it is for parents of children in older settings. Soon children will be doing more of the creative, helpful behaviors that are supported.

- When visitors come into the classroom, say, "I want you to meet my wonderful children. I am so proud of them!" When parents come by, say, "Let me tell you something fantastic Josiah did today."

- When you are in a circle, have each child give a compliment to the child next to him or as a ball or yarn is tossed.

- Keep a "great job" box so that children can write thank you notes to each other (or ask a teacher to do so). These can be read at the end of the day or sent home.

Principle 9: Put It in Writing

Start a tradition of sending good thoughts in writing. Leave "I care about you" notes in surprising places.

Writing and receiving messages help children learn a spirit of gratitude and affirmation. If the child can read, write a note of thanks or encouragement. When planning a special classroom event, ask the children to write an RSVP. When children are too young to read, send notes home and have parents read them. Leave notes on desks or in cubbies of children who show generous actions to their friends. Encourage children to leave thank you notes for each other.

Start a "Heroes" bulletin board and make sure you find ways to highlight every child for acts of kindness and courage. It takes a conscious effort to create a culture of kindness and counteract the negative attitudes they may see modeled. A spirit of gratefulness can be talked about often and encouraged.

Write notes home to the parents, letting them know how much you appreciate their love for their child, investment into his development, or support of the classroom; or you may thank them for a specific contribution they have made. Let parents know how much you enjoy having their child with you during the day.

Principle 10: Kiss Your Brain

When a child is exhibiting behavior that makes you proud or is making great choices, be sure to praise, thank, and draw attention to his great contributions. Tell him to "kiss your brain!" (Children love this!) They will respond by kissing their hand or finger and patting their head. You can model this action, as well.

Our role as teachers is not to provide empty praise, but to counteract messages that a child may have heard that have discouraged his motivation. Our praise can uplift his perceptions. One child was encouraged to "Kiss your good math brain" when she figured out an alternative solution. Later, she told her teacher it felt good to be good at math. We want to celebrate effort and successes, especially in the early childhood years when children are learning new skills every day.

Positive verbal support encourages children to try as they work toward a goal. Everyone appreciates a "silent round of applause," a "silent cheer," or an outright genuine cheer for a job well done. Make your classroom a place where children are encouraged to be proud of themselves and each other.

 ### *Principle 11: Positive Closure*

At the end of the day, remind children that they are special and loved. Help them look for something good, both about the day that is finished and the one that lies ahead.

Infants and toddlers can hear a special "good bye and see you tomorrow" song that is familiar and soothing. Younger children can dictate something special that happened each day. Older children can keep a journal of a treasured memory of each day. Make sure the children know you are looking forward to tomorrow, when you can be with them again. For younger children, this is comforting, and for older children, this can be their lifeline.

● **THINK ABOUT IT!**

Can you remember negative words someone said about you as a child? What were they? How have those words affected you since then?

_____

_____

Can you remember positive words someone said about you as a child? What were they? How have those words affected you since then?

_____

_____

Think of a child whose behavior you find annoying. What are some positive statements you can tell others about this child?

_____

_____

Summary

Every investment we make into connecting to children and families will yield a positive benefit to children's daily experiences in the classroom. We will create the kind of caring community where children feel safe and enjoy the company of adults and other children. In this safe, responsive community, children will form their first impressions about themselves as confident learners. The early meaningful experiences with us will build a strong foundation for their future social, emotional, cognitive, and physical development. The quality teacher–child interactions and positive experiences with peers will set a lasting foundation for mutually rewarding relationships and for effective positive guidance of children.

Using the Principles in Your Classroom

Love: *Practice smiling in the mirror.*

One of the most effective ways to show our care and invite children to share our space, time, and energy is to smile! Children look for happy faces. Unless you practice looking at yourself in the mirror, you might think you are smiling when you aren't. If you had a problem with your bank account and needed a teller to help you, which one would you choose when you walk into the bank? Wouldn't you choose the one who looked most genuinely pleasant? Children gravitate to those who feel and look trustworthy. A way to get started connecting is to practice smiling in the mirror.

Connect Before You Correct: *Take time to see the world through a child's eyes.*

Sit on the floor and children will gravitate to you. Have no agenda—the child knows right away that you have joined his world. Be ready to look and listen. Are you on the child's eye level? Are you looking at him directly? What is the child's mood? How is his tone of voice and rate of speed? Responsive, reciprocal listening is a way of "staying with" the child's pace, pitch, and speed. Let him guide you in the conversation. "Stay with" his or her thoughts. Repeat back what he is saying. Communicating with a child is like walking up steps. You want to extend your hand and help him come to you one step at a time.

Teachers can create consistent opportunities to build on what children are saying to add to their vocabulary. Expand on a child's words and phrases by repeating what is said back to him, and add additional thoughts or descriptions. For example, if a toddler says, "Truck!" you might respond, "Yes, that's a red truck. Where do you think the truck is going?" or "What do you think the truck is carrying?" For older children, these verbal extensions play an important role that creates a positive context for learning. Talking about emotions and experiences can support higher level concepts and processes and build meaningful exchanges between teachers and children.

Establish Routines and Traditions: *Me Bags are a wonderful way to share.*

A Me Bag is a wonderful tradition to create connections and greater understanding. Place favorite objects that represent special people and experiences into a favorite tote bag to share that shows others what you are all about. Teachers can share a Me Bag with parents or with the children in their classroom. Have one or two children bring in a Me Bag each week, or one a day. You can let the children bring in a Me Bag every few months, with different objects each time. Children love to talk about themselves, and sharing their Me Bag is a way to help them to connect to each other.

Teacher Tips

The following are comments from teachers who have been trained to use the 101 principles in their early care and education settings and elementary classrooms.

If you create a loving, safe environment where you give children confidence, they will perform for you because they feel safe with you. When someone believes in you, it gives you license to have confidence. It's amazing what that power will do in a human life. How can you communicate to your students, "I believe in you"?

I believe with all my heart and soul that this is the only plan that is in the best interest of the children. The children in my class had a year full of learning and are now capable of solving their own problems. Best of all, I did not have to spend my day solving disputes. My principal has received letters, calls, and visits from parents who can't stop raving about class meetings and positive principles. The principles are the tools I needed to make my classroom a happy, productive place where children feel safe, cherished, and excited to learn.

The principles have been the most effective tools in working with my students. I gave a copy of them to my each of my parents. I feel so lucky that I have them now and can incorporate them into my teaching style while I'm still learning to tune it, versus getting them after I've been teaching for 20 years!

I have worked with children for many years, but have found my behavior toward them and how I interact with them changing. I am now more aware of my words and actions and try to consider how the children will interpret them.

I use the principles every day. Working as a tutor in an early childhood center for children at risk gives me opportunities to observe the power of a positive attitude toward students, compliments, smiles, and bringing the best out in others on a daily basis.

I have always made every effort at the beginning of each year to connect with my new students in meaningful ways. After sharing my own Me Bag, I allowed one child each morning to share his or her bag. I teach in a multicultural community where more than half of my students are English language learners. The pictures and items they brought to share created a bridge between their common interests and similarities. This was the first time I have used Me Bags, and I feel I saved weeks of time in helping my children create meaningful relationships. The parents loved helping the children put together the bags, so it was an extra bonus for them to know we cared about the children and their families.

More than any other element of the classroom, the quality of relationship I have with my students creates a defining foundation for everything else. Having high expectations and

(continued)

following through to give children the very best in instruction and responsive care matters. But the most important influence is when a child senses my honest investment into his success. He knows I always want the very best for him, and that I am going to stick with him to help him be successful. He knows I believe in him and that I genuinely care and am invested in him. When this relationship is present, it changes everything for the child.

Research on the Run

Teachers Have a Powerful Influence

Positive teacher–child interactions and positive emotional climate are a critical part of quality programs that increase academic and social outcomes (Early, Maxwell, Burchinal, Alva, Bender, Bryant, et al., 2007; Fuller, Gasko, & Anguiano, 2010). Children with risk factors depend on the responsiveness of the teacher to connect to their needs and support their success. When teachers are warm and emotionally responsive, these children can achieve in school without as many behavior adjustments. However, if a teacher is controlling and demanding or uses coercive discipline methods, this has a distinct negative impact on these children. At-risk children rely on positive, responsive support in order to gain the skills and strategies they need for school and social success (Connell & Prinz, 2002; Murray, Waas, & Murray, 2008).

Positive relationships encourage children's feelings of worth and foster their sense of belonging in the community (NAEYC, 2008). "The close attachments children develop with their teachers/caregivers, the expectations and beliefs that adults have about young children's capacities, and the warmth and responsiveness of adult–child interactions are powerful influences on positive developmental and educational outcomes" (NAEYC, 2010, p. 34).

Positive Relationships Matter

The research shows that positive, responsive social and emotional support compensates for skills children may not get outside of school. When they receive high-quality responsive care in school, this support predicts (both directly and indirectly) how well they will do in school later on, and affects their ongoing adjustment in school and in life (Schultz, 2008; Shonkoff & Philips, 2001).

A positive, responsive teacher–child relationship:

- **Increases positive behavior.** Positive discipline and sensitive, responsive teaching strategies directly positively affect children's behavior (Bennett, Elliott, & Peters, 2005; Rimm-Kaufman, 2002; Snyder, Cramer, Afrank, & Peterson, 2005).
- **Decreases negative behavior.** When teachers model and teach emotional understanding, it decreases behavior problems (Ackerman & Youngstrom, 2001; Raikes & Thompson, 2006).
- **Helps children like school.** Having positive relationships with teachers helps children see school as a safe place where they can be successful—and where they want to be (Baker, 2006).
- **Overcomes risk factors.** Responsive, emotionally sensitive care can make up for the impact of stress, lack of maternal attachment, and other

risk factors a child experiences. Stress factors are mediated through positive climate, responsive relationships with teachers, and a consistent environment with low stress (Burchinal, Campbell, Bryant, Wasik, & Ramey, 1997; O'Connor & McCartney, 2006). These experiences make a difference academically and socially for children with risk factors (Fuller et al., 2010).

- **Strengthens healthy choices.** The ability to connect meaningfully with teachers when they are young will make a positive difference when children face the social pressures and challenges of the upcoming middle school years (Birch & Ladd, 1997; Kersey & Masterson, 2011).

- **Enhances empathy.** When adults respond empathetically to a child's distress, a child will be more empathetic to us and to others (Davidov & Grusec, 2006; Kestenbaum, Farber, & Sroufe, 1989).

- **Fosters emotional competence.** Positive interactions with teachers increase cooperation, empathy, and compliance (Blair, Denham, Kochanoff, & Whipple, 2004; Denham, Renwick, & Holt, 1991; Denham, Zinssler, & Bailey, 2011).

- **Increases self-regulation.** Positive relationships increase social skills and emotional regulation, whereas negative interactions result in higher levels of disruptive behavior and aggression (Denham, 2005).

- **Influences future relationships.** Children's relationships with their caregivers make an emotional pattern or blueprint that lasts for their lifetime. If they feel significant and important, they will bring this belief into their future relationships. If their early experiences are negative, this also creates a lasting pattern (Spencer, Jordan, & Sazama, 2004).

- **Fosters respect.** Creating a sense of community in schools is critical so that every child feels cared for, respected, and valued. Taking time to know

children and help them know one another is important (Norris, 2009).

- **Supports positive peer relationships.** When caregivers are emotionally available, sensitive, and responsive to children's needs, words, and actions, these "back and forth" (reciprocal) caring interactions have a strong positive impact on children's development, education, and social interactions with peers and others (Ahnert, Pinquart, & Lamb, 2006).

- **Creates positive role modeling.** Children's responses are strongly influenced by the way a teacher guides behavior (Herrera & Dunn, 1997; Lepper, 1981; Macoby, 1992; Snyder et al., 2005).

- **Provides life relationship skills.** Social skills gained early in school and early quality experiences with teachers affect future relationship success with peers and teachers, as well as better school outcomes (Denham, 2005; Hamre & Pianta, 2006).

The Impact of Responsive Teaching on Academic Outcomes

Responsive teachers give sensitive attention to individual needs, stay aware of changes in children's learning and emotional patterns, and work to meet their needs in consistent ways. The influence of this commitment to supporting children's development has lasting impact on important learning dispositions. Responsive teaching has lasting results:

- **Fortifies school readiness and health.** Social–emotional well-being is a critical determinant of school readiness and is related to both educational and health outcomes (Briggs-Gowan & Carter, 2008).

- **Enhances self-regulated learning.** When children can control their emotions and have self-regulation, they are more ready for school and do better in academics from the beginning (Raver, 2002).

- **Enhances learning skills.** Children with better social skills are better learners, and they get along better with friends and other adults in school (Denham, Blair, DeMulder, Levitas, Sawyer, Auerbach-Major, et al., 2003; Miles & Stipek, 2006; NICHD-ECCRN, 2005).

- **Enhances overall development.** The quality of early interaction experiences has a significant impact on developmental, cognitive, social–emotional, and language outcomes for children, with particular efficacy to children at risk (Ochshorn, 2011; U.S. Department of Education, 2009).

- **Enriches brain development.** The way adults relate and respond to young children directly affects the formation of neural pathways (Cozolino, 2006; Perry, 2001; 2005).

- **Increases school engagement.** When children have a warm, caring relationship with adults, they are more self-controlled and develop more advanced cognitive and social skills, which allows for more focused time learning and is linked to later positive outcomes in life (Barnett, 2008; Downer & Pianta, 2006; Downer, Rimm-Kaufman, & Pianta, 2007).

- **Supports high-quality learning.** High-quality learning depends on consistency in teacher–child interactions and warm, emotionally responsive relationships (Connell & Prinz, 2002; Haynes, 2009; Pianta & Hadden, 2008).

- **Promotes language development.** Children come to school with differences in the level of enriched language experiences; children from poverty tend to experience fewer words of encouragement at home. Teachers who use meaningful conversations and positive interactions can meet this need. Language thrives in the context of safe, responsive relationships and emotionally warm interactions, which nurtures positive feelings about learning in the brain (Hart & Risley, 1995; Hernandez, 2011; Landry, 2005).

- **Increases achievement.** Warm, sensitive responses help children achieve more and become more successful in school (Berry & O'Connor, 2009; Pianta, Hamre, & Stuhlman, 2003).

- **Mediates risk.** At-risk children with low socioeconomic or minority status who receive strong instructional and emotional support from teachers achieve academic outcomes equal to students with no risk factors (Hamre & Pianta, 2001).

- **Lowers referral to special education and future remediation.** Prevention of social and academic difficulties is more effective than remediation (Gallagher & Lambert, 2006; Office of Head Start, 2012).

- **Creates a more positive future for children.** The quality of strong, caring relationships between teachers and young children affects future social and educational outcomes (Bennett, Elliott, & Peters, 2005; Stipek, 2006).

The Impact of Responsive Relationships on Physiological Development

Within the context of a warm, responsive relationship with a caring teacher, children gain important developmental anchors:

- **A secure relationship bond.** A secure attachment with caregivers is an important protective factor in resilience regardless of a child's risk factors (Howes & Hamilton, 1992; Sroufe, 1995). The elements of a warm, caring relationship allow a child to internalize self-control and increase cognitive development (Kestenbaum et al., 1989). Emotional attachments between children and caregivers create social–emotional patterns that inform future relationships (Ahnert et al., 2006; Ainsworth, 1982; Bowlby, 1988). Children who experience secure attachment relationships with their caregivers have more positive relationships and show higher prosocial skills with their peers, and these effects last over time (Howes & Hamilton, 1992).

- **Healthy relationship interdependence.** The relational–cultural theory explains the influence of significant relationships with adults to create emotional patterns for self-appraisal and to form a lasting blueprint for future relationships (Spencer et al., 2004). Positive, sensitive interactions provide a secure base for children's healthy psychological growth and frame the formation of relational competence. This undergirding foundation includes mutual respect based on equality, children's fundamental need for secure relational connections with others, the establishment of trust and cooperation rather than use of coercion or punishment, and the need for relational skills as essential life competencies (Adler & Stein, 2005). The child's need for belonging and significance within a trusting relationship is a core foundation of the 101 principles and this approach to responsive practice.

- **Psychological and physical health.** Multidisciplinary research and advances in biological and neurological science shed light on the need for positive, responsive relationships to support optimal brain development, physiological regulation, and psychological health (Cozolino, 2006). Children's early experiences have lasting implications for their health, well-being, and social adjustment. The role of teachers in providing mediatory and protective factors for children is essential.

Understanding Early Education Contexts

Children may spend more time under the guidance and nurturance of non-parental caregivers than in the care of parents. The following statistics illustrate the importance of quality relationships between young children and the adults who care for them.

- The U.S. Department of Education indicates that two-thirds of all 3- to 5-year-olds in the United States attend childcare or preschool 40 hours a week or more (NICHD Early Child Care Research Network, 2005).

- In settings with high concentrations of military service personnel, children may spend 60 or more hours a week in childcare (Lucas, 2001).

- National reports show that 72% of working mothers have children under the age of 5 in the care of someone besides a parent. Of these childcare service arrangements, 48% are placed with relatives, 31% at profit or non-profit childcare centers, and 21% with other providers (U.S. Department of Labor, 2007).

- Other figures show that up to 60% of 4-year-olds are already in some type of care (Magnuson & Waldfogel, 2004).

- Of the 11 million 3-year-olds, five million will spend at least 25 hours a week in the care of someone other than a parent (Ehrle, Adams, & Tout, 2001).

- Nationally, nearly 1.3 million children attend state-funded preschools, more than one million at age 4 alone (Barnett, Hustedt, Friedman, Boyd, & Ainwsworth, 2010).

Getting Positive Results Using the Principles in Action

What happened or led up to the interaction?

_____

_____

_____

Which principle did you use?

_____

_____

_____

How did the situation turn out? (How did the child/children respond?)

_____

_____

_____

What did you learn?

_____

_____

_____

· ·

What happened or led up to the interaction?

_____

_____

_____

Which principle did you use?

_____

_____

_____

How did the situation turn out? (How did the child/children respond?)

_____

_____

_____

What did you learn?

_____

_____

_____

Guide to the Principles

1. **Connect Before You Correct:** Find multiple ways to connect with a child. Get to know him and show that you care about him before you begin to try to adapt his behavior. Help him discover his strengths, his uniqueness, and his special gifts by calling attention to them.

2. **Time In:** When you are near a child, give him a gentle touch, a thumbs-up, or a high-five. Think about it. Words don't always covey the message you want to give someone. However, touching is different. Children are less likely to seriously misbehave when they sense a love and respect on the part of an adult who matters to them. What you do is as important as what you say. We need to seize every opportunity to show our personal interest and make sure each child has received individual time and focus from us.

3. **Belonging and Significance:** Remember that everyone needs to feel that he belongs and is significant. Help each child feel important by giving him important jobs to do and reminding him that if he doesn't do them, they don't get done! Help him feel important by being responsible.

4. **Love:** Every child needs an adult who cares and wants to spend time with him. Make an effort to show him how special he is to you.

5. **Class Meeting:** Gather children together any time you sense the need to connect or address a particular issue. Starting the day off with a meeting is a good way to show that you care. Give them an opportunity to reflect, listen, empathize, and problem-solve. Focus on two-way communication. Listen more than you talk. Teachers and children will learn from each other.

6. **Make a Sacrifice:** Make sure you have taken care of your personal business (checking your social networking site, e-mail, texting, or grading papers) before school begins so you can give full attention to the children.

7. **Establish Routines and Traditions:** Children behave better when they know what they can count on. Establish traditions they can anticipate and that provide them with fond memories and feelings of belonging and security.

8. **Talk About Children Positively to Others:** Let children overhear you speaking positively about them—bragging about their good qualities, efforts, and actions—to others.

9. **Put It in Writing:** Start a tradition of sending good thoughts in writing. Leave "I care about you" notes in surprising places.

10. **Kiss Your Brain:** When the child is exhibiting behavior that makes you proud and is making great choices, be sure to praise, thank, and draw attention to his great contributions. Tell him to "kiss your brain!" (Children love this!) They will respond by kissing their hand or finger and patting their head. You can model this action as well.

11. **Positive Closure:** At the end of the day, remind your children that they are special and loved. Help them look for something good, both about the day that is finished and the one that lies ahead.

Study Guide

a. **Goal Setting:** What are the characteristics of a caring teacher? If you needed to tell someone something embarrassing or ask for help with a situation that meant a lot to you, who would you choose? What qualities would that person possess?

b. **Questioning and Reflection:** What are some ways you can connect meaningfully with children in your classroom? How do you think these specific connections will make a difference in the way children will respond to you later?

What principles in this chapter would make a difference in the quality of your connection with them?

c. **Case Study:** Mrs. Jones' kindergarten class has been "wound up" and distracted for the last month since the holidays. After trying everything, she decides to use Principle 5, Class Meeting. Which strategies presented would be most appropriate to ensure a relational connection with the group and to provide an opportunity for calming and reassurance?

d. **Personal Examples/Group Brainstorming:** When are children hardest for you to love? Do you feel it is when they are disobedient, angry, upset, whiny, or disrespectful? How do you feel at these moments? Can you give an example? What do you think children need from you at these times?

e. **Learners as Experts:** In the "Creating a Unique Identity for Your Classroom," "Creating Traditions That Connect School to the Home," "Creating Traditions That Connect Home to the School," and "Creating Traditions That Value and Honor Diversity" sections of this chapter,

what strategies are most appealing to you? Explain two strategies you want to use (or have implemented) from the reading, and what you feel the impact on your children or families will be (or has been).

f. **Principles in Action:** Using the "Getting Positive Results Using the Principles in Action" sheet, share one principle you have already implemented from this chapter. What happened or led up to the interaction? Which principle did you use? How did the situation turn out? (How did the child/children respond?) What did you learn?

g. **Research on the Run:** In this section, identify the top three priorities that you want to target in your students. What impact of responsive teacher–child relationships and interactions are most important to you?

h. **Looking Ahead:** Set the purpose for upcoming study by introducing chapter objectives. Thank you for sharing your personal insight about responsive, positive guidance and for your commitment to making a difference in the lives of children.

References

Ackerman, B., & Youngstrom, E. (2001). Emotion knowledge as predictor of social behavior and academic competence in children at risk. *Psychological Science, 12*(1), 8–23.

Adler, A., & Stein, H. (2005). *Case readings and demonstrations: The problem child and the pattern of life.* Bellingham, WA: Alfred Adler Institute.

Ahnert, L., Pinquart, M., & Lamb, M. (2006). Security of children's relationships with non-parental care providers: A meta-analysis. *Child Development, 7*(3), 664–679.

Ainsworth, M. D. (1982). Attachment: Retrospect and prospect. In J. Stevenson-Hinde & C. M. Parks (Eds.), *The place of attachment in human behavior.* New York: Basic Books.

Baker, J. (2006). Contributions of teacher-child relationships to positive school adjustment during elementary school. *Journal of School Psychology, 44,* 211–229.

Barnett, S. W. (2008). *Preschool education and its lasting effects: Research and policy implications.* National Institute for Early Education Research, Rutgers Graduate School of Education. Retrieved February 23, 2012,

from http://nieer.org/resources/research/PreschoolLasting Effects.pdf

Barnett, W., Hustedt, J., Friedman, A., Boyd, J., & Ainsworth, P. (2010). The state of preschool: 2007: State preschool yearbook. The National Institute for Early Education Research, Rutgers Graduate School of Education. Retrieved October 28, 2010, from http://nieer.org/yearbook/pdf/ yearbook.pdf

Bennett, P., Elliott, M., & Peters, D. (2005). Classroom and family effects on children's social skills and behavioral problems. *The Elementary School Journal, 105,* 461–480.

Berry, D., & O'Connor, E. (2009). Behavioral risk, teacher–child relationships, and social skill development across middle childhood: A child-by-environment analysis of change. *Journal of Applied Developmental Psychology, 31*(1), 1–14.

Birch, S., & Ladd, G. (1997). The teacher-child relationship and children's early school adjustment. *Journal of School Psychology, 35,* 61–79.

Blair, K., Denham, S., Kochanoff, A., & Whipple, B. (2004). Playing it cool: Temperament, emotional regulation, and social behavior in preschoolers. *Journal of School Psychology, 42*(6), 419–443.

Bowlby, J. (1988). *A secure base: Parent-child attachment and healthy human development.* London, United Kingdom: Basic Books.

Briggs-Gowan, M., & Carter, A. (2008). Social-emotional screening status in early childhood predicts elementary school outcomes. *Pediatrics 5*(121), 957–962.

Burchinal, M., Campbell, F., Bryant, D., Wasik, B., & Ramey, C. (1997). Early intervention and mediating processes in cognitive performance of children of low-income African American families. *Child Development, 68,* 935–954.

Connell, C., & Prinz, R. (2002). The impact of childcare and parent-child interactions on school readiness and social skills development for low-income African American children. *Journal of School Psychology, 40*(2), 177–193.

Cozolino, L. (2006). *The neuroscience of human relationships: Attachment and the developing social brain.* London, United Kingdom: Norton & Co.

Davidov, M., & Grusec, J. E. (2006). Untangling the links of parental responsiveness to distress and warmth to child outcomes. *Child Development, 77*(1), 44–58.

Denham, S. A. (2005). The emotional basis of learning and development in early childhood education. In B. Spodek (Ed.), *Handbook of research in early childhood education* (pp. 85–103). Mahwah, NJ: Lawrence Erlbaum.

Denham, S., Renwick, S., & Holt, R. (1991). Working and playing together: Prediction of preschool social-emotional competence from mother-child interaction. *Child Development, 62,* 242–249.

Denham, S., Zinssler, K., & Bailey, C. (2011). *Emotional intelligence in the first five years of life.* In R. E. Tremblay, M. Boivin, & Peters, R. (Eds)., *Encyclopedia on early childhood development.* Montreal, Canada: Centre of Excellence for Early Childhood Development.

Downer, J., & Pianta, R. (2006). Academic and cognitive functioning in first grade: Associations with earlier home and child care predictors and with concurrent home and classroom experiences. *School Psychology Review, 35,* 11–30.

Downer, J., Rimm-Kaufman, S., & Pianta, R. (2007). How do classroom conditions and children's risk for school problems contribute to children's behavioral engagement in learning? *School Psychology Review, 36*(3), 413–432.

Early, D., Maxwell, K., Burchinal, M., Alva, S., Bender, R., Bryant, D., Cai, K., Clifford, R., Ebanks, C., Griffin, J., Henry, G., Howes, C., Iriondo-Perez, J., Jeon, H., Mashburn, A., Peisner-Feinberg, E., Pianta, R., Vandergrift, N., & Zill, N. (2007). Teachers' education, classroom quality, and young children's academic skills: Results from seven studies of preschool programs. *Child Development, 78*(2), 558–580.

Ehrle, J., Adams, G., & Tout, K. (2001). Who's caring for our youngest children? Child care patterns of infants and toddlers. *Early Childhood Research Quarterly, 15*(4), 497–514.

Fuller, B., Gasko, J., & Anguiano, R. (2010). Lifting pre-K quality: Caring and effective teachers. UC Berkeley, Institute for Human Development Policy Report. Retrieved November 1, 2011, from www.brookespublishing.com/newsletters/downloads/lifting_pre-k_quality.pdf

Gallagher, P., & Lambert, R. (2006). Classroom quality, concentration of children with special needs, and child outcomes in Head Start. *Exceptional Children, 73*(1), 31–52.

Hamre, B., & Pianta, R. (2001). Early teacher-child relationships and the trajectory of children's school outcomes through eighth grade. *Child Development, 72,* 625–638.

Hamre, B., & Pianta, R. (2006). Student-teacher relationships. In G. G. Bear & K. M. Minke (Eds.), *Children's needs III: Development, prevention, and intervention* (pp. 59–71). Bethesda, MD: National Association of School Psychologists.

Hart, B., & Risley, T. R. (1995). *Meaningful differences in the everyday experience of young American children.* Baltimore, MD: Paul H. Brookes.

Haynes, M. (2009). Promoting quality in PreK–grade 3 classrooms: Findings and results from NASBE's early childhood education network. *Issues in Brief,* National Association of State Boards of Education.

Hernandez, D. (2011). Double jeopardy: How third-grade grading skills and poverty influence high school graduation. Annie E. Casey Foundation Report.

Herrera, C., & Dunn, J. (1997). Early experiences with family conflict: Implications for arguments with a close friend. *Developmental Psychology, 33*(5), 869–831.

Howes, C., & Hamilton, C. (1992). Children's relationships with child care teachers: Stability and concordance with parental attachments. *Child Development, 63,* 867–878.

Howes, C., & Shivers, E. (2006). New child-caregiver attachment relationships: Entering childcare when the caregiver is and is not an ethnic match. *Social Development, 15*(4), 574–590.

Kersey, K., & Masterson, M. (2011, July). Learn to say yes! when you want to say no! to create cooperation instead of resistance: Positive behavior strategies in teaching. *Young Children, 66*(4), 40–44.

Kestenbaum, R., Farber, E., & Sroufe, L. A. (1989). Individual differences in empathy among preschoolers' concurrent and predictive validity. In N. Eisenberg (Ed.), *Empathy and related emotional responses: No. 44. New directions for child development* (pp. 51–56). San Francisco, CA: Jossey-Bass.

Landry, S. (2005). *Early language and literacy development* [In Support of Children series]. Norfolk, VA: Old Dominion University.

Lepper, M. R. (1981). Intrinsic and extrinsic motivation in children: Detrimental effects of superfluous social controls. In W. A. Collins (Ed.), *Aspects of the development of competence: Minnesota symposium on child psychology, Vol. 14* (pp. 155–213). Hillsdale, NJ: Lawrence Erlbaum.

Lucas, M. (2001). The military child care connection. *The Future of Children, 11*(1), 128–133.

Macoby, E. (1992). The role of parents in the socialization of children: An historical overview. *Developmental Psychology, 28,* 1006–1017.

Magnuson, K., & Waldfogel, J. (2004). Early childhood care and education: Effects on ethnic and racial gaps in school readiness. *The Future of Children, 15*(1), 169–196.

Miles, S. B., & Stipek, D. (2006). Contemporaneous and longitudinal associations between social behavior and literacy achievement in a sample of low-income elementary school children. *Child Development, 77*(1), 103–117.

Murray, C., Waas, G., & Murray, K. (2008). Child race and gender as moderators of the association between teacher-child relationships and school adjustment. *Psychology in the Schools, 45*(6), 562–578.

National Association for the Education of Young Children. (2008). NAEYC Accreditation Standards for Relationships. Retrieved September 1, 2008, from www.naeyc.org/academy/standards/standard1

National Association for the Education of Young Children. (2010). *Standards for initial & advanced early childhood professional preparation programs.* Retrieved February 23, 2012, from www.naeyc.org/files/ncate/file/NAEYC%20Initial%20and%20Advanced%20Standards%206_2011-final.pdf

NICHD Early Child Care Research Network. (2005). Early childcare and children's development in the primary grades: Follow-up results from the NICHD study of early childcare. *American Educational Research Journal, 42*(3), 537–570.

Norris, J. (2009). Authoritative classroom management: How control and nurturance work together. *Theory into Practice, 49,* 122–129.

Ochshorn, S. (2011). *Forging a new framework for professional development: A report on "The Science of Professional Development in Early Childhood Education: A National Summit."* Washington, DC: Zero to Three. Retrieved February 23, 2012, from www2.ed.gov/programs/eceducator/forging.pdf

O'Connor, E., & McCartney, K. (2006). Testing associations between young children's relationships with mothers and teachers. *Journal of Educational Psychology, 98,* 87–98.

Office of Head Start, Early Childhood Learning and Knowledge Center. (2012). *Head Start leaders guide to positive child outcomes: Domain 6: Social and emotional development.* Retrieved February 23, 2012, from http://eclkc.ohs.acf.hhs.gov/hslc/tta-system/teaching/eecd/Domains%20of%20Child%20Development/Social%20and%20Emotional%20Development/edudev_art_00016_061705.html

Parpal, M., & Maccoby, E. (1985). Maternal responsiveness and subsequent child compliance. *Child Development, 56,* 1326–1334.

Perry, B. (2001). *Maltreated children: Experience, brain development and the next generation.* New York: W. W. Norton.

Perry, B. (2005, March 22). The impact of childhood trauma and neglect on brain development: Implications for children, adolescents and adults. Remarks to Old Dominion University In Support of Children Lecture Series, Norfolk, VA.

Pianta, R., & Hadden, D. (2008, June). What we know about the quality of early education settings: Implications for research on teacher preparation and pofessional development. *The State Education Standard,* 20–27.

Pianta, R., Hamre, B., & Stuhlman, M. (2003). Relationships between teachers and children. In W. M. Reynolds & G. E. Miller (Eds.), *Handbook of psychology: Educational psychology, Vol. 7* (pp. 199–234). Hoboken, NJ: Wiley.

Raikes, A., & Thompson, R. (2006). Family emotional climate, attachment security and young children's emotion knowledge in a high-risk sample. *British Journal of Developmental Psychology, 24,* 89–101.

Raver, C. (2002). Emotions matter: Making the case for the role of young children's emotional development for early school readiness. *Child Development, 16*(3), 535–555.

Rimm-Kaufman, S. E. (2002). Early behavioral attributes and teachers' sensitivity as predictors of competent behavior in the kindergarten classroom. *Journal of Applied Developmental Psychology, 23*(4), 451–470.

Schultz, T. (2008, June). Tackling PK–3 assessment & accountability challenges: Guidance from the national early childhood accountability task force. *The State Education Standard,* 411. Retrieved June 15, 2008, from www.nasbe.org/index.php/file-repository?func=startdown&id=764

Shonkoff, J. P., & Philips, D. A. (Eds.). (2001). *From neurons to neighborhoods: The science of early childhood development.* Washington, DC: National Academy Press.

Snyder, J., Cramer, D., Afrank, J., & Patterson, G. (2005). The contribution of ineffective discipline and parent hostile attributions about child misbehavior to the development of conduct problems at home and school. *Developmental Psychology, 41,* 1–12.

Spencer, R., Jordan, J., & Sazama, J. (2004). *Empowering children for life: A preliminary report.* Wellesley, MA: Wellesley Centers for Women.

Sroufe, L. A. (1995). *Emotional development: The organization of emotional life in the early years.* New York: Cambridge University Press.

Stipek, D. (2006). No Child Left Behind comes to preschool. *The Elementary School Journal, 106*(5), 455–465.

U.S. Bureau of Labor Statistics. (2010/2011). Child care workers. Retrieved from www.bls.gov/oco/ocos170.htm

U.S. Department of Education. (2009). *The early learning challenge fund: Results-oriented, standards reform of state early learning programs.* Retrieved February 23, 2012, from www.ed.gov/print/about/inits/ed/earlylearning/elef-factsheet.html

U.S. Department of Labor. (2007). *America's dynamic workforce: 2007.* Retrieved from www.dol.gov/asp/media/reports/workforce2007/ADW2007_Full_Text.pdf

c h a p t e r   2

Guiding Behavior

This chapter will introduce opportunities to create healthy outcomes for children by using positive, relational guidance. As you interact with the text and activities, you will gain insight and self-awareness about the ways that a teacher's words, actions, and responses can influence the behavior of children. You will discover how much your contribution changes the outcome of interactions and affects children's understanding and cooperation. By guiding behaviors effectively in the first place, you will be able to avoid many common behavior challenges.

The strategies presented will help you develop new ways of seeing and thinking about children. They will assist you in becoming more sensitive and responsive to children's needs. You will be able to redirect behavior with strategies that work to support children's developing social and emotional competence. The principles are intended to help teachers become more effective; however, children will learn the strategies as they see you model them. They will influence the way that children treat each other. The 101 principles provide a way to communicate with others that will enhance the quality of interactions for both adults and children.

Chapter Principles

12: Modeling

13: Make a Big Deal

14: Incompatible Alternative

15: Choice

16: When–Then/Abuse It–Lose It

17: Follow-Through/Consistency

18: Validation

19: Extinction

20: Take Time to Teach

21: Punt the Plan

Chapter Objectives

As you explore the text and activities in this chapter, you will be able to:

- Activate the powerful influence of adult responsiveness on children's behavior
- Recognize the difference between discipline and punishment
- Understand the unintended consequences of punitive practices
- Avoid power struggles and ultimatums as you shift to positive guidance

- Gain effective strategies to promote cooperation and engagement
- Learn essential strategies to boost social skills

Children Learn by Watching and Listening to Us

Children come into the world vulnerable and dependent. They form their sense of self by the way adults respond to them, as well as to others. When adults are kind, children feel they are worthy of kindness. As a result, they will treat others with kindness—as well as be kind in the way they treat themselves.

It is our responsibility to be sensitive to children's unique traits and temperaments. We want to match our response to a child's needs and stay aware of how much each one trusts and depends on us to help him be successful. Children who naturally laugh and have outgoing personalities are more likely to engage adults in conversation and find it easier to get their needs met. Children who are active may need adults to be patient and provide outlets for their energy. We may need to reach out to a quiet or sensitive child to include him and draw him into active conversation. We want to assist him by creating opportunities to interact successfully with other children. For a child who is impulsive, we want to respond in gentle ways, guiding with patience as we support skills that help him create positive outcomes. With our guidance, children can get what they need in healthy ways.

What children do is modeled on what we do—and what they say is based on what we say. Unless we reflect on our actions and work to make our responses conscious, most of us will do to children what was done to us when we were their age. Our responses will come from what we experienced. Even though an adult may have a degree in child development, when a 2-year-old throws food in her face, the emotions she feels can be influenced by the way someone once responded to her. If we were raised in a strict environment, we may react to that loss of control by becoming permissive. Those who have children of their own know that adults often become like the parent(s) who raised them. We might be surprised to hear the words we say sound like the ones that our parents said to us.

Most of us are committed to creating positive experiences for children. However, we know that when adults are frustrated, they may resort to comments such as, "Stop it!" "Don't!" "You're just asking for trouble." "What's wrong with you?" "It serves you right!"

How many times do we hear these statements coming out of the mouths of frustrated parents and teachers? How many times do we say them ourselves? Often children themselves are present when adults comment on behavior frustrations. "He's a handful!" "You should see what she did now!" "What's gotten into him?" "My children are all wild today. There must have been a full moon!"

Without realizing it, we tend to focus on what children are doing *wrong* instead of focusing on what they are doing *right!* It makes sense to be drawn to disruptive, self-defeating, unproductive behaviors, because those are the ones that embarrass and distract us. Our words show our frustration. However, are we putting our energy where it will pay off?

The truth is that what we focus on will grow! Like a weed that is fed and watered, the behavior that gets our attention will thrive. The impact of frustrating experiences can be long lasting. Children take their cues about themselves from our responses, so we need to think carefully before we speak. Remember that words have the power to influence children's perceptions about themselves and others.

Children internalize the labels they hear, and they remember the experiences that make them feel either inept or competent. When a child is successful in negotiating a new situation, he will feel confident about handling the challenge the next time. When he is not successful, he may continue to respond in ways that are frustrating to himself and others.

We need to think carefully about how we respond to children—and then choose to speak and act purposefully. It is easier to say, "That child needs to change his behavior," than to admit that the behavior that needs to change is our own. It's important to put the camera on ourselves to see how our own actions and words influence the child's reactions. Rather than rely on interactions that don't help, we can use productive strategies that will create cooperation instead of resistance. The following principles work to change our own behaviors—as well as our children's responses—so that we can help them learn the skills they need to be successful in school and life. What children learn from watching us will determine how they will respond to others in the future.

● **THINK ABOUT IT!**

Describe the child who, when present, makes the day go better for everyone. Next, describe the child who, when not present, makes the day seem easier. What skills does the first child have that the second one does not?

_____

_____

What do you think can be done to model, practice, and create a positive experience and outcome for the child who needs to learn the skills you have listed?

_____

_____

The Goal of Discipline

Discipline refers to teaching and training. The goal of discipline is self-discipline. We want children to learn the skills they need to navigate through life on their own. The sooner they have skills for getting along with others, the better. Children are capable of developing those skills early.

In order to help children make good decisions and take responsibility for their own lives, we need to shift our focus to ways we can teach and train them effectively. First, instead of putting the primary focus on what children are doing wrong, we want to concentrate on what children are doing right. Next, we need to consider what we ourselves do or say that contributes to the behaviors we do _not_ want to see. Children need a safe environment where they can feel confident to take risks and learn from their mistakes. We want to focus on teaching children healthy ways to get along and solve challenges with results that are satisfying and successful.

Many people confuse the word *discipline* with the word *punishment,* and even use the words synonymously. We often hear, "What this child most needs is a little discipline," when what is meant is, "This child needs a little punishment." Many of us think of punishment as a penalty for misbehavior. In contrast, positive relational discipline teaches children to become self-disciplined without needing to rely on punishment or coercion. This is a shift away from "stopping misbehavior." Instead, we put all of our effort and energy into ensuring that children have the strategies they need to be successful in relational and learning interactions. They will need our support to learn effective skills, language, and strategies for self-regulation and emotional regulation. These are the building blocks of healthy social interactions and success in school.

Positive relational discipline uses empowering interaction practices that assures respect for every child, models healthy relationship patterns, and fosters social and emotional competence. Through meaningful relationships, children gain a deeper understanding of respect, empathy, and care for themselves and others.

● THINK ABOUT IT!

Punishment refers to inflicting pain on purpose. There are many ways that we purposely inflict pain on others. There are many ways that do not include physical punishment that can hurt others. Can you think of some examples?

_____

_____

_____

Can you think of some ways that others hurt us, maybe without even realizing it?

_____

_____

_____

Many of us were raised to feel that children will be more likely to change their behavior if they feel remorseful about what they did. So without realizing that there are more effective ways to motivate change, we may inadvertently resort to punitive habits without understanding that this approach works against the outcome we really want. Besides physically hitting, other ways that can leave a lasting impact include yelling, insulting, name-calling, being sarcastic, or embarrassing or shaming others. If someone embarrassed us by calling attention to what we were wearing, or made us feel silly, what might we feel like doing? We might feel like leaving, retaliating, or embarrassing that person back. Some of us might turn our anger inward and cry. It is important to consider that children feel this way, as well.

Whenever someone humiliates us, talks down to us, or embarrasses us, it sets up a negative reaction. We probably want to withdraw or retaliate in some way. The connection we had is broken and it will take time and energy to repair it. The more often the connection is broken, the weaker it becomes. We need to learn and use strategies that are positive—that keep us connected to children, so that they will want to come to us whenever they need help or guidance and know that we will always be trustworthy, authentic, supportive, and helpful.

Guiding Behavior in Positive Ways

Teachers need the ability to guide behavior in positive ways. As Chapter 1 suggests, the most important goal for teachers is to develop an authentic relationship with children based on respect and caring. The resulting connection formed is critical for children who may spend between 40 and 60 hours a week in childcare, before and after school care, or in a classroom.

Even a caring teacher may respond punitively if she lacks effective strategies to redirect and guide children in positive ways. A teacher's beliefs and prior experiences may influence her response to misbehavior. She may think that losing a desired privilege will help a child learn a lesson. She may be frustrated with her own inability to respond effectively and frustrated with a child who has difficulty following directions. Yet research consistently shows that punitive approaches create more problems than they solve.

The skills for positive redirection and social–emotional competence given in this chapter are critical for children. The strategies are also important for teachers, who research tells us most often leave the profession because they do not have the skills they

● **THINK ABOUT IT!**

Can you think of some reasons why punishment might be unfair?

_____

_____

_____

What kinds of feelings may arise when children do not respond to what you ask or need?

_____

_____

In what way might your upbringing or beliefs about discipline affect the way you feel about or respond to children?

_____

_____

_____

need to deal with discipline issues. Punitive practices not only break the relational connection with children, but sap teachers of needed energy and enthusiasm for teaching.

Considering the Unintended Complications of Punitive Responses

We need to consider the importance of teaching skills instead of punishing, or we run the risk of complicating the issue and creating long-term problems for the child. We need to understand the issues, even if we ourselves are committed to positive approaches, so that we can speak knowledgeably about the challenges and become strong advocates for positive practices.

What are some reasons why teachers punish?

- Teachers are more likely to respond negatively to children when they are stressed, frustrated, or under a deadline.
- Teachers may not see everything that happens and punish a child without realizing what preceded the incident.
- When several children are involved in misbehavior, often only one is singled out by the teacher.
- If a teacher feels a child is "out to get her" or "did it on purpose," she is more likely to punish him.
- If a teacher has frequent conflict with a child, the child will be punished more often.
- Children with academic challenges often get in trouble.
- Children who are active get punished more often.
- Children from low income, minority, ethnic, or culturally different backgrounds are more likely to be punished.
- Teachers may be inconsistent in their responses and respond punitively one day, but not another—for the same behavior.
- Teachers may use punishment without realizing the deeper life lessons that are modeled, such as "might makes right" and "it's OK to make other people feel bad if they do something you don't like."

What unintended consequences result from punishment?

- The child feels embarrassed and may withdraw emotionally to protect his self-esteem.
- The positive connection between the child and teacher is weakened.
- The punitive response decreases the child's motivation.
- Resulting resentment blocks the child's ability to learn.
- The frustration over being singled out may cause a child to retaliate.
- A child's lack of success may cause him to disengage from school.
- Punishment doesn't teach the child needed skills to be successful next time.
- Over time, a child responds with anger and feels school is not a place for him.

- A child loses motivation, effort, interest, and enthusiasm for learning.
- Other children are influenced by the teacher's negative response to a child and form lasting perceptions about him.

Discipline and Punishment: What's the Difference?

It is important to distinguish between the terms *discipline* and *punishment* and to clarify the benefits of positive responsive interactions for all children.

Discipline	Punishment
Discipline means to teach and train.	Punishment means to inflict purposeful pain.
Discipline focuses on what we *do* want children to do.	Punishment focuses on what we *don't* want children to do.
Discipline teaches children that responsibility comes from self.	Punishment makes a child dependent on external control.
Discipline increases long-term positive behaviors.	Punishment decreases motivation and effort.
Discipline teaches permanent skills.	Punishment only stops behaviors temporarily.
Discipline strengthens the bond between adult and child.	Punishment breaks the connection and causes a child to retreat or pull away from an adult emotionally.
Discipline teaches emotional competence and self-regulation.	Punishment that embarrasses the child will make him turn his anger outward by acting out.
Discipline gives children skills to be successful in school.	Punishment makes a child feel school is not a pleasant place for him to be.
Discipline shows children that they can be successful.	Punishment makes a child feel like a failure.
Discipline makes children resilient, empathetic, and caring toward others. The child turns these feelings outward.	Punishment causes self-doubt, shame, and embarrassment. The child turns these feelings inward.
Discipline creates responsibility and significance that turns into cooperation.	Punishment causes retaliation and anger that turns into uncooperative behavior.
Discipline inspires a child to *be* like you.	Punishment inspires a child to *act* like you.

Positive Principles for Guiding Behavior and Relationships

The benefits of positive redirection and responsive support are lasting. Children need to learn how to be cooperative, pay attention, follow directions, get help, enter a group, understand the emotions of others, and respond in appropriate ways to various social interactions. These *prosocial skills* are socially responsible behaviors that include emotional regulation, empathy, cooperation, and compliance. They form the foundation of self-control and help a child problem-solve and get along well with others. These are essential skills for academic success and for healthy social relationships.

We want to focus all of our energy to help children become independent, motivated, and responsible human beings. When we replace punitive practices with positive connections, children will respond in new ways, and the benefits will be experienced each day in the classroom—and long into the future. Using the 101 positive redirection skills will increase your confidence as a teacher, and will create positive outcomes for all of your children in their interactions with you and with their peers.

The following principles work to change our own behavior—as well as children's responses—to elicit cooperation and motivation.

 ## Principle 12: Modeling

Model the behavior you want. Show the child, by example, how to behave. Children are watching us all the time, and they will grow up to be like us—whether we want them to or not.

- If you want children to develop character traits that you value, then you need to demonstrate those traits in your daily interactions. If you want children to be gentle, kind, patient, self-controlled, faithful, honest, generous, persistent, hard working, and caring, you must live those traits yourself!

- If you want children to be polite, then you can say, "please," "thank you," and "excuse me" in a pleasant voice when you ask for something or take something from a child.

- If you want children to be neat, it is important to show pride by keeping the classroom neat and clean.

- If you want children to be quiet in the hall, be sure you and other teachers refrain from conversation as well.

- If you want children to show a sense of humor and genuine pleasure interacting with their peers, you must demonstrate this same spirit.

● **THINK ABOUT IT!**

What are two things you do because your own parent modeled that behavior?

1. _____

2. _____

What are two ways you have seen children imitate you?

1. _____

2. _____

What are some of the qualities you want children to have when they leave you? How will you model those each day?

_____

_____

- If you want children to be kind, be respectful about children's space and belongings. For example, before you help a child with his zipper or food wrapper, ask if he can do it himself or if he would like help. Showing children how to be thoughtful is much more powerful than telling them.

Principle 13: Make a Big Deal

Make a big deal over responsible, considerate, appropriate behavior—with eye contact, thanks, praise, thumbs-up, recognition, hugs, special privileges, or incentives (not food). Children want and need our attention. We need to train ourselves to watch when children are behaving in productive ways (for themselves and others) and give our attention to those behaviors.

Stay "tuned in" and aware, so that when children negotiate good decisions and solutions, you can support these positive contributions. When we call attention to their successes, we influence their perceptions about their ability to make positive contributions to others and to make good decisions for themselves. Next time the child encounters a similar challenge he will know that you noticed and will be more likely to remember the successful experience.

Birth to Age 3

- Focus on reciprocal interactions with smiles, nods, and personal conversation.

- Help children feel secure through predictable routines.

- Respond with positive comments about new milestones and discoveries.

- Be mindful to respond to behaviors you want children to repeat. For example, if an adult laughs as an infant dribbles food out of her mouth, she may repeat the behavior to gain a similar reaction. She learns that she can make things happen!

- When a child shows empathy toward another child, be sure to support his developing emotional competence. "That was kind for you to help Sondra."

Ages 3 to 8

- Give attention to the children as often as possible when they are doing what you want them to do, and let them know how proud you are of their good choices. Use positive, specific feedback. Tell them what they are doing that you want to see more of!

- Send home "Great Moments" certificates every day highlighting children who are kind helpers, hard workers, and good friends.

- Let children see that making positive contributions and doing the right thing pays off by recognition, privileges, praise, and value in your classroom community.

- Focus on the positive. Take a clipboard with you and give children checks for doing the right thing when walking in the hall.

- Draw a smiley face on the board and let children sign their name underneath for making good choices. (Or let children draw smiley faces of their own!)

- Focus on the behaviors you want to see grow!

Children are motivated by positive relationships. They feel that they matter and are significant. They gain a sense of purpose when they contribute to positive experiences with others. They are excited by new discoveries, curious about their interests, and enjoy the positive sensations they gain through interaction with the environment. Imagine their enthusiasm as they snap a needed puzzle piece into place. During this rapid time of intellectual and emotional growth, children benefit from a teacher's verbal support and positive feedback, especially when they have learned a new skill or worked hard to achieve a goal.

Incentives may be used to "jumpstart" new behaviors and encourage new habits. They should be used to support (in addition to, rather than in place of) the relational and positive strategies of the 101 principles. They should also be used only with a child's full participation and assent under the following circumstances:

- **When skills are achievable.** Make sure the child understands what is expected and that he has the skills to accomplish the skill independently.

- **When the child participates.** The child should participate in defining the goal and choosing the incentive he wants to achieve. For example, an older child may decide to keep track of assignments completed. When he reaches four, he wants extra time to read with a friend.

- **When there is intrinsic value.** Encourage relational incentives, such as earning lunch with the teacher, partnering with a friend on an assignment, or earning the coveted job of washing the whiteboards with a friend. These activities provide healthy social engagement and responsible contributions that benefit everyone.

- **When they are developmentally appropriate.** Use incentives for younger children with care. For example, in Mrs. Hammond's class, a 5-year-old continues to drop his coat on the floor instead of hanging it in his cubby after recess. She is certain that he is able to hang it independently, but keeps forgetting. She laminates several cards with a picture of a coat on a hook. Each time Isaiah hangs his coat successfully, he drops one of the cards into a container. When he earns five cards, he earns the incentives he has worked for: He wants to get the bag of balls from the closet and bring them outside for recess. The cards work as a cue, without Mrs. Hammond needing to speak to him. This incentive was appropriate for Isaiah. (He was thrilled to be the ball boy on Friday!)

- **When the accomplishment is secure.** Children should never lose the incentive (or the step towards the incentive) once it is earned. Each step toward the goal is gained when the child is able to achieve it, until he reaches the agreed-on number. The incentive is based on the number of times that a child has completed a task rather than restricted by a time frame.

- **When they support children's success.** Cooperative incentives can encourage children to work together and inspire team spirit. For example, Mr. Anglan's second graders decide on a dance party once they reach 50 books (together as a group) that they have read at home. He doesn't set a time frame, but lets them gain points until the goal is reached. All children are to be included in the party.

There are many reasons why food should not be given as a reward or incentive, however. We want to encourage children to have a healthy relationship with their bodies. Food is for nourishment. We don't want to contribute to issues such as anorexia, bulimia, body image obsessions, or the use of food to soothe emotions. Later in life, adults may use food as a substitute for love, caring, comfort, or relief. We should eat when we are hungry and stop when we are full. We should make healthy food choices and stay tuned in to our body's needs. Food is associated with the warmth and comfort that we received as infants. Yet while food may seem to work as an incentive, it is not in a child's best interest to use food in this manner, especially in a school or early childhood setting.

● **THINK ABOUT IT!**

What are five behaviors you want to emphasize and notice in children?

1. _____

2. _____

3. _____

4. _____

5. _____

Name some behaviors in your classroom that you want to stop giving attention to. How can you turn your response around to be sure that you are focusing your attention on the behaviors you *do* want?

_____

_____

_____

_____

Accepting the Challenge to Focus on the Positive

It is very tempting when we see a child engaged in a non-productive activity to scold him, say "no," or tell him to stop. Our focus on what the child is doing wrong can actually backfire when we give our attention to the very behavior we are hoping to stop. We will be much more successful if we can quickly think of an incompatible alternative that is useful or interesting to the child. An *incompatible alternative* is an activity that cannot be done at the same time as the undesired behavior, such as walking instead of running, or whispering instead of yelling. Our ultimate goal is to engage him in something that is productive and OK for him to be doing.

It is much more effective for us to focus the child's attention on what we want him to do. We do not even mention the behavior we want to stop. Because we have not given any attention to the previous activity, we do not invite a power struggle. The incompatible alternative replaces the unwanted behavior immediately—without making an issue of it—as it encourages the child to engage in a behavior that is constructive and helpful.

A specific challenge in the early childhood classroom is redirecting behavior within the context of a group setting. The use of the incompatible alternative is very effective for groups of children. Rather than focus on what you do not want children to be doing, simply state what you want them to be doing—and how you want it accomplished.

Principle 14: Incompatible Alternative

Give the child something to do that is incompatible with the inappropriate behavior. Say, "Let's pretend we are on a secret mission and see if we can walk all the way to the cafeteria without anyone hearing us." "Help me pick out six markers" (when the child is unfocused or annoying). If a child is bothering you by playing with his shoestrings, instead of mentioning it, simply ask him to help you by sorting the papers or crayons by color.

When we want to stop one behavior, we need to put something else in its place. If we give the child something to do that is incompatible with the inappropriate behavior (that he can't do at the same time), we will discover how quickly this encourages cooperation. Instead of asking a child to stop running, we can suggest something positive for him to do, such as, "Use your walking feet" or "Come tiptoe beside me."

When a child is wandering around aimlessly, we can say, "Come read a book with me." When a child is talking with a friend instead of doing his work, we can say, "Please show me your writing." The child learns what we want him to be doing, while our positive focus on his help, cooperation, and contribution reinforces our goals for him. We have redirected his attention and not wasted our energy addressing his mistakes. The behavior becomes a non-issue. As we provide purposeful and meaningful ways for the child to be successful, he will learn how to think of good options for himself in the future. Remember that what we focus on will grow, so all of our energy should be spent focusing on productive, healthy outcomes.

● **THINK ABOUT IT!**

List an incompatible alternative for the following behaviors:

1. Running _____

2. Talking during silent reading time _____

3. Rocking back and forth in a chair _____

4. Rattling the paintbrush container _____

5. Bothering another child _____

6. A most frustrating classroom challenge _____

You will find that it requires practice for adults to think of positive alternatives. In the same way, it can be a struggle for children to redirect their own thinking about what *to* do. As they hear you model constructive options, they will become better at generating their own solutions!

🦋 *Principle 15: Choice*

Give the child two choices, both of which are positive and acceptable to you. "Would you rather tiptoe or hop over to the carpet?" "We need to clear off our desks. Do you need one minute or two?" Then set the timer.

The Choice Principle gives the child two incompatible alternatives. The teacher states the desired goal and then gives the child two choices about how it can be accomplished. "We need to hold hands while crossing the walkway. Do you want to hold my left hand or right hand?" "We need to put away the toys. Would you rather help with the puzzles or the blocks?"

Instead of saying, "Stop running," say, "We need to be quiet in the hall. Would you rather tiptoe or sneak?" This takes the focus off of running, and you have given the child a choice of two positive alternatives. "Would you rather walk on clouds or pillows? Let's do it together." Children will quickly make a choice.

It is important to use only two choices, and for both choices to create a positive outcome for the child and be acceptable for you. If the child refuses or decides on a third choice not provided by you, simply say, "You choose, or I'll choose."

For example, when you say, "It's time to clean up. Would you rather do it in one minute or two?" there may be a child who will say, "I want three." Then, you say, "One minute or two. You choose, or I'll choose." The child will want to choose for himself and will make the decision to go with one of the choices you have provided. He wants and needs to have *some* control over his life. If you have to choose, do so quickly and move on to keep the focus on what is interesting and inviting.

"It's chilly outside. Do you want to wear your coat or your sweater?" If you have offered a specific choice, and the child hesitates, then *you* choose one—while quickly making cheerful conversation about what is going to happen next. It is important to move on. Practicing choices with a teacher gets the child in the habit of looking for positive alternatives when he can't have what he originally wanted.

Children will feel more in control of what is happening to them and more willing to be cooperative when we support their need to feel competent. When we offer them options, they are likely to cooperate, because they can choose the response that works best for them.

When working with infants and toddlers, the Choice Principle works just as effectively. If a baby is crawling toward another child's toy, rather than talk about it, quickly provide a physical incompatible alternative (another blanket, baby doll, rattle, etc.) that will distract him. Staying aware and present will allow you to intervene with many incompatible alternatives and choices that can prevent common frustrations for children. In the same way, it is important to redirect a toddler's attention toward a positive option rather than talk about what we don't want him to be doing. We can say, "Here is the apple juice. Would you like to drink it from the pink or blue cup?" "It's time to put your shoes on. Do you want to do it alone or with my help?" "It's time for a nap. Would you like to snuggle with your teddy bear or your blanket?" Helping children focus on positive choices is a respectful way to reinforce needed routines and instill a sense of cooperation.

● **Think About It!**

A child is climbing on a chair. What are two alternatives that you could give the child to choose from that would help him do something different?

_____

_____

_____

_____

Can you think of an example of the Choice Principle? Remember, *both* choices need to be acceptable to you and provide positive outcomes for the child.

_____

_____

_____

_____

What should you say if the child offers a third possibility or replies, "Neither"? (Don't forget to repeat the needed goal and your two choices. Then say, "You choose or I'll choose.")

_____

_____

_____

_____

Understanding Power Struggles

None of us like it when another person orders us around. It usually brings out the worst in us and causes us to disrespect, dislike, or challenge the one who gave the order. Whenever we issue an ultimatum or tell a child what to do, we are setting ourselves up for a power struggle. We have given away our power—and now it rests with the child. It can become like a carefully orchestrated chess game. The next move is his—and he might choose to respond with, "No" or "Make me." Many small children rebel by saying, "You're not my momma." This puts us in the precarious role of either trying to force obedience or backing down.

A teacher once asked, "What would you do if you tell a child to move and he doesn't?" That is the problem with *telling* a child to do something. What will you do if the child refuses? This is a critical question in behavior guidance with groups of children, because when you interact with a particular child, other children are watching. The lessons learned are not only critical for you and the child, but for all of the other children as well.

Demands such as "Move over here" or "Stop touching the wall" invite the child to test you. Unfortunately, many well-meaning teachers and adults do not understand that using a demand sets up a power struggle with children for whom they are responsible and then wonder why they do not get cooperation. When we need something to be done, we can either invite children to "come with us" (cooperate) by the way we use our words, or we can make them "push back" by the way we challenge or demand something from them.

In order for us to gain a child's cooperation, we need to be respectful when we see that a child needs to change his behavior. Such statements as, "It's time to line up" or "I need your help," followed by a choice of how it is done, such as, "You may bring your book with you or leave it in your desk" or "You can collect the papers or the crayons," encourage cooperation and show the child that you respect his willingness to help by giving him some control over how he accomplishes the goal. (The Incompatible Alternative and Choice Principles give every chance for success. The Demonstrate Respect Principle, described in Chapter 3, will gain respect in return.) We have wisely handed to him a reason to be cooperative instead of the power to become an adversary.

Avoiding Ultimatums

It is critical to recognize the kinds of communication that adults inadvertently use to set up power struggles. An ultimatum causes children to resist and invites a power struggle. This can take three forms, and it always implies or states a threat.

1. A demand: "Come here right now." (Do this because I said so.)
2. A demand with a threat of something the child does *not* want: "If you keep talking, you will eat lunch alone." "If you don't do what I say, I am going to call your mother." "If you don't come now, I am leaving you."
3. A demand with a threat to remove something the child *does* want: "Either stay on your mat by yourself, or you will not go to recess."

● THINK ABOUT IT!

What is one ultimatum you have given or that you have heard someone else give?

_____

_____

What does the child learn when he is given an ultimatum?

_____

_____

How does an ultimatum place the adult in a precarious role?

_____

_____

_____

An ultimatum brings out the worst in children. Because they become fearful of not getting or of losing something they want, they will naturally feel resistant. Even if they do comply, they do not do so willingly, and their resentment can lead to further trouble down the road. They will not develop the respect, empathy, and cooperation they need for close relationships and a desire to make good choices in the future. When we become aware of the ways that we set up power struggles, we can replace them with new skills that will build cooperation.

Principle 16: When–Then/Abuse It–Lose It

"When you put your books on the shelf, then you may put on your coat."

"When you finish putting the play-dough away, then you may choose a partner for the game."

The When–Then Principle links a specific expectation to a positive outcome. It is important to use *when* rather than *if*. The word *if* may cause the child to respond, "Suppose I don't?" Then a power struggle has begun. However, the word *when* communicates your belief that the child will follow through.

The When–Then Principle uses a logical contingency and communicates our expectations. "When you clean up, then we can have lunch." "When you come, then we'll choose a book to read together." "When your table is clear, then you may go to the library." Children handle transitions more easily when they understand our expectations. Using *when* invites cooperation.

Until the child completes the first responsibility, he loses out on the promised privilege. "When you put your markers away, then you may go to the sand table." Until he puts the markers away, he can't go on to the next center. We want to say and communicate to children what we would want to hear ourselves—respectful, positive words about what needs to be done.

"If you don't clean up, you aren't going to have lunch." "If you don't come now, you don't get a book in the car!" "If you don't put your markers away, you aren't going to the library." This is not the When–Then Principle, but an ultimatum, and results in a power struggle, which the child usually wins. He may become resentful and find a way to retaliate if he feels forced to comply. He may decide he would rather not get the book or go to the library than complete the task. But the child needs his lunch, should be encouraged to read a book in the car, and will benefit from a visit to the library. Instead of issuing ultimatums, we need to always consider, "What is in the best interest of the child?"

It is important to focus on the positive side of the principle (when–then) instead of the negative implication. Children need to understand that behavior choices bring about reliable results that are linked to their actions. They need to see that we are paying attention and setting expectations and limits that are in their own best interest.

Children learn by our consistency in using both parts of the When–Then/Abuse It–Lose It Principle that they must follow through on the clean up before they may move to another activity. They realize that in order to read a book, they cannot throw it or tear it. They learn to handle materials with respect knowing someone else will be using them, too. They know that to play with their friends, they need to be gentle and careful, and that these guidelines are in place to help them be productive and happy. If we are consistent in insisting on the positive behavior, then removal of an object (a book that continues to be thrown, for example) will be infrequent. "I am sorry. I need to make sure you know how to read the book carefully. Why don't you choose another one and show me that you can use it gently." When we do need to step in, it should be with kindness, support, and matter-of-fact follow-through so that children understand it is necessary to ensure their safety, the safety of others, and respect for the classroom environment.

The When–Then Principle helps children feel respected and gives them a consistent opportunity to be successful. It presents a logical connection between responsibility and success before misbehavior occurs. It allows for a child to self-correct the next time, because he was responsible for the choice he made. Children want to choose—and want to feel proud of their success. In doing so, they develop self-regulation and self-discipline. This approach gives them ownership of their own decisions and motivation to be responsible for themselves and their own behavior.

We can "practice" the When–Then Principle by talking and "thinking out loud" to babies and toddlers about what we are doing: "When we finish our nap, then we will sing songs (play, etc.)." We can explain our own "When–Then" sequences to pre-verbal children. "When I have finished putting away my book, then I will come and color with you." Over time, children will see and hear the important follow-through that connects self-regulated behavior and responsibility to the pay off of positive experiences.

● **THINK ABOUT IT!**

What are two If–Thens that can be changed into When–Thens?

1. _____

2. _____

 ### *Principle 17: Follow-Through/Consistency*

Don't let the child manipulate you out of using your better judgment. Be firm (but kind)! Trust your intuition. If it doesn't feel right, don't let the child do it. Come up with choices and alternatives that can help every child to focus on more appropriate behavior and positive learning experiences.

"We've tried *everything,*" sigh some teachers. That may be the problem. When we are inconsistent in our responses—sometimes scolding or punishing and sometimes ignoring—we can be sure that the child's behavior will continue and probably increase. When we constantly change the way we respond to misbehavior, the child keeps trying, not knowing which response he might receive. The child knows that he may get to do it anyway, because the adult may look the other way,. He knows that he may even get laughed at for doing it—which pays off in gaining more attention. Even though he may be stopped, the risk is worth it to him. By being inconsistent, the teacher is creating more problems than she is solving.

Teachers who are consistent and responsive have a great advantage. Their children demonstrate greater compliance and show fewer behavior challenges. They seem to expend less energy, yet gain reliable results. Here are some important ways to be consistent.

- Keep consistent expectations. Don't fault one child for something you let another child get by with. For example, telling one child to sit up straight during circle time, and then allowing another to lie down is certainly inconsistent.

- Ask yourself if what you are requiring is realistic. Can you follow through with the request you have made? For example, you may tell children that they cannot turn upside down on the monkey bars, and then go ahead and let them after you see all the children are doing it. Some teachers tell children to line up and then get distracted talking to another teacher. They have taught their children to wait until she sounds like "she really means it," since they realize that she often does not follow through.

● **THINK ABOUT IT!**

What type of behavior is most likely to cause teachers to be inconsistent? What do children learn as a result?

_____

_____

Describe one scenario where an adult you observed asked a child to do something, but then did not follow through. What could the adult have done differently to create a more positive outcome?

_____

_____

Describe one scenario where an adult you observed followed through effectively with a child. What happened as a result? What did the child learn?

_____

_____

🦋 *Principle 18: Validation*

Acknowledge (validate) the child's wants and feelings. "I know you feel frustrated with your friend and want to keep both books to yourself. I don't blame you. I would feel the same way. However, she needs to have one. Do you want to choose which one, or shall I?"

When you validate a child's feelings, you align yourself with the child. Then you can go on to deal with the underlying issues. "I understand you feel frustrated, Michael. I would be upset too, if someone took my puzzle. Thank you for telling me and for using your words." "I know you don't want to stop playing your game. I don't blame you. I would feel the same way. However, when the bell rings, you need to line up with the other children."

Children are less likely to act out when they can use their words. We can help by giving them words to describe how they feel, and validate their experience.

When a child is upset, you can say:

"Thank you for telling me."

"I am sorry that happened."

"I am sorry you feel sad. I would never do that to you."

For young children, we often say, "I am sorry your eyes had to see that." Or "I am sorry your ears had to hear that." In this way, we validate their experience without reinforcing what they just saw or heard. When we model using specific emotional language, children learn how to use their words, instead of acting out their feelings.

● **THINK ABOUT IT!**

What are some emotion words that children can learn to describe their feelings in addition to feeling "mad"?

_____

_____

_____

_____

You will be able to use these words when you validate children's experiences. You will be teaching them multiple ways to express themselves in healthy ways when they feel frustrated.

Principle 19: Extinction

Ignore minor misbehavior that is not dangerous, destructive, embarrassing, or an impediment to learning. (Pretend that you didn't hear, move away, or focus on something else.)

Remember, children want our attention. Children repeat the behaviors that work and eliminate the ones that don't work. Teachers often don't realize how much attention they give to behaviors they would prefer to eliminate! We are naturally drawn to disruptive, self-defeating, unproductive behaviors, because those are the ones that distract us. But, by giving the behavior our attention, we inadvertently reinforce it!

When teachers stop teaching and focus on these minor behaviors, teaching time is lost. We need to train ourselves to catch children doing the right thing, and as often as possible look away from the negative behavior so that it does not get reinforced and escalate.

Examples of behaviors that are not dangerous, destructive, embarrassing, or an impediment to learning include:

- Wiggling
- Waving arms in your face (young children)
- Pencil tapping
- Playing with a shoelace
- Facial expressions that communicate an "attitude," such as eye-rolling

You will learn how to address behaviors that are dangerous, destructive, embarrassing, and an impediment to learning in Chapters 8 and 9.

THINK ABOUT IT!

Can you think of more examples of annoying behaviors that you can ignore?

_____

_____

_____

_____

Transforming Teaching Times

We want children to love learning by making our lesson times captivating and interesting. We can do this by noticing and giving attention to positive behaviors and contributions. Here are some constructive approaches to guiding behavior while you are teaching.

Principle 20: Take Time to Teach

Often we expect children to read our minds and know how to do things they have never been taught. Although our expectations may be clear to us, children may not have a clue.

- Be specific! Don't wait until things are going wrong. Start out by teaching what you expect. If you find things still aren't working, instead of focusing on what not to do, review—teach what you want children to be doing.
- Be proactive! Think ahead about how you will engage children in learning. Talk about what you will do next and let children ask questions about what they will be doing.
- Be creative! Use many resources (puppets, props, drama, songs, movement, textural materials, etc.) to involve children through "hands-on" multisensory interaction.
- Be flexible! Vary your teaching. Start whispering. Sing or stand. Stay responsive to children's needs. If one or two children are distracted, vary your plan to engage and involve all of the children.

- Be organized! Prepare materials ahead of time and have them within easy reach. Good organization can head off many behavior issues for children because it reduces frustration. Classroom organization is an important component of a quality classroom.

- Be active! Add movement, activity, and motions to learning, and give children time to stretch and be physically involved with songs and actions that match concepts and lesson plans. Planned physical exercise routines (jumping, skipping, hopping, etc.) that involve motor control, following directions, and adjusting actions to improve performance can increase self-regulation, memory, and planning. These abilities are essential to learning.

- Be individual! Pay individualized attention to children. Move around the room often and spend time with children, supporting their understanding and encouraging their involvement in active learning.

- Be patient! Prepare and practice. It takes regular repetition and rehearsal to make a skill a habit. Practice one skill a day to keep children "on board" with your plans.

- Be purposeful! Teach a new daily skill to build confidence. Encourage children to:

  - Say, "May I help you?" to at least one person every day.

  - Give someone else a genuine compliment every day.

  - Practice balance: Stand on one leg for one minute every day.

  - Stand up straight. (Pretend there is an orange between your shoulder blades and squeeze for one minute a day.)

  - Say at least one thing out loud that you are thankful for every day.

When teachers combine positive guidance with meaningful learning opportunities, children become engaged. We want to help children connect to learning by developing their interests and abilities. They need daily opportunities to explore, create, and discover. Step in frequently to facilitate social–emotional skills by talking often about how to solve problems. Remember to ask questions that link what children are learning to their real-life experiences, and help them develop understanding about concepts in their world. Meet regularly with a trusted colleague to find ways to use the principles in this chapter—and apply them to the needs of your school in ways that are creative and caring.

● **THINK ABOUT IT!**

When you meet with colleagues to talk about teaching and discipline approaches, what are three changes you would like to make?

1. _____

_____

2. _____

_____

3. _____

_____

What steps do you need to take to make these positive changes permanent?

_____

_____

Strengthening Transitions

There are many incompatible alternatives to prevent boring or extended transitions. Use a variety of educational, creative, and fun ways to use the time. Plan to read a story or sing a song while children are putting on their coats or hum a tune while cleaning up. Use your imagination! Here are some good ideas for walking to another room or out to recess:

- Plan ahead! Take along a 4-by-6 card with clues the children can look for in the environment. (Play I-Spy for colors, shapes, sounds, letters, or words.)
- Count steps. Count artwork. Count people. Count smiles. Count doorways.
- Look for favorite drawings or sculptures. Let the children imagine what they will draw or write about when they return to the room.
- Find something with a motor, a moving part, or a specific purpose.
- Have each child think of a compliment to give the child in front of him when they return to the room.
- Play mental math games, so that children have to think about a problem and discuss the solution when they arrive back in your room.

When you return or are finished with a transition, don't forget to compliment the children and tell them how proud you are of how creative and thoughtful they are!

Here are some good ideas for in-room transitions:

- For infants and toddlers, keep music, supplies, and materials lined up in order of their use for the day. Ziplock baggies make great reusable containers to keep the next activity at your fingertips.

- When one activity is completed, make sure the next is already waiting, such as books set out and ready for reading after hands are washed.

- Allow time in the morning for active brain stimulation—so while children are waiting for others to arrive, there are multiple projects and challenges underway that draw children to engage in learning.

- Keep a fantastic book on hand related to the season or unit of study, or just read for fun, but never let a moment pass without engaging minds.

- Have activities and materials waiting when children return from recess or lunch.

- Touch children on the head without talking when it is time for them to line up. Call children by color of shoes, or by letters in names. Ask questions from a lesson and when a child gives the answer, he or she may line up.

- For older children, let them place their materials for the next subject (like writing) on their desks, so that when they return, they know exactly what to begin doing next.

- Create a morning board with a message and assignments for immediate work.

- Leave an envelope on each desk every morning, so that when children arrive, they find instructions and materials enclosed.

- Give time for physical activity and movement throughout the day—before, during, and after transitions. Try yoga, deep breathing, balancing poses, or a meditation (quiet) moment. These brain and body breaks will provide needed exercise, increase concentration, and assist children in learning.

THINK ABOUT IT!

What are some other goals or ideas suitable for your specific age group or school that will transform transitions into constructive learning moments?

_____

_____

Principle 21: Punt the Plan

In the middle of something that is not working, move on to something else. De-stress yourself. Be willing to stay flexible and quickly switch directions when you see that children are unable to focus or need a break.

Stay flexible and responsive to the needs of the children. This will help you meet their needs and enjoy your interactions with them more, knowing that you are responding to their capabilities and interests. If you see that children are having difficulty sitting, vary your teaching to include times for movement, or let them sit on the floor or stand to complete an activity. Keep on hand additional activities, materials, songs, finger plays, and motion activities so that children can switch tempo. You can come back to your scheduled activity later after the children have stretched and are ready to refocus.

No matter how conscientious you are, and how much you hope things might go a certain way, many interruptions will come into your day. Parents may stop in, the principal or director may visit, or a child may get sick. Keep in mind the best interest of the children first, and trust your judgment to make good decisions about how to stay flexible. You will enjoy the day so much more, and the children will enjoy being with you.

Interactions in the classroom are often focused on the whole group. Sometimes you will want to focus on dyadic or one-on-one interactions. The 101 principles work in both situations. They can be used alone and in combination: "When you have put away the tray of sorting blocks, then you may sit with Tabitha" (the When–Then Principle). "Would you like her help, or can you do it yourself?" (the Choice Principle). "Can you arrange the blocks in order by size?" (the Incompatible Alternative Principle). "You and Tabitha used great teamwork in order to put the blocks away. Now you may read sooner!" (the Make a Big Deal Principle). As you become proficient in using them, you will be able to stay flexible in using a variety of approaches that are geared to the needs of the child and situation.

The Punt the Plan Principle, just like all of the 101 principles, places the first priority on the relational aspects of supporting behavior, recognizing that children who are calm and connected are ready to learn. Creating positive memories about learning is as important as the learning itself. Lighten up and enjoy your time with the children each day, because the relationship and experiences you have with them will help them see themselves as the capable and delightful learners they really are.

● **THINK ABOUT IT!**

What are some signs in children's behavior that indicate it's time to move on to another activity, or to present a movement or music break?

_____

_____

Bringing Out the Best in Children

When we use these principles, we will be amazed to see that a change in our own behavior has paid off in a change in the way children respond to us. In the past, we have often thought, "That child needs to change his behavior." Now we will see clearly that our own actions and responses caused or created a reaction or negative response on the part of the child.

It will be exciting to realize that by changing our own behavior, we will begin to see children taking more responsibility for their own actions. We will see a reduced number of conflicts and acting-out behaviors. Children will have improved ability to focus attention, curb impulsivity, and show greater engagement in the classroom.

As you try the principles for the first time, you will see how simple these techniques are to use. The change you feel in yourself and see in your children will definitely be worth the effort. You will notice a difference in how your children respond to you. You will feel calm, rewarded, and confident; energetic at the end of the day; and proud of your children as others notice how well-behaved they have become. You will be making a difference every day by bringing out the best that is in them—by bringing out the best that is in you!

Summary

The goal of positive guidance is to shift your energy into supporting the skills you want to establish. Adding the 101 principles to your guidance tool box will help you redirect behavior effectively and support the growth of social and emotional skills. The strategies from this chapter will refocus your own attention toward becoming more responsive and proactive with children. Each one is designed to help you to individualize support and assist children in developing self-regulation. The positive skills will help you maximize each opportunity to model and teach effective relationship interactions. By implementing each principle from this chapter, you will encourage independence and healthy interdependence as you enhance the positive climate of your classroom.

Using the Principles in Your Classroom

The 101 principles provide 101 options to connect with children so that we can stay connected, enhance relationships, and create positive outcomes without the use of punishment. It is important to learn the principles for guiding behavior in this chapter before moving on to additional principles. The skills you gain will give you lasting solutions that will serve you well in the long run and will equip children with skills for self-regulation and success. To get started:

1. Review the chapter daily.
2. Begin with one new principle.
3. Use the strategy until you feel comfortable. Add the others one at a time.
4. Use the "Getting Positive Results Using the Principles in Action" form at the end of this chapter to practice each principle: "What happened or led up to the interaction? Which principle did you use? How did the situation turn out? (How did the child respond?) What did you learn?"
5. Practice until the strategies become second nature. Those who use them are seen as "magical" teachers because they model skills that help children to become responsive and cooperative. Soon, each one will feel comfortable, and you will see the results in the behavior of your students. You will be thinking of new ways to use all of these strategies each day.

6. Keep track of your efforts. You may want to find a "buddy" and have another teacher watch you—or work as a team with your co-teacher. The more you approach the 101 principles as a schoolwide system of support and encouragement, the more effective you will be in sustaining their use.

7. Print and cut principles from this chapter into strips. Put the principles you have cut into a jar, and pick one each day as you come into the classroom to remind you of your new strategy.

8. Have children pick a principle to focus on for the day. The 101 principles are for everyone, and children will soon be using them as quickly as you do!

9. Apply the 101 principles to common behaviors that you have identified as those you would like to influence.

Here are two scenarios to help you practice. Read each one. Then list five ways you could use principles from this chapter to solve them.

- Martin is a very fidgety child in your classroom. He finds many reasons why he needs to run out of line, lay on the floor during circle time, and roam around the room. He seems constantly distracted. What would/should/could you do?

- Carlos, age 6, is a child in Mrs. Pinneli's first-grade classroom. This is his first year in an inclusive classroom. When he wants something someone else is holding, he tries to grab it away, often hitting the other child to get it, if necessary. Students, and even a few parents, have begun to complain that Carlos's behavior is detrimental to the learning of the other children in the classroom. What would/should/could you do?

Teacher Tips

The following are comments from teachers who have been trained to use the 101 principles in their early care and education settings and elementary classrooms.

I was playing Ping-Pong with a little boy in the gym. At first the child just slammed the ball. I decided to see if I could focus on only what he was doing right. "I'll tell you every one you are doing right." Every time he did anything remotely right, I said, "That's a good one!" It took a lot of focus on my part not to be irritated when he slammed the ball or when he got carried away. But by focusing on every good one, he finally got to 16! "I won," he said. It's not easy to focus on only the positive. It is our natural inclination to focus on what is going wrong. We see the results when we focus on the positive because it keeps us connected.

At the end of the day, a mother came in to pick up her 2-year-old. The little boy came up to me with a toy train that had the same name as his. I asked him, "What is the train's name?" He responded, "It's Thomas!" "That's right! And who is this other train?" I pointed to him! I had a big smile on my face and told him that he was doing a really good job cleaning up his train set. Thomas ran over to put the rest of his train set in the bin—which his mother had been trying to get him to do for 10 minutes! She could not believe how much her little boy's attitude changed in a matter of seconds. I used the Make a Big Deal Principle to put a smile on his face.

Sam was out of his seat during project time. I told him that he needed to sit. He could sit next to me on my right side or my left. He thought about it and then sat on my right side. I have done this every day with Sam, and it always works.

I have learned to make a big deal out of positive behavior. A little girl was feeling bored, so she asked me if she could help wash the table. I let her do it and made such a big deal by thanking her a lot. The next day, I had about five volunteers for washing the table.

I used the Validation Principle in a situation where a child wanted a second snack for the day. At my school, they can only get one snack, so I decided to try one of the principles. I told Jonah that I understood why he wanted a snack and that I wanted a snack, too—but we are only allowed one snack a day. To my surprise, he said, "OK!" and he walked away.

We use fun incompatible alternatives and tell children to try not to "wake the bunny" when they tiptoe down the hall. Some pretend there is a big bird on the roof and that the bird cannot see them, but he can hear them. That was with first graders, and they loved it. They tried to "sneak" past the big bird on their way down the corridor. I think the most important thing is that if you are enjoying being with the children, they will enjoy being with you.

One of my students, Davioun, with whom I have frequent behavior issues, was on the playground and refusing to go inside. This seems to be a recurring problem. I found myself chasing him, which he loved. Then I resorted to yelling at him. "Line up right now!" All of a sudden I actually heard myself and what I was doing. I changed my ways. I started hopping up and down and said, "Davioun, I am going to hop inside. Will you hop with me?" and I started hopping towards the door. It took all of one second before he was down the slide and hopping right inside with me all the way to his cubby! Amazing!

Research on the Run

For further reading and information about the research that supports this chapter, you may want to locate the following articles and resources listed at your local library or on the Internet. By knowing the latest research, you will have the background to sustain positive changes in your classroom with lasting benefits to children.

As can be seen in the following extract from the performance standards for the Head Start program, the 101 principles support Head Start standards.

§ 1304.21 Education and early childhood development.

(1) In order to help children gain the skills and confidence necessary to be prepared to succeed in their present environment and with later responsibilities in school and life, grantee and delegate agencies' approach to child development and education must:

(i) Be developmentally and linguistically appropriate, recognizing that children have individual rates of development as well as individual interests, temperaments, languages, cultural backgrounds, and learning styles;

(ii) Be inclusive of children with disabilities, consistent with their Individualized Family Service Plan (IFSP) or Individualized Education Program (IEP) (see 45 CFR 1308.19);

(iii) Provide an environment of acceptance that supports and respects gender, culture, language, ethnicity and family composition;

(iv) Provide a balanced daily program of child-initiated and adult-directed activities, including individual and small group activities;

(2) Parents must be:

  (i) Invited to become integrally involved in the development of the program's curriculum and approach to child development and education;

  (ii) Provided opportunities to increase their child observation skills and to share assessments with staff that will help plan the learning experiences; and

  (iii) Encouraged to participate in staff-parent conferences and home visits to discuss their child's development and education (see 45 CFR 1304.40(e)(4) and 45 CFR 1304.40(i)(2)).

(3) Grantee and delegate agencies must support social and emotional development by:

  (i) Encouraging development which enhances each child's strengths by:

    (A) Building trust;

    (B) Fostering independence;

    (C) Encouraging self-control by setting clear, consistent limits, and having realistic expectations;

    (D) Encouraging respect for the feelings and rights of others; and

    (E) Supporting and respecting the home language, culture, and family composition of each child in ways that support the child's health and well-being; and

  (ii) Planning for routines and transitions so that they occur in a timely, predictable and unrushed manner according to each child's needs.

(4) Grantee and delegate agencies must provide for the development of each child's cognitive and language skills by:

  (i) Supporting each child's learning, using various strategies including experimentation, inquiry, observation, play and exploration;

  (ii) Ensuring opportunities for creative self-expression through activities such as art, music, movement, and dialogue;

  (iii) Promoting interaction and language use among children and between children and adults; and

(iv) Supporting emerging literacy and numeracy development through materials and activities according to the developmental level of each child.

Early childhood is a critical time for teachers to build trust and establish positive relationships. The more energy that is invested in teaching, modeling, and supporting social competence, the more children experience success in school expectations (Masterson, 2008). The commitment to fostering a positive climate and building interpersonal skills is a hallmark of relational guidance. This approach is congruent with NAEYC standards that promote competence by using every available resource.

NAEYC Standard 1.E.03. Rather than focus solely on reducing the challenging behavior, teachers focus on teaching the child social, communication, and emotional regulation skills and using environmental modifications, activity modifications, adult or peer support, and other teaching strategies to support the child's appropriate behavior. (Reprinted with permission from the National Association for the Education of Children [NAEYC]. Copyright 2008 by NAEYC.)

Benefits of Positive Interactions

- Emotional support increased the quality of a child's social experience at school. Quality teaching practices, when combined with strong emotional support, were found to have a strong impact on children's behaviors (Rimm-Kaufman, LaParo, Downer, & Pianta, 2005).

- For young children at risk, relationships with teachers are important, as early experiences with low stress and positive climates protect children from stress and risk factors they experience at home (O'Connor & McCartney, 2006).

- For the 30% of children at risk prior to kindergarten, responsive social–emotional support mediates against all other risk factors and provides for increased development for children in every area (Hamre & Pianta, 2005; Silver, Measelle, Armstrong, & Essex, 2004).

- The long-term benefits of positive, sensitive teacher–child interactions include improvements in academic and reading achievement, higher graduation rates, higher IQ, greater cognitive development, better outcomes for children with disabilities, and less referral to special education overall (Shonkoff & Phillips, 2001).

- Compliance and self-control are affected by the quality of the adult–child relationship (Eisenberg, Zhou, Spinrad, Valiente, Fabes, & Liew, 2005).

- Cooperation and social skills are influenced by responsive teacher–child interactions (Wachs, Gurkas, & Kontos, 2004).

- High expectations and equity in practice thrive in classrooms that are characterized by positive, responsive support for all children. Positive discipline practices and positive instructional practices are both critical and necessary for children's school success (Gregory, Skiba, & Noguera, 2010).

- Behavior interactions are central to teacher–child interactions in the preschool environment. Teachers report dealing with behavior problems as their most difficult challenge (Jalongo, 2006).

- Children depend on the caregiver to provide positive, responsive interactions. When they are present, they are the hallmark of a quality preschool environment (Haynes, 2009; Raver, Jones, Li-Grining, Metzger, Champion, & Sardin, 2008).

- Children need time to practice social competence. Teachers must provide learning opportunities for them to master social skills (Vaughn, 2001).

- Positive interactions predict high-quality care (Lara-Cinisomo, Fuligni, Daugherty, Howes, & Karoly, 2009).

- Interactions with teachers (negative or positive) provide a lasting blueprint for the way children feel about themselves, school, teachers, and peers, both now and in the future (Cozolino, 2006; Denham, 2005; Miles & Stipek, 2006; Shonkoff & Phillips, 2001; Spencer, Jordan, & Sazama, 2004; Sroufe, 2000).

- "We know that all children benefit from early learning opportunities that are developmentally appropriate and instill a sense of excitement and joy for exploration and discovery. Responsive, reciprocal, respectful relationships with caring adults who have a deep understanding of the unique stages of child development and effective strategies for stimulating active learning are critical" (CCSSO, 2009, p. 6).

Consequences of Punitive Practices

- "When teachers are frustrated with children's behavior, they often resort to saying 'no' or responding punitively" (Brown, Mangelsdorf, Neff, Schoppe-Sullivan, & Frosch, 2009; Lane, Stanton-Chapman, Roorback Jamison, & Phillips, 2007). What comes next is almost inevitable; the child asks "Why?" or resists and then the adult wants to say, "Because I said so" or "Do it right now." What teachers really need is for children to be respectful and cooperative. They want children to trust their guidance, to take their lead and willingly follow directions as opposed to resisting or engaging in power struggles (Kersey & Masterson, 2011).

- Teachers respond more punitively to behaviors of minority students, and refer them to special education three times more often than white students (NEA, 2007).

- Even when poverty is taken into account, minority students are still punished more often in response to the same behaviors as white students (Zehr, 2010).

- Ethnic and cultural differences play a factor in children receiving more punishment (Serwatka, Deering, & Grant, 1995; Skiba, Michael, & Nardo, 2000).

- Cultural differences play a role in our expectations and in the way we interpret a child's behavior (Suizzo, Chen, Cheng, Liang, Contreras, Zanger, et al., 2008).

- The way we interpret words, body language, and behaviors can trigger our response (Gregory, Skiba, & Noguera, 2010).

- We may perceive low-income students as having low competence. Our perception affects our response, such as yelling, separation, and searches, as well as more severe consequences (Skiba, Michael, & Nardo, 2000).

- Children who get punished the most are the ones who we think are "out to get us," "did it on purpose," or had spiteful intent (Thijs, Koomen, & van der Leij, 2008).

- Children who irritate us or with whom we have frequent conflict also receive more punishment (Snyder, Cramer, Afrank, & Patterson, 2005).

- Children who are more physically active present a challenge (Wenar & Kerig, 2000).

- Teacher's responses to children are complicated by the fact that they may be inconsistent from day to day, and reactions may be influenced by mood, stress, or deadlines (Forman, 1990).

- Teachers are not always aware of their own contribution to behavior interactions (Cassidy, Hansen, Kintner, & Hestenes, 2009; Halberstadt, Denham, & Dunsmore, 2001).

- "Disproportionate discipline of minority students is consistent across state and national sources. Teacher training in appropriate and culturally competent methods of classroom management is likely then to be the most pressing need in addressing racial disparities in school discipline" (Skiba, Michael, & Nardo, 2000, p. 17).

Getting Positive Results Using the Principles in Action

What happened or led up to the interaction?

_____

_____

_____

Which principle did you use?

_____

_____

_____

How did the situation turn out? (How did the child/children respond?)

_____

_____

_____

What did you learn?

_____

_____

_____

· ·

What happened or led up to the interaction?

_____

_____

_____

Which principle did you use?

_____

_____

_____

How did the situation turn out? (How did the child/children respond?)

_____

_____

_____

What did you learn?

_____

_____

_____

Guide to the Principles

12. **Modeling:** Model the behavior you want. Show the child, by example, how to behave. Children are watching us all the time, and they will grow up to be like us—whether we want them to or not.

13. **Make a Big Deal:** Make a big deal over responsible, considerate, appropriate behavior—with

eye contact, thanks, praise, thumbs-up, recognition, hugs, special privileges, or incentives (not food).

14. **Incompatible Alternative:** Give the child something to do that is incompatible with the inappropriate behavior. Say, "Let's pretend we are on a secret mission and see if we can walk

all the way to the cafeteria without anyone hearing us." "Help me pick out six markers" (when the child is unfocused or annoying). If a child is bothering you by playing with his shoestrings, instead of mentioning it, simply ask him to help you by sorting the papers or crayons by color.

15. **Choice:** Give the child two choices, both of which are positive and acceptable to you. "Would you rather tiptoe or hop over to the carpet? You choose or I'll choose." "We need to clear off our desks. Do you need one minute or two?" (Then set the timer.) The Choice Principle gives the child two incompatible alternatives. The teacher states the desired goal and then gives the child two choices about how it can be accomplished. "We need to put away the toys. Would you rather help with the puzzles or the blocks?"

16. **When–Then/Abuse It–Lose It:** "When you put your books on the shelf, then you may put on your coat." "When you finish putting the play-dough away, then you may choose a partner for the game."

17. **Follow-Through/Consistency:** Don't let the child manipulate you out of using your better judgment. Be firm (but kind)! Trust your intuition. If it doesn't feel right, don't let the child do it. Come up with choices and alternatives that can help every child to focus on more appropriate behavior and positive learning experiences.

18. **Validation:** Acknowledge (validate) the child's wants and feelings. "I know you feel frustrated with your friend and want to keep both books to yourself. I don't blame you. I would feel the same way. However, she needs to have one. Do you want to choose which one, or shall I?"

19. **Extinction:** Ignore minor misbehavior that is not dangerous, destructive, embarrassing, or an impediment to learning. (Pretend that you didn't hear, move away, or focus on something else.)

20. **Take Time to Teach:** Often we expect children to read our minds and know how to do things they have never been taught. Although our expectations may be clear to us, our children may not have a clue.

21. **Punt the Plan:** In the middle of something that is not working, move on to something else. De-stress yourself. Be willing to stay flexible and quickly switch directions when you see that children are unable to focus or need a break.

Study Guide

a. **Goal Setting:** Describe the child who, when present, makes the day go better for everyone. Next, describe the child who, when not present, makes the day seem easier. What skills does the first child have that the second does not? What could be done to model and practice the needed skills and create a positive experience for this child? In what areas do you need help or support in improving your interactions and reactions to this child?

b. **Questioning and Reflection:** *Topic 1: Punishment* refers to inflicting pain on purpose. There are many ways to hurt others that do not include physical punishment. Can you think of examples? What are some ways that others hurt us,

maybe without even realizing it? Can you think of some reasons why punishment might be unfair to children? *Topic 2:* How do you feel when you need to teach a classroom of children, yet several are not following instructions? In what way might your upbringing or beliefs about discipline affect the way you feel about or respond to children at that time?

c. **Case Study:** *Scenario 1:* Jason is a very fidgety child in your classroom. He finds many reasons why he needs to run out of line, lie on the floor during learning time, and roam around the room. He seems constantly distracted. What could you do? Use the principles in this chapter to create solutions. *Scenario 2:* Carlos is a child in Mrs. Pinneli's first-grade classroom. This is his first year in an inclusive classroom. When he wants something someone else is holding, he tries to grab it away, often hitting the other child in order to get it. A few parents have begun to complain that the behavior is detrimental to the learning of the other children. What could you do? Use the principles in this chapter to create solutions.

d. **Personal Examples/Group Brainstorming:** *Topic 1/Ultimatums:* What is one ultimatum you have given or that you have heard someone else give? What does the child learn when he is given an ultimatum? How does an ultimatum place the interaction in an unstable place? *Topic 2/Consistency:* What type of behavior is most likely to cause teachers to be inconsistent? What do children learn as a result? Describe one scenario in which an adult you observed asked a child to do something, but did not follow through. What could the adult have done differently to create a more positive outcome?

e. **Learners as Experts:** Review the "Strengthening Transitions" section. Which strategies for transitions would be most effective for the children in your classroom? What are some other goals or ideas that fit the specific age group (or school community) that will transform your transitions into constructive learning moments?

f. **Principles in Action:** Using the "Getting Positive Results Using the Principles in Action" sheet, share one principle you implemented from this chapter. What happened or led up to the interaction? Which principle did you use? How did the situation turn out? (How did the child/children respond?) What did you learn?

g. **Research on the Run:** After reviewing this section, what benefits listed did you personally experience through positive interactions with a teacher when you were a child? Do these benefits still affect you? Consider a time when a teacher or someone else responded punitively towards you. How did you feel then? Does that interaction still affect you today?

h. **Looking Ahead:** Set the purpose for upcoming study by introducing chapter objectives. Thank you for sharing your personal insight about responsive, positive guidance and for your commitment to making a difference in the lives of children.

References

Brown, G., Mangelsdorf, S., Neff, C., Schoppe-Sullivan, S., & Frosch, C. (2009). Young children's self-concepts: Associations with child temperament, mothers and fathers' parenting, and triadic family interaction. *Merrill-Palmer Quarterly, 55*(2), 184–216.

Cassidy, D., Hansen, J., Kintner, V, & Hestenes, L. (2009). Teacher ethnicity and contextual factors: The implications for classroom quality. *Early Education and Development, 20*(2), 305–320.

Council of Chief State School Officers. (2009, November). A quiet crisis: The urgent need to build early childhood systems and quality programs for children birth to age five: A policy statement of the Council of Chief State School Officers. Retrieved June, 15, 2011, from www.ccsso.org/Documents/2009/Policy_Statement_A_Quiet_Crisis_2009.pdf

Cozolino, L. (2006). *The neuroscience of human relationships: Attachment and the developing social brain.* London, United Kingdom: Norton & Co.

Denham, S. A. (2005). The emotional basis of learning and development in early childhood education. In B. Spodek (Ed.), *Handbook of research in early childhood education* (pp. 85–103). Mahwah, NJ: Lawrence Erlbaum.

Eisenberg, N., Zhou, Q., Spinrad, T., Valiente, C., Fabes, R., & Liew, J. (2005). Relations among positive parenting, children's effortful control, and externalizing problems: A three-wave longitudinal study. *Child Development, 76*(5), 1055–1071.

Forman, E. (1990). Contextual constraints that empower children: Review of *Social interaction and the development of children's understanding* (Ed. Lucien Winegar). *Educational Researcher, 19,* 32–33.

Gregory, A., Skiba, R., & Noguera, P. (2010). The achievement gap and the discipline gap: Two sides of the same coin. *Educational Researcher, 39*(1), 59–68.

Halberstadt, A., Denham, S., & Dunsmore, J. (2001). Affective social competence. *Social Development, 10,* 79–119.

Hamre, B., & Pianta, R. (2005). Can instructional and emotional support in the first-grade classroom make a difference for children at risk of school failure? *Child Development, 76*(5), 949–967.

Haynes, M. (2009). Promoting quality in PreK–grade 3 classrooms: Findings and results from NASBE's early childhood education network. *Issues in Brief,* National Association of State Boards of Education.

Jalongo, M. (2006, May). Professional development: Social skills and young children. *Scholastic Early Childhood Today, 20*(7), 8–9.

Kersey, K., & Masterson, M. (2011, July). Learn to say yes! when you want to say no! to create cooperation instead of resistance: Positive behavior strategies in teaching. *Young Children, 66*(4), 40–44.

Lane, K., Stanton-Chapman, T., Roorback Jamison, K., & Phillips, A. (2007). Teacher and parent expectations of preschoolers' behavior: Social skills necessary for success. *Topics in Early Childhood Special Education, 27*(2), 86–97.

Lara-Cinisomo, S., Fuligni, A., Daugherty, L., Howes, C., & Karoly, L. (2009). A qualitative study of early childhood educators' beliefs about key preschool classroom experiences. *Early Childhood Research and Practice, 11*(1). Retrieved from http://ecrp.uiuc.edu/v11n1/lara.html

Masterson, M. (2008). *The impact of the 101s: A guide to positive discipline training on teacher interaction practices, attitudes and prosocial skill outcomes in preschool classrooms.* Ph.D. Dissertation. Norfolk, VA: Old Dominion University.

Miles, S. B., & Stipek, D. (2006). Contemporaneous and longitudinal associations between social behavior and literacy achievement in a sample of low-income elementary school children. *Child Development, 77*(1), 103–117.

NAEYC. (2012, January). Relationships: Accreditation of programs for young children. *National Association for the Education of Young Children Trend Brief, 3*. Retrieved February 23, 2012 from www.naeyc.org/files/academy/file/TrendBriefsStandard1.pdf

National Education Association. (2007). Truth in labeling: Disproportionality in special education. Retrieved February 23, 2012, from www.nea.org/assets/docs/HE/EW-TruthInLabeling.pdf

O'Connor, E., & McCartney, K. (2006). Testing associations between young children's relationships with mothers and teachers. *Journal of Educational Psychology, 98,* 87–98.

Raver, C., Jones, S., Li-Grining, C., Metzger, M., Champion, K., & Sardin, L. (2008). Improving preschool classroom processes: Preliminary findings from a randomized trial implemented in Head Start settings. *Early Childhood Research Quarterly, 23*(1), 10–26.

Rimm-Kaufman, S., LaParo, K., Downer, J., & Pianta, R. (2005). The contribution of classroom setting and quality of instruction to children's behavior in kindergarten classrooms. *The Elementary School Journal, 105*(4), 377.

Serwatka, T. S., Deering, S., & Grant, P. (1995). Disproportionate representation of African Americans in emotionally handicapped classes. *Journal of Black Studies, 25,* 492–506.

Shonkoff, J. P., & Phillips, D. A. (Eds.). (2001). *From neurons to neighborhoods: The science of early childhood development.* Washington, DC: National Academy Press.

Silver, R., Measelle, J., Armstrong, J., & Essex, M. (2004). Trajectories of classroom externalizing behavior: Contributions of child characteristics, family characteristics, and the teacher-child relationship during the school transition. *Journal of School Psychology, 43,* 39–60.

Skiba, R., Michael, R., & Nardo, A. (2000, June). The color of discipline: Sources of racial and gender disproportionality in school punishment. Policy Research Report SRS1. Bloomington: Indiana University, Indiana Education Policy Center.

Snyder, J., Cramer, D., Afrank, J., & Patterson, G. (2005). The contribution of ineffective discipline and parent hostile attributions about child misbehavior to the development of conduct problems at home and school. *Developmental Psychology, 41,* 1–12.

Spencer, R., Jordan, J., & Sazama, J. (2004). *Empowering children for life: A preliminary report.* Wellesley, MA: Wellesley Centers for Women.

Sroufe, L. A. (2000). Early relationships and the development of children. *Infant Mental Health Journal, 21,* 67–74.

Suizzo, M., Chen, W., Cheng, C., Liang, A., Contreras, H., Zanger, D., & Roginson, C. (2008). Parental beliefs about young children's socialization across ethnic groups: Coexistence of independence and interdependence. *Early Childhood Development and Care, 178,* 467–487.

Thijs, J., Koomen, H., & van der Leij, A. (2008). Teacher-child relationships and pedagogical practices: Considering the teacher's perpective. *School Psychology Review, 37*(2), 244–260.

Vaughn, B. (2001). A hierarchical model of social competence for preschool-age children: Cross-sectional and longitudinal analyses. *Revue Internationale de Psychologie Sociale, 14,* 13–40.

Wachs, T., Gurkas, P., & Kontos, S. (2004). Predictors of preschool children's compliance behavior in early childhood classroom settings. *Journal of Applied Developmental Psychology, 25,* 439–457.

Wenar, C., & Kerig, P. (2000). *Developmental psychopathology from infancy through adolescence* (4th ed.). London, United Kingdom: McGraw Hill.

Zehr, M. (2010). School discipline inequities become a federal priority. *Education Week, 30*(7).

c h a p t e r   3

Showing Respect

This chapter will explain the role of respect in helping children develop kindness and empathy toward others. As you highlight the power of respect, you will activate respect in children. You will learn specific techniques that will help children gain relationship skills and support engagement in learning. The philosophy of relational respect will permeate every aspect of your teaching and have a significant impact on the way children get along with others.

The strategies and activities in this chapter will help you and the children in your classroom become more sensitive to the needs of others. Respect will be realized in practical ways as you promote both autonomy and interdependence. As you consider your own experiences and those of children and families, you will develop a new understanding of the ways that respect connects children to common goals and ensures dignity and equity for all.

Chapter Principles

22: Golden Rule	**28:** I-Message
23: Demonstrate Respect	**29:** Apology
24: Whisper	**30:** Get on the Child's Eye Level
25: Privacy	**31:** Think of the Outcome
26: Turtle Time	**32:** Anticipation
27: Owning the Problem	**33:** Don't Put the Cat with the Pigeons

Chapter Objectives

As you explore the text and activities in this chapter, you will be able to:

- Create environments that are respectful and supportive for every child
- Know, understand, and use strategies to promote self-control, self-regulation, and problem-solving
- Facilitate outcomes of respect: honesty, kindness, and empathy
- Prompt active listening, mutual understanding, and collaboration
- Uphold high standards of professional ethics, confidentiality, and respect for children, families, and colleagues
- Develop positive respect for diversity and a common commitment to shared purpose

Living by the Golden Rule

How does it feel when someone treats me with respect? How do I know if I am being respectful toward someone else? Whether we are being respectful can be easily answered with the question, "Would I want someone saying or doing that to me?" This is the Golden Rule, a universal understanding across cultures and religions.

 ## *Principle 22: The Golden Rule*

Do unto children what you would have them do unto you! Children will (eventually) treat us the way we treat them. It pays to take a deep breath and think twice, so that we will tread gently. Ask yourself, "How would I want someone to do that to me? How would that make me feel?"

We show children that we are respectful by our tone of voice, by our body language, and by the way we listen. This requires us to become aware of the way we come across to others. This perspective can inform our words and actions. Thinking about what the other person needs from us and being careful to honor others will make us more aware of the way we come across.

Children learn a lot from the comments we make and the way we treat ourselves. If we share the ways that we respect ourselves, such as modeling good eating habits or talking about how we got enough sleep, children will see the importance of taking good care of themselves. If we are positive and thankful when we make comments about our activities and responsibilities, this helps them develop an attitude of respect for themselves and others.

Treat children as you would other special and important people in your life. They are less likely to seriously misbehave when they sense they are loved and respected. What you do is as important as what you say. When we are thoughtful in the way we talk to children, they are more likely to be thoughtful to us in return.

● **THINK ABOUT IT!**

Remember a time when you were in a group setting and you felt out of place. Give words to describe how you felt (alone, scared, mad, helpless).

_____

_____

What would have made this experience different for you?

_____

_____

_____

We need to realize that children often feel like they don't belong. When we try to put ourselves in their place, we can be more intentional about creating an environment where they will feel comfortable and accepted.

Demonstrating Respect in Our Beliefs and Attitudes

The 101 principles help us think about what is in the best interest of children and give us skills to respond with respect. We want them to see us as an adult who is on their side. We show them through our words and actions how we would like them to speak and act toward us.

Remember a time when someone spoke to you in a disrespectful manner? How did you feel? Most of us felt stressed, disappointed, ashamed, angry, or defensive. How did you feel when someone supported you when you really needed it? Most of us felt reassured, encouraged, or empowered. Which of these experiences do we want children to have? Children need for us to be the kind of person who is safe, respectful, trustworthy, and who never gives up on them.

In order for children to have respect for you, you need to honestly have respect for them. It has to be genuine. If you have trouble respecting a particular child, ask for help from a trusted friend to help you sort out the issues. Children who are respected respect themselves and others.

The following principles can help us to stay respectful in our interactions with children. We will see an immediate difference in the way children respond.

 Principle 23: Demonstrate Respect

Treat the child the same way you treat other important people in your life—the way you want him to treat you, as well as others. Ask yourself, "How would I want him to say that to me?" Think before you speak.

Respect provides the setting for all healthy interactions. Here are some suggestions that can help you become more conscious about focusing on respect in your interactions with children.

Birth to Age 3

- Use an infant's name each time you talk with him.

- As you change a diaper, give eye contact and focus your attention without distraction.

- Anticipate when children are hungry or tired and have a bottle, food, or nap items ready. Take time to talk softly about what you are preparing, Describe what you are doing together to enhance the child's awareness and verbal growth.

- Stay responsive to a child's cues. Mirror his sounds and give reciprocal (back and forth) responses to his initiations and responses.

- Learn from his family what interactions, routines, and special songs comfort him.

Ages 3 to 8

- Practice saying "Come here" three different ways. Which way would make a child *want* to come to you?

- Imagine there is a video camera focused on you. At the end of the day, how will you feel watching yourself? This is how children see you and feel about you.

- Consider how children learn to treat each other. Have you seen a child take something from another child without asking? How can your own attitude and actions show them a different way?

- Ask before you pick up something that belongs to children. "May I look at your drawing?" "Will you share your writing with me?" We demonstrate respect by honoring children's physical boundaries and belongings. They will quickly pick up this attitude and pass it on in the way they treat their peers.

- Respect children's ideas and thinking. Engage them in conversation and let them express their views and questions. Incorporate their ideas and experiences as you assist their exploration.

- Help children learn from their mistakes. Give support, respect their need for time to process learning, and respect their differences in understanding. Children want and need to figure out how to make things work for themselves. We can encourage them by asking, by listening, and by assuring them that we are a resource for them.

- Be a teacher of influence! Bring your "best self" each day to the classroom. More than anything else, your positive attitude and confidence in them will make children want to be their best selves. Your modeling and expectation will influence their belief that they can be successful in reaching their goals.

Think About It!

Name one trait you like about yourself that is a positive influence on the children with whom you work.

_____

_____

Name one trait you would like to change in yourself that will affect the way you come across to others. How will this change in you create a change in them?

_____

_____

Demonstrating Respect in Our Words

How we talk about another teacher, the president, the news, or even our dog affects children's attitudes about the world. Our words can influence their values and can change the way they feel about themselves. *Children are listening to everything.* We don't realize the lasting impression we make or the legacy we leave.

Are we kind? What children see and hear from adults is what they will say and do, yet we can be so unaware of how we come across. If we pay attention, we can hear our expressions coming out of their mouths. When we treat children with kindness, they will return the favor and become kind to themselves and others. We need to counteract the culture of unkindness that children often see or hear in the media and in the world around them.

Are we thinking ahead? Interactions that come before a request have a direct impact on the way others respond to us. Words that are positive and respectful are more likely to result in cooperation. A child who is misbehaving is giving us a clue that we need to work extra hard to build a caring relationship and model respectful words. We can show him how to be responsive to us by staying responsive to him.

Are we living the values we want to instill? Children are wired to become like their role models. The honesty, integrity, empathy, kindness, and love that we show to children are the mirror in which they see themselves and the measure of how they understand the world. Would we like for them to be more empathetic? When they experience our empathy, they will realize how it feels to show empathy to others.

Recognizing the impact of our modeling in the way children speak, respond to us, and treat others is significant. The extent to which they internalize respect shows us how much influence is present in the way we communicate. The 101 strategies will help us focus our energy on creating positive outcomes by recognizing our own influence on the children we teach.

● THINK ABOUT IT!

In order to understand children's feelings, it is helpful to reflect on our own previous experiences and to consider how they affected us. Describe a time that a person in a position of authority said something disrespectful either to you or about you. What did they say? How did their words make you feel? How did this experience change the way you felt about that person or change your level of respect for him or her?

_____

_____

_____

Describe a time that a person in a position of authority said something that made you feel respected. What did they say? How did their words make you feel? How did this experience change the way you felt about that person? How did it make you feel about yourself?

_____

_____

_____

Principle 24: Whisper

Instead of yelling, screaming, or talking in a loud voice, surprise children by lowering your voice to a whisper. It helps you to stay in control, think more clearly, and most often evokes immediate attention.

What all children need are teachers who keep their cool. When young children flip out, melt down, or fall apart, what they really need is for *you* to stay unflappable. Right at that moment, children need you to step back, think, and stay calm.

- When you feel like yelling, whisper instead. (You may have to count to 10 first.)

- Realize that children respond to a teacher's tone of voice like an emotional thermostat. A whisper is an incompatible alternative to raising your voice—and can capture their attention!

- Other quiet sounds can be used to precede a whisper, such as a soft bell, a gentle chime, a rain stick, or a small xylophone. Children will enjoy taking responsibility to help you make these sounds (ringing the bell, striking the chime).

- Stay calm! Whispering helps you to be in control . . . of yourself.

Children take their emotional cues from you. If you want children to be calm and respectful, whispering can help you to remain calm and respectful. When you stay in control of yourself, children learn how to be in control of themselves. Your calm response will show children how to manage their emotions and to know they are worthy of respect from others.

● **THINK ABOUT IT!**

Describe the kind of experience that makes you feel most like yelling. How would whispering affect the situation?

_____

_____

_____

_____

Describe a situation that you found frustrating. How would improving the way you respond or talk to children affect the outcome?

_____

_____

_____

_____

Principle 25: Privacy

Always move to a private place to talk when there is a problem. Discuss issues with a child where he feels safe.

Many of us would say the trait we value most in another person when we come to them with a problem is trustworthiness. We want someone to keep a confidence. When children find we are trustworthy, they will be more likely to open up to us and share their real thoughts and feelings. It is important that they know we will not talk to others about what they have told us in private. The same principle of privacy is true for our communication with parents.

Confidentiality is a very important part of professional ethics in teaching. When a child shares a story or experience, keep it between you, unless you have permission to share it. When a parent talks with you, refrain from discussing the situation with other teachers. When you overhear a conversation, it should "go no further." The reputation you gain by being discreet will mark you as a person of integrity. Confidentiality is an important foundation of respect.

In the classroom, as well as in transit between school and home, be sure to keep papers, photos, or files containing children's personal or academic information safe. At school, these should be protected in a locked cabinet. If stored digitally, they must be password protected and not left on a computer screen for someone else to view accidentally if you have stepped away. Be certain that you understand all legal requirements for protection of school and medical records so that you don't inadvertently disclose information that is private.

Any time there is a problem you want to discuss with a child, move quickly to talk privately with him. The connection you build will be as important as the words you share. Private conversation creates a special bond between you and makes a child feel connected to you. Your confidentiality and respect will help him feel safe and he will be more likely to remember.

If you have a concern or question about child abuse, you may discuss the situation with your director, principal, or school counselor. Reporting anything that is inaccurate can ruin a parent's reputation and can damage your relationship with parents and/or cause them to remove the child from a school. Be sensitive as you listen and be certain that your perceptions are correct. However, your primary role is to be an advocate for children. You want to be sure that you do not overlook serious needs or issues where you can protect children. You may request training from your local or state department of social services if you would like further guidance about this issue.

Creating a quiet place in the room where children can go to be alone and have privacy is also important. This may be a quiet corner with pillows, an alcove, or a beanbag chair that is not used for any other purpose. When children know they have a place to "get themselves together" or take a break, they will be able to seek help and comfort when they need it. These principles need to be taught to children so that they will be able to use calming techniques when they are upset. Be sure to plan time in a class meeting and on a repeated basis to discuss and support calming strategies and to let children know that they can use the quiet area when they need it.

Principle 26: Turtle Time

Encourage a child to withdraw into his "turtle shell" to calm himself down, think more clearly, and keep from reacting in a negative or unproductive way.

We want to help children to practice self-control, and be able to stop and think about the best way to respond, especially when they feel frustrated. Talk with them about positive choices: They can get help, take a deep breath, put their head down, sit quietly for a minute, take three steps back, or count to five. Providing the Turtle Time option (using cute turtle signs or cards as a reminder) can help children stop and think before they react. Children may choose a Turtle Time card for themselves as well.

Remember that Turtle Time is a self-selected option. Children can use the quiet place in the room where they can withdraw or calm down. Adding a few stuffed turtles or turtle pillows to the quiet spot can reinforce Turtle Time. Be sure that this area is visually accessible so you can ensure safety at all times.

● **THINK ABOUT IT!**

Describe a place in your classroom that can be used for Turtle Time. What materials do you need to add? What plans can be made to create and help children use this safe, private area?

_____

_____

_____

_____

 Principle 27: Owning the Problem

Decide who owns the problem by asking yourself, "Who is it bugging?" If it is bugging you, then you own the problem and need to take responsibility for solving it, or you can opt to not let it bug you and let it go. When you realize that the problem is yours, then you can deliver an I-message.

 Principle 28: I-Message

Own your own feelings. "When you make a mess with the paper towels, the floor gets wet, and I feel frustrated. I would like for you to throw your towels away when you are finished washing your hands." I-messages only work within the context of a caring connection.

Instead of getting stuck revisiting a problem, the I-Message Principle creates solutions by helping us take responsibility for saying what we want or need. The I-message moves the problem toward a successful solution. The listener is more willing to respond positively when the expectations are clear.

Often there is not an immediate reaction on the other person's part, but you will see a change in a later response. You may need to repeat I-messages often. Stating our feelings gives the listener a chance to understand what we need.

School-aged children can use I-messages as an effective way to express their feelings and problem-solve with peers. We can help them practice by role-playing. Children can say, "When you took my seat, I didn't have a place to sit and I felt frustrated. I would like for you to move." "When you got in front of me, I didn't get to be the line leader. I feel mad and would like for you to wait for your turn." "When you and Laura wouldn't share with me, I felt sad. I would like to play in the sandbox too." Children will need our ongoing support as they learn to listen to each other and become more respectful of others' feelings.

● **THINK ABOUT IT!**

Here's how to practice the I-Message Principle.

1. State the problem: "When you are playing with your friend while I am giving directions . . . "

2. Explain the effect: " . . . then it is hard for people to hear me."

3. Explain how it makes you feel: "I feel frustrated . . . "

4. Describe exactly what you need or want: "When I am talking, I would like for you to listen carefully to what I am saying."

Use an I-message that relates to a situation you would like to change.

1. State the problem: _____

2. Explain the effect: _____

3. How it makes you feel (Use a feeling word. Say, "I feel ____." Resist the urge to say, "You made me feel . . . " or "That made me feel . . . " Your ownership of the feeling is what makes this principle so powerful.): _____

4. What you need or want: _____

Try this principle with a child at school or at home. How did it turn out?

_____
_____
_____

Principle 29: Apology

Apologize easily when you goof or "lose it." ("I wish I could erase what I just said." "You must have been scared by my reaction." "I didn't mean to hurt your feelings." "I was wrong." "I'm sorry.") Apologize *for* the child. ("I'm sorry he knocked you down.")

But don't make the child apologize—you might be making him lie or think that wrong-doings can be rectified with an apology.

Many adults are in the habit of making children apologize, feeling this practice teaches good manners. Others feel that an adult should "help" a child apologize. It is critical that we understand the issues involved, so that we establish the honesty and empathy we hope to instill.

If we ask a child to say he is sorry, we are asking him to lie, if this is not his true emotional experience. We are also teaching a child that it's OK to continue the behavior . . . as long as he apologizes afterwards. Instead, when we apologize *for* a child, the child is able to step back and become aware of the impact he has had on others. We want to apologize on behalf of the child until he is able to say it honestly for himself.

You can say to the child who has been hurt, "I'm sorry. I would never do that to you. I am sorry your feelings were hurt." Soon, children will be following your example and will want to apologize for themselves. Rather than forcing them to apologize when they may not feel sincere, it is better for you to encourage empathy by comforting and reassuring the other child. The child who has caused the hurt (as well as other children) will be watching and will be more careful and caring the next time.

The words "I would never do that to you" serve a distinct purpose. You might want to say instead, "I would never hurt you." Often children suffer from abuse, teasing, and hurtful words and actions from others. We want to give them a strong message that hurtful behavior toward them is not okay. We want to be certain that children understand that they are worthy of respect rather than of being hurt. We want to encourage empathy and give an opportunity for all children to think about how aggression or hurtful words have affected the other child. For strategies to help support children who are teased or bullied, see Chapter 6.

Demonstrating Respect in Our Actions

Our shared experiences create ongoing opportunity to promote learning. We can facilitate relationship connections, as these boost the child's confidence in our respect toward them. Thinking ahead about the results we want—the child's responsiveness, engagement, and cooperation—can help us be more mindful of our own contribution to creating positive outcomes. Focusing on the way we treat others keeps our personal connection strong. Children will remain open and trusting as we guide them. Here are principles that will help strengthen respectful interactions.

Principle 30: Get on the Child's Eye Level

When talking with the child, get down on her eye level and look her in the eye while talking softly to her.

When a child comes to you, it helps first to get on his eye level. Stop what you are doing and give him your full attention. Focus on the child and really listen. Pay attention to non-verbal behavior. Match your tone and rate of speed with his. Nod and use positive facial expression to show you understand. Responsive listening is one of the greatest gifts you can give. It takes commitment and practice to become good at it.

When talking with preschool and school-aged children, ask open-ended questions that promote problem solving and higher-level concepts. "What would you do if . . . " "What would happen if . . . " "What do you need to do to when . . . ?" Our engagement helps them keep their minds active.

Children want to solve their own problems and can often do it when they have an empathic and authentic listener. When you get on a child's level, you are inviting him to share the moment with you in a respectful way. You are letting him know how important he is to you, and that what you share between you is significant and confidential.

- Sit on the floor with young children and really focus on their world. This simple technique, even when you simply watch, will bring about surprising experiences and open new perspectives for you. Try this with infants, toddlers, or preschoolers. Look for a funny moment, evidence of learning, or the emotions a child is experiencing. What would make this child's experience more enriched or soothing? Observe the child's interactions with the environment and see what you can learn.

- When a child comes to you with a problem, make sure to stop what you are doing, listen, and ask him what he thinks is a good solution. Making eye contact on his level helps him feel respected and heard.

THINK ABOUT IT!

Did you ever try to talk with someone who was distracted? Did you keep talking or give up? What did you do to get that person's attention?

_____

_____

_____

How do children feel when they want to have your full attention? Do you feel they have a sense of urgency? Why or why not?

_____

_____

_____

Principle 31: Think of the Outcome

What is your intention? What outcome are you trying to achieve? Are you trying to take care of an issue for the moment, or are you trying to help the child learn important problem-solving skills? Keep your eye on your goal.

It is always helpful to think about what is in a child's best interest before we respond. Maybe a child needs validation for his feelings. "I understand. I would feel the same way if I were you." Perhaps he needs someone to help him figure out a better solution to a problem. Asking questions will encourage healthy resolutions. "What could you do to solve it?" "What might work better?" "What could you do differently?" We want to support ongoing growth and success for the child.

A helpful option is to state what you see the child experiencing, and then offer some solutions in the form of choices. "I can see you are frustrated trying to get your friend to help you with the puzzle. Would you like to work it out together, or do you need my help? "I see that you are stuck. Can you think of a way to ask for help?" "What can you do to get help putting your books onto the shelf?" "I can see how your papers are mixed up. Can you straighten them, or would you like a friend to help?" Perhaps the child needs an extra moment of your time: "Yuridiana, I can see that you are tired. Would you like to come and read next to me?"

Our interactions with children have a lasting impact. What we say when a child is having a struggle can change the way he will react the next time he faces the same dilemma. Sometimes we may realize that we have inadvertently contributed to behavior issues rather than solving them. Thinking of the outcome can help us become more intentional about the ways we respond.

● **THINK ABOUT IT!**

Many times, when teachers feel frustrated, they need to step back and think about what has happened and plan a response that will be supportive of the child. It is possible to reframe a response by replaying the scene in our mind. When we analyze our previous response, we can be more intentional the next time we encounter the behavior.

Describe the last time you felt you felt frustrated with a child or a group of children. What led up to the situation? What did you say?

_____

_____

_____

_____

After reading the Think of the Outcome Principle, what will you plan to do or say differently the next time the situation occurs? What is the outcome you want to achieve?

_____

_____

_____

Demonstrating Respect in the Environment

 ## Principle 32: Anticipation

Think ahead about whether the child is capable of handling the situation. Be realistic and remember to focus on the children's needs, not just your own agenda. Staying proactive will make a difference in avoiding behavior issues.

In the classroom, make sure to place puzzles, blocks, and other materials in stations or boxes around the room, so that young children won't need to compete to gain access. Be sure there are enough items to go around. (This will significantly reduce biting for toddlers and cut down on squabbles for preschoolers!)

Children need enough time to transition from one activity to the next. Having a set routine helps, but they also need advance warning to be able to shift their attention. Give them time to wrap up one activity with a timer, bell, or verbal reminder, so that they can mentally switch gears. Always review what will be needed next, such as procedures, materials, rules, and activities. This shows respect and communicates clear expectations of success for everyone.

 ## Principle 33: Don't Put the Cats with the Pigeons

Keep temptation away from children. Place materials for an upcoming lesson that may be particularly colorful and attractive away from curious eyes and hands. Set materials out of reach until after you have given instructions and are ready to have the children use them. "Don't place candy out in a dish if you don't want children to eat it!"

If we put birds in front of a cat, wouldn't the cat want to chase the birds? If we place enticing items in front of children, they will want to play, as they are naturally curious. When you plan an activity, be sure that you think through the steps ahead of time. It might help to complete the activity yourself first. By doing so, you will discover what will work best for the children. Most problems can be avoided completely through thoughtful planning and preparation.

Keep in mind what is developmentally appropriate. If you have manipulative work that you want done at tables, offer a "sitting" table and a "standing" table. Some children need more space around them to spread out or to help them focus. Others may work more independently seated on the floor. Let children choose what will work best for their body and concentration level. Be flexible in supporting their physical needs, as your goal is their engagement in learning.

Conduct a full review of your room. If you notice repeated behavior issues that come up, evaluate the placement of supplies, materials, timing, and physical space. Moving a shelf, table, or divider three feet one way or the other can create more space for children to move during circle time and activities without bumping into each other. Changing the physical environment, shifting a schedule, or moving supplies can make a big difference in supporting positive behavior outcomes.

● **THINK ABOUT IT!**

It is important to learn from our mistakes when things are not working. Have you ever passed out crayons, pens, or balls and given instructions to young children afterward? What happened? Brainstorm at least two creative ways to adapt your approach the next time you encounter a similar situation.

_____

_____

_____

_____

What can you change about your environment, schedule, or materials that will provide more opportunities for behavioral success?

_____

_____

_____

_____

_____

Demonstrating Respect in Supporting Diversity

The 101 principles and effective strategies provide positive, respectful alternatives that help teachers and children respond to each other with greater sensitivity. If we are respectful to all children, our consistency will be beneficial to everyone. However, there may be cultural differences that we misinterpret or wonder about. We may overreact to something that happens and not really understand why we feel so upset. Taking time to identify our feelings, issues, and concerns can help us respond calmly to situations that might otherwise have bothered us.

Taking a few minutes to think about our past experiences and feelings can help us be more mindful and careful about new choices we make. Nurturing a respectful interaction environment is as important as creating an enriched learning environment. Our responses to children and families require thoughtful planning, in the same way that we plan for other aspects of teaching.

Often children wonder about the differences they observe. Adults may make the mistake of thinking that if they do not talk about differences that children will not notice. When children ask questions, address them honestly and let them know that we value their perceptions. Responding sensitively will help children learn how to talk openly about important issues and will foster deeper respect for others.

Children may ask questions such as, "Why does he look like that?" This is a good time to have a meaningful discussion. Answering with kindness and respect will transfer the same values to the child. "He uses a wheelchair because he has cerebral palsy and can't walk. The wheelchair assists him in coming to school to learn just like you do."

We can incorporate books that deal with different abilities and exceptionalities (special needs) and plan meaningful discussions to facilitate understanding. Every room should have books and materials that represent many ethnicities, cultures, and abilities, and that show children equitably in work and play. It is important for young children to be exposed to different perspectives so that they can begin to move beyond their own egocentric view.

Respect is the essential foundation for positive guidance and will always affect the way we relate to others. Talk often to parents and ask questions to help you gain understanding about the unique needs of their children. They are the expert source of knowledge about their children. Each child is unique and needs our individual understanding and support. Using the principles from this chapter will ensure that all children and families feel valued and respected. Chapter 9 will provide many more strategies to help you build bridges of communication and trust that will benefit everyone.

● THINK ABOUT IT!

Describe the cultural or language differences of children in your classroom. Do you think these are always obvious? How might these unique characteristics affect a child's experience in your classroom?

_____

_____

_____

How can you focus more on building bridges between cultures in your classroom? What resources would you need to make this happen? What conversations would you like to have and with whom?

_____

_____

_____

Summary

Every day we have the opportunity to show respect to children and families. If we are honestly trying to be respectful in our conversations, actions, and responses, we need to consider the experience and needs of the other person. By practicing respect, we grow in our ability to take on others' perspectives and to become more sensitive about the ways we communicate and connect.

By reflecting on what has worked well and what we would like to change, we can dedicate ourselves to continuing growth as teachers. When we utilize the principles that focus on respect, we become more mindful about the impact we have on children and families. We begin to appreciate the influence we have in their lives. We realize that, in many ways, they have influenced our lives as well. This cycle of respect will leave a lasting impression on children in our classroom and will affect their understanding of themselves and others for years to come.

Using the Principles in Your Classroom

The following are some approaches to building respect that will help you become more intentional as you implement the principles in your classroom.

Demonstrate Respect

Start the day with a Daily Respect Moment—a moment of silence for children to think about and plan something special they can do for someone today.

Model the Golden Rule

Use an acronym that has special meaning to your children that reinforces character traits you want to highlight. You can use any creative idea that your children can brainstorm. One option is to use the acronym FROG: Friends Respect Others Graciously.

One teacher said that she teaches her students from the first day that she wants them all to be like FROGs. They talk a lot about what that means and she encourages their ideas frequently. When she sees a child being kind or demonstrating respect, she stops and makes an announcement: "We have a FROG moment." Then she highlights the positive character trait, staying sensitive to the children's needs.

Often the children will call out, "Teacher, Sarah is being a FROG!" She stops to give attention to the child whose act of kindness or caring showed respect. She has a frog necklace for children to wear and small plastic frogs that she places on desks when children are especially helpful. This teaches her class to take pride in being a caring community where children show genuine concern for others.

Use your own interests and imagination to create a system that teaches character and reinforces the Golden Rule in your classroom. It might be a FROG or another system that promotes respect and recognizes caring kindness when it is demonstrated.

Teach Children to Think of the Outcome

Cut out a large paper cardboard man. Give him facial features and ask children to "crinkle" him up. Tell children to be careful not to tear him, but they can use one or both hands to crinkle him. By the time they have each had a turn passing him around, he has turned into a crumpled ball. Then, try to straighten him out. Show the children that it is not possible to get all the crinkles out. Name him "Mr. Crinkle Man" and post him on the bulletin board. Tell the children that Mr. Crinkle Man is there to remind us that whenever we hurt someone's feelings, we put a crinkle in him, and there is no way to erase it. Remind them that we all want to be careful not to "crinkle" another person's feelings. Children frequently report, "Kristin crinkled me." Be sure to validate their feelings and tell them that you are sorry. Usually, children will apologize spontaneously.

Demonstrate Respect Throughout Daily Routines and Activities

- All children can learn. Our job is to discover where they are—and meet them there!
- All children need success. Find ways for each child to be competent.
- If you give a child something to do, support him so that he can be successful.
- Be sure to fill the day with meaningful learning. Give children topics to investigate; projects to work on; and books to read, listen to, and discuss.
- Keep children involved with engaging work. Children *want* to learn.
- Praise each child for something every day.
- Remember the limited attention span of children. Give them physical breaks.
- Start every day with a "clean slate" and a positive attitude.
- Treat children the way you would want to be treated. Never say to a child what you wouldn't want someone to say to you.

Use the Golden Rule as Your Foundation

Stay flexible and adaptive. Know any accommodations that your students need and be sure you are using them. Don't wait for formal requirements. Make sure every child can participate freely and feel respected and successful. Use common sense to consider what is needed to help children feel secure and included.

Teacher Tips

The following are comments from teachers who have been trained to use the 101 principles in their early care and education settings and elementary classrooms.

I have learned to stay calm. No matter what is going on, a calm and respectful demeanor really matters. As soon as a teacher gets upset or frustrated, so do the students. I really admire how my advising teacher always walks into the classroom with a big smile on her face. Regardless of how she is feeling on a particular day, the children notice her smile and smile back. If you are smiling, they are smiling. This is a very valuable lesson. It seems like such an easy and very effective way to guide a good attitude in the classroom.

I had many interruptions one morning, including a little boy with a bloody nose and a parent who stopped by unannounced, so I felt irritated when several children were acting silly in the line to go outside while putting on their coats. I stopped and remembered the Think of the Outcome Principle. So instead of fussing at them, I told them I was sorry it had been a frustrating morning and I wanted them to have a happy time at recess. They responded right away and cooperated to go outside. I thought about how useful it was to use the Apology Principle because they were probably feeling the same way I was. Taking time to be respectful really paid off.

Respect is really important. When Charlie was chewing on a crayon, I just went over

(continued)

to him and said, "Crayons are for coloring." He pulled the crayon out of his mouth right away and went back to work. I didn't have to remind him again. I made sure to whisper it in his ear, so he wouldn't feel embarrassed.

To really show respect to my second graders, I always ask first before I look at their papers or touch their belongings. I would want them to do the same to me. They are always respectful of my desk and my things in return.

I decided that when my toddlers needed a diaper change, I would go privately to them and whisper in their ear, "I need to change your diaper."

I thought I would want someone to do that for me before they swooped in to change my diaper. I find that the more respectful I am of them, the more respectful they are of each other and me.

I keep a locked box where children can write notes to me about issues they want to discuss. They know I will never break their confidence and that no one else will see what they have written. When I talk with them, it is private between us. By opening this communication of respect, I have seen children engage in school, finish homework, be kind to friends, and completely change their attitude about school.

Research on the Run

Influencing Children's Perspectives Through Demonstrating Respect

- Relationship quality matters. When teachers provided strong emotional support and respect, children respond positively. They are more caring and empathetic. Their teachers demonstrate higher levels of positive regard, are calm and consistent, and have low levels of stress (Bridges, Denham, & Ganiban, 2004; Denham, 2007; Denham & Grout, 1992; Denham, Renwick-DeBardi, & Hewes, 1994; Stipek, 2006; Warren, Bassett, & Denham, 2008).

- The more we stay respectful and connected to children, the more they want to please us and become like us. They learn what is important to us. We want to model kindness, courage, empathy, and responsibility. When children see us truly caring and giving, they will internalize those values (Deci & Ryan, 1985; Ryan & Deci, 2000).

- Being respectful is an essential part of the teaching profession and is integral to all other practices (LePage, Darling-Hammond, & Akar, 2005).

- Seeing from the child's perspective is critical. Teachers need to be aware of a child's communication (verbal and non-verbal) and respect his wants and needs. Children need to experience a lasting emotional bond with the caregiver (Bergin & Bergin, 2009).

- If a teacher is constantly calling out a student's name to correct his behavior, this negative association is picked up by the child's peers. Instead, celebrate positive behaviors, so that the children who are watching will respect this child as being socially competent. He will begin to act in the way he is treated (Reinke, Lewis-Palmer, & Merrill, 2008).

- Children develop social skills, self-confidence, and positive perceptions about themselves by the way they are treated by their teachers and by the way teachers express their feelings about children (Bierman, Nix, Domitrovich, Welsh, & Gest, 2009; Bierman, Nix, Greenberg, Blair, & Domitrovich, 2009).

- NAEYC Standard 1.D.05 states: "Teaching staff [should] promote prosocial behavior by interacting in a respectful manner with all staff and children." (Reprinted with permission from the National Association for the Education of Children [NAEYC]. Copyright 2008 by NAEYC.)

Getting Positive Results Using the Principles in Action

What happened or led up to the interaction?

_____

_____

_____

Which principle did you use?

_____

_____

_____

How did the situation turn out? (How did the child/children respond?)

_____

_____

_____

What did you learn?

_____

_____

_____

What happened or led up to the interaction?

_____

_____

_____

Which principle did you use?

_____

_____

_____

How did the situation turn out? (How did the child/children respond?)

_____

_____

_____

_____

What did you learn?

_____

_____

_____

Guide to the Principles

22. **Golden Rule:** Do unto children what you would have them do unto you! Children will (eventually) treat us the way we treat them. It pays to take a deep breath and think twice, so that we will tread gently. Ask yourself, "How would I want someone to do that to me? How would that make me feel?"

23. **Demonstrate Respect:** Treat the child the same way you treat other important people in your life—the way you want him to treat you, as well as others. Ask yourself, "How would I want her to say that to me?" Think before you speak.

24. **Whisper:** Instead of yelling, screaming, or talking in a loud voice, surprise children by lowering your voice to a whisper. It helps you to stay in control, think more clearly, and most often evokes immediate attention.

25. **Privacy:** Always move to a private place to talk when there is a problem. Discuss issues with a child where he feels safe.

26. **Turtle Time:** Encourage child to withdraw into his "turtle shell" to calm himself down, think more clearly, and keep from reacting in a negative or unproductive way.

27. **Owning the Problem:** Decide who owns the problem by asking yourself, "Who is it bugging?" If it is bugging you, then you own the problem and need to take responsibility for solving it, or you can opt to not let it bug you and let it go.

28. **I-Message:** Own your own feelings. "When you make a mess with the paper towels, the floor gets wet, and I feel frustrated. I would like for you to throw your towels away when you are finished washing your hands." I-messages only work within the context of a caring connection.

29. **Apology:** Apologize easily when you goof or "lose it." ("I wish I could erase what I just said." "You must have been scared by my reaction." "I didn't mean to hurt your feelings." "I was wrong." "I'm sorry.") Apologize *for* the child. ("I'm sorry he knocked you down.") But don't make the child apologize—you might be making him lie or think that wrong-doings can be rectified with an apology.

30. **Get on the Child's Eye Level:** When talking with the child, get down on his eye level and look him in the eye while talking softly to him.

31. **Think of the Outcome:** What is your intention? What outcome are you trying to achieve? Are you trying to take care of an issue for the moment, or are you trying to help the child learn important problem-solving skills? Keep your eye on your goal.

32. **Anticipation:** Think ahead about whether the child is capable of handling the situation. Be realistic

and remember to focus on the children's needs, not just your own agenda. Staying proactive will make a difference in avoiding behavior issues.

33. **Don't Put the Cats with the Pigeons:** Don't place temptation in front of the child. Place materials for an upcoming lesson that may be particularly colorful and attractive away from curious eyes and hands. Set materials out of reach until after you have given instructions and are ready to have the children use them. "Don't place candy out in a dish if you don't want children to eat it!"

Study Guide

a. **Goal Setting:** (1) Name one trait you like about yourself that you feel is a positive influence on the children with whom you work. What respectful practices do you recognize from this chapter that are working well for you? (2) Name one trait that you would like to change in yourself that will affect the way you come across to others. How will the change in you create a change in them?

b. **Questioning and Reflection:** In order to understand children's feelings, it is helpful to reflect on our own previous experiences. (1) Describe a time that a person in a position of authority said something disrespectful to you or about you. What was said? How did the words make you feel? How did this experience change the way you felt about this person? (2) Describe a time that a person in a position of authority said something that made you feel respected. What was said? How did the words make you feel? How did this experience change the way you felt about this person? How did it make you feel about yourself?

c. **Case Study:** Mrs. Taylor had been confiding in another colleague and felt that her conversation was safe. However, at a teacher's meeting, the private information Mrs. Taylor had shared about a child in her classroom was repeated to another staff member. After the meeting, Mrs. Taylor decided she needed to use the I-Message Principle with her coworker. What would Mrs. Taylor say—and how would she say it—in order to communicate her feelings in a respectful way? (See the I-Message Principle on page 74. Be sure to use the full verbal sequence. For information about confidentiality, see Principle 25, Privacy, on page 73.

d. **Personal Examples/Group Brainstorming:** Many of us grew up being told to apologize after we had done something wrong. Why do you think we make children apologize? Do you feel having the adult apologize for a child provides a benefit? Do you think the child will eventually apologize for himself? What behaviors have you encountered and felt the child should apologize? (See Principle 29, Apology, on page 75.)

e. **Learners as Experts:** Consider the section "Demonstrating Respect in Supporting Diversity." How do you feel the tips provided in Principle 23, Demonstrate Respect, will affect children who have differing home languages or cultural backgrounds? How will the strategies introduced in "Using the Principles in Your Classroom" impact children's perspectives of one another? (See FROG and Mr. Crinkle Man on page 82.)

f. **Principles in Action:** Using the "Getting Positive Results Using the Principles in Action" sheet, share one principle you implemented from this chapter. What happened or led up to the interaction? Which principle did you use? How did the situation turn out? (How did the child/children respond?) What did you learn?

g. **Research on the Run:** Review this section. We realize that the more we can honestly evaluate our own words and actions, the more effective we will be in communicating with others. Why do you think it is hard for us to realize how we come across to others? Do we know how others see us? How can we become more sensitive and aware of the way we come across?

h. Looking Ahead: Set the purpose for upcoming study by introducing chapter objectives. Thank you for sharing your personal insight about responsive, positive guidance and for your commitment to making a difference in the lives of children.

References

Bergin, C., & Bergin, D. (2009). Helping children and families in need: Using a primary bonding model in a shelter child care setting. *High Scope Resource,* 4–8.

Bierman, K., Nix, R., Domitrovich, C., Welsh, J., & Gest, S. (2009). Fostering school readiness with preschool interventions that promote social–emotional learning and language skills: The Head Start REDI project. Health and Early Childhood Development: The Impact of Health and School Readiness and Other Educational Outcomes, Human Capital Research Collaborative Fall conference, October 14, 2010, Minneapolis, MN. Retrieved from http://humancapitalrc.org/events/2010/hcrcconf/papers/bierman.pdf

Bierman, K., Nix, R., Greenberg, M., Blair, C., & Domitrovich, C. (2009). Executive functions and school readiness intervention: Impact, moderation, and mediation in the Head Start REDI program. *Development and Psychopathology, 20,* 821–843.

Bridges, L., Denham, S., & Ganiban, J. (2004). Definitional issues in emotion regulation research. *Child Development, 75,* 340–345.

Deci, E., & Ryan, R. (1985). *Intrinsic motivation and self-determinism in human behavior.* New York: Plenum.

Denham, S. (2007). Dealing with feelings: How children negotiate the worlds of emotions and social relationships. *Cogniţie Creier Comportament, 11*(1), 1–48.

Denham, S. A., and Grout, L. (1992). Mothers' emotional expressiveness and coping: Topography and relations with preschoolers' social-emotional competence. *Genetic, Social, and General Psychology Monographs, 118*(7), 5–101.

Denham, S. A., Renwick-DeBardi, S., & Hewes, S. (1994). Affective communication between mothers and preschoolers: Relations with social-emotional competence. *Merrill-Palmer Quarterly, 40,* 488–508.

LePage, P., Darling-Hammond, L., & Akar, H. (2005). Classroom management. In L. Darling-Hammond & J. Bransford (Eds.), *Preparing teachers for a changing world.* San Francisco, CA: Jossey Bass.

National Association for the Education of Young Children. (2012). Trend Brief. Relationships: Accreditation of Programs for Young Children Standard 1. Retrieved February 25, 2012, from www.naeyc.org/files/academy/file/TrendBriefsStandard1.pdf

Reinke, W., Lewis-Palmer, T., & Merrell, K. (2008). The classroom check-up: A class-wide teacher consultation model for increasing praise and decreasing disruptive behavior. *School Psychology Review, 37*(3), 315–332.

Ryan, R., & Deci, E. (2000). Self-determination theory and the facilitation of intrinsic motivation, social development, and well-being. *American Psychologist, 55,* 68–78.

Stipek, D. (2006). Relationships matter. *Educational Leadership, 64*(1), 47–49.

Warren, H., Bassett, H., & Denham, S. (2008, May). Early emotional development, social cognition, and relationships with others. *Zero to Three,* 32–39.

chapter 4

Giving Nurturance

This chapter will help you create the kind of high-quality interactions in your classroom that will nurture authentic personal connections with each child. When children are nurtured, they feel safe, secure, and nourished. The dependable safety of your warm interaction supports their growing sense of relational competence and well-being. Nurturance builds children's self-esteem and gives them a sense that they are OK. Their intellectual growth, curiosity, interests, values, and dispositions require this secure space in which to grow.

Sensitive teachers ensure a low-stress classroom, so that children can freely discover and explore the world around them. As they experience your caring responsiveness, they will be able to invest their energy into positive engagement in learning. As you implement the strategies from this chapter, you will be able to encourage children's confidence and provide the kind of environment where they can develop their full potential. By providing nurturance, you will infuse your teaching with new vitality and create a happy and inviting place where children enjoy being with each other and with you.

Chapter Principles

34: Get Help

35: Take Care of Yourself

36: Nap/Take a Break

37: Bunny Planet

38: Read a Book

39: Have Fun Together

40: Humor

41: Jump Start a Belly Laugh

42: Make It Fun

43: Give Life to Inanimate Objects

44: Institute Mailboxes

Chapter Objectives

As you explore the text and activities in this chapter, you will be able to:

- Apply strategies for positive emotional modeling and relational competence
- Help children manage impulsivity and reduce stress
- Teach children effective methods to disengage and reorient perspective

- Use explicit approaches to facilitate play, fun, and humor in learning
- Teach children manners, coping, and communication skills
- Foster creative activities to promote positive social interaction and learning

Nurturing Trust

When children have a caring adult to guide and encourage them, they do better in school, make friends more easily, and develop healthy social skills. Children need a reliable relationship with at least one significant adult who consistently validates their experiences so that they can trust themselves and others. Children measure themselves by what they see in their caregiver or teacher's body language, tone of voice, expression, and words.

We need to carefully evaluate ourselves to make sure that we are putting aside our worries and concerns and truly focusing on each child at all times. This takes work on our part. It means that we are willing to stop what we are doing, give our full attention, and focus with our eyes, our ears, and our responsive presence. Our safe, secure connection to them allows them to trust us and to trust their own perceptions. When children experience this kind of unconditional caring, they gain confidence in their inner strength and resources.

It is inspiring and motivating to consider that the way we treat children will have a lasting impact in their lives. Once they experience the safety and trust with a teacher in early childhood, they will carry this impression with them into future experiences in

● **THINK ABOUT IT!**

As a child, who knew you the best? Who inspired you to find your passion? What did this person (or people) do for you? Did they spend time with you? What do you remember about them?

_____

_____

_____

What traits do people who inspire others have in common?

_____

_____

_____

school. Our consistent support and belief in them gives them courage to make decisions wisely and to work hard to achieve their goals.

Nurturing Yourself

There are many ways to become nurturing. The first is to take good care of yourself. Finding new strategies for handling stress, laughing more, and engaging in meaningful conversations with others will help you become better available for the children in your life. The following principles will help you focus on keeping a balance in your personal and professional life while creating a nurturing environment for children.

 Principle 34: Get Help

Staying aware of your limits and getting support from others is vitally important. You may want to ask another teacher to cover for you while you focus on, or spend extra positive time with, a child who seems troubled. Be sure to prioritize and ask for help when you need it.

Children reflect our moods and are sensitive to our fatigue. They can hear frustration in our words or voices. When a child enters a room where a teacher is happy, he feels a sense of security. When he walks into a room that is filled with tension, he picks up this message quickly. It is essential that we plan time to provide for our own needs so that children sense stability and consistency in our care.

All of us need time to recharge. Set aside time for coffee with a special friend or devote time to a passion or personal interest to refuel your energy. Our inner vitality and the attention we give to our own needs set an example to children for healthy life choices. Asking for help when we need time to regroup or refocus will help us get a better perspective. Personal satisfaction will spill over into our teaching and we will come to school refreshed and eager to return to our responsibilities.

● **THINK ABOUT IT!**

In what ways do you wish you had more help or support at school? Who could you ask for help at school?

_____

_____

_____

How can you reprioritize, reorganize, or review routines to give children more responsibility to help and contribute in your classroom?

_____

_____

_____

Principle 35: Take Care of Yourself

Children pick up on our emotions and model our ways of handling our feelings, so we want to do our best to be a good example of healthy and mature behavior.

It is important for us to stay in control of our emotions and stop ourselves before we "lose it" and say or do things that we'll regret. We need to develop the ability to calm ourselves—by counting to 10, taking deep breaths, or walking away while we have a chance to thoughtfully consider our options.

Sometimes we may need to take a walk or call a trusted friend for comfort and advice. We may need to take a break while we collect our thoughts and decide the best course of action. Take time to regroup and reorganize essential priorities. Keep focused on the important goals.

● **THINK ABOUT IT!**

How would you like to take better care of yourself at home?

_____

_____

_____

_____

 Principle 36: Nap/Take a Break

A nap usually puts everything into better perspective. Teachers and parents are often sleep deprived. Make it a goal to go to bed sooner at night, so that you will feel more energetic during the day. At school, when you see children becoming tired or lethargic, take a stretch break, a music break, or a brain break.

We also may be experiencing stress and taking on many responsibilities in our personal lives. As we become older and wiser, we can learn many ways to step back and take a break, so that we always have options ready to help us keep our perspective.

It is not always possible to stop and take a break when we are on duty and responsible for the children around us. However, children need breaks as well. Many children come to school sleep deprived, and for those, a break or rest in the middle of the morning and another in the middle of the afternoon is critical. Wise teachers are careful to watch for children who need to take a break and know ways to provide this important escape for them.

We can turn off lights, turn on soft music, and ask children to close their eyes. Teach them to visualize a tranquil place where they can go in their mind, which will bring them to a peaceful perspective. Visualizations can be related to lessons, such as the process of seeds sprouting, weather changing or animals hibernating; or descriptions of peaceful places like mountains or rainforests. These word pictures can provide a creative way to help children refocus and restore energy.

We need to watch for signs of stress in children as well as in ourselves, and encourage opportunities to take some deep breaths, chill out, cool off, and think different thoughts. When we return to the daily challenges, we see them differently. We see our purpose more clearly. We can guide children across another "bump in the road," and help them (and ourselves) feel more confident that we can negotiate it again successfully in the future.

THINK ABOUT IT!

Is there a particular time of day that is difficult for you? Consider the last half hour of the school day, for example. Describe the situation and how you feel about it. (You also may interview a teacher.)

_____

_____

_____

What could you change to make this time of day more pleasant? What could you do to make this time less stressful and more fun?

_____

_____

_____

Keeping Calm

Retaining a sense of perspective and calm is an important skill. Being able to stay cool under stress or when things don't go as planned requires practice. The following are principles that will help maintain—and allow you to return to—a sense of emotional stability, in spite of challenges. Your ability to model these strategies will become a strong resource for you, and also will reinforce and teach very needed calming and coping skills to each child.

Principle 37: Bunny Planet

The Bunny Planet Principle is named for a book series by Rosemary Wells. Close your eyes and tell the children that you are going to the Bunny Planet (or another imaginary place). Ask them to tell you when they are ready for you to come back, once things are quiet and they are ready to make good choices.

The children were gathering around Mrs. DeRolf in the reading circle. She was ready to read a story, but the children were shuffling, poking each other, and talking.

Quietly addressing the children, she said, "I am going to go to the Bunny Planet and I will come back when everyone is sitting quietly ready to listen to the story." She sat still, closed her eyes, and listened. She waited for the children to join her. In just a few moments, she heard the quiet response she hoped for. Opening her eyes, she began to read to the children.

You may have an imaginary place you want to go to take a momentary mental break and give children the opportunity to behave appropriately. This short break will allow them the chance to adjust their own behavior without further prompting. The Bunny Planet Principle can also be encouraged with children as a calming strategy. As a result of seeing us model a "trip to the Bunny Planet," children will soon use it themselves.

We want to model self-control to children and show them that when we feel the need to take a break, it is OK for us to remove ourselves temporarily to do so. Giving ourselves a break allows a stressful situation to diffuse, helps us feel better, and gives children a chance to take a break as well. Taking a visit to the Bunny Planet (or any other place that suits our fancy) allows children (and ourselves) to take time to change our behavior or frame of mind, and to return with fresh perspective and new energy.

● **THINK ABOUT IT!**

When is a time that you might need to go to the Bunny Planet or model self-control? Try this principle today and describe how the children responded. (This strategy works well with children of all ages.)

_____

_____

_____

Principle 38: Read a Book

Sit down and read to the children. Take your attention away from the child who is behaving inappropriately. Read something engaging and helpful to them until you have cooled off and can deal with the situation in a productive manner.

When a teacher is frustrated with the way things are going, she can switch gears and get a favorite book to read to the children. She can turn off the lights and get a flashlight to read to the class in a whisper—or at least a calm and pleasant tone—just to change the atmosphere from chaos to peaceful.

We can teach this principle to younger children as a way of diffusing their energy or frustration. They can learn to walk away and get a book when they are upset or need to disengage. A teacher can read a book as a cue, or read a poem that will be calming to children. The book can focus on feelings or emotions, or simply be used as a constructive way to disengage or reengage with a fresh frame of mind.

When we feel on the verge of "losing it," we need to give ourselves a mental break. Sitting down to read a book to refocus and get our mind off of frustration or stress accomplishes two important objectives: It gives our minds a chance to rest and be more relaxed and creative, and it also gives the children time to refocus their own behavior and self-correct.

It takes two to engage in a power struggle or to escalate a situation. Modeling alternative strategies to calm and to reorient our feelings is a helpful way to respond. By choosing disengagement, we are allowing both the child and ourselves a chance to regroup and think more creatively about appropriate solutions.

● **THINK ABOUT IT!**

Think about a time you felt frustrated with children's behavior. What do you think would have been their response if you had given them a book to read—or read a book yourself—to help diffuse the situation?

_____

_____

_____

Nurturing Confidence

Too often, adults are task oriented and in a hurry, yet children need time to explore. We may say no out of habit. With children, we should say yes as often as possible. Then when they need to be stopped for important reasons, they are likely to quickly comply. The more we say yes to children's wishes, ideas, strengths, and interests, the more they will grow to be creative and responsible. Although our role is to support, protect, guide and teach, we want to encourage initiative and confidence.

Changing from "no" to "yes" requires a shift in thinking. However, once we reframe the direction of our responses, the "yes" approach makes sense. For example, instead of saying, "No, you cannot go outside," we can say, "Yes, you may go outside after centers." Instead of, "No, the paints are put away now," we can rephrase it as, "Yes, we will be setting up the easel and paint after lunch."

Older children may offer to help at an inconvenient time. Rather than say "no," we can respond, "Yes, how thoughtful of you to offer to help. I would love for you to collect the books after science rather than now." These affirming responses acknowledge a child's initiative, interest, and enthusiasm, and are more likely to keep him engaged and motivated than if we say no.

The environment also plays a role in the way children interact with each other and with you. Sit on the floor or at a child's desk. Imagine that you are the child. What do you see that is interesting to you? What catches your attention and makes you want to get up to investigate? How would you feel about completing activities or assignments? What materials would prompt your engagement with other children? If you work with infants, close your eyes and listen. What sounds do you hear? What emotions do the voices in the room communicate to you? All of the sounds, sights, and emotions set the stage for successful interactions and learning.

● **THINK ABOUT IT!**

Remember a time when you wanted to try something new and an adult encouraged and supported you. What was it? How did you feel? Do you still enjoy that activity or experience today?

_____

_____

_____

_____

Imagine you are a child in your own classroom. What would you discover there that is thrilling to you? What would make you want to come in and explore?

_____

_____

_____

What changes could you make to enrich or enhance a child's experience after seeing your classroom from his or her perspective?

_____

_____

_____

_____

Relating to Children

"Tanisha, we missed you yesterday. How are you feeling?" "Gloria, how did your dentist appointment go?" "Ben, good for you for bringing in a book to share!" These are the kinds of greetings children need to hear from their teachers when they arrive in the morning.

When we see a teacher interacting in a nurturing way, we hear meaningful conversation, warm exchanges, and shared laughter. These encounters between the adult and child provide a safe place for the child. These interactions are the soil where a child's gifts and abilities can take root and grow. Nurturing includes protecting the spirit of a child and encouraging curiosity. If we share a sense of purpose, love of learning, and healthy communication, these are the qualities children will gain.

Nurturing also means taking the time to lighten up and have fun together. Ask children, "Was this a regular day, or a special day? What made it special?" Ask them to compliment the child next to them, and focus on the special qualities of friendship like kindness and cooperation. Look for "funny moments" together. Smile. Laugh often. Celebrate the joy in common experiences.

Birth to Age 3

- Encourage nurturing behaviors for both boys and girls. Provide infant care items (small blankets, beds, bottles) and dolls that reflect a variety of skin tones and ethnicities. Use the dolls to model emotionally nurturing behaviors such as comforting, feeding, and rocking. "Homemaking" skills are helpful in supporting emotional regulation and empathy. Include picture books in the housekeeping area so that toddlers can "read" to their babies by pointing to pictures.

- Be sure to ask questions that nurture emotion knowledge and planning. "Is your baby hungry? What will you feed her?" "Are you taking her to the store? How will you carry her?" "Is it cold outside? What will keep your baby warm?" Young children can comfort themselves when they act out nurturing and soothing behaviors with a baby doll or stuffed animal.

- Be sure to add and change items frequently in play areas. A basket of colorful flannel squares can serve multiple functions as scarves, blankets, or picnic cloths. These encourage imagination and provide soothing engagement.

- Label items and place needed materials at eye level to support security and confidence.

Ages 3 to 8

- Survey the environment with children's needs and perspectives in mind. Provide materials and space that promote nurturing activities. Provide pet grooming accessories (for stuffed animals) that inspire engaging play. Provide individual tubs of beans or other safe materials to "plant" in, measure, and dig that also provide tactile comfort to eager hands. Make sure children have access to molding materials that promote relaxation as well as creativity.

- Drawing and art activities can help children express their feelings in pictures and can be used to foster conversations about important events and experiences.

- Poetry can be shared, dictated, written, or read to help children communicate their point of view.

- Provide books that reflect the emotional needs of your particular children. For example, books about a new baby in the family or an upcoming move can give assurance to children about events and changes in their lives.

- Let children decorate their cubbies or lockers to give them a sense of connection and ownership.

How were you nurtured as a child? Where were you when you felt most safe to explore and grow? Who was with you and what were you doing?

_____

_____

_____

How did a teacher nurture your confidence to "be yourself"?

_____

_____

Enjoying Children

Do you remember a time when you were having such a great day that you did not want it to end? Do you feel that way about teaching? If you are enjoying the day, the children will be able to enjoy it along with you. It is likely that you came into this profession because you love to work with children. Appreciate your time with them, and look for every opportunity to make each day special and full of good memories.

The following principles will help you infuse your teaching with a new sense of purpose and vitality.

 ### *Principle 39: Have Fun Together*

Children love to know that they bring us joy and pleasure. Lighten up and have fun. Have you watched a child entertain himself while adults were talking or otherwise engaged? Have you seen him dance around, play with his shadow, or practice jumping, skipping, and hopping? Have you seen him make funny faces and little noises—completely absorbed in his play?

If you have, you know how delightful, unencumbered, free, and joyful a child can be. Have you wondered if you used to be that way? When did it stop? Do you know why?

Adults laugh about 15 times a day, whereas children laugh about 400 times a day. Research shows that the act of smiling even when you don't feel like it elicits positive responses from others. Genuine smiles (or even pretend smiles) reduce stress and promote a sense of well-being by releasing positive, healthy endorphins. Not only are children drawn to adults who have a smile and positive attitude, but the one who is smiling will have a happier day.

All children are born with the capacity to laugh, have fun, and bring joy into the lives of others. In order for them to hold on to this ability, we need to recognize it, reinforce it, and let them see their positive effect on us. Children constantly watch our faces to see our reactions and feel satisfied when they can make us happy. The more they see us respond favorably to them, the more they see the world as a happy place and develop confidence in their ability to find positive solutions to life's challenges.

When we can make things fun instead of serious or threatening, children are much more likely to be willing to do what we need them to do, even if it seems unpleasant to them at first. Sometimes it takes effort on our part to make a needed activity engaging and interesting, but it is worth the energy and time. When we choose to be positive and patient, we change the tone and quality of the experience.

Each day brings a new adventure for children. They bring a sense of joy and wonder, and have much to share. If we "join their world," try to see it the way they see it, and watch, listen, and learn from them, we not only strengthen their confidence, but we brighten our own days with energy and perspective.

● THINK ABOUT IT!

The more you look for funny moments, the more you will find. Describe a humorous moment you observed or something funny you heard a child say or do. (Be sure to write it down and share it with the parent.)

_____

_____

_____

Think about the last time a child found something to be truly funny in class. Did you stop and let the children enjoy the moment? Why or why not?

_____

_____

_____

You may want to keep a "funny moment" journal to remind yourself of why you enjoy being with children and to capture unique and special moments of laughter and joy.

Principle 40: Humor

Make a game out of it. Have fun. Laugh a lot together. ("How would a rabbit brush his teeth?") Look for the funny moments. Enjoy the child's sense of humor.

Do you remember a time when you got the giggles and couldn't stop laughing? Do you remember how good it felt to share that experience with a friend? Children need to have those same kinds of experiences with us. The one thing they love more than making themselves laugh is making others laugh. We need to have fun and laugh together.

There is humor to be found in the way children deal with life. Children who are singing "My Country 'Tis of Thee" have no idea what they are saying, but they are singing it with gusto and joy because they have seen the patriotism of adults during the music.

If we sit back and really appreciate children, we can learn from their wonderful sense of humor. They love to laugh and will laugh at everything possible!

Young children enjoy tall tales, knock-knock jokes, and riddles. Have children (or parents) share a riddle in a designated riddle box. When you need a moment to lighten up, you (or a child) can pull one out and share it. Humorous books can make children laugh out loud at the descriptive words or far-fetched plots.

When children see us approaching them with patience, a sense of humor, and good will, they realize that life is what you make it, and learn to approach their own stressful moments with humor. Life is so much better when we can find ways to laugh and have fun together. These happy times build memories—and relationships—that will never be forgotten.

● **THINK ABOUT IT!**

Describe the last time you were learning with children and laughing at the same time. What were you doing? What were the children doing? What materials were being used? How could you make this happen more often?

_____

_____

_____

Find and read at least one hilarious book to the children in your classroom. Consult your school or local librarian for a list of materials that are appropriate for the age level you teach. When you read it, emphasize the aspects of humor and let children laugh as long as they want. Watch, listen, and enjoy. What did you learn through sharing this experience? (Did the positive mood last beyond the shared experience of humor?)

_____

_____

_____

🦋 *Principle 41: Jump Start a Belly Laugh*

Surprise children by teaching them to jump start a belly laugh. Grab hands and jump up and down together, saying, "ho, ho, ho" really fast, until you are genuinely laughing. You will be surprised how good it feels to laugh. Your body and your brain both get a chance to take a break. When you come back to where you were, you will be more relaxed and have better perspective.

Sometimes, we need to restart an activity due to interruptions or unforeseen events. A principal had come in to talk with a teacher about a serious matter. After he left, Ms. Jacobs realized that the children had gotten tired of waiting. Some were wandering around the room unfocused, and others had started bickering. She immediately realized the need for a change of pace and wanted to energize them quickly.

"I want you to stand up and each take both hands of one partner and face him or her. See how quickly you can do it." Ms. Jacobs sounded serious, so all the children jumped up, wondering what she was doing. "Holding both of your partner's hands, start jumping up and down—saying 'Ho, ho, ho' with every jump." She grabbed Shanika's hands and started bobbing up and down. Soon everyone else had joined in. Before long, every child in the room was laughing. "Oh, I feel better now," Ms. Jacobs said, "and I hope you do too. Let's close our eyes and take a deep breath."

This very wise teacher had saved the day. Realizing that the children needed to refocus, she interjected some fun into the day, broke the spell of the recent interruption, and gave them a chance to give their brains a rest. After a few minutes, everyone was ready to get back to work. It is worthwhile to take the time to have fun, shed the tension, regroup, and get a fresh start. All of us need to lighten up at times and take time to readjust. Jump starting a belly laugh is a great way to make this happen.

● **THINK ABOUT IT!**

Before or after lunch, regardless of what mood you are in, jump start a belly laugh with your class. What did the children say? How did it change the mood of the day? (If you work with infants, try this with a coworker, or gently say, "ho, ho, ho" while rocking a baby.) What was the result?

_____

_____

_____

 Principle 42: Make It Fun

See if you can turn a chore into a challenge; a job into a game; a "must" into a "want to." Model pleasure in doing hard work.

It takes a bit of creative energy to think of a fun way to teach an important lesson or to get a job done, but it is well worth the effort. We can put music on and dance when we clean up the classroom. We can set a timer and see how quickly we can get chores done. We can sing as we work, make up songs, or harmonize with each other. It makes positive memories of the times we spend together.

Recently a teacher let her students play a math game using the desk tops as a tic-tac-toe board. They lined up in teams and she asked them a math question. If they got the answer right, they got to be the human game pieces and sit on the desks. They practiced for the upcoming math test and had fun at the same time.

Many teachers have been creative in finding beanbag, baseball, or Jeopardy games they can use to teach children needed skills. A pre-K teacher made hopscotch grids on the floor with masking tape and put letters in each space. During indoor

recess when it was raining, children rolled a letter cube and jumped to the correct space. Both children and adults will enjoy the time together when they find creative ways to get involved.

We are attracted, just like children are, to the face of someone who reflects a smile! An attitude of fun is always contagious. One person with a cheerful heart and happy words can inspire cooperation from others. When children see the twinkle in our eye and know we will be making the job a pleasant one, they will look forward to being with us. Nothing inspires cooperation more than someone who makes a job fun.

Birth to Age 3

- Sing to babies about whatever they are eating. "Oh, these peas are yummy. Can you feel them in your tummy?" (Any rhymes that you make up will be perfect!)

- Make funny faces together. Describe the activity: "Lift your eyebrows high! Drop your chin down low! Bunch up your nose." You can also add body poses, being sure to describe the action. This is entertaining to infants and teaches toddlers to follow directions.

- Get toddlers to sing "Whistle While You Work." They may not know how to whistle, but they love to try.

- Make up rhyming poems while serving lunch or changing a diaper.

- Sing silly bubble songs while assisting children with washing their hands. (To any familiar tune, sing the words "Bubble, bubble, bubble.")

- Chant familiar nursery rhymes, such as "Jack Be Nimble." Have children jump or skip while they are picking up toys.

- Use music, games, and finger plays to build connections and share experiences.

- Provide soft and soothing music when a child has been crying, or when calming or comforting is needed.

- Encourage motor skills by using a variety of music, each for a few minutes: lively and quick, high and sweet, stately and low. Dance with children, imitating the sounds of the music with your body motions. You can ask them what the music "sounds like" or "feels like" to them, and encourage them to act out that sound. This activity connects emotions and imagination to motor control. You may add the use of soft scarves or streamers to this activity.

- Tap, clap, or rub your hands together; click your fingers; tap your feet; or have fun making mouth noises (buzzing, whistling, tweeting, zipping, etc.) to encourage sound and body awareness. These movements and sound activities can be rhythmic or random, enjoyed with one child or with a group. Patterns can be created along with music or alone. Having the children repeat sound patterns is a fun and effective cognitive regulation activity.

- Try tapping on different objects and listening to the sounds. Describe whether the sounds are high or low. Have children march or walk to the tempo as you tap or clap. This is a great attention-focusing activity.

- Fill water bottles with dry beans or rice, and tape securely shut so that children can use them as shakers (or use commercial shakers). Shake to music or shake while dancing. "Shake high! Shake low. Shake fast. Shake slow!" They won't realize they are practicing following directions!

Ages 3 to 8

- Nurturing cooperation and confidence are a benefit of planned physical activities for children. Games such as "Mother, May I?" and "Simon Says" promote confidence, coordination, and shared fun. Physical games require memory to practice rules, planning for body adjustment, and practice for self-control as children inhibit the desire to move or to get ready for the next action. There are many books available with physical games for children that include concept development as well. Be sure to check out your local library, bookstore, and the Web for more information. Nurturing a spirit of fun and cooperation will pay off in the way children relate to each other throughout the day.

- Board games are highly recommended for preschool and school-aged children to facilitate self-regulation, attention, planning, and reflection. Many games like dominos, card games, and board games promote one-to-one correspondence, math skills, and math logic. Incorporate board and card games into lesson plans for "minds-on" activities that promote social interaction as well as learning.

- Providing music for soothing, stimulation, or mood enhancement is as important for school-aged children as it is for preschoolers. Using a familiar routine song can make transitions go more smoothly. For example, instead of announcing time for writing in journals, simply put on the writing music. Gradually shifting from the use of verbal to music cues will establish routines where children are able to self-direct their transitions.

- Preschool and school-aged children benefit from dance and motion as much as younger children, and will appreciate the spirit and involvement. Setting aside time at the end of lunch for a music and movement break will reinvigorate the afternoon of learning. If you can, let children bring in their favorite music to share during these times.

- Bring a jump rope to recess for group chants and games, and be sure to facilitate and monitor involvement. Resources are available online for great jump rope games and chants for young children.

Creating opportunities for children to contribute, cooperate, practice social skills, and have fun together will support a nurturing, caring environment. What feels like games to them are actually purposeful learning activities that will stimulate self-control. Music and movement activities coordinate children's bodies, develop body awareness, and promote self-regulation and planning. These shared activities support listening and following directions and give children needed activity as they promote a nurturing environment.

● **THINK ABOUT IT!**

Describe a person who you love to be around because he or she is always having fun. What characteristics are appealing to you?

_____

_____

Name two ways you can make learning or work more engaging and meaningful for yourself and others.

_____

_____

Principle 43: Give Life to Inanimate Objects

Tell the child that "the books are calling," or "the trash is saying that it wants to be taken out to the hall." Give your voice a believable "squeaky" tone to make it more dramatic (and fun).

A child's imagination is in constant gear. A child can make the leap to the land of pretend without skipping a beat. To make cleaning up a room fun, adults can make toys come to life. Children will love to help with their requests. The airplane asks in a low, slow voice, "Will somebody please fly me back home?" The blocks sigh, "Oh dear, I am lonely down here, can someone help me find my friends?" The plastic turtles lying in a heap exclaim in a croaking voice, "I am so hungry, can you please lead me back to the pond for dinner?" This simple game of pretend makes common moments seem like fun and encourages young children to jump in to help.

Children will laugh out loud when they see the puzzle piece of a giraffe waiting to be picked up and hear it say in a silly voice, "Help me find the rest of my neck!" A paintbrush asks, "Will someone please give me a bath?" With no further request, a child will hurry over to pick up the puzzle pieces or to rinse off the brush in the sink.

As students are lining up to go into the hall, Mr. Micah says, "I hear the floor saying, 'I am asleep. I hope nobody wakes me up while they walk on me.'" The children know just what that means, and so not a sound is heard as they tiptoe into the library.

The reason giving life to inanimate objects works so well is that it creates a word picture for children. When an object "comes to life," it captures a child's imagination.

Children will respond eagerly as they hear a request—in fun—coming directly from an inanimate object.

● **THINK ABOUT IT!**

Complete the following, using the Give Life to Inanimate Objects Principle.

Your food is spilled on the table. What does the food say?

_____

_____

The crayons have rolled onto the floor. What do the crayons say?

_____

_____

You have come in from outside and need to wash your hands. What do your hands say?

_____

_____

Talking Together

There are many creative ways to make personal connections with each child. One way to create a meaningful bond is to share writing or drawing. Not only do you nurture the child's attachment with you, but you show that writing can share feelings and express thoughts and ideas with others. Writing can multiply the impact of our words, because it a tangible reminder to the child of your personal care and relationship together. He can revisit and "keep close" the message that you have shared.

Principle 44: Institute Mailboxes

Put a mailbox inside your classroom, and attach one to each child's desk or cubby. Write personal notes (suggestions, thanks, etc.) to put inside the child's mailbox. Be sure to have one on your desk for their messages back to you.

Ms. Lopez teaches third grade. Her students created mailboxes that express their personalities and attached them to the sides of their desks. Ms. Lopez takes a few moments every day to notice acts of kindness and special contributions made to the class, and then tucks a note about it in the student's mailbox when the student doesn't notice. It's a great place for her to leave written "Great Moments."

One afternoon, Ms. Lopez left a note for her student saying, "Dear Ethan, Thank you for being a friend to Nick today when he came to visit our class. You made our classroom a friendly place to be." The next day, Ms. Lopez found a return note in her box from Ethan: "I appreciate you because you don't yell. I want to be a teacher just like you. P.S.: You are just right." We want to weigh our words with care, remembering that what is written has lasting impact.

A journal is another way to open safe communication with children. A child can write to the teacher, who promises that the writing will remain confidential. The teacher can respond in writing to the child with validation and thoughtful comments. This is a beautiful way to influence a child's life.

"You've got mail!" Those are words that we love to hear! It means someone took time to stop everything and think about us. Every time we write the words, "Thank you for listening, thank you for caring, thank you for being kind," we affirm how much a child contributes to others. In classrooms where teachers use the 101 principles, children are in the habit of noticing acts of kindness and enjoy sharing their thanks in writing.

Birth to Age 3

- For young children who are too young for desks but ready for early writing opportunities, encourage drawing pictures. If a child wants to dictate a note to go along with the picture, the teacher or another adult can help. Children at this age can still have individual mailboxes, or the class can have a group mailbox that the teacher empties and reads at large group times. (Parents can leave positive notes for the group as well.)

- Place a box where parents can write or leave notes to you about their child. Reassure them that their communication with you is confidential.

- Take photos of infants (or older children) during happy moments and write a note on the back to give to parents.

- Toddlers will want to pretend to mail pictures, photos, and letters to their parents. This is a wonderful opportunity to support pre-literacy skills and dictation as you help them tell their parents about a special experience in the classroom.

- Remember that stick figures can tell a story, so a simple drawing of a teacher and child holding hands with a heart drawn where the heart should be will give a toddler the wordless message. He will soon be drawing you pictures back.

Ages 3 to 8

- Have each child decorate an envelope or box to attach their desk, cubby, or locker. This is a perfect opportunity for them to decorate their mailbox to reflect their personality and interests.

- Encourage children to create or write letters or cards to each other. The purpose can be to celebrate special experiences, wish happy birthday, share poetry and art, or simply express positive thoughts and messages.

- Create "Kindness Crowns" and "Happy Hearts" by cutting out colored paper shapes. Put these shapes in a bowl or bag so that the children can take one, sign their name on the back, and insert it into a friend's mailbox whenever they want to share a hug or cheer. This concept is similar to social networking "gifts," in which friends are sent a heart, hug, or word gift. Plan ideas together and let the children brainstorm what shapes and meanings they want to create and use.

● **Think About It!**

Can you remember a time a teacher or someone special wrote something special about you? What was it? How did it make you feel? Do you still have it?

_____

_____

_____

_____

Summary

Nurturing children's sense of security, self-confidence, and competence will pay off in increased engagement and a sense of belonging. Nurturing others begins by taking good care of your own resources and energies, so that you are prepared to be a nurturing role model. Taking stock of your priorities, your schedule, and your responses to previous experiences can provide insight and reveal opportunities to realign your balance. Reevaluating components of the classroom and emotional climate can help you identify opportunities to implement new strategies and increase support for children's development. As you infuse each day with new purpose, you will become more effective at nurturing others.

Using the Principles in Your Classroom

Nurture Passion by Launching Expert Projects

Ms. Driscoll asked her second graders to share their passion with the class. Each child was to bring in something they were passionate about and explain to the other children how to create, do, or try their topic. Some of the projects included hair braiding (on dolls), needlepoint, learning how to draw, motor and emergency vehicles, whales, creating comics on the computer, dinosaurs, how to make pancakes, trash to treasure, making paper airplanes, how to Greek dance, how to take care of a dog, and how to fish. The children brought the ingredients or supplies and demonstrated their interest, sport, or activity. Ms. Driscoll posted photos on her class website. Through sharing of interests and passions, the children got to know each others' gifts and abilities and admire their classmates in new ways.

This activity is perfect for children ages 4 to 8 (pre-K to third grade). Children ages 2 to 3 can bring in a book on a topic they enjoy and tell the class about their interest, or bring an object from home that they love and tell about it with the teacher's assistance. For example, a child could bring a book about tractors or share a book about a favorite animal and explain the animal's care.

Nurture Leadership

Appoint a Star of the Week. Be sure every child receives a turn to be honored.

- Music Freeze: Let the chosen child select music and lead the "music freeze" of their choice. For music freeze, the teacher stops the music and all the children must follow the leader's pose and "freeze" like him/her.

- Guest of Choice: Let the child choose who will be the classroom guest of choice for the week. This invited guest can be a parent or guardian who has a special skill or hobby to share. The guest can demonstrate cooking, woodworking, playing an instrument, flower arranging, crafts, story reading, a sport, or any other skill or interest. Community members such as a dentist, medical or emergency technician, scientist, mail carrier, or trash collector can be invited to share their vocation. Whoever is available in your community can be invited in to talk with your class. By year end, this effort exposes children to the social interdependence of communities as well as to available services and potential careers.

- Teacher's Helper: Let the chosen child be the assistant during teaching times. They may help turn pages (if younger), be the reader (if older), help explain the lesson, or demonstrate an activity. This assigned role should provide a way for the child to feel competent and use his efforts toward helping others learn. This responsibility is age appropriate for all children from toddler to third grade.

Nurture Manners

Create fun and engaging opportunities for children to practice good manners. Here are a few words children can use to interact in socially positive ways. Have children brainstorm others and practice together.

- Meeting others: "Hello! How are you?" "I am glad to meet you!" "Thank you for letting me play."

- Entering a group: "I have a great idea!" "I like the way you are . . ." "What would happen if . . . ?"

- Asking: "May I please?" Can you please help me?"

- Meal skills: "Please pass the _____ " "Thank you!" "Please may I be excused?"

- Waiting for a turn: "Excuse me. May I please have it when you are finished?" "When will you be finished?" "Wear a patient hat!" (The teacher uses a sign for hat, pointing her fingers together over her head, and the children copy this cue as a reminder to themselves that they need to wait. This is an external cue for internal self-regulation. Using cues can help even toddlers develop the ability to postpone a desire.)

- Saying no when needed: "No, thank you." "Please stop." "Thanks, but no thanks!" "I'm not ready to play."

- Saying words for safety: "Walk away." Teach children as soon as they are verbal that they can "walk away" and move themselves from another child if they are being bothered or if someone is being aggressive toward them. This is a critical skill. A child can say "walk away" to himself. In addition, teach children to say, "Walk away" to a child who is taking their toy, pushing them, or doing something uncomfortable. The phrase "Walk away" has been used successfully with children as young as 12 months and up to three years. Very young children understand this concept clearly and can respond to it even before they can say the words themselves. If a teacher needs to say, "Walk away" to a child who is heading toward a frustrating or potentially harmful situation, he understands that he needs to go the other direction. You will be surprised to see toddlers walk backwards when they hear "Walk away!" These words can be a helpful safety tool for children and for teachers. It is a good idea to practice this skill when children are comfortable and happy, so that they can internalize and be able to use it when needed.

Nurture Language

The more children are able to use words to express themselves, the fewer behavior issues there will be. The ability to use words to think and express emotions fosters reasoning, self-regulation, and problem solving. When we engage children in enriched language interactions, they not only grow intellectually, but they develop the verbal skills to get along socially. Language supports a child's ability to self-regulate. Every time you read, talk, and listen together, you are practicing skills for positive relationships and successful learning. We can encourage language development with children in the following ways:

- Read books daily with expression and enjoyment. Comment and ask questions to invite the children's participation. Talk about what is familiar in the book. What is similar to and different from the children's experiences? Use colorful and descriptive vocabulary to explain the story. Ask questions about what is happening and what children think will happen. Read aloud poems, songs, stories, or chapter books. Consult your librarian or library for a list of appropriate titles.

- Use responsive conversation. For infants and toddlers, use "back and forth" interaction, which includes responsive listening and empathetic vocalization. Listen to the tone of voice, rate, and inflection. Respond by mirroring a child's movement and sounds.

- Be sure to describe activities, actions, and feelings of the child, such as, "Let's put you up in the high chair so you can eat some yummy green peas." "You have the brown puppy. Is he feeling sleepy? Are you putting him to sleep under the blanket?"

- Use picture books that are large enough for groups of children to see, and that show people, places, objects, and experiences that extend children's connection between words and their current experiences. Read with animation, pointing to objects in the book and describing what you see. "Do you see the baby? He is eating his cereal with a spoon." "The boy is happy! There is his mother. He is hugging his momma. Do you hug your momma?"

- Enrich vocabulary. Have "real-life" conversations that let children discuss and ask questions about the topics they are currently learning. *Photosynthesis* may not be a first-grade vocabulary word, but the children will be excited to use "real" words that describe the reason leaves are green in the spring and turn colors in the fall. *Metamorphosis* is another good word that children love to know!

- Label objects in the classroom. Use both English and languages spoken by English language learners. When conversation turns to a specific subject (pets, animals, the ocean, etc.), follow through and provide books and websites that support children's extended learning in each needed language.

Teacher Tips

The following are comments from teachers who have been trained to use the 101 principles in their early care and education settings and elementary school classrooms.

A child in my class was tearing up a box and throwing the pieces onto the floor. I thought to myself, "It is now or never!" I had wanted to try the Bunny Planet Principle, and now was my chance. I told him that I was going to close my eyes and go to the Bunny Planet and that I hoped that all the paper on the floor would be gone when I opened my eyes. Perhaps he thought I had taken leave of my senses, but he did actually clean up the paper! I was amazed that this worked.

This past week, snack time was a bit chaotic. I decided to let the children do something silly to let them show me what they wanted and to keep them calm. If they wanted a peanut butter and jelly sandwich, then they put their finger on their nose. If they wanted an apple, they touched their ear. This really helped to keep it quiet and to get everyone their snack without me feeling frustrated or everyone raising their voices to tell me what they wanted. This was so effective that the next day, I saw a couple of the other teachers using my Make It Fun technique!

Braydon was getting distracted from writing and was watching his tablemates work. I told him that his journal was calling him and that it wanted to be finished so it could go into his backpack. He thought that was funny and went right to work. He even told his journal, "Here you go!" when he was finished and put it in his backpack. Give Life to Inanimate Objects made my reminder for him to follow through friendly and fun.

This week was extra hectic, with an assembly and school concert practice. I decided to use the Institute Mailboxes Principle. I gave each child a manila envelope to decorate. When they were finished, the children taped them to the back of their chairs. The children have been putting in notes thanking each other for random acts of kindness. The amazing thing is that they have really stepped up to show each other respect and helpfulness.

Research on the Run

Nurturing Quality Interactions

- Teachers need to nurture children as well as foster their learning (Burchinal, Howes, & Pianta, 2008).

- Children need a deep, emotional attachment to an adult caregiver that includes sensitivity and responsiveness (Seigel, 2001).

- Warm, enriched verbal environments with shared understanding and support for social interaction affect children's intellectual and social growth. The teacher's responsiveness and consistency plays a key role in scaffolding development (Seigel, 1999; Vygotsky, 1978).

- Children are concerned with pleasing adults and experience stress and anxiety if they feel an adult's displeasure. They need to feel they are not a disappointment to the adults in their lives (Honig, Miller, & Church, 2007).

- Healthy social and emotional development is critical to school readiness and positive long-term outcomes (Thompson & Raikes, 2007).

- Positive perceptions about self and self-confidence in the classroom can be influenced by the child's perception of the teachers' feelings about the child (Bierman, Nix, Domitrovich, Welsh, & Gest, 2010).

- Emotional stress for children can result when teacher turnover affects the long-term consistency of caregivers (Mims, Scott-Little, Lower, Cassidy, & Hestenes, 2008).

- A child's relationship with his teacher or caregiver can provide an important secure base, but depends on consistent supportive interactions. These are the qualities linked to greater emotional support, positive interactions, positive climate, and quality instructional practices (Thijs, Koomen, & van der Leij, 2008).

Nurturing Positive Behaviors

- Early connections are supported through "growth fostering relationships" where reciprocal empathy is central. The authentic inter-relationship provides a secure base for a child's healthy psychological growth (Rolfe, 2004).

- Within the relational–cultural theory, interactions are guided by respect rather than by power and coercion (West, 2005).

- Nurturing interactions include mutual respect as well as responsive listening and interacting. The supportive emotional interactions empower a sense of relational competence for the child (Raver, 2002).

- Core components of this approach support the development of healthy interdependence. The relational–cultural model has strong ties with the work of Alfred Adler. Similarities include mutual respect based on equality and a fundamental faith in the child. An important assumption of Adler's theory is that the more human beings develop, the more they connect to others (Adler & Stein, 2005).

- Intentional reflection and purposeful awareness of the impact of one's words, emotions, and actions on others are central to nurturance and the support of social–emotional competence (Epstein, 2007; Masterson, 2008).

- The mutual empathy that is established between adult and child builds trust and cooperation. The ability to develop emotional regulation and share emotional understanding allows children to succeed in the social interactions of learning (Brownell & Kopp, 2007; Denham, 2005).

- Because significant relationships create emotional patterns for self-appraisal as well as interaction with others, adult–child interactions create a lasting blueprint for future relationships. The supportive emotional interactions empower a sense of relational competence for the child (NICHD ECCRN, 2006; Spencer, Jordan, & Sazama, 2004; Trevarthen, Barr, Dunlop, Gjersoe, Marwick, & Stephen, 2005).

- Warm, positive relationships support factors of resilience and include many variables necessary for healthy social, emotional, and academic adjustment (Nash & Hay, 2003; Pianta, Hamre, & Stuhlman, 2003).

- Interactions that involve shared laughter and enjoyment positively affect body chemistry for participants and support increased physiological health and well-being over time (Berk, Felten, Tan, Bittman, & Westengard, 2001; see www.laughingrx.com/15.html).

- Higher quality social–emotional interactions between the teacher and child enhances learning in language, literacy, and academics (Mashburn, 2008).

- A sense of humor increases children's ability to handle stress and negotiate challenges, as well as sensory awareness, high expectations, and a sense of competence. All of these can be boosted through interactions with a responsive teacher (Breslin, 2005).

Getting Positive Results Using the Principles in Action

What happened or led up to the interaction?

_____

_____

_____

Which principle did you use?

_____

_____

_____

How did the situation turn out? (How did the child/children respond?)

_____

_____

_____

What did you learn?

_____

_____

_____

What happened or led up to the interaction?

_____

_____

_____

Which principle did you use?

_____

_____

_____

How did the situation turn out? (How did the child/children respond?)

_____

_____

_____

What did you learn?

_____

_____

_____

Guide to the Principles

34. Get Help: Staying aware of your limits and getting support from others is vitally important. You may want to ask another teacher to cover for you while you focus on, or spend extra positive time with, a child who seems troubled. Be sure to prioritize and ask for help when you need it.

35. Take Care of Yourself: Children pick up on our emotions and model our ways of handling our feelings, so we want to do our best to be a good example of healthy and mature behavior.

36. Nap/Take a Break: A nap usually puts everything in better perspective. Teachers and parents are often sleep deprived. Make it a goal to go to bed sooner at night, so that you will feel more energetic during the day. At school, when you see children becoming tired or lethargic, take a stretch break, a music break, or a brain break.

37. Bunny Planet: Close your eyes and tell the children that you are going to the Bunny Planet (or another imaginary place). Ask them to tell you when they are ready for you to come back, once things are quiet and they are ready to make good choices.

38. Read a Book: Sit down and read to the children. Take your attention away from the child who is behaving inappropriately. Read something engaging and helpful to them until you have cooled off and can deal with the situation in a productive manner.

39. **Have Fun Together:** Children love to know that they bring us joy and pleasure. Lighten up and have fun.

40. **Humor:** Make a game out of it. Have fun. Laugh a lot together. ("How would a rabbit brush his teeth?") Enjoy the child's sense of humor.

41. **Jump Start a Belly Laugh:** Surprise children by teaching them to jump start a belly laugh. Grab hands and jump up and down together, saying, "ho, ho, ho" really fast, until you are genuinely laughing. You'll be surprised how good it feels to laugh. Your body and your brain both get a chance to take a break. When you

come back to where you were, you will be more relaxed and have better perspective.

42. **Make It Fun:** See if you can turn a chore into a challenge; a job into a game; a "must" into a "want to." Model pleasure in doing hard work.

43. **Give Life to Inanimate Objects:** Tell the child that "the books are calling," or "the trash is saying that it wants to be taken out to the hall." Give your voice a believable "squeaky" tone to make it more dramatic (and fun).

44. **Institute Mailboxes:** Put a mailbox outside your classroom, and attach one to each child's desk or cubby. Write personal notes (suggestions, thanks, etc.) to put inside the child's mailbox. Be sure to have one on your desk for their messages back to you.

Study Guide

a. **Goal Setting:** How were you nurtured as a child? Where did you feel most safe to explore and grow? Who inspired you to find your passion? What did this person (or these people) do for you? What traits do people who inspire others have in common?

b. **Questioning and Reflection:** How can you re-prioritize, reorganize, or review routines to give children more responsibility in your classroom to help, lead, and contribute?

c. **Case Study:** Mr. Charles reviewed his room to evaluate the perspective of his third-grade students. He decided to add nature displays and use the microscopes that had been in the closet. The children enlisted the librarian's help to choose books for the center. Many chose butterflies, insects, and nests. A student's father offered a collection of butterflies and nests to complete the study area. What could Mr. Charles do to give his students complete responsibility over this new science area? What would help even the most active children be successful in taking ownership of the collection?

d. **Personal Examples/Group Brainstorming:** Is there a particular time of day that is difficult for you? Consider the last half hour of the school day, for example. Describe the situation and how you feel about it. What could you change or modify to make this time of day more pleasant? What could you do to make this time less stressful and more fun?

e. **Learners as Experts:** *Topic 1:* Describe the last time you were learning with children and laughing at the same time. What were you doing? What were the children doing? How could you make this happen more often? For strategies to discuss, see Principles 40 (Humor), 41 (Jump Start a Belly Laugh), and 42 (Make It Fun). What would work best with your students? *Topic 2:* Which of the strategies from "Using the Principles in Your Classroom" will help you best nurture children's engagement: passion, leadership, manners, or language? (See pages 107–110.)

f. **Principles in Action:** Using the "Getting Positive Results Using the Principles in Action" sheet, share one principle you implemented from this chapter. What happened or led up to the interaction? Which principle did you use? How did the situation turn out? (How did the child/children respond?) What did you learn?

g. **Research on the Run:** Rate yourself on a scale of 1 to 5 (with 5 being the highest) in the characteristics discussed in the "Nurturing Positive Behaviors" section. Which areas do you want most to develop? Which areas are you best in giving? (See pages 111–112.)

h. **Looking Ahead:** Set the purpose for upcoming study by introducing chapter objectives. Thank you for sharing your personal insight about responsive, positive guidance and for your commitment to making a difference in the lives of children.

References

Adler, A., & Stein, H. (2005). *Case readings and demonstrations: The problem child and the pattern of life.* Bellingham, WA: Alfred Adler Institute.

Berk, L., Felten, D., Tan, I., Bittman, B., & Westengard, J. (2001). Modulation of neuroimmune parameters during the eustress of humor-associated mirthful laughter. *Alternative Therapies, 7*(2), 62–76.

Bierman, K., Nix, R., Domitrovich, C., Welsh, J., & Gest, S. (2010). Fostering school readiness with preschool interventions that promote social-emotional learning and language skills: The Head Start REDI project. Paper presented October 14, 2010, at the Human Capital Research Collaborative Fall conference, Minneapolis, MN. Retrieved October 28, 2011, from http://humancapitalrc.org/events/2010/hrcconf/papers/bierman.pdf

Breslin, D. (2005). Children's capacity to develop resiliency: How to nurture it. *Young Children, 60*(1), 47–52.

Brownell, C. A., & Kopp, C. B. (Eds.). (2007). *Socioemotional development in the toddler years: Transitions and transformations.* New York: Guilford.

Burchinal, M., Howes, C., & Pianta, R. (2008). Predicting child outcomes at the end of kindergarten from the quality of pre-kindergarten teacher-child interactions and instruction. *Applied Developmental Science, 12*(3), 140–153.

Denham, S. A. (2005). The emotional basis of learning and development in early childhood education. In B. Spodek (Ed.), *Handbook of research in early childhood education* (pp. 85–103). Mahwah, NJ: Lawrence Erlbaum.

Epstein, A. (2007). *The intentional teacher: Choosing the best strategies for young children's learning.* Washington, DC: National Association for the Education of Young Children.

Honig, A., Miller, S., & Church, E. (2007). What makes children fearful and anxious. *Early Childhood Today, 21,* 23–17.

Mashburn, A. (2008). Quality of social and physical environments in preschools and children's development of academic, language, and literacy skills. *Applied Developmental Science, 12,* 113–127.

Masterson, M. (2008). The impact of the 101s: A guide to positive discipline training on teacher interaction practices, attitudes and prosocial skill outcomes in preschool classrooms. Ph.D. Dissertation, Norfolk: Old Dominion University

Mims, S., Scott-Little, C., Lower, J. K., Cassidy, D. J., & Hestenes, L. L. (2008). Education level and stability as it relates to early childhood classroom quality: A survey of early childhood program directors and teachers. *Journal of Research in Childhood Education, 23*(2), 227–237.

Nash, A., & Hay, D. (2003). Social relations in infancy: Origins and evidence. *Human Development, 46,* 222–232.

NICHD Early Child Care Research Network. (2006). Infant–mother attachment classification: Risk and protection to changing maternal caregiving quality. *Developmental Psychology, 42*(1), 38–58.

Pianta, R., Hamre, B., & Stuhlman, M. (2003). Relationships between teachers and children. In W. M. Reynolds & G. E. Miller (Eds.), *Handbook of psychology: Educational psychology, Vol. 7* (pp. 199–234). Hoboken, NJ: Wiley.

Raver, C. (2002). Emotions matter: Making the case for the role of young children's emotional development for early school readiness. *Social Policy Report of the Society for Research in Child Development, 16*(3), 535–555.

Rolfe, S. (2004). *Rethinking attachment for early childhood practice: Promoting security, autonomy and resilience in young children.* Allen, Australia: Crows Nest, NSW.

Siegel, D. J. (1999). *The developing mind: How relationships and the brain interact to shape who we are.* New York: Guilford Press.

Seigel, D. (2001). Toward an interpersonal neurobiology of the developing mind: Attachment relationships, "mindsight," and neural integration. *Infant Mental Health Journal, 22*(1–2), 67–94.

Spencer, R., Jordan, J., & Sazama, J. (2004). *Empowering children for life: A preliminary report.* Wellesley, MA: Wellesley Centers for Women.

Thijs, J., Koomen, H., & van der Leij, A. (2008). Teacher–child relationships and pedagogical practices: Considering the teacher's perspective. *School Psychology Review, 37*(2), 244–260.

Thompson, R. A., & Raikes, H. A. (2007). The social and emotional foundations of school readiness. In D. F. Perry, R. F. Kaufmann, & J. Knitzer (Eds.), *Social and emotional health in early childhood: Building bridges between services and systems* (pp. 13–35). Baltimore, MD: Paul H. Brookes Publishing Co.

Trevarthen, C., Barr, I., Dunlop, A., Gjersoe, N., Marwick, H., & Stephen, C. (2005). *Supporting a child's needs for care and affection, shared meaning and a social place. Review of childcare and the development of children aged 0–3: Research, evidence and implications for out-of-home provision.* Edinburgh, Scotland: The Scottish Executive.

Vygotsky, L. S. (1978). *Mind in society: The development of higher psychological processes.* Cambridge, MA: Harvard University Press.

West, C. (2005). The map of relational-cultural theory. *Women & Therapy, 28*(3/4), 93–110.

c h a p t e r 5

Fostering Independence

This chapter will explore the ways that teachers can support children's growing need for independence and examine the community environment that shapes children's developing skills. You will discover effective ways to help children solve problems and self-correct when issues arise. These strategies will help them establish healthy independence as you support their increasing social and emotional resources.

As you teach children routines and responsibilities, you will create a sense of teamwork and cooperation that will encourage positive interactions. You will be able to use multiple approaches to help children take responsibility for their personal needs and become aware of the needs of others. Children will know that you are in their corner and are ready to assist them in their continuing journey toward independence.

Chapter Principles

45: Good Head on Your Shoulders

46: Thank You

47: Trust

48: Logical Consequences

49: Third Party

50: Self-Correction

51: Ask the Child

52: Let the Child Be the Teacher

53: Values Are Caught, Not Taught

54: Teach—Don't Reteach

55: Successive Approximations

56: Prompt and Praise

57: Sing

58: Allow Imperfection

59: Encouragement

Chapter Objectives

As you explore the text and activities in this chapter, you will be able to:

- Support independence and healthy interdependence
- Facilitate growing exploration, mastery, and leadership
- Utilize trust and collaboration to build children's growing competence
- Prepare children to problem-solve and take on challenges
- Develop children's active engagement in caring for themselves and others
- Support meaningful purpose and motivation for learning

Building the Road to Independence

All children need to belong and feel significant. Our role is to support growing independence and help children develop responsibility for their emotional, social, and physical responses and choices. At the same time, they are developing a sense of interdependence as they learn to help, participate, and cooperate with others. We need to make sure that children learn the skills they need to become competent and to feel confident about looking out for themselves and others. We want to help them take ownership of their belongings and contribute positively to the physical and emotional climate of the classroom. Early accountability has a great pay off in later life.

By the time children are teenagers, they need to know how to make good decisions, how to say no to dangerous options, and how to take care of their bodies and possessions. It is important for us to convince children that they can do it, that they have a good head on their shoulders, and that we trust their judgment. It is important to remember that the early childhood years are a critical period, during which children form their sense of purpose. We want to empower every child to become excited about the adult he will someday be. We need to keep our eyes on the goal of preparing children for life.

Understanding Social Factors That Affect Independence

Learning about our surrounding community can help us become more sensitive to children's unique needs. Many families are involved in outside activities, busy with work, spending less time eating and playing together, and feeling frustrated by the growing responsibility to "keep up." Young children are using social media networks, video games, and media entertainment earlier than ever, which can draw them away from traditional family activities and extended periods of play.

At the same time, young children are introduced to increasing social pressures. Children have early access to cell phones and to the Internet. They are exposed to the influence of sexuality and risk-taking activities within a climate of hypersexuality promoted by the media, advertising, clothing, and music industries. Product placement and media role models urge conformity to accepted body images and participation in consumerism. Children may adapt their behaviors to match what is popular without the maturity or understanding to support their decisions or to make wise choices. They confront intense peer pressure, social exclusion, and cyberbullying without a protected period of childhood to develop self-respect, confidence, self-regulation, and independent thinking.

When families are in a state of change or stress, children often need to take on increased responsibility for themselves and for siblings. According to the Center on the Developing Child at Harvard, one out of every seven children experiences some form of chronic neglect or physical, emotional, or sexual abuse. Nearly half of children living in poverty witness violence or are indirectly victims of violence. Families in poverty are more likely to face issues related to drug abuse and social isolation. Early health problems and stress can present a challenge to families. As we better understand the contributing social, economic, and environmental influences within our communities, we can become more sensitive to the needs of children and families. (For more information about the role of early stress in childhood, see Research on the Run.)

In 2009, the poverty rate in the United States was 19% (almost one in five) for children under the age of 18. Forty-two percent of children under age 6 (more than 10 million) live in low-income families. Sixty-one percent of Latino children, 61% of black children, 28% of Asian children, and 26% of white children live in low-income families. Families in poverty move more frequently than higher-income families, and 51% of low-income children live with a single parent. Resources containing more specific demographic information can be located in Research on the Run.

It is important to consider the strengths and assets of families as well as the challenges. Many children from poverty rate highly in self-help skills, and are expected to prepare meals as well as dress and bathe themselves. Often they are responsible for siblings and take on added roles in the home. However, they can be lacking access to medical and dental care, and may experience food insecurity—anxiety about whether they will have enough to eat.

In an elementary school lunch line, a seven-year-old first grader was assisting two younger girls. A visitor was impressed with his attentiveness and commented to his teacher. The teacher explained that the boy was responsible for waking up these girls—his sisters—and getting them ready for school each morning, and that his concern for them extended throughout the school day. Some children have many concerns besides learning and play.

These responsibilities have a tremendous impact on a child's focus and engagement at school. Children from poverty experience a higher rate of absenteeism and move more often, which affects their ability to assimilate and become comfortable with expectations in the classroom. A caring teacher shared that several homeless shelters were present in her district. She was committed to making sure the children who came to her school received needed clothing and supplies and that they were warmly accepted into her classroom community.

The need to take on adult roles at an early age can foster hypervigilance, and as a result, children can have difficulty filtering out external distractions. They can enter the classroom in a heightened state of physiological stress, and need to experience a teacher's calm consistency as well as practical support. Many teachers make healthy snacks available, secure warm clothing in cold-weather climates, and extend their commitment and care well beyond teaching and learning. Stocking extra school supplies and providing time during school hours for older children to complete homework can provide an ongoing boost for children who need responsive assistance.

Stress factors affect families of all socioeconomic backgrounds during times of recession, economic hardship, and illness. It is important to remember that these factors are not always visible, so staying aware of the needs of all children can help us be responsive to their need for support. Even when resources are limited, children bring a remarkable energy and inner determination to learn. Schools, families, and communities working together can positively affect the direction of children's lives and provide skills and practical help for healthy independence that will continue to serve them well.

Children are not only resilient, but vibrant and creative, with a natural drive to communicate their stories, connect with others, and share their hopes and dreams. Children need caring adults who will respect and recognize their strengths and aspirations—and help them develop skills for independence as well as healthy interdependence with others.

● **THINK ABOUT IT!**

What are some unique characteristics of your community? How might the children with whom you work need extra support as they grow toward independence?

_____

_____

_____

Name several skills that you want to encourage the children in your classroom to learn that will support their growing independence. If you work with infants or toddlers, describe the skills that you want to encourage and model.

_____

_____

_____

Helping Children Be Competent

Our goal is to help children become capable of creating relationships and outcomes that are healthy and that bring happiness to themselves and to others. We want to empower children to believe in themselves and to have confidence in their ability to make good things happen. We have to build their competence by giving them many opportunities to explore, practice, and master successful social and learning experiences.

In order to develop independence, children need to become responsible, learn to make good decisions, and acquire strategies to become creative problem solvers. When we use positive language of affirmation, we see children rising to the occasion—working hard, putting forth effort, and surprising themselves with achievements they didn't even know were possible!

The following principles will demonstrate many ways to help children develop their strengths, identify their gifts, and make meaningful contributions to their world.

Principle 45: Good Head on Your Shoulders

Tell a child frequently, "You have a good head on your shoulders. You decide. I trust your judgment." This brings out the best in the child and shows him that eventually he will be in charge of his own life and responsible for his own decisions.

There is a tendency to give a quick response when children ask us if they can do certain things, but it is better to allow the child to practice his skills of decision-making. When a child asks a question, respond by asking the child, "What do you think is the best way? You have a good head on your shoulders. I trust your judgment." If he comes to you with a problem, reply, "How do you think you can solve it? I trust your judgment."

If you work with younger children, affirmation is important. With infants, you can say, "I see you are a good rattle shaker!" "Look at you roll over. You are so strong." For toddlers, you want to be encouraging. "You can carry your bag all by yourself. What a good helper you are."

It is important to realize that you are not simply giving unqualified compliments. Young children are learning new skills daily. Give helpful feedback about what worked well. Support specific accomplishments when toddlers are in the process of hanging up their own coats and sweaters, or when preschoolers put away belongings or successfully clean up after a meal. Let them know when their effort has really paid off, and a solution they chose was productive or helpful.

With school-aged children, you need to encourage increasing responsibility for academic learning and for making thoughtful social decisions. Of course, you will want to stay near to provide scaffolding as children develop confidence. When you have a conversation with them, you can repeat back what they have said (or what you have seen) and then extend their thinking with a question: "It was good thinking to ask Joanna for help. How did you decide to solve the issue? What did you agree would work best?" If children need your assistance, you can help them generate ideas for consideration. Giving strong support for their developing judgment and independence is the goal.

If a child offers a solution that doesn't fully address or solve an issue, encourage him to talk to peers about his decision. The purpose is to promote problem-solving skills and critical thinking. When children make suggestions, try them out, and adjust their own behavior based on how well something worked for them, they are likely to use the strategy again in the future. It takes practice for children to develop effective solutions.

When working with younger children and toddlers, remain consistent and calm, yet always act quickly to ensure the safety of all children. Be patient as they are learning new skills. Try to anticipate and step in before problems occur. This age group needs constant repetition and cuing. It is necessary to guide children many times to support and reinforce needed or desired actions. As children "use their words" and get help when needed, they will be better able to relate with their peers and to solve issues. Meanwhile, keep focusing on their accomplishments and make a big deal over their successes.

Transferring the opportunity for problem-solving to the child helps him gain confidence that he can work things out. It shows him that you have faith in his actions. Support for independence can take time. It is often easier for an adult to suggest a solution than to assist a child in doing it. However, encouraging independence pays off in children's growing confidence and enthusiasm. As you stay present to support and guide them, you honor children's growing ability to make constructive decisions. These are the skills they are going to need to negotiate their lives.

You encourage independence when you say, "You have a good head on your shoulders. I trust your judgment." This conveys confidence and challenges each child to rise to the occasion. Setting high expectations shows him that eventually he will be in charge of his own life and responsible for his decisions. Then when he reaches a new goal, say "I knew you could do it!" Let him know that you believe in him and affirm him. You will be there to support and guide him, should he need your wisdom or assistance, but the message you convey about his positive decision-making and trust is essential.

Ultimately every child has to assume responsibility for his own life. The sooner that you convey to him that you trust his capacity to make good decisions, the sooner he can draw on his inner resources to help himself. It feels good to hear someone say to you, "You decide! I trust your judgment!"

● **THINK ABOUT IT!**

What was something you did that made you feel proud as a child? How did others respond?

_____

_____

_____

Do you remember a time when someone trusted you to do something important, and you wanted to "live up" to their belief in you? What happened?

_____

_____

_____

Teaching Children to Be Responsible

One of the greatest gifts we can give to children is to model and teach the joy of being responsible. The result is a sense of competence and an "I can do it" attitude. A sense of determination and pride forms when adults expect children to invest effort in the responsibilities of the classroom. Children will be more likely to volunteer when work needs to be done and stick with a task until it is completed. Our attitude and high expectations can be enhanced through effective strategies that invite cooperation.

 Principle 46: Thank You

Thank the child for doing the right thing—*before* he does it! "Thank you, Sarah, for dropping your paper scraps into the trash can" (before they land on the floor). "Thank you, Sam, for tucking your pencil in your desk before you line up" (before the pencil is put away). Children want to be helpful and cooperative, and a gentle reminder (with respectful thanks) encourages success.

Thanking a child ahead of time is one of the most effortless techniques for creating immediate positive cooperation. It is such a simple thing to thank someone ahead of time. You will find that it is effective with other adults, such as your co-teacher or assistant, as well. "Thank you, Ms. Davis, for helping Danny with his coat." The chance is great that she will step in quickly to help him.

● **THINK ABOUT IT!**

Name one thing that was expected of you as a child that, if you didn't do it, no one else did.

_____

_____

_____

How did this responsibility make you feel? Were you held accountable? (If you cannot think of an example from your own life, explain why you think it helps children to feel that their contributions are important to others.)

_____

_____

_____

Clarifying Expectations

Remember that expectations at home may be much different from those at school. A child's parents may happily hang up his clothes, clean his room, and tie his shoes for him. So when he comes to school, he will need assistance to learn skills and responsibility. Once, a two-year-old came to school and wouldn't eat during snack or lunch time. She cried for several weeks during meals. It took the bewildered teachers some time to realize that as part of this family's culture, the child was still being hand-fed by the parents. She had never before eaten without dependence on an adult to hold the spoon and help her.

It is important to discuss situations like this with the parents. You will be able to assist in feeding at first, with the goal of gradually turning over the responsibility to the child. Be sure to communicate often with parents about home expectations. Include questions on parent surveys and a daily communication sheet, with a section for notes to be exchanged between teacher and parents about feedings and routines. The more you are committed to communicating with parents about how you can best coordinate expectations, the better. In addition to solving daily issues, you will become more sensitive to the ways that daily routines can be affected by cultural expectations and practices.

Clarify specific details with parents about what will be needed at school. A list of expectations can be sent home at the beginning of the year and discussed at parent meetings. Ask parents how things are done at home and what would help you best meet the needs of the child. Make sure that parents have the opportunity to ask questions and raise concerns. Follow up your conversations with "What Happened Today" sheets to support a child's growing independence. The more we communicate openly, the more the child benefits.

If you work with infants, be sure to find out what routines for comforting and preferences for holding, rocking, and sleeping are used at home. If you work with toddlers and preschoolers, be sure to ask about nap routines, eating, and what the child is expected to do alone at home. Without ongoing communication, even the most caring teachers can miss an obvious reason for a child's difficulty in adjustment.

At an inner-city school, a multi-aged class of 3- to 5-year-olds was adjusting well. However, one little boy continued to cry inconsolably after his nap. The teachers thought the child was simply tired or waking up too soon. They thought he was crying for his "momma." Finally, they understood that he was saying, "I want my bottle." They realized he was given a bottle at home upon waking. Since that practice was not followed at school, the child was understandably upset. Realizing the situation, the teachers provided a drink and read him a book until the other children woke up. They talked with his parents, who decided to wean him off the bottle after naptime at home, as well. This kind of open and ongoing communication is needed to prevent and resolve issues related to expectations for growing independence.

For older children, differences in expectation may show up in issues surrounding completion of homework. If a teacher asks a parent to help a child with his homework, this request takes on different meanings to different families. You need to make sure that your system and materials make sense to them. Cultural, language, and social understandings must be considered. Often teachers hold a child responsible for requirements that don't get completed. Sometimes, parents feel that it is their responsibility to complete the homework for their child. Successful communication takes practice and ongoing attention.

Be sure to understand the resources available to a child at home; whether a parent or older sibling is available and if there is a quiet, consistent place for reading or study. If children need additional support, it is equitable and fair to provide time and opportunity for children to complete homework at school. Time can be given when children first arrive or while others are busy with centers or activities. It is extremely important that children feel they have the resources to accomplish requirements and that they know you are there to ensure their success.

Preschool and school-aged children need the same depth of communication between home and school, and extra communication and connection with the teacher. Be sure that assumptions about what children know and understand do not hinder their progress. Walk through the steps of each responsibility or requirement with children until you are certain that they understand what is needed. Ask questions to be sure they have the background knowledge and concept understanding to carry out the needed tasks and procedures. In addition, be certain you provide all the materials that children need to complete an assignment both in and away from the classroom. This collaboration is essential to create a lasting sense of teamwork and trust.

● **THINK ABOUT IT!**

It will benefit parents and children when you are able to take on their perspective. Can you think of a time that something didn't work as expected and you realized that perhaps your expectations were not clear to children or to parents? What did you do (or could you do) to communicate and work out a better solution?

_____

_____

_____

Principle 47: Trust

Let the child know—often and in many ways—that you trust his judgment and his ability to make good choices.

Our words and influence have the power to change the outcome of a child's life. Children will always remember when they were in a tough situation or at a life-altering point of decision and a teacher came to stand behind them with the belief that they would do the right thing.

Ms. Jones taught her students that her class was a family and that they could always rely on one another. When a pocket calculator was missing from a drawer, the principal wanted to come in and question the students until one of them confessed. Ms. Jones asked to speak with her class first. She addressed them in a steady voice, "I know that there is an item missing from a drawer. I am certain not one of my students would ever do anything to tear apart the trust we have built. If something is missing, then it is an oversight or mistake. So I want to go about our day and give you the opportunity to live up to the expectation I have for you. I know you will do the right thing." By lunchtime, the calculator was replaced, with a note that said, "I am sorry."

Children need to experience trust. Even the smallest inclination to believe in children's strength, purpose, or character will influence their belief and commitment. Teachers can affirm children with words of trust. Children will want to live up to the words of confidence. They need to hear every day, "I trust your judgment." "I admire your honesty." "I value your insight." "I honor your decision." Infants and toddlers can be encouraged with the words, "You can do it!" "Good for you to . . . " (describe the activity or action they have just completed).

There are many ways to give affirmations of trust. "When you are the 'guest greeter' for our room, I know that you will remember to be polite and shake the hand of each guest when he arrives." "When you are helping Jolanda with her project, I know you will use your best problem-solving skills." "When you are on the playground, I know you will remember to come down the slide safely." "When you all have to share the game, I trust you will figure out just how to handle sharing." "I know I can count on you to tell the truth."

We want to keep the highest expectations for children and let them know we believe they can be successful. Children are learning and just developing self-regulation, so we want to be supportive and caring when a child makes mistakes. These are times when our positive guidance and affirming words will build a child's character and cause him to develop honor and trust.

● **THINK ABOUT IT!**

Did your parents trust you to make good decisions? Did their attitude and words make you more or less likely to be responsible? How do you feel this affects you today?

_____

_____

_____

Think about a child in your classroom whom you would not necessarily trust to carry out a task independently. Perhaps something happened and the child was distracted, or maybe there is an ongoing issue with self-regulation.

Now imagine that this child has done something in the classroom that you want to correct and make sure it doesn't happen again. *Without describing to the child what he did wrong*, role-play a conversation using the Trust Principle that focuses on the child's strengths and on your faith in his positive character traits. What will you say to the child?

_____

_____

_____

🦋 *Principle 48: Logical Consequences*

Teach the child that behavior has consequences. If he forgets his sweater, he gets cold. If he forgets his boots, he cannot play on the grass. If he throws his lunch on the floor, it is all gone. If he forgets his homework, he needs to finish it during puzzle time.

It is important that the consequence relates directly to the behavior. For example, if a child throws a book, he does not lose recess; he loses the book. Logical consequences should always teach—never punish. Continue to provide proactive guidance, support, cuing, or redirection for success, rather than rely on consequences to teach. The purpose of a logical consequence is to enforce needed rules and to support learning.

To intervene when a behavior needs to be stopped, simply state the rule: "The balls roll on the floor. When you can roll the ball on the floor, then you may play with it." If the child then throws the ball, he loses the ball. To make this principle work, the adult must be there, first to model the desired behavior, and then to supervise the activities and materials given to children.

Toddlers are told, "When you sit in the chair with your feet on the floor, then you may eat. I want you to be safe." If an older infant throws food, the teacher can say, "Food is for eating. Are you finished now?" If an older child is being silly at lunch and spills his drink, the logical consequence is that he needs to take immediate responsibility for cleaning up the mess. The goal is never to punish, embarrass, or upset a child, but to let circumstances become a natural teacher. The follow-through should be immediate, but respectful and calm, so that the child can see the direct connection between his behavior and the consequences.

Logical consequences should not involve "take aways" that are unlinked to the child's behavior. For example, we would not remove something that is in a child's best interest to have or to experience. Computer time is important, as are recess and other needed resources and enrichment activities. The child who threw the book had the book removed, but he did not lose the opportunity to read during reading time. (Of course, first we will support him in holding the book with care, but if the behavior continues or is dangerous or destructive, we need to intervene.) He should be allowed to choose another book, with the words, "When you are able to be gentle and handle a book with care, you may choose another book." We want to make the most of every opportunity for learning.

Expectations and materials should be age and developmentally appropriate. When a baby throws a block, simply say, "Blocks are for building, beanbags are for throwing," and quickly replace the block with a soft beanbag as you help him toss it into the bucket. For young children, redirecting behavior is the most effective strategy. Remember that our goal as teachers is to support positive behaviors and to help children make safe decisions.

● **THINK ABOUT IT!**

We want to avoid removing a child from instructional or learning times and focus on creating responsibility about a specific behavior. What is one specific behavior expectation that a child you work with has struggled to uphold? What responses have you used in the past?

_____

_____

_____

_____

Describe a logical consequence that could be used to support the desired goal.

_____

_____

_____

_____

Preparing Children to Problem-Solve

Often adults are tempted to step in to solve problems for children when they need help. Children need practice in finding solutions to the challenges they face. We do them a favor when we give them opportunities to talk about their own ideas as much as possible. By facilitating conversation, adults can help children learn the skills and strategies they need to successfully negotiate issues.

🦋 Principle 49: Third Party

Tell a story about a particular situation they might encounter. For example, "There is a mom who would like her son to take out the trash. Should she (a) ask him to do it, (b) tell him to do it, (c) let him know the trash is full and needs to be taken out, (d) tell him the 'trash is calling,' (e) ask him to help her with the trash, or (f) other? What should the mom do?"

Describe to the children a situation that mirrors a challenge encountered in your classroom. "I heard that some children needed to learn better manners in the lunchroom. What could they do?" This lets them consider options objectively without singling out anyone involved. By using their own insight and proposing solutions, children will have much more investment in seeing that their solutions are successful. Children can give advice individually or work together. They love the opportunity to have input and to be taken seriously.

● **THINK ABOUT IT!**

Name a behavior issue that you have faced repeatedly in your classroom. Next, make up a story about other children (animals, pets, etc.) that presents the same kind of problem or dilemma. Tell the story to the children in your classroom. Ask what they think the children in the story should do to solve the problem. What story did you tell? How did the children respond? What solutions did your children suggest?

_____

_____

_____

_____

_____

🦋 Principle 50: Self-Correction

Give the child a chance to self-correct. Without talking or lecturing, give him space and time. Tell him you will check back with him later.

It is so easy to jump in to remind a child what he did wrong! Instead of preaching or lecturing, give him time to think and reflect or cool off. Often, if we let words hang in the air, the person who said the words will hear himself in a different way. He will often regret what he said and make an effort to make things right.

When we lecture or confront a child, we may "push him into a corner," and the chances are great that he will only want to defend himself or become angry. It is good to back off and give him the respect he needs, knowing that on reflection, he will reconsider and be more likely to make amends.

● **THINK ABOUT IT!**

When is the last time you confronted a child, but on reflection, feel that allowing self-correction might have been a better alternative? What did you say during that encounter? How do you think the child might have responded differently if you had given him the chance to cool off or self-correct?

_____

_____

_____

Encouraging Independent Thinking

How can we encourage independent thinking? The best way is to ask the child.

 ## Principle 51: Ask the Child

Ask the child for input. "Do you think this was a good choice?" "What were you trying to accomplish or tell someone with your behavior?" "What could you have done instead that would have worked better?" "How can I help you?" "What do you think could help you in the future to remember to make a better choice?" "How would you like for things to be different?" "How about drawing a picture of how you feel right now?" Children have wonderful insight into their own behavior and great suggestions for ways to make things better.

It doesn't help children to have someone to fuss, get mad, or reward unproductive behavior by giving it a lot of attention. By asking them to reflect on what they could have done differently, you will give them the opportunity to make better decisions. Ask, "What did you hope would happen?" "How did you want this to turn out?" Help them rehearse some new strategies so that the next time they face the same situation, they will be prepared to choose better options. Remember that it takes multiple times with patient support for children to be able to think ahead and use new skills independently. Our goal is that next time children face the same situation, they will make more positive choices and the experience will lead to a better outcome.

 ## Principle 52: Let the Child Be the Teacher

Let the child assume the role of teacher (or parent). Ask him to teach you a skill.

Allow a child to sit in your chair and give him a "teacher" job to do, such as read a book, tell a story, or teach a skill. This will have many benefits: You will quickly learn

how you come across, you will see the child's strengths emerge, and you will be able to understand where the child needs academic support or has misunderstandings.

● THINK ABOUT IT!

Try letting a child be the teacher. Write three things you noticed or learned about the child or about yourself.

1. _____

2. _____

3. _____

Training Children to Develop New Skills

Talking about skills for "being a good friend" will give children relationship tools they will use all of their lives. Have frequent conversations about treating others with kindness. The more we focus on positive character traits like sharing, caring, and helping, the more children will demonstrate those traits. The following principles will help you support children's growing social skills.

 ### Principle 53: Values Are Caught, Not Taught

Expose children to role models who are passionate about their work. Take piano lessons yourself and watch children absorb your love for music. Eat well and exercise, and watch them imitate your example. Don't talk about what you want to do—do it! Invite professionals and parents to your classroom to present their passion about a job or a hobby.

We cannot choose what children will be or what they will love to do. In the presence of a mentor who is passionate about his career, children connect to their own interests and passions. Young children long to have role models who will capture their imagination.

One teacher had a passion for airplanes. She was a licensed pilot and when she became a third-grade teacher, she brought her passion into the classroom—with model airplanes everywhere. When she retired, she said that more than 25 children through the years had caught her passion and had become airplane pilots. She felt elated that she had been able to influence them at such an impressionable age. When we are passionate about our own lives and are enthusiastic about activities we care about, children will discover their own meaningful purpose.

It is important to encourage active participation when guests come or activities are presented to children. When you invite a guest to share an interest, career, or hobby, be sure to prepare children ahead of time. Have them think of questions they can ask, perhaps writing these down ahead of time. Find out what they know and don't know. They will be excited to ask (or have you ask) their questions when the guest comes. When we actively foster curiosity and participation, children become engaged with new ideas. When we let them experiment with materials, activities, and topics without stress or pressure, this hands-on involvement can spark an interest that may develop into a lifelong hobby or career.

When we are gentle and caring toward ourselves and take care of our needs and our health, children learn it is natural to nurture and respect their bodies. When we share our passion for scrapbooking, cooking, gardening, sewing, or geography, children can see our love of learning. We may build models, love to run, or share our love for music or the arts or books. Motivation and engagement are the traits we most want them to catch.

● **THINK ABOUT IT!**

What do you feel passionate about? What hobby or interest do you bring to the classroom that has a positive influence on children?

_____

_____

_____

_____

Principle 54: Teach—Don't Reteach

Teach children the correct procedures and behaviors as soon as you have an opportunity. It is much harder to go back and undo a learned behavior. Personal items on your desk or a remote control are not toys. Keep them high up out of the reach of a toddler. Children need to know your expectations for entering your classroom on the first day of school. Lining up, cleaning up after a snack, and washing hands are not negotiable. Children need to shift their attention and refocus each time they begin a new activity, so we want to practice routines and procedures until they become automatic.

We are always teaching children. *Discipline* means to teach and train. This responsibility requires constant vigilance on our part. It is easy to look the other way when routines haven't been followed, or to give a child something to distract him from bothering others when we wouldn't otherwise like for him to play with it. However, the pay off for doing so has serious consequences. We have now taught the child that is OK to play with this item at least some of the time. He will not be sure if the next time he can get by with it, and so we have taught him that we are inconsistent. It is much kinder to teach children from the beginning what our expectations are and then follow through each time. This is important for younger children as well as for older children.

When a teacher sees that a child comes into a classroom running and accidentally knocks something off of a table or goes to visit with a friend instead of to his desk, the time to address that situation is immediately. The teacher needs to kindly say to the child, "I need for you to go back to the door and come in the proper way." Of course, this is better done quietly and privately, but it needs to be done. If at any time you let it go or look the other way, the child concludes that this behavior is acceptable. He will then come to question you every time to see if you will allow the exception again.

It is tiring but necessary for us to think through all of the procedures and rules in our classrooms and frequently reassess whether they are necessary and enforceable as well as whether we are requiring enough of our children. It is just as important to make sure our expectations serve a purpose and are developmentally appropriate.

As children mature, they are capable of handling more responsibility. We should be turning over more to them as they grow older. It is much more difficult to "unlearn" something than to learn it correctly from the very beginning.

Birth to Age 3

- Take time to review needed routines in a group format. You may use dolls, puppets, or simply describe activities as needed.

- Give each child a tour of each area in the classroom to show how things can be done.

- Give careful attention to personal routines and care. These include hand-washing, storing belongings, using the bathroom (or having diapers changed), knowing how to ask for help, and how to find needed classroom items, such as the tissue box.

- Stay sensitive and aware, knowing that very young children need continued support to accomplish needed routines successfully.

- Practice proceeding down ramps or stairs and using the bathroom. Flushing the toilet can be a concern for children, so teach them to plug their ears if the sound bothers them. All of these activities require sensitivity to children's feelings of dependence as they are learning to master independence.

- Treat potty training with respect and consistent positive support. There are a variety of supports for potty training on the market, including books, videos, and songs. Remember that how children feel about the experience (positive, accepted, supported) is the most important goal.

- Eating times should be relaxed and pleasant, with children involved in happy conversation with caregivers and peers. Children need to be offered healthy choices and be able to choose how much and what they eat. Communicate often with parents about their expectations as you focus on creating positive memories with children during meals.

- Remember to provide positive feedback and encouragement as children are learning routines. Help them feel proud of their efforts and contributions.

Ages 3 to 8

- Establish simple routines from the first day children enter your room. They need to know what is expected. What is the first thing they will do? What will they do next? Effective teachers will spend a great deal of time teaching the skills they want their children to have and practicing them until they become routine.

- Use music to establish transitions. When a certain song is played, children automatically know what to do next: clean up, wash their hands, line up, prepare for snack, get ready for lunch, or nap.

- Make eating times pleasant. Put on soft music. Sit with children and engage in happy and meaningful conversation. Get to know more about them.

- Provide a specific place to hang coats and keep belongings. Children can individualize as much as possible to make it feel that it is "theirs."

- Keep a distinct school-to-home communication system. Use a zipped pocket folder or other system of choice. Parents will know to look in their child's folder for papers, reminders, pictures, belongings, or requests.

- Rotate jobs on daily or weekly basis. Use a clip system (clothespin with child's name clipped onto the job card) or a pocket system (child's name is written on a card or stick and placed in pocket describing job responsibility). Children will keep the classroom environment safe, friendly, and interesting. Some jobs include:

  - Conductor (line leader)

  - Door Holder (second in line)

  - Table Washer (wipes tables and desks)

  - Paper Helper (helps pass out papers)

  - Book Helper (helps pass out and hold books)

  - Trash Collector (helps pick up trash around classroom; puts trash can in hall at end of day)

  - Disk Jockey (responsible for music in room)

  - Light Keeper (turns the lights on and off when needed)

  - Substitute (takes on job of those who are absent)

  - Messenger (takes messages to office or other teachers)

  - Recess Helper (assists teacher in gathering up children to come in from recess)

  - Equipment Engineer (moves equipment to playground or within room)

  - Teacher's Helper (helps teacher with special jobs, such as calendar procedures and lunch count)

  - Behavior Monitor (finds students doing the right thing; awards "caught being good" stickers)

  - Feelings Helper (takes a tissue to a sad child)

  - Caboose (last in line; closes room door)

  - Librarian (keeps classroom library neat and tidy)

  - Time Keeper (starts/stops timer throughout the day)

  - Germ Buster (squirts hand sanitizer before lunch or snack)

  - Guest Greeter (welcomes all guests into room; carries out guest routines in accordance with safety procedures of your school)

● **THINK ABOUT IT!**

List three routines you want to review with your children that, if followed, make the day easier for everyone. How can you review or teach these so that they become a habit for everyone involved?

1. _____

2. _____

3. _____

🦋 *Principle 55: Successive Approximations*

Don't expect perfection. Acknowledge small steps in the right direction.

We often expect children to know what is in our head when we ask them to do something, without breaking it down into steps or procedures. We need to divide the larger task into smaller goals that can be accomplished. Even skills like washing hands and eating routines need to be taught. Be patient with children and make sure they are successful in reaching the goals you set for them.

For older children, break down expectations, routines, and tasks into steps that are manageable. As they make progress, be sure to let them know you see their effort and improvement. Help them learn the steps that lead to competence. Ask them to explain what they are thinking. In this way, you can find out what skills or procedures need support.

A toddler can help put away his covers from his cot or put away toys into a basket. Older children may wipe up the table after snack time or put books away. Young elementary-aged students may clean their desks. None of these may be done exactly as you hope, but you can reinforce their effort with your enthusiasm and give positive feedback about their good progress.

Children at morning meetings may not talk as much as you like, or others may go on and on. It takes practice and active discussion to teach them how to be good listeners and good at sharing. You can work with them by letting them know what is appropriate behavior during discussions. (We turn our head towards the person who is talking and nod our head when we agree. We wait until someone finishes before asking a question. We smile to encourage others.) Patience and attention to successive approximations communicates a strong message that learning is an ongoing process that is rewarding!

● **THINK ABOUT IT!**

Describe a learning or behavior skill that you want children to have. What are the steps this skill can be broken into so that children can master it? How will you know the steps are manageable? How will you encourage success?

_____

_____

_____

_____

Helping Children by Being Consistent

We want children to be valued as human beings, not "human doings." We want to be certain that they know we accept them for who they are and that we value all the traits that make their personality unique and special.

Make sure to create opportunities for every child to feel competent. Let them know that we are there for them to support their success. When we are consistent in our actions, expectations, and responses, children can relax, knowing they can trust us—and themselves—to create a day that is happy for everyone in the classroom.

Here are four principles that will help you to hold high expectations and encourage children to be successful. Like a coach who is on the same team with children, you will be working toward the same goals. These principles will help children gain skills and make progress until they become competent.

 ## Principle 56: Prompt and Praise

Explain the expected behavior in a non-critical way and praise the child as soon as the behavior occurs.

Children are often given general requests: "Please settle down!" "I told you to cut it out!" "Sit still." The teacher may make the assumption that a child understands exactly what she means for him to do. Even though she means well, the child actually may want to comply but have no real idea what is expected!

Instead of telling a child to settle down or be quiet, give positive feedback instead. "Thank you for tucking your hands in your lap and crossing your legs." (We thank him for doing it, even before it is done.) Simple, direct instructions help the child understand. Sometimes a child doesn't notice what he is doing, so we want to make sure to show him patience and courtesy. He will be likely to return the attitude to us.

As soon as the child has cooperated, he also needs to hear praise in the form of specific detailed words. "I am glad that you and Anna shared the blankets." "I appreciate that you sorted the papers with Jose." Having a supportive adult say, "I know you can do it!" is necessary for young children who are just learning many new skills.

When we are consistent and patient, children give their willingness in return. When we train a child with respect and gentle regard, he will give back to us because he does not feel threatened. A child is always looking for approval, so receiving a ready smile along with quick praise will help him want to cooperate again.

It is necessary to review expectations often. We can review how to sneeze properly or how to greet an adult. Teaching manners while having fun and allowing for humor will go a long way toward giving children confidence in themselves. Set aside time to review needed routines and be sure to praise cooperation and effort. Children will become much more competent in following through.

● **THINK ABOUT IT!**

Explain a behavior that continues to frustrate you or that you would like to address. Describe some ways that you may address it before it happens.

_____

_____

_____

What specific instructions will you give next time *before* the behavior occurs? What questions can you ask children to be sure that they understand (e.g., ask them to explain the expectations back)?

_____

_____

_____

Principle 57: Sing

Surprise children by singing what you want them to do. Get in the habit of making up songs with familiar tunes (e.g., "The Farmer in the Dell," "Jingle Bells") and using words to describe your expectations. This approach works well with children of all ages.

Singing songs with surprising words creates a spirit of fun and teamwork. When you sing with children, it helps them engage. The songs you choose may be the same every time or can be new and invented on the spot. You may use a song you know or make up a sing-song nonsense tune.

Stay aware that transitions may provoke anxiety for young children and songs provide a consistent cue and comforting routine. Making up songs provides comfort and familiarity. Sing songs for routines and giving directions: "This is the way we wash our hands." "We are holding on the railing going up" (to the tune of "If You're Happy and You Know It").

Singing catches a child's attention and draws him toward your positive attitude and invitation to join in. It attracts immediate attention when a job needs to be done and lightens the load while the work is being accomplished. It also motivates him to get a job completed before the music ends.

The songs you choose can be simple, but they will provide a backdrop for connection and consistency. Singing eases transitions and soothes and comforts children throughout the day. We create special occasions out of daily activities for children by singing with them.

● **THINK ABOUT IT!**

What are the easiest tunes to sing? See how many jobs you can sing to the tune of "Twinkle Twinkle Little Star" (or another favorite tune). This activity is for children of all ages!

_____

_____

_____

_____

 Principle 58: Allow Imperfection

Don't demand perfection. With perfection as the goal, we are all losers. When we tell children they are the best or encourage them to be "at the top," we are setting them up for disappointment. It is not possible for them to sustain that position; nor do we want them to value this mindset. We want to follow through to help them pursue realistic goals that have meaning and purpose to them. Rather than a competitive frame of mind, we want to focus on the inherent value of hard work, determination, and love of learning. We want to reinforce teamwork and cooperation. We also need to be careful to only ask of children what is appropriate at their developmental level and to allow for setbacks and imperfections.

 Principle 59: Encouragement

Give encouragement as often as possible. Help the child see the progress he has made. "You got three spelling words correct. That is better than last week!" "Doesn't it feel good to be able to zip your own zipper?" "You cleaned up your own spill. You must be proud to know that you did that all by yourself."

There are creative ways to encourage children by giving "Great Moment" certificates for a job well done or a kindness shown. Use the certificate to write out a description of the contribution the child made and send it home with him, or display it on a bulletin board. We can ask children to help us solve a problem that needs addressing in the room. Be creative and thoughtful about creating opportunities for success.

Develop and focus on character traits. Find a child's "sweet spot" (what he likes to talk about or what interests him). Ask, "What are you good at? What do you love to do?" Bring in role models who are passionate about their work and give children opportunities to develop and use their gifts in meaningful ways. Encourage them to try new things!

Consider a child about whom you have concerns or worries. What skills does he have that you can capitalize on? Describe a skill that he is good at. How will you give him the opportunity to teach (or help) someone else to do that skill?

_____

_____

_____

Summary

A primary goal of positive behavior guidance is to support children's growing need for social competence and independence. We want to model caring, kindness, empathy, and patience while children are learning, because the perceptions children develop about themselves while learning are as important as the skills they gain. Activities and interactions should be designed to promote the child's sense of safety and confidence.

We want to encourage natural exploration while we remain flexible and supportive. The need and desire of the child to figure things out in his own way must be considered. When we do need to encourage conformity for health and safety reasons, we want to do so gently and with support for children's growing understanding. We want to always be sensitive to the developmental needs of each child. Desire for independence is a strong motivator. Helping children gain mastery through respectful, consistent encouragement is an important role of a teacher.

Using the Principles in Your Classroom

Create Opportunities to Problem-Solve

Ask children what problems they think need to be solved in the classroom. Encourage them to list or tell you their own solutions to the problems they have presented. What did they suggest? You will be surprised what they tell you!

Ask Questions

Ask questions to encourage independent thinking. When the children are successful, respond, "That's a great solution. You have a good head on your shoulders. You can trust your own judgment." When there are still challenges ahead, you can ask:

- What do you need to do next?
- What else can you do?
- What is another option?
- What makes sense?

- How do you think that worked out?
- What will help you solve the problem?
- What can you do differently next time?
- Why don't you work together with a friend?
- Why don't you think about it?

For Pre-Verbal Children, Ask Guiding Questions

Provide descriptive conversations that focus on children's sense of taste, smell, or touch and give words to their experiences. Ask them to show you what they know by touching, getting, bringing, pointing, and doing.

- For an infant, try looping the conversation by answering your own questions: "Is this your diaper? Here is your diaper. Is this your bottle? Here is your bottle. Is it warm? It feels warm." "How can we get the truck down? Let's reach up high for the red truck." Conversations like these should describe the infant's actions and activities as well as yours.
- For a toddler, extend his thinking and activities: "Is your baby doll cold? Show me how you keep your baby warm." "Do you want to hang up your coat? Show me how to hang up your coat."
- For a preschooler, assist with problem-solving: "Can you work with a friend to untangle the string (stack the blocks, put away the balls)? What is a good way to do that? Can you show him how?"

Practice the Principles

Use the principles in this chapter with your co-worker and other adults in your life. Remember that our goal is to focus on and change our own behavior, and to watch what happens in the way others respond to us. Each principle will help us take responsibility for our own contributions, and will encourage maturity and independence for the people with whom we live and work.

Teacher Tips

The following are comments from teachers who have been trained to use the 101 principles in their early care and education settings and elementary classrooms.

At lunch today, Bryce realized that his juice box didn't have a straw. He looked so disappointed, so I asked him what he could do to solve the problem. He thought for a minute and then announced that he could ask the teacher on lunch duty for a milk straw. I allowed him to solve his own problem and to feel good about himself! He grinned when he came back with his straw. The Ask the Child Principle is wonderful.

A student wasn't paying attention to the fire safety lady. Instead he was reading a book.

(continued)

I walked over to him and thanked him for paying attention. He quickly put the book away and started listening. Thanking him before he did it worked.

Olivia was trying to get her leftovers into her lunch box and was very frustrated. I was tempted to help her, but I decided to "ask the child." When I asked her how she was going to arrange her container and sandwich to fit, she said, "I will put some paper towels in my lunch to make my food more comfortable." I would have missed that sweet moment if I hadn't asked her to solve her own problem.

When I noticed the children carrying buckets of sand away from the box and over to the playground area, I quickly walked over. The children looked at me like they knew I was going to correct them, but instead, I asked the child: "Oh dear, what shall we do when the sand falls out all over? How shall we get the buckets back to the box?" A little boy piped up, "Let's take the sand over to the sandbox so we can make a birthday cake!" The buckets were returned to the sandbox in record time, right along with the children. I didn't have to do a thing.

I have a new group of kindergarteners that I meet each morning at the bus. We have been practicing how to get off the bus and line up. Each day, they progressed closer to what I expected of them, and I cheered them on. After five days, they got off the bus, lined up in a safe manner, and patiently waited for me to lead them inside. I was very pleased with their behavior and gushed over how well they cooperated. I walked by each one and gave him or her a high-five. Their eyes lit up with enjoyment and pride.

I have a student in second grade who answers questions before the other children get a chance. One day, I decided to try something different. I approached Rebecca before the review and told her that I expected her to raise her hand calmly and quietly (Prompt and Praise Principle). It took her a few tries, but once she sat patiently with her hand up, I immediately called on her and thanked her for raising her hand nicely.

My kindergarteners were taking so long to line up for recess and the biggest issue was getting their shoes tied. I started singing, "We need to tie our shoes, we need to tie our shoes, *hi ho the dairy-oh,* we need to tie our shoes." They smiled at me and quickly tied their shoes. The next day, they started singing (and tying their shoes) without being reminded. The Sing Principle made a big difference!

Robert continued to have difficulty with his spelling words. He had practiced alone and with his partner. The next time he took a quiz, even though it wasn't perfect, he had improved so much. I told him how proud I was of his hard work and how excited I was about his improvement. He was encouraged and kept on trying. I loved to see him happy with himself, and encouraging him was a great way to show it.

Research on the Run

Experiencing the Benefit of Strength-Based Approaches

- Secure, healthy attachment influences school success, grades, test scores, emotional regulation, and social competence. This effect is particularly significant for at-risk children (Bergin & Bergin, 2009).

- Academic gains are related to the extent of a teacher's positive interaction with students and promotion of enriched language. Teachers need to nurture children as well as foster learning (Burchinal, Howes, & Pianta, 2008).

- Children need high-quality experiences in social–emotional support along with enriched learning to promote positive outcomes in language, literacy, and academics (Mashburn, 2008).

- A strength-based system for children includes a sense of belonging, mastery, independence, and generosity, as opposed to a punitive demerit-based system. The focus should be on "relationship building, problem solving, skill development and support for success" (Rubin, 2005, p. 143; Sigler & Aamidor, 2005).

- The experience of secure attachment in the preschool years is correlated with academic, social, and personal competencies later in life. Children need frequent opportunities to develop these critical attachment relationships (Honig, 2002).

- Children need adults to show interest and pay attention to them. When prosocial behavior is reinforced and children are given important responsibilities, everyone benefits. Adults need to be aware of the developmental needs of children and be sensitive to their response to stress. Children need environments that help them thrive (Waterston, 2000).

- An atmosphere of respect, encouragement, and enthusiasm for learning helps children see school as a safe place where they want to be and where they can be successful (Baker, 1999; Howes, Bryant, Burchinal, Clifford, Early, Pianta, et al., 2006).

- Warm, sensitive responses help children achieve more and become more successful in school (Pianta, Hamre, & Stuhlman, 2003).

- In order to reflect on learning, children must see reflection modeled and understand that process (Jones & Dotson, 2010).

- The literature suggests the remedial, compensatory, and predictive nature of social–emotional support leads to direct and indirect effects on prosocial skill development and academic outcomes, both in the short term and over time (Schultz, 2008; Shonkoff & Phillips, 2001).

- The ability to connect meaningfully when they are young will make all the difference when children face the social pressures and challenges of the upcoming middle school years (Birch & Ladd, 1997; Hamre & Pianta, 2001; Knitzer, 2007).

- Motivating children by engaging their interests and allowing them opportunities for mastery and exploration is a critical part of learning (Dwenk, 2006).

Finding Information About the Impact of Poverty

- For information about children's development and the impact of poverty, see Center on the Developing Child, Harvard University; National Scientific Council on the Developing Child; National Forum on Early Childhood Policy and Programs, "The Long Reach of Early Childhood Poverty: Pathways and Impacts," Q & A with Drs. Greg Duncan, Katherine Magnuson, Tom Boyce, and Jack Shonkoff, 2010; and Center for the Developing Child at Harvard University, www.developingchild.net.

- You can locate the specific information about your state and community through the National Center for Children in Poverty: www.nccp.org.

- You can gain resources about homeless populations at the National Coalition for the Homeless website: www.nationalhomeless.org/factsheets/education.html.

Getting Positive Results Using the Principles in Action

What happened or led up to the interaction?

_____

_____

_____

Which principle did you use?

_____

_____

_____

How did the situation turn out? (How did the child/children respond?)

_____

_____

_____

What did you learn?

_____

_____

_____

What happened or led up to the interaction?

_____

_____

_____

Which principle did you use?

_____

_____

_____

How did the situation turn out? (How did the child/children respond?)

_____

_____

_____

What did you learn?

_____

_____

_____

Guide to the Principles

45. Good Head on Your Shoulders: Tell a child frequently, "You have a good head on your shoulders. You decide. I trust your judgment." This brings out the best in the child and shows him that eventually he will be in charge of his own life and responsible for his/her own decisions.

46. Thank You: Thank the child for doing the right thing—*before* he does it! "Thank you for dropping your paper scraps into the trash can" (before they land on the floor). "Thank you for tucking your pencil in your desk before you line up" (before the pencil is put away). Children want to be helpful and cooperative, and a gentle reminder (with respectful thanks) encourages success.

47. Trust: Let the child know—often and in many ways—that you trust his judgment and his ability to make good choices.

48. Logical Consequences: Teach the child that behavior has consequences. If he forgets his sweater, he gets cold. If he forgets his boots, he cannot play on the grass. If he throws his lunch on the floor, it is all gone. If he forgets his homework, he needs to finish it during puzzle time.

49. Third Party: Tell a story about a particular situation they may encounter and elicit sugges-

tions. For example, "There is a mom who would like her son to take out the trash. Should she (a) ask him to do it, (b) tell him to do it, (c) let him know the trash is full and needs to be taken out, (d) tell him the 'trash is calling,' (e) ask him to help her with the trash, or (f) other? What should the mom do?"

50. Self-Correction: Give the child a chance to self-correct. Without talking or lecturing, give him space and time. Tell him you will check back with him later.

51. Ask the Child: Ask the child for input. "Do you think this was a good choice?" "What were you trying to accomplish or tell someone with your behavior?" "What could you have done instead that would have worked better?" "What do you think could help you in the future to remember to make a better choice?" "How would you like for things to be different?" "How about drawing a picture of how you feel right now?" Children have wonderful insight into their own behavior and great suggestions for ways to make things better.

52. Let the Child Be the Teacher: Let the child assume the role of teacher (or parent). Ask him to teach you a skill.

53. Values Are Caught, Not Taught: Expose children to role models who are passionate about their work. Take piano lessons yourself and watch children absorb your love for music. Eat well and exercise, and watch them imitate your example. Don't talk about what you want to do—do it! Invite professionals and parents to your classroom to present their passion about a job or a hobby.

54. **Teach—Don't Reteach:** Teach the children the correct procedures and behaviors as soon as you have an opportunity. It is much harder to go back and undo a learned behavior. Personal items on your desk or a remote control are not toys. Keep them high up out of the reach of a toddler. Children need to know your expectations for entering your classroom on the first day of school. Lining up, cleaning up after a snack, and washing hands are not negotiable.

55. **Successive Approximations:** Don't expect perfection. Acknowledge small steps in the right direction.

56. **Prompt and Praise:** Explain the expected behavior in a non-critical way and praise the child as soon as the behavior occurs.

57. **Sing:** Surprise children by singing what you want them to do. Get in the habit of making up songs with familiar tunes (e.g., "The Farmer in the Dell," "Jingle Bells") and using words to describe your expectations. This approach works well with children of all ages.

58. **Allow Imperfection:** Don't demand perfection. With perfection as the goal, we are all losers.

59. **Encouragement:** Give encouragement as often as possible. Help the child see the progress he has made. "You got three spelling words correct. That is better than last week!" "Doesn't it feel good to be able to zip your own zipper?" "You cleaned up your own spill. You must be proud to know that you did that all by yourself."

Study Guide

a. **Goal Setting:** Name several skills you want to encourage the children in your classroom to develop that will support their growing independence. If you work with infants or toddlers, describe the skills that you want to encourage and model.

b. **Questioning and Reflection:** What was something you did as a child that made you feel proud? How did others respond? Do you remember a time when someone trusted you to do something important and you wanted to live up to their belief in you? What happened? Were you held accountable for a responsibility that was important to others?

c. **Case Study:** Mrs. Hardy had trouble with Max following through after instructions were given. She really wanted to avoid removing him from instructional times and focus instead on creating responsibility for specific behaviors like getting

started right away on learning activities. What is a behavior expectation that Max might struggle to uphold? What positive behavior guidance strategies could be used to support success? See Principles 49 (Third Party), 50 (Self-Correction), 51 (Ask the Child), and 52 (Let the Child Be the Teacher). Talk through how these approaches will help Max.

d. **Personal Examples/Group Brainstorming:** *Topic 1:* Imagine that a child in your classroom has done something that you want to correct and ensure never happens again. Without describing anything at all to the child about what he did wrong, role-play a conversation using the Trust Principle, focusing on the child's strengths and your faith in his positive character traits. What words will you say to the child? *Topic 2:* What is one skill or procedure you need to review with your students? See Principles 54 (Teach—Don't

Reteach), 55 (Successive Approximations), and 56 (Prompt and Praise). What approaches would be effective for your classroom? (See pages 131–136.)

e. **Learners as Experts:** Using the "Getting Positive Results Using the Principles in Action" sheet, share one principle you implemented from this chapter. What happened or led up to the interaction? Which principle did you use? How did the situation turn out? (How did the child/children respond?) What did you learn?

f. **Research on the Run:** Consider a child about whom you have concerns or worries. What skills does he have that you can capitalize on? Describe a skill that he has. How will you give him the opportunity to develop that skill and share it? (See the justification for strength-based practices in Research on the Run.)

g. **Looking Ahead:** Set the purpose for upcoming study by introducing chapter objectives. Thank you for sharing your personal insight about responsive, positive guidance and for your commitment to making a difference in the lives of children.

References

Baker, J. (1999). Teacher–student interaction in urban at-risk classrooms: Differential behavior, relationship quality, and student satisfaction with school. *Elementary School Journal, 100,* 57–70.

Bergin, C., & Bergin, D. (2009). Helping children and families in need: Using a primary bonding model in a shelter child care setting. *High Scope Resource,* 4–8.

Birch, S., & Ladd, G. (1997). The teacher-child relationship and children's early school adjustment. *Journal of School Psychology, 35,* 61–79.

Burchinal, M., Howes, C., & Pianta, R. (2008). Predicting child outcomes at the end of kindergarten from the quality of pre-kindergarten teacher-child interactions and instruction. *Applied Developmental Science, 12*(3), 140–153.

Center on the Developing Child, Harvard University; National Scientific Council on the Developing Child; National Forum on Early Childhood Policy and Programs. (2010). The long reach of early childhood poverty: Pathways and impacts. Q & A session with Drs. Greg Duncan, Katherine Magnuson, Tom Boyce, and Jack Shonkoff at the 2010 American Association for the Advancement of Science (AAAS) Annual Meeting Symposium, February 21, 2010, in San Diego, CA. Retrieved February 26, 2012, from http://developingchild.harvard.edu/index.php/download_file/-/view/623

Dwenk, C. (2006). *Mindset: The new psychology of success.* New York: Random House.

Hamre, B., & Pianta, R. (2001). Early teacher-child relationships and the trajectory of children's school outcomes through eighth grade. *Child Development, 72,* 625–638.

Honig, A. (2002). *Secure relationships: Nurturing infant/toddler attachment in early care settings.* Washington, DC: National Association for the Education of Young Children.

Howes, C., Bryant, D., Burchinal, M., Clifford, R., Early, D., Pianta, R., Barbarin, O., & Ritchie, S. (2006). National Center for Early Development and Learning (NCEDL) issued statement. Chapel Hill, NC: NCEDL, FPG Child Development Institute.

Jones, J., & Dotson, K. (2010). Building the disposition of reflection through the inquiry-focused school library program. *School Libraries Worldwide 16*(1), 33–46.

Knitzer, J. (2007, January). Testimony on the economic and societal costs of poverty. National Center for Children in Poverty Hearing on Economic and Societal Costs of Poverty. Retrieved October 28, 2011, from www.nccp.org/publications/pdf/text_705.pdf

Mashburn, A. (2008). Quality of social and physical environments in preschools and children's development of academic, language, and literacy skills. *Applied Developmental Science, 12,* 113–127.

Pianta, R., Hamre, B., & Stuhlman, M. (2003). Relationships between teachers and children. In W. M. Reynolds & G. E. Miller (Eds.), *Handbook of psychology: Educational psychology, Vol. 7* (pp. 199–234). Hoboken, NJ: Wiley.

Rubin, R. (2005). A blueprint for a strengths based level system in schools. *Reclaiming Children and Youth: The Journal of Strength-Based Interventions, 14*(3), 143–145.

Sigler, E., & Aamidor, S. (2005). From positive reinforcement to positive behaviors: An everyday guide for the practitioner. *Early Childhood Education Journal, 32*(4), 249–253.

Schultz, T. (2008, June). Tackling PK–3 assessment & accountability challenges: Guidance from the national early childhood accountability task force. *The State Education Standard, 411.* Retrieved October 28, 2011, from http://nasbe.org/index.php?option=com_zoo&task=item&item_id=196&Itemid=1033

Shonkoff, J. P., & Phillips, D. A. (Eds.). (2001). *From neurons to neighborhoods: The science of early childhood development.* Washington, DC: National Academy Press.

Waterston, T. (2000). Giving guidance on child discipline. *British Medical Journal, 320*(7230), 261–262.

c h a p t e r   6

Building Resilience

This chapter will help you develop sensitivity to the needs of children and create the kind of responsive environment that they need in order to become resilient. Resilience includes the ability to deal effectively with stress and pressure and to bounce back from hardship. It is a child's self-righting capacity that helps him "land on his feet," even when he is faced with obstacles. Resilience helps him stay flexible when confronting challenges. It helps a child to persevere, rebound from adversity, and choose healthy solutions when problems present themselves.

A hallmark of resilience is the ability to connect meaningfully with others. In order for this to happen, the child will need the support of a caring adult. The sensitive, attentive caregiver can help him regulate his emotions and assist him with developing relational competence. As a result of this trusted connection, he is able to develop a lifelong pattern of trust and hope. He realizes that others are there for him—and that he is worthy of their care.

Chapter Principles

60: Availability

61: Wants and Feelings

62: Empowerment

63: Make up a Story

64: Role-Playing

65: Brainstorming

66: Stay Healthy

67: Keep Your Perspective

68: Frog Suit

69: Help Me Out

70: Teach Children to Stand Up to Bullies

71: Best Friend

Chapter Objectives

As you explore the text and activities in this chapter, you will be able to:

- Develop strategies to help children cope with stress and foster resilience
- Encourage healthy solutions and creative approaches to solving problems
- Understand multiple influences on resilience, including diverse cultural, community, and family contexts

- Implement skills to protect children during vulnerable situations
- Deal effectively with bullying and teasing
- Give children strategies to promote self-efficacy and persistence

Helping Children Cope

It is important to teach children at an early age not to despair when things don't go the way they had hoped. Being resilient means knowing what to do—when you don't know what to do. When plan A falls through, it is the ability to consider other options and find plan B. When a door is shut (or slammed in your face), it is the determination to look for another window of opportunity. When you are given lemons, it is the willingness

to make lemonade. These are common themes that express the idea of resilience.

A resilient child keeps going when the going gets tough. He learns early on that life has ups and downs and that he needs to find a healthy way to cope with its constant challenges. He needs to have a healthy role model who exhibits these traits, believes in him, and will never give up on him. When a child has a cheerleader and champion to provide a safe, steady emotional home base, he will develop flexibility and find resources to deal resiliently with difficult situations. Through this empowering relationship, he will learn how to get the help he needs and look for workable solutions when confronted with challenges.

● THINK ABOUT IT!

Can you think of a time when someone in your life helped you feel comforted, understood, or accepted? How would you define the relationship you had?

_____

_____

_____

Have you ever sat on a sofa and snuggled up with someone you loved? What were the benefits to you? (For example, when you snuggle with your cat, your blood pressure lowers and heart rate slows.)

_____

_____

_____

Being Available

Pre-verbal children develop perceptions about themselves and others using their senses. Their understanding is internalized through emotional feelings and physical sensations. By the time a child is one year old, he has formed a "relational image" of himself.

He learns whether his needs are significant and have value to those around him. Through these sensations and ongoing evaluations, his own sense of value is formed. If he has experienced consistent, positive connections, he will continue to make healthy connections when he is older. His early experiences create a pattern that will determine the kind of relationships he will seek and create for himself throughout his lifetime.

If a child experiences shame or disconnection from others, physiological responses such as anxiety and fear can work against the formation of resilience. Increased trauma and anxiety raise stress chemicals (corticosteroids) in the brain and continue to affect the way his body will react to future stress. Safe relationships provide comfort and reassurance and make him feel good. If he experiences this comfort through positive interactions, he learns to comfort himself. However, if he is unable to create good feelings in healthy ways, he may turn later to risky behaviors to experience needed positive feelings.

When a child does find a caring adult with whom he can connect and who is invested in his well-being, resilience has a chance to take root and grow. When he has experienced stress, insecurity, or trauma, teachers can provide a therapeutic relationship model that has a powerful influence on a child's physiological responses (Cozolino, 2006; Perry, 2001; 2005). He needs the security of a calm and reliable adult to help him filter and process his emotions. The consistency of this safe environment allows him to develop new responses to better adapt and thrive.

Every child needs at least one adult who is there for him, believes in him, wants to be with him, and cares about him unconditionally. When he has this person in his life, he can come to believe in himself and discover his unique potential. The research tells us that the one difference resilient children have from others is the presence of a significant adult (an "enlightened witness") in their lives (Miller, 1996, 2001). This adult is able to validate the child's experiences and perceptions and remain a stable presence in his life. A teacher can be an effective enlightened witness, providing meaningful validation and consistent support.

Principle 60: Availability

At school and at home, a child wants—and needs—time spent with the undivided focus of an adult. We need to stop what we are doing, make eye contact, and really take time to talk with and listen to a child. Encourage parents to spend 15 minutes a day with their child at home.

If we realized how important our undivided attention is to a child, most of us would be more careful to meet this need. We play an important role in providing active listening at school. We can show personal interest, note concerns, and recognize needs or changes, so that we can better support a child's social, emotional, and learning needs.

Parents can also plan to spend 15 minutes alone with their child each day. This time should be spent listening carefully, watching the child's responses, asking the child's advice, learning what is important to him, trying to see life from his eyes, and understanding his perspectives. The parent should set everything aside and give him full attention. It might be a good idea to meet with the child in his room or to choose another place where there are few distractions. The parent can ask questions or simply spend time doing something together that the child enjoys.

The parent also will want to make a note of any changes in behavior, interest, attitude, or enthusiasm. If a parent has concerns, these can be talked about with the child. When additional support is needed, the parent can meet with the teacher, talk to a guidance counselor, or seek professional help. The primary goal of the 15 minutes is to build and support the connection between the adult and child. Teachers can encourage parents to use this practice at home.

Children need a sense of capability and confidence in their ability to overcome life's challenges. We can help them by being their champion and cheerleader—their advocate—who is always in their corner. We want to become a good role model and create an environment where they can become strong and self-confident. We do this by being available to them, spending time listening and being attentive. This helps us to understand their needs and learn how to be more responsive to them. They need to know that we are thankful for their company and that we value them in our lives.

● **THINK ABOUT IT!**

Who was a significant adult for you when you were a child? Who provided a stable, caring presence where you gained a sense of strength and purpose? Was this someone who you could count on to tell you the truth and guide you when you needed to trust your perceptions? How did the presence or absence of this kind of person affect you?

_____

_____

_____

Helping Resiliency Grow

Resilience is supported within a climate of kindness and caring. When a child watches a caregiver helping another child who is hurt, he experiences a similar emotional response of being comforted. This is the result of activated "mirror neurons," a sympathetic reaction that causes the body and brain to experience the physiological effects of the interactions around it.

Likewise, if a child observes fighting or arguing, he experiences a vicarious response of stress. This is what happens when we watch television and see something frightening—sometimes, our heart pounds and our hands sweat. If we watch a romantic movie, we may cry or feel strong emotions along with the characters. Children respond the same way when watching emotional experiences of others. This involuntary response makes children vulnerable to the emotional moods, feelings, and interactions around them. Understanding young children's sensitivity to the surrounding emotional climate can help teachers become reflective about the impact of the emotional climate in a classroom.

Words have the power to build children up or tear them down. Words that belittle, embarrass, or tear down work against the development of resilience. A child needs us to help him turn his challenges into opportunities for growth and help him learn skills and strategies to negotiate satisfying outcomes. He needs emotional support to affirm his experiences and to let him know he is OK.

Children are vulnerable to the impressions others leave behind. In early childhood, interactions are like wet cement. The imprint is made and it can influence the way a child will think about himself and his relationship with others for years to come.

● **THINK ABOUT IT!**

What words have you heard in a school setting that you feel have built a child up? What words have you heard that you feel have torn a child down?

_____

_____

_____

Describe a time you had a strong emotional reaction to another person's experience.

_____

_____

_____

Describe an experience where you think a child might have an emotional reaction to something he observes. How does this affect your thinking about what children need from you?

_____

_____

_____

Creating a Calm and Consistent Environment

Temporary stress may occur for a child when he has been woken up early, when a parent is angry, or when his morning is disorganized. Over time, or if a family is in prolonged crisis, the stress may accumulate. A child may experience more lasting trauma due to life-changing events in a family or community. Prolonged stress can result from economic stress on the family, health and disability, the need to negotiate different cultural contexts, and by events that interrupt the normal family routines. These may include violence, earthquake, terrorism, weather-related trauma, abuse, or the death of a significant caregiver. Long-term stress can interfere with a child's ability to pay attention, to respond calmly, and to bring all of his needed energies to the tasks required for learning.

When children come to school, they need a transition period—a bridge—where they find a calm atmosphere, predictable routines, and time for connection. A quiet morning circle or class meeting can assist with the transition from home to school. Familiar activities such as soft music, established routines, books read in small groups, or other interactive materials fulfill this purpose.

The first interactions between teacher and children serve as a buffer and give them time to reorient into a safe environment. It is critical for a teacher to understand his or her role in supporting resilience. Daily interactions should be CALM: caring, available, loving, and meaningful. This CALM approach mediates stress by ensuring a safe, secure emotional environment.

Principle 61: Wants and Feelings

Allow the child to want what he wants and feel what he feels. Don't try to talk him out of or feel guilty for his wants and feelings.

Allowing a child to want what he wants and feel what he feels has real impact on a child's self-esteem and also on our future relationship with him. Simple words make such a difference. "I am sorry that hurt you. I know you must feel sad." "I can understand why you wanted to run away. Sometimes I get scared, too." "I can understand why you want that puzzle. It looks like a lot of fun. Why don't you work on the shapes puzzle until the other one is available?"

Children are still learning to self-regulate, postpone immediate gratification, and adjust to new environments. Younger children may say, "I miss my momma." The teacher can respond, "I miss my momma too!" Five minutes after the snack has been cleared and put away, a child may say, "I want more snack." The teacher can respond, "I can see that you are hungry. I am still hungry, too. I am glad that lunch is coming." An older child may announce, "I want to go outside." The teacher can respond, "I can understand, because it's so sunny today. When math is finished, then we will be going outside for recess." When we acknowledge and validate their experience, it helps them feel that we understand.

If we affirm children's wants and feelings when they are young, they will trust adults with their wants and feelings when they are older. It is critical that we build a foundation of trust with a young child. The next time he or she feels strongly about an experience, he will stay open and want to connect, rather than shut down or discount his feelings. We want him to trust that it is safe to come to an adult to share what he sees, feels, and needs.

If we are respectful, the child respects himself and learns to use his awareness to be reflective and wise. If we discount or make a child feel guilty about what he wants or feels, he becomes unsure of himself. That insecurity can be lasting. Being aware of his feelings will be an emotional resource for him as he develops resilience. A child who is listened to and feels validated stays open with himself and trusting of others. He learns how to give empathy and believes he has something important to offer to others—his true self.

Birth to Age 3

- Sing a variety of songs as you rock children gently. Repetitive motion is soothing and calming.

- Be sure to talk about feelings with children even before they can use their own words. They will absorb the feelings and ideas of the words you use, interpret your tone of voice, and internalize the physical sensations of their environment and interactions. These early sensory perceptions are an important foundation for the emotions they will understand and express in the future.

- Wordless picture books can be used to talk about what children feel. They relate to pictures of other children and focus on the expressions of faces. You can describe the scene and ask questions about feelings: "Is the boy happy? What is he doing?"

- Provide music and encourage free movement that lets children "describe with their bodies" what they feel.

- Stay "tuned in" to the textures of art materials, toys, food, soap, stuffed animals, the carpet, blankets, and other materials in children's environments. Describing these physical feelings and sensations supports children's awareness.

Ages 3 to 8

- Encourage expression. Let children draw pictures or work with art materials to describe an event or to show their feelings. Encourage self-portraits, which allow the children to talk about or reveal their emotions. Provide a small mirror to let children look at themselves as they draw.

- Provide (and read) books that tell stories about feelings and experiences that children have in common.

- Incorporate music and movement to encourage children to talk about how they are feeling.

- Use music as a background for writing activities that matches the emotion, idea, theme, or experience that children are describing in their writing. Support young children by asking questions as they color or paint. When children are engaged with the creative arts, their thinking and expression is activated. They are more likely to talk about their feelings when engaged in creative work.

- Invite a parent who has experience in a special area, such as an emergency medical technician, doctor, police officer, or social worker, who can reassure children about issues that concern them.

- Be sure to use the Validation Principle and Wants and Feelings Principle to support children in understanding and expressing their own and others' experiences.

● **THINK ABOUT IT!**

Describe two examples when a child in your classroom has needed extra support. How will you use the Wants and Feelings Principle to provide security and assurance for him?

1. _____

_____

_____

2. _____

_____

_____

Identifying Risk Factors

It is not always evident which children in your classroom are at risk. *At risk* means that a child will need additional support or intervention to have optimal school success, development, physical, or mental health outcomes. Each additional risk factor makes children more vulnerable to the impact of the challenges they face.

Rather than limit children by low expectations, we must dedicate ourselves to providing the social, emotional, and academic resources they need to thrive. Supporting resilience is a key ingredient to children's ability to rebound and thrive in the future.

Any stress factor can affect a child during early childhood. Cumulative risks (exposure to multiple risk factors) increase the level of vulnerability for social and academic adjustment. The following is a list of potential risk factors that may affect children:

1. The child or child's family is experiencing short- or long-term emotional stress.
2. The child lives in poverty.
3. The child is homeless, either temporarily or long term.
4. The child's parents or guardians are school dropouts or have limited education, or are chronically ill.
5. The child's family is under stress, as evidenced by violence, crime, underemployment, unemployment, or incarceration.
6. The child has health or developmental problems, including (but not limited to) developmental delays, low birth weight, or substance abuse.
7. The child's family member has experienced mental health issues, alcoholism, drug use, or sexual or physical abuse.
8. The child has experienced frequent moves due to a parent in the military, a divorce, or other separation. Military families may move up to 15 times before high school graduation (Bloom, 2004).

9. The child's parent is a teen mother.

10. The child is an English language learner.

11. The child experiences a death in the family.

12. The child has experienced acts of nature or war that result in long-term crisis to the community.

13. The child's family includes migrant workers or others without U.S. citizenship. Along with other implications, these circumstances may affect medical care and health insurance.

It is important to realize that other risk factors are invisible. A child may come to school well-dressed and keep up academically, but may be experiencing severe stress. A child may be bullied or teased. There may be stress due to a change in the family, the birth of a sibling, the death of a pet, or an upcoming move. Sometimes a child shows his need through behavior or academic issues, but other times, the need doesn't present such clear symptoms. All children need our help to support resilience.

THINK ABOUT IT!

What risk factors can you describe that affect the children you teach? Be sure to list as many as you can. Which of these present the greatest challenge to you? What can you do to support developing resilience?

_____

_____

_____

_____

_____

_____

_____

Experiencing the Benefit of Support

The early childhood years have a profound impact on a child's overall development and on his future ability to rebound and recover from stress. The role that a caring teacher can play in fostering resilience is powerful. Figure 6.1 illustrates the direct connection between the adult's supportive behaviors and the many benefits to children. When the caregiver is consistent in providing warm, responsive emotional connections, the benefits affect the child's current relationships and behaviors and continue to have a significant, positive influence for the rest of his life.

Figure 6.1   How to Support Resilience

When the Adult:	The Child Gains the Ability to:
Makes meaningful connections with child	Reach out to other caring adults in the future
Creates safe and secure environments for exploration and learning	Engage in learning with motivation
Welcomes and supports child in healthy and rewarding activities	Develop competence and confidence in being able to achieve goals (boosts self-efficacy)
Listens responsively, pays attention to physical needs, encourages success, mirrors tone of voice	Learn how to get needs met through constructive methods—and in turn will meet his own needs in healthy ways in the future
Provides security in times of stress (is physically present, emotionally aware, and reliable)	Stay calm physically and recover from stress experienced at home and school
Chooses calm, consistent, and frequent interactions	Trust that someone will be there for him in the future
Makes emotional connections and responds with empathy to children	Look for a trusted adult to turn to in times of stress
Creates environments that are consistent and calm	Show higher levels of prosocial skills and empathy toward others
Helps children identify and verbalize their own and others' feelings	Have fewer behavior problems and higher emotional competence
Offers children choices, respect, and empathy	Help, listen, and cooperate with others
Responds to children's needs in a warm, caring tone of voice and with gentle, kind responses	Become self-controlled and have greater cognitive development
Assists child to process and problem-solve when confronted with challenges	Handle stressful experiences better in the future

Dealing with Stress

In addition to the stresses children experience at home and in their daily lives, they are also exposed to environmental and media images that may be disturbing or confusing. On the average, children ages 2 to 5 watch more than 32 hours of television a week, and children 6 to 11 watch more than 28 hours a week (National Institute for Early Education Research, 2009). When children see repeated violent or frightening images during news broadcasts or weather-related events, they may think the event is happening over and over. They may have fear or anxiety that something similar may happen again. They may not understand the difference between "pretend" and reality. It is important to assure children that they are safe and that adults are looking out for them. Limit exposure the images and respond reassuringly when children ask questions. We need to watch for signs of stress.

Sometimes children want to talk about their experiences, such as the death of a pet, a divorce, or other family concerns. When we respond to questions, we must listen carefully and provide information that is developmentally appropriate. It is best to answer children's questions in terms they can understand. The important thing is to tell them the truth and answer their questions honestly.

You will want to continue to establish open communication so that when stresses and challenges arise, you understand the wishes of the family concerning what to tell the child. It requires sensitivity and professionalism to respect the way a specific situation is to be handled. Parents should be the ones who decide how much they want their children to know. If we are unsure, we can tell children that they will need to discuss it with their parents.

Children can handle stress better if they are told the truth. They often sense when something is amiss, and need to have their perceptions and feelings validated. When children are not told the truth, they can become hypervigilant and distrustful, traits that can follow them into adulthood. When situations arise, we can answer questions, making sure they know that adults are there to support and protect them from harm and to give them resources that will help provide stability through changing circumstances and transitions.

Sometimes, traumatic events happen to our students. One family found out that their daughter, Melanie, had cancer. She was diagnosed with leukemia when she was 18 months old. They learned that she could have a bone marrow transplant and that their 10-year-old daughter, Megan, was a perfect match. The parents constantly reassured Megan that it may or may not work and that if it didn't work, it wasn't anyone's fault. They answered all of her questions honestly.

Ultimately, when they knew Melanie was going to die from the leukemia, they told Megan that she had done everything she could to help and that she had been able to do something many people would never have the chance to do. They explained to her that she had given them extra time with her sister.

Megan was present in the hospital room when her sister died. She had the opportunity to say goodbye. Her sister Melanie was four-and-a-half years old when she died. Her parents have since had another daughter, Savannah, who is now four. Megan is now 15. Today they have a trusting relationship with their teenager. They feel it is because they were honest with her during this very traumatic situation.

Sometimes grief and loss can affect students in the classroom when there is a death in a family. A young teacher explained that the mother of a child in her second-grade class died during the fall semester. Some days she seemed fine, but other days, Alicia was very quiet. Even though she had been told that her mother was "in heaven," she often went to the school counselor to talk about her mother's illness. The counselor affirmed how hard it was for Alicia to watch her mother be sick for so long. The children in her class were told what had happened; that Alicia's mother had been very sick and had died. The children were able to show kindness and empathy to their friend. Because Alicia had such a strong support system, she was able to talk about her feelings as they arose. The school continued to watch for signs of grief and stress and to provide ongoing support for the family.

We can help children feel safe and adapt more quickly as they process their feelings. We can reassure them that we understand their feelings and will be there to support and encourage them. Children are remarkably resilient. The support we give them can make all the difference in helping them feel secure and confident in themselves.

● **THINK ABOUT IT!**

What event has happened recently in the news or affected your area that children have been talking about? To what extent have they needed reassurance? What have you said or done to help them understand or cope?

_____

_____

_____

_____

Encouraging Healthy Solutions

There are four principles that support children's self-regulation and lead them toward healthy options and choices. The following strategies help them solve problems rather than pull away or act out in self-defeating ways. The Empowerment, Make Up a Story, Role-Playing, and Brainstorming Principles will help you make great strides as you encourage children to respond productively to challenges and develop determination and courage to find healthy solutions.

 Principle 62: Empowerment

Encourage children to solve their own problems. Develop their competency, skills, mastery, and independence. Let them know that their choices will determine their future.

We want to empower children to do things for themselves every time they can. Our job is to work ourselves out of a job! Children love to take pride in responsibility: zipping their own zipper, putting trash in the bucket, putting away a game, helping to dry the dishes. These early experiences teach children competence. As they get older, they want to make their own decisions, solve problems, and know we trust them to do so. Resist the urge to do things for a child that he can do for himself. Then he will learn confidence and mastery rather than inferiority and dependence.

Likewise, when children encounter frustrations—a squabble with a playmate, a homework problem in need of a solution—all too often adults may be tempted to swoop in and help, confident they are fixing something for a child. Instead, children need to know we trust their ability to think for themselves and choose good solutions.

We can use verbal encouragement to let a child know we trust his ability to solve a problem. "Why don't you think up some rules that make you both happy?" "Listen to your brain. What does it tell you?" "I am proud you can talk that out with your friend!" "What solutions do you see?" "Wow! You figured it out all by yourself!" Letting the child solve the problem with our support builds skills and develops confidence. Our affirming words motivate him to try again.

● THINK ABOUT IT!

Use the Empowerment Principle at least twice today with the same child in your classroom who needs to be encouraged. Describe what you said and how the child responded.

_____

_____

_____

Children who are successful are eager to repeat their successes. We want to notice when children need our support and encourage them to try. When they make progress and we cheer them on, we give them the opportunity to be proud of themselves. We want to empower children to have confidence in their own decisions.

Principle 63: Make Up a Story

Make up a story giving an account of an incident in which the child was at fault, but using another child's name. Ask the child what the character in the story did wrong—and what he should do differently the next time.

Mrs. Brady was upset about what happened in her room. She was trying to think of a way to help the children be more sensitive to a child who had just gotten a haircut and was miserable when others laughed at him. She brought the children together in a circle and told them a story (of course, she changed the names of the characters). She most of all wanted to impress Nathan, the boy who had been unkind, and to see if she could help him to be a better friend.

This is the story she told the class: "Ryan's mother took him to get a haircut. When they left the barbershop, Ryan was upset that his hair was so short. He ran to the car and jumped in the back seat, hiding his head. As soon as he got home, he found a cap to wear and even wore it to bed that night. The next day in school, when Ryan walked into the room, Nicholas started pointing at him. 'Why are you wearing a hat to school?

What's wrong with your hair?' He grabbed Ryan's hat and took it off. 'Look at Ryan's haircut. It is too short!' Ryan started crying."

After she told the story, Mrs. Brady went on to ask the children, "What do you think Ryan should do? What do you think of what Nicholas said to Ryan? If you were Nicholas, what would you have said?" Then, she got to Nathan and asked him what he thought Nicholas should do. Nathan replied, "I think Nicholas should apologize to Ryan and tell him that his haircut looks nice."

Children are often insensitive to each other and they desperately need our help and intervention. Teachers need to stay tuned in to what is going on between children, especially on the playground and other places where children may not think they are being heard. It is the teacher's responsibility to teach children how to get along with each other. Making up a story using other names is an effective tool to use. Nothing more needs to be said to the children who actually were involved in the incident.

By making up a story, we create a teachable moment where a child can realize his own mistake and see a better alternative for the future. We don't want to preach and nag or shame a child for his behavior. We want instead to be forgiving and understanding and help children find a socially more acceptable way to get along with each other.

● **THINK ABOUT IT!**

Describe an incident in your classroom where you wish you had been able to help one child consider the impact of his or her actions on another child.

_____

_____

_____

Write a brief story that uses other names yet describes a similar situation.

_____

_____

_____

_____

Try out the story with your students. (If you work with infants and toddlers, try out a story on a friend or co-worker with whom you have wanted to discuss an issue!) How did it turn out?

_____

_____

🦋 *Principle 64: Role-Playing*

Have children act out different roles or ask a child to exchange roles with you. Let him tell you what he would do if he were in your place. Have him sit in your chair and show you how he perceives you. Taking on other roles helps children gain perspective.

Ms. Tanella realized that there seemed to be a few children who constantly talked to each other. It was not only hard for her to concentrate on what she was saying, but she knew the talking was distracting other children.

The next day, during a class meeting, Ms. Tanella said, "I would like several of you to role-play a situation that I have experienced. Eva, I would like for you to be the teacher, take my book, and read page 34. Adriana and Vince, I would like for you to start talking while Eva is reading. Please carry on a conversation at the same time that Eva is trying to teach you."

The children did as they were asked for several minutes. By this time, all of the children understood. Then Ms. Tanella thanked them and asked, "OK, Eva. Tell me how you felt while you were trying to teach." Eva confessed, "It was hard! I wanted Adriana and Vince to be quiet." "Adriana and Vince, how did you feel when you were interrupting while Eva was reading?" asked Ms. Tanella. "It felt funny," they replied.

"When I am trying to teach and you are talking, it's hard to concentrate. I need you to be respectful of our learning together, and listen carefully when I am teaching." Rather than lecture, Ms. Tanella had let the children discover for themselves how she felt.

Role-playing helps children see things from another perspective. Most of us assume that others are like us and see life the way we see it. But that is not the case. When we let children role-play the part of another person, they can begin to feel differently about the situation. Young children respond well to puppets who act out a situation or problem and show a resolution. We can let a bully role-play a child who is bullied, or vice versa. This helps them see how it feels to be on the other side of the fence.

Children who role-play are often able to come up with strategies to help another child who has to deal with an unpleasant situation. After the children watch the role-playing, they can brainstorm solutions. This technique helps everyone become more tuned in to the feelings of others and more able to find strategies and look for solutions to their problems.

For younger children, role-playing can yield remarkable understanding and insight. Children are able to express their feelings and role-play experiences they are going through. Many children who have parents who travel or who are separated through military deployment keep pictures of their absent parent and want to talk about when their parent will return. Using puppets or dolls and drawing pictures are good ways to facilitate conversation about this important experience in their life.

Children love to hear stuffed animals or puppets "come to life" and act out situations that they recognize. Role-playing how to get ready for a nap will yield giggles for children when the puppet begins to ask for a drink, another story, a muffin, and another hug. It's amazing to see children "believe" the scenarios they see demonstrated.

Younger children also love to role-play manners and are full of enthusiasm when they are asked to take on the roles of teacher or students. Acting out feelings and situations fits in line with the developmental make-believe play that they enjoy. Using children's naturally occurring ability to take on other perspectives and imitate allows a teacher to talk about important issues, such as feeling sad when parents leave, saying goodbye to a friend who is moving, or talking about a storm or other event that has happened in the community. Using role-play has lasting benefits because it allows very young children to watch their own feelings come to life and to talk about those experiences. This is a wonderful way to communicate reassurance and to alleviate concerns or fears.

 ## *Principle 65: Brainstorming*

Help the child brainstorm possible solutions to the dilemma, problem, or predicament.

When problems don't have easy solutions, it is a good idea to get several people or even an entire class together and come up with possible solutions. Many heads are better than one. When children think outside the box, they often can come up with ideas that no one else has considered. After we brainstorm solutions, we can vote on which one to implement and then give a time limit for the implementation. Next, we agree to come back within a certain amount of time to revisit the issue.

It is always better to consider all of the options when problems arise. Often, brainstorming brings about permanent solutions.

Here is a procedure for problem-solving that even young children can learn. We can model it by talking through the steps as a group.

1. State the problem
2. Brainstorm the alternatives
3. Select one possible solution
4. Implement the solution
5. Set a time to reassess the plan
6. Start over if unsuccessful

● THINK ABOUT IT!

Use the Brainstorming Principle with the children in your classroom (or with colleagues, if you work with infants):

State a current problem.

_____

Brainstorm the alternatives.

_____

_____

Select one possible solution.

_____

Make a plan to implement the solution. When you have done so, describe what happened. (Don't forget to set a time to reassess the plan. And start over if necessary!)

_____

_____

_____

To practice these steps, ask the children to brainstorm what to do when the class-room water fountain is leaking. Make a list of their alternatives. You will find that the solutions children suggest will be imaginative, fun, and useful. They quickly learn that it makes sense to brainstorm solutions to problems as they arise.

Becoming Your Best Self

Health is critical to resilience. When the body is functioning well, it is more able to deal with challenges and rely on energy reserves, as well as to fight off infection and sustain a strong immune system. A well-cared-for body provides strength when we need to focus on work or problem solving. Children developing resilience will benefit from having physically healthy bodies. Our enthusiasm for mental and physical health will influence them. Being a role model concerning healthy habits is critical. Children need to learn healthy habits for themselves, as well.

There are many other dispositions and habits that children learn from us. Children will gain an understanding of creativity when they see us being creative. Children will learn to be reflective when they hear us being reflective. When they see us model the process of thinking in new and divergent ways, it makes more sense when they need to use those skills. The more we are maximizing our own gifts, abilities, dispositions, and energies, the more we will bring this sense of self-efficacy to children. This means that they see in us a sense of confidence about where we are headed and see our belief in our ability to reach our goals.

 Principle 66: Stay Healthy

Remember the importance of taking good care of yourself—physically as well as emotionally. Eat well, sleep well, and get plenty of exercise. You will not only be able to cope better, but you will also become a good role model for the children you teach.

It is amazing how children pick up our habits. When we choose healthy food to eat, our children are likely to reach for the same things. A 3-year-old in a preschool room was recently heard to say, "Mmmm! I love these raw green snap beans!" Everyone in the room was surprised to hear a little girl in the midst of her morning snack gushing with delight over snap beans! With certainty they knew that her parents were modeling good eating habits at home.

We want to make sure we aren't living close to the emotional edge and that we keep a reservoir of strength and energy. These resources of flexibility and resilience are daily requirements for parents and teachers. When we are detached, children become clingier. When we are anxious, children become concerned. When we are rested, our reactions to everyone are gentler, our responses are easier, and our tempers less likely to be short.

Adults are like thermostats. They set the temperature for the children around them. If the adult's emotional thermostat is set at "comfortable," then the children will relax. When we are calm, children pick up on our calm. When we feel good and are rested, our energy and positive attitude affect the people in our world. When we are looking for the positives, our children will be looking for the positives right along with us. Problems that seem insurmountable when we are tired, haven't eaten recently, or haven't been exercising seem so much smaller when we have slept well and taken good care of ourselves.

We need to be loving and kind to ourselves and to our bodies. Our physical selves do so much for us and ask so little in return. When we do take good care of ourselves, our days will go so much easier and better, and children will realize the importance of taking care of themselves, too.

● THINK ABOUT IT!

What changes do you want to make to be your "best self"?

_____

_____

_____

Focusing on What Is Important

Keeping a healthy balance and staying flexible in our responses is a critical component of responsive teaching. It is also an important factor in psychological health! By setting priorities, keeping our goals in mind, and maintaining a balanced perspective, we will be able to deal constructively with issues that are important to us.

🦋 *Principle 67: Keep Your Perspective*

Is it really that important? If not, let it go. It's hard to make a quick decision about whether to let a child do what he wants or stop him. If we tell a child to stop, then we have to

follow through and make sure that he does. Sometimes we realize that it wasn't worth the hassle.

We need to think quickly, "Is it important?" "Is it in the child's best interest?" "Is it worth the energy that it will cost me to make an issue of it?" "Am I willing to enforce my decision?" If you can possibly let it go, then you probably should.

On the playground, teachers sometimes ask children to stop running or playing rough. Then when their back is turned, the children continue to run or play rough. It may be that the teacher needs to let go of the requirement before making an issue of it. But once the decision is made, the teacher needs to follow through and make sure the children follow the rule. This is why it is so important to consider ahead of time whether it would be wise to let the issue go.

Children are watching us constantly and will imitate the attitudes and responses they see in us. If we get upset over small, unimportant issues, they will do the same. Our responsibility, then, is to model mature behavior and let go of those issues over which we have little or no control. The best way to teach a skill is to model it. Children will follow our example when we do not make mountains out of molehills.

● **THINK ABOUT IT!**

Describe an experience when you made a mountain out of a molehill and soon after realized it was not such a big deal. What could you have said to yourself at the time it first happened to release the experience and move on?

_____

_____

_____

_____

Staying Responsive

Young children are vulnerable to experiences around them. As they get older, they need help knowing what to do when they hear unkind words said about themselves or others. We can help children understand that even when others tease them, these words are not a true reflection of them or their character. It is critical that adults take a proactive role and teach children skills to help them manage their emotions and to protect themselves from taking another person's uncaring words personally.

 ## Principle 68: Frog Suit

Teach the child to "put his frog suit on." The imaginary, invisible frog suit protects the child from being hurt by other children's careless or cruel comments.

It is a pretend suit that is available any time the child needs to use it, so when others make him feel sad, he feels protected. It will shield him and keep others' unkindness from harming him. We can show the child how to pull on the suit and zip the magic zipper so the unkindness won't seep in. When he puts on a frog suit and holds very still, he will see that other people's words don't have anything to do with him. By giving the child a frog suit, we empower him to manage his hurt feelings and feel in control of the situation.

Adults can also use this principle to keep a clear perspective. A teacher recently shared that she came to school "out of sorts" and was unkind to her assistant. The assistant responded, "I am going to go to the supply room to take care of some things. I will be back before the bell rings." Rather than get involved in an exchange of words, she kept herself detached from the hurtful words that were said. The teacher realized her assistant was protecting herself until the climate changed.

We want to ensure that children can learn and play in places that are safe; however, we cannot always be there to protect them. We want them to stay open emotionally and to be sensitive and empathetic to the needs of others. We hope they will never experience times when others hurt or embarrass them. However, we must prepare them for times when they need to disengage in order to be safe. Giving them an imaginary frog suit will provide a special tool they can use to guard themselves until they can discuss the situation with a caring adult.

THINK ABOUT IT!

Describe a time you regretted the way you handled a situation with a child—perhaps said something you wish you could take back. What happened? What did you say? How did you act?

_____

_____

_____

How would the situation have been different if you had put on a frog suit (gone within) and waited until you could think of a better response? How would that have affected the immediate situation? What would the long-term impact have been?

_____

_____

_____

When you do wish you could take back what you just said, apologize quickly. Don't wait until later to reconnect. Whenever the connection is broken, it takes energy to reconnect. We want to protect the positive bond we have with children. When we show them that they are worthy of respect, they can stand tall and better handle challenges. The skills they learn with us—to protect and respect themselves—will serve them well all of their lives.

Building Confidence

Children are naturally caring and genuinely express their feelings. They like to look out for others and want to do what they can to help us. Helping is a habit of the heart we want to cultivate. When children are young, we want to build their confidence by asking them to help and letting them know that what they do makes a big difference to us.

We also want to model for children how to ask for help. The ability to get help for themselves and to turn to others for help when they are in need is an important part of resilience. We want to help children stay flexible and find the best solutions to turn a frustrating experience into a more positive result. We want them to know they are capable of figuring out a plan for themselves and creating healthy solutions that bring happiness to themselves and others.

Principle 69: Help Me Out

Elicit the child's support by asking him to help you out.

To children, play is imitating life. The more they feel they are helping us, the happier they are. This spirit of joy in helping others can last throughout their lives, so we want to nurture this sense of generosity. We feel important—and gain a sense of meaning—when we know we are helpful to another person.

At one time or another, all of us can feel at wit's end. In those moments, we may need to gain children's cooperation. We can call on their natural spirit of helpfulness when we say, "You may not understand why this needs to be done. I know this is frustrating to you. I need to ask you to follow through. I really need your help." Children will be more likely to shift their point of view when they understand how significant their helpfulness is to us. They will feel appreciated and valued when we thank them for their help.

● **THINK ABOUT IT!**

Have you ever asked a child for advice? What did you ask? Were you surprised by his wisdom and judgment? What did you learn?

_____

_____

_____

Teaching How to Get Help for Bullying

Bullying is any intent to hurt another person and to receive pleasure in being unkind until the other person's suffering or distress can be seen. Bullying makes others feel bad by disregarding their feelings and inflicting physical or psychological pain. This is a learned behavior and it can be changed. Bullies need to learn constructive ways of expressing their anger and resolving conflicts. They need adult intervention to learn appropriate outlets for their feelings and to understand the impact of their actions and words on others.

Unfortunately, when children come to tell an adult, most adults tend to push them away, telling them to go find another friend and to ignore the bullies' actions. Instead, we need to address the consequences of bullying in a proactive way. Victims of bullying and those who see bullying happen need to be trained in how to intervene and stop the damaging behavior.

Principle 70: Teach Children to Stand Up to Bullies

Empower children by role-playing and letting them practice speaking up (loudly, if necessary) to bullies.

Children need help knowing when to walk away, when to speak up when someone is bothering them, and when to go to others for help.

Teach these three alternatives in order.

1. Ignore the bully. If you can, walk away. If someone else needs help, offer to walk away with him or her.
2. Tell him to stop—loudly. Say you will tell an adult. Children need words to say: "No, thank you!" "I don't like that." "Please stop." "Cut it out." "That hurts my feelings."
3. Tell an adult.

The most important thing is to let children know that it's OK to come to a teacher for help. Once a child comes, it's critical that a teacher does not send him or her away, saying, "Go find another friend." Instead, this is a perfect opportunity to *connect*—and to give the child what he or she needs. Be available to listen.

First, validate and provide support: "I'm sorry. Thank you for telling me!" "I am sorry your eyes had to see that." "I am sorry your ears had to hear that." "I'm glad you told me. You must have felt so sad. I am sorry your feelings were hurt."

Next, children need problem-solving skills: "What do you think you could do to work it out? Can you tell him how it made you feel?" "Do you want me to go with you so you can tell him how that made you feel?" We want to empower children by teaching them to use their words and stand up to bullies. Children can affect the outcome for themselves or for another child who is being bullied by going to get help from an adult. Adults need to listen and remember the plight of children who suffer long-term consequences from bullying. We all must work together to become part of a lasting solution.

What to Do When Bullying Continues

It is important to help children understand that not all people show kindness. Children must be reassured, so that they do not take personally the disrespectful things people might say about them. When someone is mean, the child needs to get help immediately. We need to teach children strategies to empower them to know how and when to speak up, and encourage them to tell an adult. Children who observe bullying *should not wait*. They should immediately report what they have seen or heard.

Teachers need to remain alert and responsive to bullying. We need to follow through with children who bully. Punitive responses to bullying do not work and can further alienate children. If we determine the situation is something we can handle ourselves, ask the child if he understands how his actions and words made the other child feel. Work with him to learn and practice new skills: "What other strategies can you use

● **THINK ABOUT IT!**

Print out the following lists of skills and teach these responses to the children in your classroom. Share them with the teachers in your school. Plan an event or meeting to talk about how to teach empathy and kindness to counteract the impact of bullying and teasing.

What We Can Say to Children

- I'm sorry.
- Thank you for telling me.
- I would never do that to you.
- I am sorry your ears had to hear that.
- I am sorry your eyes had to see that.
- I am glad you told me.
- You must have felt so sad.
- I am sorry your feelings were hurt.

What Children Can Do or Say

- Walk away.
- "No, thank you."
- "I don't like that."
- "Please stop."
- "Cut it out."
- "That hurts my feelings."

What Children Can Do to Practice Confidence

- Stand tall.
- Give eye contact.
- Smile.
- Give compliments.

Problem Solving with Children

- Would you like my help?
- What do you think you could do to work it out?
- Can you tell him/her how that made you feel?
- Do you want me to go with you so you can tell him how that made you feel?
- Could the two of you choose a third person to help you solve this problem?
- What is your brain telling you about that?
- Kiss your brain for doing the right thing—coming to tell an adult and not hitting or hurting someone else!

when you feel frustrated and angry?" Ask for his commitment: "Will you come and talk to me next time, instead of bullying?" Tell him that it is your job is to ensure the safety of every child. He must know that you will keep him as well as others safe. However, if the behavior continues, you will have to take further action.

While it can be uncomfortable, it is important to talk with parents when a child bullies. If your school has a policy in place, it is important to follow the steps provided.

Inviting your school counselor to collaborate in talking with parents is a critical step. When having a conversation about what happened, the child should be present. Just as in a parent conference, you should ask the parents if there is anything they want to tell you about their child. Calmly share the facts about what you saw or heard. Assure the parents that you want the very best for their child. Ask if they and the child will address this issue at home, while you support him at school. Make a plan together and agree to meet again. End the meeting with a positive assurance and commitment to the child.

It is critical that every parent receives information about the ways children bully. Many parents think their child won't participate, but unfortunately, when under peer pressure, all children have the capability to participate in unkind acts and words toward other children. This can be a life-and-death issue for older children, and the time to address bullying head on is in the early childhood years. Children do not outgrow bullying, so intervention must happen early. If you do not already have an ongoing training program, ask your administrator to invite a child psychologist or other professional to address the issue of bullying with you and your colleagues.

While some states are passing important legislation that deals with bullying protection, ensuring children's safety has to be everyone's responsibility. Policies and rules do not stop bullying. Caring, vigilant adults who are willing to speak out and step up must take responsibility to intervene. Bullying is a human problem. Adults face this cycle in the workplace and in the world. People of all ages need to learn skills to negotiate, intervene, and make a difference. This text provides a foundational philosophy of respect for the dignity of each human being that must be continually discussed, taught, reinforced, and put at the center of schools and childcare centers. Adults must step in immediately to ensure the emotional, physical, and psychological safety of children.

Providing Extra Support

Children benefit from the support of their peers. Whether there is stress at home or a child simply needs encouragement, the role of a peer's availability in social and academic growth is essential. For children who are English language learners, for a child who has recently moved, or for one who simply needs a boost of encouragement, teachers can use the following principle to provide assistance.

Principle 71: Best Friend

Elicit help from the child's best friend. Ask a friend to see if he can support the child's behavior, emotions, or learning.

This principle works well for a child who is struggling to stay on task or overcome a behavior challenge. In academic tasks, consider which child can facilitate and prompt growth for the other. In a social situation, pair a child with a friend who will encourage him to cooperate and think about what choices would help him be successful in the activity.

Because children share the same perspective and speak the same language, they can often help each other with essential learning and growth. Sometimes "language" means "the language of a child." Sometimes, it means a home language. Children teach and learn from each other in ways that work best for them.

We can elicit assistance from a child's friend when he needs extra support. It can help to ask another child to sit beside his friend or to play with him on the playground. Sometimes you may want to ask him in front of the other child; other times it may be better to ask for support from the friend privately. This technique is almost always successful in welcoming a child into smaller groups, helping improve connections between peers, and supporting children socially and emotionally as well as academically.

● **THINK ABOUT IT!**

Describe the behavior of a child for whom you have been meaning to provide additional attention and assistance.

_____

_____

Explain how you can use the Best Friend Principle to gain support from another child or children in your room for at least two specific activities.

_____

_____

Summary

Teachers can have lasting influence in the lives of children. The way we respond and provide validation for their experiences can have a permanent impact on the way they view themselves and their relationship with others. Establishing support for resilience is an ongoing process. A trusting and reliable relationship with a caring teacher can make a difference to children as they face challenges or difficulties. Modeling positive skills and encouraging healthy relationships with peers can foster resilience.

The greatest point of impact lies in a child's connection to a secure, caring, and reliable adult. When we have been sensitive, trustworthy, and consistent, we provide a safety net that fosters security and a sense of self-worth. As we teach skills for self-advocacy, flexibility, perseverance, and humor, we encourage a growing sense of purpose. Children will gain understanding of who they are and who they want to become. Our guidance and strong confidence will help them gain determination to seek the best for themselves and for others.

Using the Principles in Your Classroom

Practice Active Observation

Without being obtrusive, choose a child to watch for several minutes. Sit off to the side—watch the child's face and really listen without interfering in the child's world. Adults are often amazed by what they see. Observe what the world looks like to the child. Note how many times he laughed. How often did an infant initiate sounds, but no one responded? Did she seem calm or distressed? For an older child, how often did he talk—but no one was listening? Was the child misunderstood or upset about something? With an older child, what words were used in interactions that were surprising or interesting to you? How did you see the child expressing a sense of humor? What did you learn by watching the child?

Keep a Journal

Keeping a journal for self-reflection is helpful. What did you learn about children, teaching, or yourself today? "I learned it's hard for me when children whine. I learned that gets on my nerves. It's difficult for me to know what to do with that." Take along a notebook and jot down notes. How did you use two 101 principles? What led up to the situation? How did it turn out? Many teachers continue to journal at night, because when they reflect, they grow. Consider how you handled this day and how you could have done something differently.

Help Children Keep Journals

Encourage children to write about special moments, what worked for them, or what they want to work on. Writing about their experiences serves many purposes. Help younger children by letting them dictate "the nicest thing that happened to me today." Writing about their feelings will support emotional growth, reflection, and language development. Reading and writing together will give you time to connect. For older children, write notes back to them in their journals to support their feelings and experiences.

Create a "Therapy Book"

Create a book for a child with photographs, clip art, original drawings, or pictures cut out of magazines, showing the events that led up to a certain situation (new baby, moving, deployed parent, divorce, upcoming operation)—and a healthy resolution. This will help the child accept the circumstances surrounding the upcoming change in his life and maintain his trust in the significant adults around him. It may become his favorite book, which he will carry around with him and reread frequently.

Create a Safety Zone

Be sure to provide a safety and reflection space for children. For older children, provide a table in a quiet corner of the room where they can work, write, or read without interruption. This may be a place where two children can go to "talk out" a problem they are experiencing. Also create a quiet place in a low-traffic area with a soft chair or beanbags, where they can be alone if they are upset or need support.

For younger children, make sure there is a separate area in the room with soft pillows and furniture (upholstered chairs, soft low couches, beanbags, etc.) that is used only for the purpose of quiet and safety. Some classrooms have provided a large storage carton for children to climb into that is padded with cushions. Unfortunately, the classroom safety zone is a priority that is sometimes omitted when there is limited space. Consider storing classroom materials elsewhere in order to make room for this needed safety zone.

Teacher Tips

The following are comments from teachers who have been trained to use the 101 principles in their early care and education settings and elementary classrooms.

I didn't think that a "nice" girl in my class would exclude other children, but found out she had been doing so. I was amazed that after setting aside time to Teach Children to Stand Up to Bullies that she went on her own to tell a friend she was sorry. I didn't realize how much these strategies would help the children who were doing the teasing and bullying. I wish I had taught them sooner.

This week, I told my students that I needed them to help by paying attention and following directions. I was shocked by the change in them. Now I use the Help Me Out Principle all the time. When they know I need them to help me, it makes them feel important. I am so excited!

One of my students didn't want to go to his speech class. I said, "I really need to find the speech room. Can you help me find it?" He held my hand and led me up to the room. By the time he got there, he didn't mind going in at all. The Help Me Out Principle helped him feel so proud of himself, and I felt like I had a new friend.

Research on the Run

Defining Resilience

Resiliency is:

- The ability to adjust well in adverse circumstances (Tedeschi & Kilmer, 2005)

- The capacity to deal effectively with stress and pressure; cope with everyday challenges; rebound from disappointments, mistakes, trauma, and adversity; develop clear and realistic goals; solve problems; interact comfortably with others; and

(continued)

treat oneself and others with respect and dignity (Brooks, 2005)

- The ability to cope with stress, or "stress resistance," which requires strength awareness (Smith, Dalen, Wiggins, Tooley, Christopher, & Bernard, 2006)

- The ability to adapt, even without all necessary resources (Neuman, 2008)

- Entwined with a sense of self-efficacy, which is the ability to persist toward a goal, even in the face of difficulty; and the certainty that one has the ability and resources necessary to reach that goal (Bandura, 1977; 1991)

- The ability to "bounce back" when facing difficult odds (Adler & Stein, 2005)

- A "self-righting tendency" (Meichenbaum, 1985)

- The ability to recover successfully from trauma (Neuman, 2008)

Influencing Resilience

- Positive relationships support resiliency, compensate for stress at home, and help children achieve their full potential (Hamre & Pianta, 2005; O'Connor & McCartney, 2006; Raver, Jones, Li-Grining, Metzger, Champion, & Sardin, 2008; Silver, Measelle, Armstrong, & Essex, 2004).

- A teacher's immediate responses to children each day in school strongly affect their social and academic success (Ackerman & Youngstrom, 2001; Pintrich, 2000; Miles & Stipek, 2006).

- Teacher–child conflict has negative implications for children's behavior, whereas the longer children are with teachers who are caring, sensitive, and positive, the longer these effects last into later school years (Peisner-Feinberg, Burchinal, Clifford, Culkin, Howes, Kagan, et al., 2001; Silver, Measelle, Armstrong, & Essex, 2010).

- A child is dependent on the way adults treat him, and these interactions form the way he feels about

and interacts with others (Bennett, Elliott, & Peters, 2005).

- Consistent emotional support is a strong factor in the development of resilience. A child forms his self-image and worthiness based on whether he feels acceptable to his caregivers. When he feels accepted and valued, he feels worthy to be in ongoing relationships with caring adults (Cicchetti, Toth, & Hennessey, 1989; Iwaniec, Larkin, & Higgins, 2006).

- A child's social–emotional competence is linked directly to ongoing acceptance in social interactions with peers. The more he participates with others, the more he has opportunities to practice his growing social skills. Through his successful interactions with others, his opportunities to learn are enhanced. Conversely, lower emotional competence negatively affects a child's ability to enter into learning opportunities. Lower emotional competence brings greater behavior adjustment problems such as anger and aggression, and has a negative impact on a child's future behavior and engagement in learning. Emotional competence has a lasting impact on academic achievement (Denham, 2005, 2010; Denham & Brown, 2010; Miles & Stipek, 2006).

- When interactions are consistent and sensitive, children feel better about themselves and develop a more positive framework and higher expectations for future relationships. Early high-quality, responsive interactions affect relationships, behavior, and learning and influence children's ability to adapt to stress over time (Peisner-Feinberg, 2004; Peisner-Feinberg & Burchinal, 1997; Obradovic, Bush, Stamperdahl, Adler, & Boyce, 2010; Sroufe, Egeland, & Kreutzer, 1990; Yates, Egeland, & Sroufe, 2003).

- Early stress puts children at risk because it affects the way their biochemical systems react in social interactions. The emotional and cognitive responses affect the way a child learns and adapts at school. When the child is in a state of stress (either hypervigilant or underarousal), he is not in a frame of mind (or body) to learn. This places him at risk for social, emotional, and behavioral difficulties. Sensitive, responsive, and attentive caregiving can help him regulate stress and can counteract the psychological stress responses (McCrory, De Brito, & Viding, 2010).

- Caregivers play a critical role in fostering resilience for children who are responding to current stress and trauma (Berson & Baggerly, 2009).

- While temperament, abuse, stress factors, and other environmental factors play a formational role in a child's developing resilience, warmth and emotional support along with an early secure attachment provide protective mediation. These relationship factors lead to later social adjustment and overall positive psychological development (Sroufe, Duggal, Weinfield, Carlson, & Stein, 2005).

- In spite of what is known about the benefit of responsive teacher–child interactions, children at risk are much less likely to attend high-quality, center-based preschools. They experience fewer positive, supportive affirmations at home and more negative or coercive discipline. The stress of early punitive environments negatively affects children's physical and mental health, compromises immune systems, increases behavior problems, and increases long-term incarceration and public assistance rates (Shonkoff, 2005; Shonkoff & Phillips, 2001).

- A secure attachment with caregivers is the most important protective factor for a child. It influences his resilience, competence, and ability to adapt, despite continuing challenges and risk factors (Werner, 2005; Werner & Smith, 1992).

For information about poverty and risk see the following:

- National Center for Children in Poverty and Report on the Impact of Risk Factors for Children: www.nccp.org (Romero & Lee, 2008)

- The FEMA Department of Homeland Security website (www.fema.gov/rebuild/recover/cope_child.shtm#2) provides excellent resources for meeting children's physical and emotional needs and giving reassurance and coping skills after a natural or other disaster.

- The Center for the Developing Child at Harvard website (http://developingchild.harvard.edu/initiatives/forum) provides explanations from science about the ways early experiences affect children's development, mental health, and learning. Information and the latest research about risk factors for children are available.

Getting Positive Results Using the Principles in Action

What happened or led up to the interaction?

_____

_____

_____

Which principle did you use?

_____

_____

_____

How did the situation turn out? (How did the child/children respond?)

_____

_____

_____

What did you learn?

_____

_____

_____

What happened or led up to the interaction?

_____

_____

_____

Which principle did you use?

_____

_____

_____

How did the situation turn out? (How did the child/children respond?)

_____

_____

_____

What did you learn?

_____

_____

_____

Guide to the Principles

60. **Availability:** At school and at home, a child wants—and needs—time spent with the undivided focus of an adult. We need to stop what we are doing, make eye contact, and really take time to talk with and listen to a child. Encourage parents to spend 15 minutes a day with their child at home.

61. **Wants and Feelings:** Allow the child to want what he wants and feel what he feels. Don't try to talk him out of or feel guilty for his wants and feelings.

62. **Empowerment:** Encourage children to solve their own problems. Let them know that their choices will determine their future.

63. **Make Up a Story:** Make up a story giving an account of an incident in which the child was at fault, but using another child's name. Ask the child what the character in the story did wrong—and what he should do differently the next time.

64. **Role-Playing:** Have children act out different roles or ask a child to exchange roles with you. Let him tell you what he would do if he were in your place. Have him sit in your chair and show you how he perceives you. Taking on other roles helps children gain perspective.

65. **Brainstorming:** Help the child brainstorm possible solutions to the dilemma, problem, or predicament.

66. **Stay Healthy:** Remember the importance of taking good care of yourself—physically as well as emotionally. Eat well, sleep well, and get plenty of exercise. You will not only be able to cope better, but you will also become a good role model for the children you teach.

67. **Keep Your Perspective:** Is it really that important? If not, let it go.

68. **Frog Suit:** Teach the child to "put his frog suit on." The imaginary, invisible frog suit protects the child from being hurt by other children's careless or cruel comments.

69. **Help Me Out:** Elicit the child's support by asking him to help you out.

70. **Teach Children to Stand Up to Bullies:** Empower children by role-playing and letting them practice speaking up (loudly, if necessary) to bullies.

71. **Best Friend:** Elicit help from the child's best friend. Ask a friend to see if he can support the child's behavior, emotions, or learning.

Study Guide

a. **Goal Setting:** Describe an experience when you had a strong emotional reaction while watching an event or interaction. When might a child have a strong emotion or stress reaction, yet an adult might not realize the impact? In what ways might your students be stressed on a daily basis? What will they need from you to help mediate this stress?

b. **Questioning and Reflection:** See Figure 6.1 on page 156. Consider the strategies that a responsive teacher can use to support developing resilience. Rate yourself on a 1 to 5 scale (with 5 being the highest) for each area. In which area would you like to intensify your responsiveness?

Next, identify a skill (in the right-hand column) for which children may need more proactive support. How will your intentional investment help?

c. **Case Study:** Mrs. Young was distressed to find out that her students were being bullied on the bus. The children told her that an older boy had laughed and "made fun" when someone fell down, calling him clumsy and stupid. A second student tripped a girl on her way down the aisle and blocked a place for her to sit. Using the strategies provided on page 168, how can Mrs. Young help the children stand up to bullies? In what ways do you think she should get the school involved?

d. Personal Examples/Group Brainstorming: *Issue 1:* What risk factors affect the children whom you teach? How do these risk factors influence their emotional development and achievement in school? *Issue 2:* What events have happened recently in the news or affected your area that children have been talking about? To what extent have they demonstrated fear and anxiety or needed reassurance? What have you said or done to help them understand and cope?

e. Learners as Experts: Describe a time when you regretted the way you handled a situation with a child or family. In what way do you feel that your own stress, interpretation, or feelings affected your reaction? What changes would you like to make in your own life to ensure a deeper reservoir of strength and energy, so that you can be your best self? (Keep names confidential when sharing your experiences.)

f. Principles in Action: Using the "Getting Positive Results Using the Principles in Action" sheet, share one principle you implemented from this chapter. What happened or led up to the interaction? Which principle did you use? How did the situation turn out? (How did the child/children respond?) What did you learn?

g. Research on the Run: After reviewing the definitions and influences of resilience, how well do you feel that you cope with stress and pressure? What happened in your own childhood that helps (or hinders) you today as you handle stress and find inner strength to face challenges? Who in your life provided the emotional support and secure attachment for you? How does understanding yourself help you to better understand children?

h. Looking Ahead: Set the purpose for upcoming study by introducing chapter objectives. Thank you for sharing your personal insight about responsive, positive guidance and for your commitment to making a difference in the lives of children.

References

Ackerman, B., & Youngstrom, E. (2001). Emotion knowledge as predictor of social behavior and academic competence in children at risk. *Psychological Science, 12*(1), 8–23.

Adler, A., & Stein, H. (2005). *Case readings and demonstrations: The problem child and the pattern of life.* Bellingham, WA: Alfred Adler Institute.

Bandura, A. (1977). *Social learning theory.* Englewood Cliffs, NJ: Prentice Hall.

Bandura, A. (1991). *Self-efficacy: The exercise of control.* New York: W. H. Freeman.

Bennett, P., Elliott, M., & Peters, D. (2005). Classroom and family effects on children's social and behavioral problems. *The Elementary School Journal, 105*(5), 461–480.

Berson, I., & Baggerly, J. (2009). Building resilience to trauma. *Childhood Education, 6*(85), 375–379.

Bloom, R. (2004). School connectedness: Improving student's lives. Military Child Initiative: Report for Center for Disease Control and Prevention Conference. Retrieved from http://cecp.air.org/download/MCMonographFINAL.pdf

Brooks, R. B. (2005). The power of parenting. In S. Goldstein & R. B. Brooks (Eds.), *Handbook of resilience in children* (pp. 297–314). London, United Kingdom: Kluwer Academic/Plenum Publishers.

Cicchetti, D., Toth, S. L. & Hennessey, K. (1989). Research on the consequences of child maltreatment and its application to educational settings. *Topics in Early Childhood Special Education, 9*(2), 33–55.

Cozolino, L. (2006). *The neuroscience of human relationships: Attachment and the developing social brain.* London, United Kingdom: Norton & Co.

Denham, S. A. (2005). The emotional basis of learning and development in early childhood education. In B. Spodek (Ed.), *Handbook of research in early childhood education* (pp. 85–103). Mahwah, NJ: Lawrence Erlbaum.

Denham, S. (2010). Emotion regulation: Now you see it, now you don't. *Emotion Review, 2*(3), 297–299.

Denham, S. A., & Brown, C. (2010). "Plays nice with others": Social–emotional learning and academic success. *Early Education and Development, 21*(5), 652–680.

Hamre, B., & Pianta, R. (2005). Can instructional and emotional support in the first-grade classroom make a difference for children at risk of school failure? *Child Development, 76*(5), 949–967.

Iwaniec, D., Larkin, E., & Higgins, S. (2006). Research review: Risk and resilience in cases of emotional abuse. *Child and Family Social Work, 11*(1), 73–82.

McCrory, E., De Brito, S., & Viding, E. (2010). Research review: The neurobiology and genetics of maltreatment and adversity. *The Journal of Child Psychology and Psychiatry, 51*(10), 1079–1095.

Meichenbaum, D. (1985). *Stress inoculation training.* Toronto, ON: Pergamon Press.

Miller, A. (1996). *The drama of the gifted child: The search for the true self.* New York: Basic Books.

Miller, A. (2001). *The truth will set you free: Overcoming emotional blindness and finding your true adult self.* New York: Basic Books.

Miles, S., & Stipek, D. (2006). Contemporaneous and longitudinal associations between social behavior and literacy achievement in a sample of low-income elementary school children. *Child Development, 77*(1), 103–117.

National Institute for Early Education Research. (2009). Online Newsletter, Volume 8, Issue 26, 2009. Retrieved February 26, 2012, from http://nieer.org/newsletter/index .php?NewsletterID=146

Neuman, S. (2008). *Changing the odds for children at risk: Seven principles for breaking the bleak cycle of poverty and disadvantage for children at risk.* Westport, CT: Praeger.

Obradovic, J., Bush, N., Stamperdahl, J., Adler, N., & Boyce, W. (2010). Biological sensitivity to context: The interactive effects of stress reactivity and family adversity on socioemotional behavior and school readiness. *Child Development, 81*(1), 270–289.

O'Connor, E., & McCartney, K. (2006). Testing associations between young children's relationships with mothers and teachers. *Journal of Educational Psychology, 98,* 87–98.

Peisner-Feinberg, E. (2004). Child care and its impact on young children's development. In R. E. Tremblay, R. G. Barr, & R. Peters (Eds.), *Encyclopedia on early childhood development.* Montreal, Quebec: Centre of Excellence for Early Childhood Development.

Peisner-Feinberg, E., & Burchinal, M. (1997). Concurrent relations between child care quality and child outcomes: The study of cost, quality, and outcomes in child care centers. *Merrill Palmer Quarterly, 43,* 451–477.

Peisner-Feinberg, E., Burchinal, M., Clifford, R., Culkin, M., Howes, C., Kagan, S., & Yazejian, N. (2001). The relation of preschool child-care quality to children's cognitive and social developmental trajectories through second grade. *Child Development, 72,* 1534–1553.

Perry, B. (2001). *Maltreated children: Experience, brain development and the next generation.* New York: W. W. Norton.

Perry, B. (2005, March 22). The impact of childhood trauma and neglect on brain development: Implications for children, adolescents and adults. Remarks to Old Dominion University In Support of Children Lecture Series, Norfolk, VA.

Pintrich, P. R. (2000). The role of goal orientation in self-regulated learning. In M. Boekaerts, P. R. Pintrich, & M. Zeidner (Eds.), *Handbook of self-regulation* (pp. 452–502). San Diego, CA: Academic Press.

Raver, C., Jones, S., Li-Grining, C., Metzger, M., Champion, K., & Sardin, L. (2008). Improving preschool classroom processes: Preliminary findings from a randomized trial implemented in Head Start settings. *Early Childhood Research Quarterly, 23*(1), 10–26.

Romero, M., & Lee, Y. (2008). How maternal, family and cumulative risk affect absenteeism in early schooling: Facts for policymakers. Retrieved from www.nccp.org/ publications/pub_802.html

Shonkoff, J. (2005). Excessive stress disrupts the architecture of the brain. National Scientific Council on the Developing Child, Working Paper No. 3. Retrieved July 20, 2011, from www.developingchild.net/reports/shtml

Shonkoff, J. P., & Phillips, D. A. (Eds.). (2001). *From neurons to neighborhoods: The science of early childhood development.* Washington, DC: National Academy Press.

Silver, R., Measelle, J., Armstrong, J., & Essex, M. (2004). Trajectories of classroom externalizing behavior: Contributions of child characteristics, family characteristics, and the teacher–child relationship during the school transition. *Journal of School Psychology, 43,* 39–60.

Silver, R., Measelle, J., Armstrong, J., & Essex, M. (2010). The impact of parents, child care providers, teachers, and peers on early externalizing trajectories. *Journal of School Psychology, 48,* 555–583.

Smith, B., Dalen, J., Wiggins, K., Tooley, E., Christopher, P., & Bernard, J. (2006). The brief resilience scale: Assessing the ability to bounce back. *International Journal of Behavioral Medicine, 15,* 194–200.

Sroufe, A. L., Egeland, B., & Kreutzer, T. (1990). The fate of early experience following developmental change: Longitudinal approaches to individual adaptation in childhood. *Child Development, 61,* 1363–1373.

Sroufe, A. L., Duggal, S., Weinfield, N., Carlson, E., & Stein, M. (2005). *Resilience and young people leaving care: Overcoming the odds.* York, United Kingdom: Joseph Rowntree Foundation.

Tedeschi, R., & Kilmer, R. (2005). Assessing strengths, resilience, and growth to guide clinical interventions. *Professional Psychology: Research and Practice, 36,* 230–237.

Werner, E., & Smith, R. (1992). *Overcoming the odds: High-risk children from birth to adulthood.* New York: Cornell University Press.

Werner, E. E. (2005). What can we learn about resilience from large-scale longitudinal studies? In S. Goldstein & R. B. Brooks (Eds.), *Handbook of resilience in children* (pp. 91–105). London, United Kingdom: Kluwer Academic/Plenum Publishers.

Yates, T. M., Egeland, B., & Sroufe, A. L. (2003). Rethinking resilience: A developmental process perspective. In S. S. Luthar (Ed.), *Resilience and vulnerability: Adaptation in the context of childhood adversity* (pp. 243–266). Cambridge, United Kingdom: Cambridge University Press.

c h a p t e r   7

Preventing Misbehavior

This chapter will show you how to step in before behavior becomes a challenge. You will learn strategies to turn around potentially frustrating experiences and refocus the direction of individual and group behavior. Before a situation gets out of hand, you will be able to define your objectives, establish expectations, and support the positive results you hope to achieve. You will learn to intercede and prevent misbehavior before it becomes an issue.

The activities and reflections provided will help you show respect for children's growing autonomy. You will learn when to wait and when to step in to assist children in gaining the self-regulation, emotional competence, and coping strategies they need. As you continue to connect in positive ways, you will be able to support each child's awareness of himself and of others, and ensure the learning, safety and positive well-being of your classroom community.

Chapter Principles

72: Pay Attention	78: Hand Gestures
73: Remember Who the Grown-Ups Are	79: Cueing
74: Keep It Simple	80: Switch Gears
75: Blame It on the Rules	81: Do the Unexpected
76: Shrug	82: Thinking
77: Preparation	83: Satiation

Chapter Objectives

As you explore the text and activities in this chapter, you will be able to:

* Learn how establish and carry out expectations
* Discover how and when to step in
* Master five steps that will help children turn around non-productive behavior
* Replace "take aways" with proactive principles for success
* Increase cooperation and consistency and reduce resistant behavior
* Build new strategies for self-regulation and engagement

Working Toward a Child's Best Interest

Our goal for children is for them to be able to manage their own lives and become productive, contributing members of society. Children come into the world not knowing how to behave, and they learn by watching and repeating the behaviors that get our attention and get their needs met. They rely on a caring adult to be responsible for them and guide them as they gradually learn to assume responsibility for their own lives.

It is critical to remember that children who feel connected to and respected by an adult will develop a firm foundation of trust. Connection, respect, and trust are essential pre-requisites for all meaningful interactions with children. Children can sense when an adult is genuinely looking out for their best interest.

In a school or early education setting, children need support to learn the expectations of the classroom and the social skills to work well with others in a group. The more consistent you are, the easier it will be for them. You will need to decide what is non-negotiable, and be respectful and kind about following through on those expectations. Children will need a lot of practice and support in order to be able to gain all of the skills they need. Their success in the future will depend on learning these skills from you.

You can step in and prevent misbehavior before it occurs by knowing how and when to intervene. The following sections will give you the steps and skills you need to prevent misbehavior from getting out of hand. These strategies will help you give children skills that work—before a behavior becomes a lingering issue.

● **THINK ABOUT IT!**

What are some "bottom lines" (expectations) that are not negotiable?

_____

_____

_____

_____

Using Five Steps to Turn Around Behavior Outcomes

The steps to turn around behavior follow in sequential order. You may find that step one is enough to bring about the outcome you want. If the first step does not resolve the issue, then move on to step two. You will see that each of the five steps is powerful in changing your own words, actions, and behaviors. By changing your own approaches, you will rarely need to move beyond these five steps.

As you progress through the sequence, you will see that you are actively teaching and training, which is the definition of true discipline. Each step will help you stay flexible, calm, and respectful as you empower behavior change.

1. Staying in Control of Yourself

2. Focusing on Behavior You Want to See More of

3. Giving Preparation and Following Through

4. Switching Gears and Doing the Unexpected

5. Turning Around Take Aways

Staying in Control of Yourself

The first step in preventing misbehavior is for you to stay calm and focus on the outcomes you want. Remember to treat a child as you would like to be treated. Pay attention to your own response, realizing that children are watching you. They also are watching to see what behaviors are going to get your attention. Staying in control means thinking about what you will contribute to make this situation turn out well.

It is inevitable that when you snap at a child with impatience, he will snap back at you or at his friends. If you snatch away something that you don't want him to have, he will grab toys away from his friends. The more consistent, calm, positive, and supportive you are, the more the child will respond cooperatively to your example. The stronger the bond and more sensitive the relationship between you and the child, the more easily these issues can be worked through with positive results.

In the classroom, not only is the child watching and learning from the way you react, but so are his classmates. They are learning how you will be handling future interactions—with them! They also are learning how to talk to and treat each other.

The following two strategies will help you stay in control of yourself, turn a situation around quickly, and help you achieve the outcomes you desire.

Principle 72: Pay Attention

Keep your eyes and mind on what is happening. Don't wait until the child is out of control to step in.

Children have limited perspective. They cannot look ahead and see the big picture. Children rely on adults to pay attention and to look out for them. When we are with children, we want to keep our eyes and ears focused on what is happening. It is so much easier to step in early to redirect behavior than to try to fix a problem after it has already happened.

When we stay aware of children and their experience, we help them on several important levels. When a child is young, we want to stay tuned in to his physical surroundings and make sure we look ahead to anticipate potential problems and interactions. On the playground, teachers and assistants should continually scan the area to watch for children's safety. Keeping a "global view" will let us know where children are and what they are doing at all times. We want to develop highly sensitive radar so that we can pick up signals that warn us of potential problems. Is there enough equipment so that all the children in the group can join in? Is a toddler headed to climb onto a bench that is too high? Keeping our eyes and ears open is essential.

We also want to develop emotional awareness so that we can pick up important cues. Watching for cues in body language and tone of voice will help us to intervene early when young children need help. Are the children tired? Do we see a child getting to his limit? If we step in now to support the activity, can he be successful—before he gets too frustrated? If we see patterns emerging, we can step in before things get out of control. A teacher's sensitivity and awareness is essential.

● **THINK ABOUT IT!**

What behaviors might be a signal for us to step in while we are scanning the playground?

_____

_____

What signs or behavior cues in the classroom let you know your support is needed?

_____

_____

_____

Name one behavior you have seen in the past that you didn't notice until it was too late to stop it. How will you step in and intervene in the future? (Remember, stepping in should be positive. Review Chapter 2 for alternatives for redirecting behavior: "Here is another building for your fireman to rescue. Why don't you drive your truck over to that tunnel?" "Can you read your story to me?")

_____

_____

_____

Principle 73: Remember Who the Grown-Ups Are

Always remember that you are the grown-up and that you are ultimately responsible for the way things turn out. The child does not have your judgment or history of experiences and can't be held responsible for the ultimate outcome.

Juanita loved to sit next to Francesca, but was distracting her friend from reading. Their teacher realized that it was in the girls' best interest to move them apart. Earlier, a group of boys were getting wound up and extra noisy on the playground. Their teacher knew it would be just a matter of time before the group became whiny and aggressive—not happy with each other. She stepped in quickly and made the decision to take them inside for a snack, realizing everyone needed a break.

Children need for us to take the lead and be willing to make the important decisions even when they are disappointing to the child. It is often tempting to let children have their way even when it is not in their best interest to do so. Teachers need to remember that children do not have an adult's experience and cannot possibly understand all of the ramifications of a decision. They will have more respect for us in the long run if we make decisions based on what is in their best interest.

When we are consistent, children learn that we really are looking out for them and want the very best for them. When we make decisions based on children's safety and well-being, they come to trust our wisdom and judgment.

● **THINK ABOUT IT!**

Can you think of times when you need to be firm in a decision or routine? How will your consistency be in children's best interest? How will this affect behavior in the long run?

_____

_____

_____

_____

Focusing on Behavior You Want to See More Of

The second step in preventing misbehavior is to focus on the behaviors and skills you want to see more of, instead of giving energy to what you want to extinguish! Most of us were raised with someone who gave a lot of attention to what we did wrong, so we tend to respond with anger or frustration toward a child who repeats misbehavior. Many of us are in the habit of giving our energy to the misbehavior.

You need to make sure the misbehavior does not gain your attention. Now is not the time to talk about it. Now is the time to suggest an incompatible alternative and support the child's positive choices. You will need to address the issue at another time using role-play, brainstorming solutions, or class meetings. Later, when the child is calm, and when the other children are busily engaged, you may want to take the child aside to talk about what happened. You may decide the whole class could benefit from role-playing a similar situation and asking the children what would have been a better choice.

It may seem counterintuitive to refrain from talking about a behavioral issue immediately with a child; however, you may reinforce the behavior by doing so. Your calm and consistent actions (redirecting him, moving him away, comforting and assisting the other child) communicate much more than a lecture. He will experience the immediate effect of his actions (that it did not work out or pay off for himself). Your actions speak louder than your words!

Four-year-old Russell knocked over a tower that another child was building. Mr. Cole quickly took him by the hand and led him over to another area. As he provided other building materials, he said, "Let's build on the table, and keep our friends' blocks safe." Mr. Cole gave no other attention or discussion about the incident to Russell. However, he returned and helped the other child rebuild the tower. He noted that Russell was quiet for a few minutes and watched the tower being rebuilt before starting his own activity.

Later, when there was time to talk with him alone, Mr. Cole said, "I know how much you care about your friend. He felt sad when his blocks were knocked down. Do you think you can be more careful next time?" Russell nodded, and Mr. Cole gave him a pat on the back before encouraging him to return to play.

It was important to give Russell as little attention as possible (so as not to be reinforcing) and help him learn empathy (demonstrated when the teacher returned to support the child whose blocks had been knocked over). By returning later to talk to him, Mr. Cole could assure that he had Russell's full attention to connect relationally, discuss the issue in a calm and instructive way, and ask for a reflection (commitment) for future behavior. This exchange took place privately, to protect Russell's growing sense of empathy, responsibility, and conscience development.

It takes intentional focus and practice to gain new skills. The next three principles will help you by saving your energy and using every opportunity to teach children needed skills. Each strategy will assist children in taking responsibility and choosing good solutions to issues that arise.

Principle 74: Keep It Simple

"We need to be kind to our friends." "Time for a nap." "Remember the rules." "Gentle hands." "Walking feet." Stating things simply keeps us and our listener focused on the real issue and lets us both stay level-headed about what needs to be done. The simple task stays exactly that—simple.

Young children love to help and to know they are doing the right thing. When we state the rules simply, they can quickly focus on the important idea: "Use kind words!" "Books go on the shelf." "Blocks are for building." This simple approach provides time for the child to respond and to show his cooperation.

Keep it simple means *less is more*. When we state the rules or task in a simple way, it allows the child to focus on the positive. As soon as we see a child's response, we want to affirm his cooperation and our appreciation: "Thanks for making my task so much easier!" "I appreciate your helping hands!" "Thanks for being kind." Any time we can make cooperation easy, we succeed in drawing others along with us and creating positive learning experiences.

Principle 75: Blame It on the Rules

"Our school rule is to wash your hands before eating." It is important to tell children why rules exist, so that they have a framework when they are reminded of a rule. For example, children need to know that washing hands before a meal makes sure that the germs get rinsed down the drain instead of getting on food or in mouths. Children are more likely to follow rules that make sense to them. Once the groundwork of understanding is set, "blaming it on the rules" can help the child follow through.

Children respond to "It's a school rule" better than they respond to the familiar phrase many parents and teachers use: "Because I said so." That approach challenges children, whereas blaming it on the rules makes sense to the child. In a room of younger children who may ask "why" 20 times a day, blaming the rules can reduce resistance.

Knowing they are cooperating with the rules gives children a sense of pride in being part of a caring community. We want to connect children to a meaningful identity and purpose as we help them learn to get along with others.

● **THINK ABOUT IT!**

Name five rules for your classroom that are all stated in the positive. (They state what *to* do!)

1. _____

2. _____

3. _____

4. _____

5. _____

🦋 *Principle 76: Shrug*

Learn to shrug instead of arguing. The shrug means, "I'm sorry, but that's the way it is—end of discussion."

Sometimes it's tempting to argue or discuss an issue with children when they don't want to follow the rules, but this teaches children that it is acceptable to argue about the validity of a rule. It's easier for them and for you if you simply let them know that the discussion is over and that what you have said is non-negotiable. A quiet shrug is often helpful. It is important that the shrug convey a certainty about what you are saying, but not in a callous or sarcastic way.

Sometimes if we let children debate or argue with us, we are tempted to break down and change our mind. We have also taught them that debating and arguing are permissible. The shrug is a respectful way to communicate the message that this is not negotiable. There is no need to discuss it. Move on and don't linger on the issue.

Mrs. Carter let the class take a break on a rainy day and play a spelling game in the classroom. They loved the game and it also reinforced their spelling words. After the children had been playing for 20 minutes, she knew they needed to get back to their science lesson. "OK, it's time to stop playing. I need for you to come and get your science books." The children weren't ready to comply. "Oh come on, just two more words. It's our turn! They have been up four times. We have only been up three. Please, please?"

Mrs. Carter looked at the class. She smiled, shrugged her shoulders, and said nothing. When the children saw her body language, they realized that it was no use. She was not going to change her mind. And so they returned to their seats and went back to science.

Using the Shrug Principle kept Mrs. Carter from having to explain and kept the children from debating or arguing. When children know you mean business, they will understand that they need to follow through. A shrug is a great way to convey that message.

Giving Preparation and Following Through

The third step in preventing misbehavior involves helping children get ready for what will come next. Planning ahead can be accomplished in fun and surprising ways with the consistent use of the Preparation, Hand Gestures, Cuing, and Switch Gears Principles. These strategies will be effective with children of all ages.

 Principle 77: Preparation

Let the child know ahead of time what to expect: "We can go outside and play Duck, Duck, Goose for 20 minutes. Then we have to come back and get in our seats quickly and quietly."

Children are extremely reasonable about cooperating if they know what to expect. They want to know, "How long will this take? What will I have to do while I am there?" Letting children know what to expect of upcoming situations allows them to put their best foot forward and cooperate with the plans. We want children to cooperate because they feel willing. Their desire to contribute in positive ways is our goal.

A few simple steps of preparation will make all the difference. A trip to the library will be a positive experience if children are rested and have already eaten. Talking about specific plans ahead of time will help them understand and agree to expectations. If you need them to be quiet or choose only two books, be specific. You can ask children to explain the rules back to you, so that you are certain they understand. When you "think out loud" with them about what will come next, they have the chance to practice skills as they "think along." This inner rehearsal will help them negotiate new situations more easily.

It is important to review and practice expectations for each activity until children can accomplish what is needed without extra support. In early childhood, children have varying levels of self-regulation. Rather than single out a child after he has done the wrong thing, provide explicit instructions and time for all children to practice before the activity. This creates an atmosphere where everyone can be successful.

Mrs. White noticed that the children had trouble moving from a circle to a set of four lines when getting ready for a reading activity. She stopped right away and said, "I notice we need some practice moving from a circle into our reading activity. Let's walk through it together." She followed through by assisting them: "Melody, you lead the first row. Next, Jaden, you lead the next row. Excellent! Now we have gotten it straight. Let's practice once more."

After rehearsing the transition successfully, Mrs. White congratulated the children and went right on with the reading lesson. The following day, when the children made the transition quickly, she made a big deal and told them how proud she felt of them. Without making an issue of any one child, she helped the whole group be successful.

Working with toddlers will require special preparation. Toddlers live in the present moment and need teachers who understand their need for consistency, patience, and vigilance. They repeat the behaviors that work to bring them pleasure and that reward them with positive, enjoyable experiences. It is up to the adults in charge to create a safe environment where toddlers will be free to explore, investigate, run, and play.

Those who care for toddlers need to be fun, fair, firm, and fast, all at the same time, and must be prepared to set up routines and create interesting challenges for busy, active learners. Children will quickly head in new directions, so they need to be protected from harm and given many opportunities to satisfy their curiosity.

Younger children, English language learners, and children with special needs often are responsive to picture schedules that illustrate the day's activities. The child can slide a marker across or cover each step as it is completed. The pictures are a reminder of what comes next. When the teacher needs to make a transition, she can point to the picture schedule. Going over the picture schedule at the beginning of the day helps children feel better prepared to make a shift to new activities.

Many wonderful books are available to help children prepare for trips to the doctor or dentist, travel, new siblings, moving to a new school, and other life experiences. Whether you work with infants, toddlers, or older children, be sure to describe what will happen, using pictures and books to provide reassurance and support. As a teacher, you have a strong influence in helping children think about, talk about, and prepare for what lies ahead.

● **THINK ABOUT IT!**

Think about a time when something unexpected happened in the classroom. How did the children react?

_____

_____

_____

Consider the importance of planning ahead for difficult times in your day. How could you prepare differently by talking about it ahead of time with the children and getting their input on how to help?

_____

_____

_____

Ensuring That Teachers Follow Through.   One of the most common mistakes teachers make is saying no before thinking through a situation. Then we realize that it will be hard (or maybe even unnecessary) to enforce it, so we let it slide. If we don't follow through, however, we are teaching children that they do not have to take us seriously. We should say yes as often as possible and create special words such as "danger" or "stop" for times when we really need the child to pay attention, such as in instances of safety. Children need boundaries. Children respond better and respect our decisions when our limits are consistent and always in their best interest.

At recess, a child says, "Mrs. Smith, can I put the balls inside?" She replies, "No. Not today. Just leave them where they are." Predictably, the child says, "Why not? It will only take a minute. You let Joshua get them yesterday." If the teacher responds, "Oh, OK," she has taught that it pays off to question, complain, and argue.

After returning from gym class, the teacher says, "Please return to your tables to read." Johnny asks, "May I read with Suzy?" The teacher replies, "I would like for you to read alone." Johnny waits a minute and then goes over to Suzy. The teacher is busy looking for a book with another child, and does not notice that Johnny is doing it anyway. This is another example of not following through.

There are several effective ways to improve consistency:

Birth to Age 3

- Stay aware of signs and cues that tell you a child needs soothing, comfort, or assistance. Building consistency and trust will pay off in the child's developing understanding and patience as he learns new routines and skills.

- Sing songs and act out upcoming transitions or events. For example, show how you will put on your hat, boots, and scarf before going outside; ask the children which will go on first. Practicing routines will help them feel confident when it is their turn.

- Use puppets to act out experiences children may encounter. Showing how puppets take a nap, get a diaper change, or take a trip will bring enjoyment as well as teach new skills.

Ages 3 to 8

- If we do make a hasty decision and later change our mind, then we need to address the issue directly with the child or with the group: "I have thought this through. I said no too quickly before, and I should have thought about it first." "I know that I told you I would not allow you to do that. However, I have reconsidered, because I think this might be a good opportunity for you to show responsibility."

- Another option is to let the child or children come up with an alternative solution rather than give a hasty answer. "Why don't we think about it for a few minutes? I'll give you until 10:00 to come up with a better plan that you think is fair. We can talk about it then."

- When you do make a request, and it doesn't work well the first time, you can rehearse the strategy so that the request becomes a respected procedure. For example, when the children are coming in from recess, they may still be excited. You have said, "When you get to door, be sure to walk." However, when the first few children come inside, they are running. Say, "I need each of you to go back outside. Let's practice walking in." By following through, they will understand the expectation.

- Always consider pre-emptive ways to improve a situation the next time. The teacher who needs her children to walk in after recess might decide the next day to have them do several stretching and deep breathing exercises while they are lined up ready to come inside. Then she asks if they remember the procedure. Patient preparation and practice help children (and you) to be consistent and follow through.

● **THINK ABOUT IT!**

Name at least three expectations that you want to be consistent in explaining and following through.

1. _____

2. _____

3. _____

When are you most likely to be inconsistent? What do children learn as a result?

_____

_____

Encouraging Children to Cooperate.   It is important to be sensitive to the age and developmental needs of children, realizing that they may not be able to explain or even understand all of what is happening around them. Teaching young children simple sign language is a kind way to help them communicate to others. The gestures are used along with verbal language as a support to language development.

🐝 *Principle 78: Hand Gestures*

Develop hand gestures that signify, "Please," "Thank you," "More," "Stop," "Be careful," "Use your words," and "All done."

Using hand gestures helps young children communicate before they have the words to do so verbally. This enables them to be less frustrated, because they are able to communicate their needs and wants. They also are aware that their teachers are expecting them to watch for signals and follow the directions given.

It is fun, actually, to use sign language saying "please" and "thank you," "be careful" and "now." For infants and toddlers, teaching the signs for "more" and "all done" will make meal time go more smoothly. Using sign language for "drink," "eat," and other often-used words will assist them in getting their needs met in healthy ways while their language is developing. You can find many age-appropriate DVDs and books that illustrate and demonstrate simple signs. For more information and resources that use sign language to support learning and communication, please see the Internet, your local book store, or library.

As adults, we can continue to use hand gestures to save ourselves from raising our voice when children don't seem to be paying attention. We can make up our own gestures or we can use those learned in American Sign Language. Teachers are wise to find ways to communicate silently with their classes. Children will love to help make up signals and use them, too. It is a fun and friendly way to communicate, and it cuts down on possible frustration.

● **THINK ABOUT IT!**

What hand gestures can you use as a sign for lining up, close your books, bathroom needs, or sharpen your pencils? What else might you need signs for?

_____

_____

Principle 79: Cueing

Give the child a cue to remind him—ahead of time—of the behavior you want him to exhibit.

There are many cues we can use in our classroom or at home that will have special meaning to children. We can use hand signals to let them know that we need them to pay attention. Gesturing the motions to a song, such as "The Itsy Bitsy Spider," can be your cue to the class that you need them to stop talking and give you their full attention. Signaling with your hand "5, 4, 3, 2, 1" without saying a word is another effective way to get attention. Of course, turning off the lights is an old tried-and-true signal that many teachers use effectively.

Cueing is useful for teachers to communicate privately with a particular child. Agreeing on a sign to remember a required task or to redirect a child to a specific activity is a great way to support success. Mrs. Genoa had a child who was highly sensitive and often had difficulty staying calm during transitions. She developed a cue just for him, so that he would have extra time to begin and complete putting his things away. Together, they agreed that she would quietly walk by and tap him three times on the shoulder about two minutes before ringing the bell for everyone else. Providing this support not only prepared the child for what was ahead, but it created a special bond between them.

We need to teach children many cues and help them learn to use cues as well. There are many ways that using cues can be effective for individual children as well:

Birth to Age 3

- Familiar routines are very comforting and can help infants to feel safe and secure. Familiar songs are a cue to infants that it is time to eat or take a nap.

- Teach a child that instead of interrupting when you are talking with somebody else, he is to squeeze your hand. This will let you know that he wants to talk to you (as you return the squeeze) and as soon as you can, you will stop the conversation and give him your full attention.

Ages 3 to 8

- When you make an agreement with a child, create a secret signal, such as pulling on your ear or rubbing your nose. Whenever you see the child, give the secret signal to remind him of your conversation and his promise to try new ways to get what he needs or wants.

- Children as well as adults can use "caring cues," such as the "I love you" sign, a unique handshake, or other symbolic gestures created by the children.

- Some children appreciate a green card slipped on their desk a few minutes early to give them extra time to prepare before a transition. Let children decide what kind of cues will work best for them. What they have chosen them, they are more likely to use them.

- It is wise to help children learn to cue themselves by leaving sticky notes in a prominent place reminding them to take their eye glasses with them when they leave school, or pasting pictures of a satisfied animal on one side of a poster and an unhappy animal on the other side of a poster as a cue to remember to feed the class gerbil.

- Using a cue is a wonderful way to connect with a child who needs extra support. Create a secret sign, such as a pinky hug. Every time you go by him, you can use the sign as a way to connect and let him know you are supporting him and care about him.

Cueing is a smart and effective way to remind everyone of the rules. By giving non-verbal cues, we save ourselves from having to talk loudly, yell, or become irritated when children aren't listening. Cueing is a respectful way to deal with problems that arise on a daily basis—and they provide lots of support for children's success.

THINK ABOUT IT!

Name one non-verbal cue you have seen another teacher use that you felt was effective.

_____

_____

_____

How could you replace a "worn out" cue like saying "shhhh" or flicking the lights with one that is creative and grabs children's attention?

_____

_____

_____

Try using the motions to "The Itsy Bitsy Spider" without using words and see how many children will imitate you. This works for children and adults of all ages.

Switching Gears and Doing the Unexpected

The fourth step in preventing misbehavior encourages teachers to be flexible, adaptive, and ready to adjust to the emotional and learning needs of children. Your responsiveness will allow you to provide high expectations, yet be sensitive to the developmental, social, and physical needs of children.

Principle 80: Switch Gears

When the unexpected occurs, look for a way to make the most of the situation. For example, if you have a long wait, suggest that children close their eyes and listen for what they can hear, or look around and find something they have never noticed before.

Another name for this principle is "The Plan B Principle." When plan A falls through, then let's see if we can make plan B more interesting than plan A might have been. We do this by modeling flexibility and willingness to keep a positive attitude when interruptions occur or unforeseen circumstances prevent us from doing what we had planned. We need to make an effort to help children think of an alternate plan that will be more beneficial, fun, or memorable than the original plan.

Mrs. Mitchell and her first-grade team had planned Field Day for weeks. On the morning of the event, it was pouring rain. Instead of focusing on the water games that had to be canceled, the teachers and children were given 30 minutes to come up with an activity that could be played in the gym. Rather than focus on the missed event, they quickly prepared to make plan B even better. At the end of the day, all agreed that their Field Day had been a big success!

All teachers need to be flexible. The schedule may get interrupted by a fire drill or a child may get sick. Perhaps a lesson plan just isn't working out the way you expected. When you notice that children need a break, switch gears quickly. Always be ready by keeping extra materials and ideas on hand to engage children's minds and bodies. You may need to switch gears as you answer children's questions. Staying responsive and sensitive to children's needs can bring about memorable results for everyone.

Birth to Age 3

- We want to be consistent in routines and care, yet remain responsive to individual needs. For infants and toddlers, switching activities, educational materials, and toys keeps them interested and engaged.

- Rotate and replace puzzles and provide new toys that include a variety of textures. For example, have a soft basket filled with stuffed animals, fabric squares, small blankets, puppets, multitextured balls, flexible plastic shapes, and shape-sorting activities. (Rotated toys seem "new" to the children.)

- Consistently be on the lookout for better ways to arrange the room. If there is a particular part of the room or part of the day that is a continuing problem, see if there isn't some change that could resolve the issue. It helps to brainstorm possible solutions with an assistant, teacher, or supervisor. Sometimes, the children themselves can come up with a creative plan. If it is their idea, they will have an investment in making it work.

Ages 3 to 8

- If there is something exciting happening outside, give students a chance to see and talk about it before they return to their work or activity.

- Give students the option of working independently or with a partner.

- Keep an "unexpected" bag ready. Fill it with a chapter book, brain teasers, riddles, or mental math games. If you find you are stuck while waiting for a program, access to the lunchroom, or an assembly, you will have engaging mental activities ready to employ.

- Be ready for inclement weather and indoor recess. Keep a container ready to use for times you must switch gears. Include word games (like Boggle and Scrabble Jr.), activity games (Pictionary, Twister, Charades), and action games.

- When something unexpected does occur, explain to children what has happened and provide any new expectations. They will appreciate your confidence and trust your decisions when you need to switch gears.

Every day, you will find many situations that require flexibility. You will benefit by quickly moving on and showing children how to have a great attitude and how to be creative, even when things don't go as planned.

> **THINK ABOUT IT!**
>
> When it starts raining and you are on the playground, what could you do to fill up the time in a creative way? (For example, try a treasure hunt in the building for items that start with a specific letter.)
>
> _____
>
> _____
>
> _____

Principle 81: Do the Unexpected

React in a surprising way. Start doing jumping jacks! Clap a familiar rhythm such as "Jingle Bells" to relieve the tension and get some perspective. It is amazing how much better you can think and then decide on a more rational way to handle the situation when your head is clear.

When an activity is not working or children become frustrated, it's time to do the unexpected! There are many ways to get attention that will break the cycle and help everyone refocus. Get out your harmonica, whistle a tune, or start singing the "Hokey Pokey." Try whispering, "If you can hear me, touch your nose [ear, clavicle, scapula, femur, etc.]!" It is amazing how much fun it can be when you do something startling to divert children's attention and ward off a more serious problem. It takes creativity to a think of something unusual to do, but it is well worth the effort.

A teacher will be remembered forever by the kind and funny ways she captured the children's attention as well as their hearts. Infusing joy and humor into what might otherwise be a difficult situation will create memories that will leave an impression for years to come.

● **THINK ABOUT IT!**

Visualization exercises and stories have a strong impact in calming older children. They also work well to engage infants and toddlers, who will enjoy listening to your description of the sounds of the wind or other soft imagery. Implement at least one "unexpected" with your class today. You may choose from the examples below or make up your own.

- "Close your eyes and think of your favorite cuddly toy." (Use your imagination to describe various parts in sequence.)

- "Close your eyes and listen for a song. As soon as you know it, raise your hand." (Very softly hum tunes children will recognize.)

- "Close your eyes and listen for a noise that sounds like a kitten. Raise your hand when you hear it." (Meow very softly.)

- Ask older children to stand for "The Star-Spangled Banner" (or another song you sing often)—and instead surprise them by singing (and acting out) "The Hokey Pokey."

What happened? How did the children respond?

_____

_____

_____

Turning Around Take Aways

The fifth step in preventing misbehavior involves evaluating the effectiveness of current behavior guidance systems. Children do their best to negotiate challenges. If what they are doing is not working for them, the obvious solution is to help them learn skills rather than to take something away, thus adding to their frustration. Instead of using "take away" systems, there are some great solutions that will achieve the outcome you desire.

Take-away systems involve either the threat of taking away something the child wants or the actual removal of a desired object or activity. This may be a simple card system in the room, where children are asked to "move a card down" if they do something wrong. There are many reasons these systems are unfair:

- Take aways cause resentment and anger—which can cause disengagement in learning.
- Take aways can embarrass or shame, which weaken a child's motivation. Instead of making children feel bad (with a misguided belief that this will motivate them), we can teach children moral behavior (right from wrong) and encourage them with skills to increase empathy and cooperation.
- Take aways are biased against particular children, especially against those who lack social skills.
- The adult may be inconsistent about enforcing take aways, depending on his or her mood or the stresses of the day.
- Take aways are issued only if the teacher notices or sees a behavior.

- Take aways are used less with "a teacher's pet" and more with a perceived "difficult" child.

- Take aways discourage traits that are important to learning, such as effort, interest, and enthusiasm.

- Take aways interfere with trust and motivation. When we have promised something, the incentive should not be removed, or the child will stop trying in the future.

Once we understand the discouraging impact of take-away sytems, we can reformat our own system to support motivation and cooperation. Everything that is approached negatively can be turned around to have a positive outcome. Children want to be competent and proud of their achievements. Figure 7.1 illustrates some effective ways to turn around systems to encourage and enable children's success.

Figure 7.1   How to Reverse a Take-Away System and Create a Cooperation System

Instead of This	Do This
Telling children what to stop doing	Tell them what you want them to be doing
Using a stoplight system and moving children from green to red	Let them start on red and earn the privilege of moving to yellow and green
Keeping a tally of children's misbehavior	Keep a tally of children's positive behavior
Writing names on the board when children do the wrong thing	Write names on the board when children do the right thing
Carrying a clipboard to mark names of children who are misbehaving in line	Carry a clipboard to mark the names of children who are displaying responsible behavior
Taking away a coin or ticket when children misbehave	Put a coin or ticket on a child's desk for being cooperative
Dropping stars out of the sky	Let children be shooting stars to recognize their accomplishments
Erasing the letter of a word for misbehavior	Let children earn letters to obtain a cooperative incentive (for St. Patrick's week, they can earn the word SHAMROCK to play a round of math bingo)
Leaving a "stop" sign on a child's desk as a warning	Leave a "go!" sign to let them know you notice their effort
Calling home when children misbehave	Call home and leave a positive message when children do something well
Writing rules that tell children what *not* to do	Write rules that tell children what *to* do

● **THINK ABOUT IT!**

Give two examples of take aways that you use or know that others use.

1. _____

2. _____

Now turn those examples around and explain how you can create an opportunity for children to "move up," be reinforced, or gain privileges, either individually or as a group.

1. _____

_____

2. _____

_____

Supporting Positive Outcomes

Mrs. Jordan teaches second grade. She is having concerns about Robert, who frequently wanders around the room and bothers other children when they are working. She decides to turn things around and focus on the positive skills she wants him to have. She chooses three strategies to try and writes down her plan:

1. **Make a Big Deal.** Catch Robert doing something *right* at least once every 30 minutes. Tell him what he did right and be specific. "You wrote three sentences by yourself. This is an interesting beginning to your story."

2. **Think of the Outcome.** Instead of taking away "reward dollars" (which resulted in negative outbursts), focus on changing only one misbehavior at a time. Robert is out of his seat when he really needs to be focused during lesson time. Stop using take aways and let Robert earn time when he is in his seat to do what he really likes—working with art materials.

3. **Incompatible Alternative.** Make a small basket and put in three items: a squeeze ball, a small beanbag, and a small stuffed animal. As Robert comes to circle time, he may choose an item to bring with him to hold quietly. He will only have access to these materials during the teaching times when he is sitting in his chair.

By making a conscious choice to eliminate negative take aways and to implement specific positive interventions, Mrs. Jordan saw an immediate change in Robert's motivation and cooperation. By drawing his attention toward positive opportunities to be successful, he gained confidence in himself and became more responsive to her positive guidance.

● **THINK ABOUT IT!**

Describe one behavior that has been frustrating to you. Suggest three alternatives that you can use to support positive outcomes that you have not yet used with this child. (If you are unable to think of a scenario of your own, provide three additional positive strategies from the 101 principles that could be used in the scenario with Robert.)

_____

_____

Building New Skills

When we approach children with respect and kindness, we can help them learn skills to aid their success. Instead of looking at a child and thinking he has a problem, think about what you can do to solve the problem together. "Samantha, you are having a hard day. Let's see what I can do to help you. Let's talk together and work this out."

This child needs someone to assist her in becoming productive and successful. When we oppose children and feel it is "them against us," we only frustrate the child and ourselves. When we treat the child as we would want to be treated, we realize this child is doing the best he or she can. By using new strategies ourselves, we can stop the cycle and change the pattern, not only for this child, but hopefully for his family and others who interact with him.

Knowing What to Do to Keep Misbehavior from Continuing

When you have a behavior that continues to bother you, first, review the principles from Chapter 2 to be sure that you have kept your skills finely tuned and your perspective positive. Next, if you are unsure how to handle a behavior you find annoying or bothersome, make sure to consider what is in the best interest of the child. Use good judgment and evaluate the needs of other children present.

Principle 82: Thinking

Take time to think about your options and consider the outcome. Will it be positive? How do you want this to turn out?

You want to have high expectations for every child. Use the Thinking Principle frequently. Take time to think about your options. Consider the outcome.

● **Think About It!**

1. Think about a child who needs help to change a behavior. Explain how you responded to him in the past.

2. Name three specific skills you want him to develop. Write one of the 101 principles next to each skill to help him develop that behavior. An example is provided. Describe your situation below.

The problem as I see it:	
John becomes frustrated when he plays with Abby.	
How I responded in the past:	
I separated them, but know that he feels bad when he can't play with Abby.	
First skill needed:	Principle I will use: Validation
To be able to wait his turn	*"I know it's hard to wait. I know you feel frustrated."*
Second skill needed:	Principles I will use: Choice
To be able to share	*"Would you like to use the art set or the markers while you are waiting?"*
Third skill needed:	Principle I will use: Brainstorming
To be able to use words when he wants something	*"What would work better for you next time? What could you ask Abby when you want to help her?"*

The problem as you see it:	
How you responded in the past:	
First skill needed:	Principle you will use:
Second skill needed:	Principle you will use:
Third skill needed:	Principle you will use:

Be deliberate and proactive about your choices with children so that you can turn around any negative habits, responses, and perceptions into positive outcomes. Remember that the behavior you want to change is your own. The child will respond in positive ways when he experiences your respect and learns that you are giving him opportunities to show you that he can do it! Therefore, you want to choose a principle that matches the need of the child and use it to create a positive outcome.

It may be helpful to keep a 3-by-5 card with at least two principles written on it that you can use as a reminder. You may want to cut the principles into strips and keep several in your pocket. Try at least two new ways of responding to create a new reaction from the child. Remember to focus on teaching new behaviors, rather than stopping the old.

Principle 83: Satiation

If a behavior is not dangerous, destructive, embarrassing, or an impediment to learning, let it continue until the child is tired of doing it.

It may be helpful to assign a behavior, as long as it is not embarrassing to the child. For example, a child who repeatedly gets up to sharpen his pencil can be given an entire box of pencils to sharpen. If young children get "the sillies" when a child says a harmless word like "underpants" and the giggles don't go away, let all of the children say "underpants" 10 times so that they tire of it.

Often a "misbehavior" is simply something that is best done at another time. If a child can't stop making mouth noises, try (at another time) assigning the whole class to "sing" a song with a mouth band. Let each one choose the sound they want to make. After the fun of doing it together, the child may get it out of his system and no longer want to do it. This can be used for whistling, humming, tapping, or drumming. It is a useful (and fun!) way to help children tire of a habit that might otherwise be distracting.

● **THINK ABOUT IT!**

The Satiation Principle must be used with sensitivity. What behavior/activity could be assigned that might be embarrassing to a child? What could you assign instead that would not be embarrassing? What factors might make a difference in how a child responds or feels?

_____

_____

_____

_____

_____

Maximizing Teachers' Influence on Children's Behavior

In order to prevent misbehavior, we need to understand the influence we have in turning around outcomes. We want to help children become aware of themselves (self-disciplined and responsible for their behavior) as well as aware of others (caring and thoughtful about those around them). By planning carefully and understanding our impact, we can create an environment where misbehavior is much less likely to occur. We will *actively pursue* the goal of equipping each child with the strategies he needs to develop competence.

We want children to think for themselves, learn to problem-solve, and become flexible and adaptive. The more we practice modeling these skills, the better we will become at helping children learn them. Using the 101 principles is a perfect way to model these attributes. We will gain a sense of perspective; we will think before we react; and we will develop a greater sense of humor and enjoyment in our time with children. As we show respect and support, we will see that misbehavior has been intercepted and constructive prosocial behaviors have become established.

Summary

We have seen how a teacher can utilize a purposeful plan of action to intervene in behavior issues before they become significant or challenging. Preparing children for what is expected and following through with consistent support will encourage cooperation. As you use the 101 principles, you can maximize your influence to build children's social skills while preventing misbehavior.

Using new skills requires practice on your part. When you understand how much your actions and words affect children, you will find a clearer sense of purpose in your work. Review the 101 strategies frequently. Remember to focus on what you *do* want! Talk about your efforts with your colleagues. Encourage other teachers to use the strategies. Celebrate the changes that you see. Clarify the changes you want to make. Write down the goals you want to achieve. You will contribute powerfully to creating a positive climate where all children can be successful learners.

Using the Principles in Your Classroom

Animals and Stuffed Animals

Use animals as symbols of comfort or cheer and to recognize positive contributions. This will make such a difference in the way children of all ages recognize their own feelings and respond more sensitively to the needs of others.

Place a stuffed animal on a child's desk for any positive reason. Use multiple stuffed animals, each for a different purpose. Children will love to bring them from home and create a special purpose for each one. This concept works with children of all ages. The following ideas can be modified for your classroom:

- Have a class "Puppy Buddy" that children pass around to each other when they feel a friend needs encouragement.
- Use a "School Is Cool" mascot bear in the classroom. Move the bear to the desk of a student who is making exceptional behavior choices. This will reinforce positive behavior.
- Have a "Molly Manners" stuffed bunny to give to a child who is very polite.
- Pass around a "Floppy Feeler" pup as children share their feelings during class meetings.
- Pass a "Happy Helper" around the circle as children tell something special they did to help someone else.

Be Creative with Hand Signals

Let children decide on new signals and what they mean. You will be amazed at their creativity and ideas. When children have taken part in making them, they will want to use them! Here are some ideas:

- Raise hand with closed fist to show need of restroom.
- Open hand or "quiet thumb" to answer a question.
- Put one finger up if you agree with answer.
- Put two fingers up if you want to disagree.
- Use "OK" signal to ask for a drink.
- Use a thumb wiggle to ask for help.

Partnering Up

Encourage math and reading pals by pairing a child with a stronger student or with a positive behavior model who can be a good influence. Match children with others to buddy read, solve math problems, finish puzzles, or write a story. Partner a child with an older student who can help illustrate a book or be involved in a similar constructive project. A child who is busy with meaningful work is much less likely to misbehave. Even very young children can enjoy time with an older child, and the benefit is reciprocal.

Teacher Tips

The following are comments from teachers who have been trained to use the 101 principles in their early care and education settings and elementary classrooms.

I have been working very hard on following through and being consistent. Today I walked by two boys who were poking each other under the table. I asked them to show me how they were solving their math challenge. They knew I meant they should be doing something constructive instead of fooling around. Even though I didn't say it, they knew. I stayed near to be sure they would follow through with what I expected.

During flexible time, there are two girls who like to take off their shoes and play in the back by knocking their feet together. I tried to keep an eye on them so that I could intervene before things got out of hand, but I soon realized it was better to step in ahead of time. Before the next flex time, I had two jobs waiting that they could choose. By thinking ahead and being pro-active, I stopped the issue before it got started.

A boy in my class liked to spin in the halls while he was coming back from music class. Rather than create an issue, I whispered, "Let's walk together and when we get to recess, we'll have a spinning party!" When we got outside, a group of children spun around together until that particular child tired of it. He never wanted to spin again in the hall. I was so surprised that the Satiation Principle worked. I realized how a change in my approach had a lasting impact.

This week, I used the Switch Gears Principle. I began playing a game of "Doggie, Doggie, Where's Your Bone?" with the children. After the first two times, the children became restless, so we switched to "Simon Says." This game worked out great and the children loved it. I regained their attention and everything went smoothly.

Today at school, we were interrupted by a fire drill. Mrs. Austin had the students stand up in a line and the kids were getting restless. I began to play a game of "I Spy" with part of the line. Soon, the other children joined in and we played until it was time to go back in. This activity got their minds off everything else, and they had fun.

Our old take-away system was a temperature chart. When children had to move their clip down, the result incited more misbehavior and drama than the initial behavior itself. All the attention and energy would be invested into the misbehavior. The system made behavior so much worse. We threw it out schoolwide and replaced it with a school ball field and BASE system (believe, achieve, solve, and envision). This allowed children to move their clip around the bases as they engaged in positive behavior. The best benefit is that the new system increased children's positive behavior. Using the new system also helped teachers put their energy and focus on positive behaviors. They felt more effective and enjoyed their time in the classroom more. They are no longer dealing with the negative outcomes of the take-away system. Parents, teachers, and students are "on the team" to be on BASE every day.

Research on the Run

Helping Children Learn Skills to Be Successful

- Discipline that focuses on punishment in an attempt to turn behavior around only makes behavior worse, complicates the emotional reactions of children, and makes discipline more problematic (Cornell & Mayer, 2010; Washburn, Stowe, Cole, & Robinson, 2007).

- Schools must stop being reactive to behavior and begin addressing the skills that children need to be successful in social interactions (Skiba, 2000).

- "Teacher training in appropriate and culturally competent methods of classroom management is likely . . . to be the most pressing need in addressing racial disparities in school discipline" (Skiba, Michael, & Nardo, 2000, p. 17).

- A critical role of high-quality preschool is to provide all children with the opportunity to learn needed social skills. Teachers need to receive ongoing training in positive guidance to ensure that children receive these skills. Teachers can intervene early to support children's success and should use productive rather than punitive methods, such as positive reinforcement and descriptive feedback, as well as teaching positive prosocial skills (McCabe & Frede, 2007).

- Making sure that teachers receive clear training in classroom management basics is essential, as teachers may bring prior experiences and personality factors into their discipline and teaching decisions (Decker & Rimm-Kaufman, 2008).

Knowing Which Skills Are Important

- Prosocial skills such as sharing, cooperating, and being respectful are as important to long-term success as academic strategies (McCelland & Morrison, 2003).

- Socialization skills are influenced by socioeconomic backgrounds. Adequately providing skills for all children's success is an integral part of supporting children from every cultural background, particularly children who are English language learners (Flores, 2001).

- Focusing attention on supporting emotional security and social skills such as sitting, paying

attention, and getting along are just as important as reading and math, especially to children who experience early stress (Pollak, 2008; Thompson & Raikes, 2007).

- More conversations about emotions with young children can result in greater emotional understanding, a significant factor in emotional competence (Raikes & Thompson, 2006).

- When children are able to regulate their feelings and emotions, they are more liked by their teachers and peers and are better learners. Social–emotional competence is a critical foundation block for ongoing school success and must be supported in positive and proactive ways (Denham, 2006; Denham, Bassett, Kalb, Mincic, Wyatt, Graling, et al., 2009).

- Very young children are vulnerable to the feelings others communicate about them and cannot protect themselves from the way others treat them. It is important for them to feel loved, supported, and nurtured by their caregivers (Graham-Bermann & Hughes, 2003).

- Whether a child gains emotional competence during early childhood years will affect how that child feels about himself, as well as his mental health and well-being throughout his school years and for the rest of his life (Denham, 2005; Denham, Blair, DeMulder, Levitas, Sawyer, Auerbach-Major, et al., 2003).

- "Promoting school readiness is not simply a matter of encouraging literacy and number skills. It must also ensure the secure, unhurried, focused attention from sensitive caregivers that contributes to the growth of curiosity, the eagerness to discover, self-confidence, and cooperation. . . . Sensitive caregiving underpins healthy development . . . Relationships also influence the growth of social and emotional understanding" (Thompson, 2004).

Getting Positive Results Using the Principles in Action

What happened or led up to the interaction?

_____

_____

_____

Which principle did you use?

_____

_____

_____

How did the situation turn out? (How did the child/children respond?)

_____

_____

_____

What did you learn?

_____

_____

_____

What happened or led up to the interaction?

_____

_____

_____

Which principle did you use?

_____

_____

_____

How did the situation turn out? (How did the child/children respond?)

_____

_____

_____

What did you learn?

_____

_____

_____

Guide to the Principles

72. Pay Attention: Keep your eyes and mind on what is happening. Don't wait until the child is out of control to step in.

73. Remember Who the Grown-Ups Are: Always remember that you are the grown-up and that you are ultimately responsible for the way things turn out. The child does not have your judgment or history of experiences and can't be held responsible for the ultimate outcome.

74. Keep It Simple: "We need to be kind to our friends." "Time for a nap." "Remember the rules." "Gentle hands." "Walking feet." Stating things simply keeps us and our listener focused on the real issue and lets us both stay level-headed about what needs to be done.

75. Blame It on the Rules: "Our school rule is to wash your hands before eating." It is important to tell children why rules exist, so that they have a framework when they are reminded of a rule. Once the groundwork of understanding is set, "blaming it on the rules" can help the child follow through.

76. Shrug: Learn to shrug instead of arguing. The shrug means, "I'm sorry, but that's the way it is—end of discussion."

77. Preparation: Let the child know ahead of time what to expect: "We can go outside and play 'Duck, Duck, Goose' for 20 minutes. Then we have to come back and get in our seats quickly and quietly."

78. Hand Gestures: Develop hand gestures that signify "Please," "Thank you," "More," "Stop," "Be careful," "Use your words," and "All done."

79. Cueing: Give the child a cue to remind him—ahead of time—of the behavior you want him to exhibit.

80. Switch Gears: When the unexpected occurs, look for a way to make the most of the situation. For example, if you have a long wait, suggest that each of you close your eyes and listen for what you can hear, or look around and find something you have never noticed before. Another name for this principle is "The Plan B Principle." When plan A falls through, then let's make plan B more interesting than plan A might have been.

81. Do the Unexpected: React in a surprising way. Start doing jumping jacks! Clap a familiar rhythm such as "Jingle Bells" to relieve the tension and get some perspective. It is amazing how much better you can think and then decide on a more rational way to handle the situation when your head is clear.

82. **Thinking:** Take time to think about your options and consider the outcome. Will it be positive? How do you want this to turn out?

83. **Satiation:** If a behavior is not dangerous, destructive, embarrassing, or an impediment to learning, let it continue until the child is tired of doing it.

Study Guide

a. **Goal Setting:** How do you feel your upbringing affected your views about children's behavior? What was an important lesson taught by your family about the way you should behave? Do you think this idea or belief affects the way you respond (or feel) when children misbehave?

b. **Questioning and Reflection:** Name a classroom expectation that you want to be consistent in explaining and following through. When are you most likely to be inconsistent about it? How will staying consistent affect children's behavior over time? How can the principles in this chapter help children want to cooperate? (See "Encouraging Children to Cooperate" on pages 191–193.)

c. **Case Study:** Mr. Matthews is expecting a visit from his supervisor on Friday. He recognizes the sound of irritation sneaking into his voice and hears himself starting in on a "lecture" as he tries to finish a math unit before the end of the week. He can't quite seem to get the children focused, in spite of the new counting materials. How can he accomplish the desired outcomes with much more pleasant results for himself and the children? Use Principles 80 (Switch Gears) and 81 (Do the Unexpected) along with the tips on pages 194–195 to provide a new plan of action for Mr. Matthews.

d. **Personal Examples/Group Brainstorming:** Describe a behavior or persistent interaction that has been frustrating to you. How did you respond in the past? Decide what skills the children need to be successful in negotiating this situation next time. What principle will support

each new skill? Why will the principle you have chosen be effective? (See the "Building New Skills" section on pages 199–200.)

e. **Learners as Experts:** Give two examples of "take aways" that you use or know that others use. Now turn those examples around and explain how you can create an opportunity for children to move up, be reinforced, or gain privileges individually or as a group as they reach their goals. (See page 197 for examples.)

f. **Principles in Action:** Using the "Getting Positive Results Using the Principles in Action" sheet, share one principle you implemented from this chapter. What happened or led up to the interaction? Which principle did you use? How did the situation turn out? (How did the child/children respond?) What did you learn?

g. **Research on the Run:** After reviewing this section, how do you think this chapter has helped you become more proactive—and less reactive—in preventing misbehavior? How does the use of positive guidance make discipline decisions more equitable for children of all races and cultures? How does positive guidance affect the way a child feels about himself and his relationship to learning?

h. **Looking Ahead:** Set the purpose for upcoming study by introducing chapter objectives. Thank you for sharing your personal insight about responsive, positive guidance and for your commitment to making a difference in the lives of children.

References

Cornell, D., & Mayer, M. (2010). Why do school order and safety matter? *Educational Researcher, 39*(1), 7–15.

Decker, L., & Rimm-Kaufman, S. E. (2008). Personality characteristics and teacher beliefs among pre-service teachers. *Teacher Education Quarterly, 35*(2), 45–64.

Denham, S. A. (2005). The emotional basis of learning and development in early childhood education. In B. Spodek (Ed.), *Handbook of research in early childhood education* (pp. 85–103). Mahwah, NJ: Lawrence Erlbaum.

Denham, S. (2006). Social–emotional competence as support for school readiness: What is it and how do we assess it? *Early Education and Development, Special Issue: Measurement of School Readiness, 17,* 57–89.

Denham, S., Bassett, H., Kalb, S., Mincic, M., Wyatt, T., Graling, K., & Warren, H. (2009). How preschoolers' social and emotional competence predicts their school-readiness: Development of competency-based assessments. *Advances in SEL Research Newsletter, 3*(1), 11–13.

Denham, S., Blair, K., DeMulder, E., Levitas, J., Sawyer, K., Auerbach-Major, S., & Queenan, P. (2003). Preschool emotional competence: Pathway to social competence. *Child Development, 74,* 238–256.

Flores, B. (2001). Bilingual education teachers' beliefs and their relation to self-reported practices. *Bilingual Research Journal, 25,* 276–299.

Graham-Bermann, S., & Hughes, H. (2003). Intervention for children exposed to interparental violence (IPV): Assessments of needs and research priorities. *Clinical Child and Family Psychology Review, 6,* 189–204.

McCabe, L., & Frede, E. (2007, December). Challenging behaviors and the role of preschool education, National Institute for Early Education Research (NIEER) Report, Issue 16. Retrieved from http://nieer.org/resources/policybriefs/16.pdf

McClelland, M., & Morrison, F. (2003). The emergence of learning-related social skills in preschool children. *Early Childhood Research Quarterly, 18,* 206–224.

Pollak, S. (2008). Mechanisms linking early experience and the emergence of emotions: Illustrations form the study of maltreated children. *Current Directions in Psychological Science, 17*(6), 370–375.

Raikes, A. H., & Thompson, R.A. (2006). Family emotional climate, attachment security and young children's emotion knowledge in a high-risk sample. *British Journal of Developmental Psychology, 24,* 89–101.

Skiba, M. (2000). Zero tolerance, zero evidence: An analysis of school disciplinary practice. Policy Research Report No. SRS2. Bloomington: Indiana University, Indiana Education Policy Center.

Skiba, R., Michael, R., & Nardo, A. (2000, June). The color of discipline: Sources of racial and gender disproportionality in school punishment. Policy Research Report SRS1. Bloomington: Indiana University, Indiana Education Policy Center. Retrieved July 15, 2011, from www.indiana.edu/%7Esafeschl/cod.pdf

Thompson, R. A. (2004). Shaping the brains of tomorrow: What developmental science teaches about the importance of investing early in children. *The American Prospect, 15*(11). Retrieved October 28, 2011, from http://prospect.org/article/shaping-brains-tomorrow

Thompson, R. A., & Raikes, H. A. (2007). The social and emotional foundations of school readiness. In D. F. Perry, R. F. Kaufmann, & J. Knitzer (Eds.), *Social and emotional health in early childhood: Building bridges between services and systems* (pp. 13–35). Baltimore, MD: Paul H. Brookes Publishing Co.

Washburn, S., Stowe, K., Cole, C., & Robinson, J. (2007). Improving school climate and student behavior: A new paradigm for Indiana schools. *Education Policy Brief, 5*(9), 1–8.

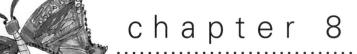

chapter 8

Creating Solutions to Common Behavior Challenges

In this chapter you will learn to apply specific strategies that ensure positive resolutions to common behavior challenges. You will be able to evaluate the environment, resources, and interactions in order to take constructive steps that result in lasting solutions. Even behaviors that previously seemed impossible to change can be guided effectively. As you add new tools to your growing set of responses, you will be able to create an effective plan of action.

The principles, strategies, and skills presented in this chapter will help you move forward with a greater understanding of behavior guidance. When children's behavior is unexpected or challenging, you will need to make intentional decisions about the kind of responses that will be most effective. You will be able to step in with confidence to help children turn around any issues that need to be addressed.

Chapter Principles

84: Nip It in the Bud

85: Use Actions Instead of Words

86: Divide and Conquer

87: Stay Detached Emotionally

88: Take a Break

89: The Timer Says It's Time

90: Get Support from Another Person

91: Change of Environment

92: Wait Until Later

93: Write a Contract

94: Collect Data

95: ABC

Chapter Objectives

As you explore the text and activities in this chapter, you will be able to:

* Keep your cool to become highly effective in supporting behavior change

* Learn and implement six steps to help children create successful solutions

- Know when to act instead of ignore behaviors
- Influence positive behavior without unintentionally reinforcing misbehavior
- Use available environmental, social, and human resources to support positive behavior change
- Maximize time, materials, and teaching strategies to make healthy behavior become permanent

Dealing with Persistent Behaviors in Multiple Contexts

In the previous chapter you learned how to prevent misbehavior by planning ahead, building skills, and helping children find solutions to challenges before they become frustrated. However, when behaviors are dangerous, destructive, embarrassing, or an

impediment to learning, we cannot ignore them and hope that they will go away. In fact, ignoring them actually makes them worse, because a child is aware that we are present and not doing anything about it. Therefore, our lack of response gives him permission to continue. Children need someone to step in and actually stop the misbehavior.

Some teachers feel that they can intervene effectively during lessons, but struggle with behavior issues while children are at centers, outdoors, during transitions, waiting in line, or in the bathroom. One situation is more structured, whereas the others require careful support of routines, procedures, and movement. Perhaps a specific child presents a persistent behavior that feels like a challenge when we are occupied with other children. We need to consider how our choices will affect the outcome.

Children respond differently to different teachers. All of us have seen a group of children engaged and motivated in one classroom, but unproductive and disorganized in another. The teacher is the one who makes the difference.

Knowing When to Take Action: Six Steps to Successful Solutions

The following sections will provide the skills a teacher needs to turn things around when you *do* need to intervene with misbehavior (that which is dangerous, destructive, embarrassing to the child or to others, or an impediment to learning). You or another adult or an assistant will follow the six steps for turning behavior around.

1. Learning when to act—instead of ignore
2. Moving close and avoiding eye contact
3. Guiding in the least reinforcing way
4. Deciding who needs to take a break
5. Getting support from another person
6. Addressing the issue later

● **THINK ABOUT IT!**

Can you describe a classroom that you would call chaotic? What were the children doing? How was the teacher responding?

_____

_____

_____

Now describe a classroom that impressed you with the attentiveness of the children and the effectiveness of the teacher. What do you think made the difference?

_____

_____

_____

Decide whether the following behaviors need to be stopped. How would you normally respond to this behavior?

- Going up the slide instead of down _____
- Throwing sand _____
- Running in the hall _____
- Yelling to friends down the hall _____
- Hitting a classmate _____
- Cutting in line _____
- Other _____

I. Learning When to Act—Instead of Ignore

Many teachers make the mistake of turning all their attention to misbehavior—looking at the child, scolding, talking about what happened, and asking reasons for it, yet not realizing that they have stopped instruction to place all their attention on the misbehaving child. In addition, the other children can see that misbehavior pays off by getting attention.

As children grow past the preschool years and move into early elementary school, the decision about when to redirect and when to intervene can have significant impact on the way a situation will turn out. We need to decide ahead of time which issues are nonnegotiable and then follow through with firm limits. The following principles will help you recognize when to intervene, how to give support, and why consistency is so important.

 ## *Principle 84: Nip It in the Bud*

When you see a child doing something that is dangerous, destructive, or embarrassing (to you or to himself), take immediate action. Don't let the behavior continue, hoping that it will go away. It usually gets worse if the child knows you are watching and you are doing nothing about it. Giving a hand signal might be enough. You might also whisper a code word, such as "red light," that always means "Stop right now!"

Remember that a child who is misbehaving may not be paying attention to you, but is focused on what he is doing. He may not be aware of your cue. You might have to move toward the child, take his hand, and move him to another place in the *least reinforcing way possible*. This means that even when you approach or move a child, you do not make eye contact or talk with him.

Remember that when you do stop a behavior, it is important to provide a new plan of action immediately. Use the 101 principles to punt the plan or switch gears, and then quickly move on to something else by redirecting the child to a new activity. Use an incompatible alternative to move the child on *without* giving attention to the old behavior. When we need to step in and "nip it in the bud," this action is never meant as punishment or to make a child feel bad about what happened. It simply is a matter-of-fact way to move the child forward into a constructive activity.

Many young children become deeply immersed in an activity and do not easily stop to shift their attention to something new. When you give instructions, it is important to be sure you are standing near a child who needs extra support, rather than across the room. Before you take action, be sure the child has a chance to focus on you and hear the directions and expectations clearly. Be sure he has enough time to shift and that he can carry out what you have asked.

It is important to be sensitive. Sometimes a child may interpret a cue in a different way or misunderstand instructions. Be sure that the child understands ahead of time what cues mean. Some cultures do not interpret "the look" as a warning sign, whereas other children are socialized to watch adult faces carefully. Hidden communication rules (assumed expectations) need to be clarified. Children may not have the background knowledge or social understanding to pick up on subtle cues. Any and all expectations must be taught and *must be explicit*, including the cues that you use to gain a child's attention.

Make sure to teach and practice a cue first. Have the child repeat the sign or words back to you, so that you are certain that he associates the cue with the expectation. For example, the teacher may touch two fingers together as she gives instructions, and ask that children who have heard and can do what is asked touch two fingers together in response. This action or cue may need to be rehearsed until you are certain a child can respond independently. However, if you are sure a child understands instructions and you can still see that it is not working for him, then it is time to intervene.

You may need to evaluate other ways a child best responds to support (e.g., a friend to help him put things away), and check to be sure that he hasn't missed the cue because his attention has been focused elsewhere. The child may need a touch on the shoulder or another "attention shifter" that works for him. (A picture card slipped on his desk to remind him to look up works well as an individual cue. A soft bell that he is asked to ring to help him to stop and listen can instill cooperation when you next need to give directions.) Children want to be competent and will appreciate your help.

However, if we sometimes let behaviors go and do not follow through consistently, then children are being trained to only pay attention when the teacher begins to sound upset or concerned. The more clear we are about the expectation and the more we review needed rules about safety and behavior, the less surprised children will be when we ask them to follow through.

● **THINK ABOUT IT!**

If you see two children shoving in the hall, how would you stop the behavior immediately in the least reinforcing way using a strategy from Nip It in the Bud? (Be sure to review pages 213 and 214.)

_____

_____

_____

If you see two children doing something dangerous on the playground, what would you do to stop the behavior immediately in the least reinforcing way using a strategy from Nip It in the Bud? (For example, state the rule and quickly get them involved in another activity.)

_____

_____

_____

There are many ways that children embarrass each other. What would you do to stop the following behaviors without embarrassing anyone further and in the least reinforcing way? (Be sure that you have seen the behaviors yourself.)

- Messing up another child's hair _____
- Shoving a child so that he cries after falling down _____

    _____
- Pulling a child's chair out from under him so that he lands on the floor _____

    _____
- Saying that a child smells when parents haven't given her a bath _____

    _____
- Calling a child "four eyes" when she has to wear glasses _____

    _____
- "Horsing around" at the drinking fountain _____

    _____
- Not letting a child be heard by talking over him _____
- Snatching away something that belongs to a child _____

II. Moving Close and Avoiding Eye Contact

Move close to the child, *giving him as little eye contact as possible*. Keep your eyes on the other children. When behaviors are inadvertently reinforced, they are more likely to increase. So we want to focus the child and ourselves on supporting positive behaviors. Investing our focus forward may seem counterintuitive, but it is important to remind ourselves that attention (even eye contact) can be highly reinforcing—meaning that it encourages the behavior to continue.

When we are encouraging an infant to go to sleep, but he is fussing, we want to pat his back to reassure him of our presence, but not talk or give eye contact. This soothes and settles the infant, rather than stimulating him with our voice and focus. He may mistake this attention as a message to wake up and play. Similarly, we want to give a child as little reinforcement as possible for misbehavior, and use every opportunity to move forward and guide, teach, and support the new skills he needs for the future. Just moving him on can be enough. He realizes by our quiet, consistent actions that the alternate activity we are showing him is a better choice. He must be certain that we are serious about enforcing it every time.

Remember that our ultimate goal is not to stop misbehavior. When we think about changing children's behavior in that way, we are simply reacting to what has already happened. To be effective, we want to give as little attention, stimulation, or reinforcement as possible to a previous incident. We want to guide the child's attention toward what we want him to be doing, and toward children who are engaging in learning. We want to focus on the primary purpose of strengthening positive relationships and interaction skills.

Sometimes the most effective strategy requires only common sense, but when the time comes, we miss the opportunity to step in because the strategy does not occur to us at the moment. Practicing the 101 principles and naming them (silently to yourself) as you use them is a good way to get in the habit of looking forward and being proactive. Creating an intentional plan for success will help you use effective guidance strategies.

III. Guiding in the Least Reinforcing Way

If a child persists in a behavior that needs to be stopped, take him by the hand and gently move him, but do not talk to him at this time. Laughter, surprise, or highly charged concern over a child's actions will teach him that he is capable of getting a lot of attention or evoking a big response with his behavior. Staying detached emotionally, using positive redirection, moving the child in the least reinforcing way, or changing the environment can all be productive ways to interrupt the behavior without reinforcing it. The following principles will let you take action to guide behavior without inadvertently reinforcing it through attention or discussion.

Principle 85: Use Actions Instead of Words

Don't say anything. Instead of responding when a child says something inappropriate or hurtful, let the words hang in the air. Walk away or take his hand and move to another place. Give him a chance to hear what he just said. Very often, he will make an effort to self-correct or apologize.

Taking a child by the hand and walking him to a quiet place without saying anything allows him to hear and reflect on what he has just said and on what has happened.

When you have moved the child to another location and walked away, he knows what he has done is inappropriate. You have given him time to think about what he should do next. Your calm actions, completed without words, show him that he is capable of changing a situation by himself, without you telling him what to do.

When we keep the atmosphere cool, we give the child mental and emotional space to deal with and think for himself. We stay connected with the child and do not waste energy becoming unnecessarily upset. We want to encourage a child to deal responsibly with his actions, self-correct, make things right, and remember to make a better choice next time. Using actions instead of words accomplishes this goal.

When one child hurts another, rather than face the child who has misbehaved, we want to turn *all of our attention* to the child who was hurt and say, "I am sorry that happened. I would never do that to you. I am sorry your ears had to hear that. I am sorry you were hurt." By turning our attention to the hurt child, the behavior does not pay off for the one who instigated it. The child who is hurt is the one directly in front of us, and the child who misbehaved receives no immediate focus. Comfort and support the hurt child. Then take the other child by the hand and walk him to a quiet place without discussion. This child will learn through your actions of empathy and comfort to the other child. The quietness you provide for him will give him time to reflect without the use of confrontation or invested energy in the misbehavior.

Consistency will require practice and effort on your part. Most people are used to talking instead of being quiet. You will need to practice until it becomes comfortable. You may need to counteract your desire to talk to the child, especially if his behavior has interrupted an activity or has been hurtful to another child. Your actions will be enough to show the children that you are protecting their safety and ensuring the best interest of all.

● **THINK ABOUT IT!**

Describe a situation where you would move a child without giving eye contact or saying anything. Do you think the child will know what he needs to correct without your saying it?

_____

_____

Principle 86: Divide and Conquer

Separate children who are reinforcing each other's misbehavior.

Two children are sitting next to each other in circle time. They keep nudging, pulling, and pushing each other and not paying attention to the story. Rather than ask one of the boys to move (which would give attention to them), ask another child to sit between them. Make a mental note to separate the children the next time they come to the circle, or have an adult sit between them.

A group of school-aged children has become distracted by loud street noises. You want them to focus on learning. Divide the large group into several smaller groups and assign specific tasks to each group. Using common sense and acting quickly will diminish most issues. Smart teaching involves being vigilant to organize children so that they stay eagerly involved in learning.

🦋 Principle 87: Stay Detached Emotionally

Try to remain objective, with your eye on the goal of self-discipline. Don't let the child "hook" you emotionally—in other words, don't take his behavior personally.

We all have "hot buttons"! Ever notice how the same issues seem to come up again and again in our relationships? Children are intuitive and can find these areas that seem to set us off. It is difficult to step outside the immediate conversation and take a third-person view of the action—and to remain objective.

An important key to staying detached emotionally is to understand how our escalating emotions actually fuel the intensity of children's response to us. The calmer we stay and the more rational the words we choose, the more likely children will match our demeanor.

Often when a child is upset, he simply needs a few minutes to calm himself down, and so we can provide him with those minutes and then return to listen calmly and validate his feelings. If we get upset with him, it keeps him from calming down, and from being able to think and let the issue go. When we stay respectful and quiet with him, then he gets a moment to get himself together within our presence.

We may need to turn away and let the child come around on his own. When we give him space and a moment to calm down and cooperate, this lets him save his dignity. For example, when we have given instructions to put things away, turn away and give the child time to get the job done rather than stand there and wait (which could feel like a challenge to the child). This is what we would want someone to do for us if we were upset, and it is extremely important to provide this anchor of stability to a child.

● **THINK ABOUT IT!**

What "hot buttons" do you have that children know how to push? Describe the experience. How do you normally react? How can you stay emotionally detached next time this happens?

_____

_____

_____

_____

_____

IV. Deciding Who Needs to Take a Break

Our aim is to help children practice a needed skill or interaction in a successful way, so that they can remember and accomplish it independently in the future. We don't want them to become dependent on us to calm or stop them, but to develop self-control. The following strategies, when used with respect and consistency, will weaken power struggles and show children that you trust their ability to meet needed expectations.

Principle 88: Take a Break

Tell the child to take a break and think about what he could do differently that would work better or be more constructive. Give him a place to go until he is ready to come back and behave more productively. This could be a place that you have created in your classroom that is comfortable and quiet. A timer is sometimes helpful. The child can determine how long he needs to reflect, refocus, and calm down. The child is in control here. He can decide when he is ready to rejoin the group or try again.

   You need to encourage a child to take a break when he has stepped over the limit, has hurt another child, can't seem to get in control or listen to an adult, or is causing disruption for others. You can provide a table in the back of the classroom where a child can go to be alone. In a young children's classroom, you might have a beanbag chair for this purpose. However, every measure should be taken to keep children present during instruction and learning activities. Be sure to review positive strategies for guiding behavior and promote active participation so that children can be successful.

   With young children, it often works well to give them a timer and ask how long they need to be upset. They may choose two or five minutes and then you can set the timer while they remove themselves from the others. When the timer goes off, they will come back, usually ready to join into the activities.

   Research shows that a break works much better when the child is able to decide for himself when the break is over and when he is ready to rejoin the group. This is not the same as a time out, where an adult is in control of assigning the duration. Instead, Take a Break allows the child to choose the amount of time and control the time away by changing his behavior. That is very critical to long-term development of positive behavior and instilling cooperation, which is our goal.

   It might be that you are the one who needs to take a break. You may need to take a deep breath, close your eyes, or count to ten while you gain a better perspective. If you realize that a child can benefit from a break, it might be helpful to send him to another teacher with

whom you have a pre-arranged agreement. An infant may calm after a few minutes with another teacher. A toddler may need time to refocus, or an older child can take a few minutes to complete reading or homework. The teacher is catching herself before she feels upset with the child and knows that a change of scenery might help.

● **THINK ABOUT IT!**

Describe a time when you think it was you who needed the break! How could you have taken it?

_____

_____

Principle 89: The Timer Says It's Time

Set a timer to help children make transitions. "When the timer goes off, you will need to put away your books." "In five minutes, we will need to line up for lunch." It is a good idea to give the child a chance to choose how long he needs to pull himself together: "It's okay to be upset. How long do you need?" Then allow him to remove himself from the group and set the timer. You may offer the child a choice (and set the timer) when it is necessary to encourage cooperation: "Do you want to pick up the blocks/let Susan have the wagon/share the computer in one minute or two?"

A teacher discovered an effective use of the timer when she said to an upset, tantruming child, "It's OK to be mad. How long do you need to cry?" The child wailed, "Five minutes!" The teacher set the timer and left it with the child. When it "dinged" after five minutes, the child turned off the tears and rejoined the group. Use your professional judgment to be sure the child is not in distress and in need in comfort or other intervention.

It's not only wise, but it is a kind gesture to give children a time signal before they need to shift gears and move on to another activity. You also can allow a child to be the timer person for the day. Attach the timer to him (or hand him the timer if it is an older child) and let him announce to the others, "Five more minutes before snack is over." When the timer goes off, the children will automatically start clearing their tables.

Adults have a clear concept of time and a preconceived idea about how the day is to be spent. It is easy to forget that children don't have this perspective and need advance notice when they will be asked to shift gears. It is upsetting to us when circumstances interrupt our day. Children need our respect and help in making successful transitions.

V. Getting Support from Another Person

A critical step in guiding behavior is to utilize all available resources. We can use others to reinforce positive interactions and make adjustments to the environment. Our planning can create a strong, interconnected system to support children's success. The following principles will encourage you to make the most of all of your available resources.

● **THINK ABOUT IT!**

Describe a behavior in your classroom that could be solved by using The Timer Says It's Time Principle. Explain how you will use it with a specific child.

_____

_____

_____

_____

_____

Principle 90: Get Support from Another Person

Ask someone else to help you reinforce the positive behavior.

Your relationship with your co-teacher and colleagues is an important asset. Make sure that your co-teacher or assistant teacher is present to fully model appropriate behavior and participate in activities such as singing, dancing, or other games. During teaching times and book reading, he or she should be nodding and paying attention. This sets a very important example to children. While children are in the classroom, they are your priority.

During group activities, young children need extra support. An assistant can quietly move to sit near and support children during lesson times by patting or rubbing their back gently if they need calming. For older children, when an assistant is not present, involving parents and other caring adults is helpful to reinforce positive social and academic behaviors.

Ms. Kim, a first-year teacher, was having trouble inspiring Jasmine to read out loud. The child seemed hesitant and acted shy when she was asked to read. Ms. Kim asked for the principal's help. Mrs. Sturdevant offered to come into the room and see if she could do anything to encourage Jasmine. Later in the day, she dropped by and went around the room, asking children to read to her, smiling at them, and validating their efforts.

When she got to Jasmine, she knelt down beside her and asked if she would read. The child looked up and said, "Why do you want me to read? Don't *you* know how?" The principal laughed. She loved the child's honest response. "Yes, I know how to read, but your teacher told me that you are good at it, too. I was wondering if we could read together." She took the child's hand and led her to the back corner of the room where no one else would hear. Happily, the little girl began to read aloud.

This teacher was very wise to get the support of another person, especially a prestigious person like a principal or a beloved grandparent. It is often easy to ask someone else to casually reinforce or pay attention to a child when he is doing the right thing and to give added encouragement. If we get the support of someone else, we may find that his or her resources can save the day!

● **THINK ABOUT IT!**

If you feel irritated by a child's behavior and you are about to lose your cool, how might you get the support of another adult before you engage in behavior you might regret?

_____

_____

_____

What are some other strategies you could use to get a better perspective?

_____

_____

_____

Principle 91: Change of Environment

If the children's misbehavior cannot be stopped, move to another room or location or go outside.

It had been raining all week and the teachers were tired of having to stay inside, as were the children. "I can't believe it's raining again," Ms. Brooke said to another teacher as they met in the hall that morning. "It looks like rain all day."

"Why don't we trade classrooms around mid-morning?" asked the other teacher. "You bring your children over and we can switch rooms. We will let them have a different environment. What do you think?" Ms. Brooke readily agreed: "Great, why don't we try it?" Each prepared their classroom, and the children were excited about the change. When they met at lunch, the teachers agreed that the change of environment had worked well.

There are many times when going outside or moving to another room can help break a cycle and give a needed change of pace. You can take children to the hall, outdoors under a tree, or to the library. Be sure to plan ahead to negotiate a different environment and bring needed materials with you. Changing environments can help both children and adults get a fresh perspective.

VI. Addressing the Issue Later

The final step in guiding behavior is to determine when and how to talk with the child about the issue that needs to be resolved. We want to help him see all of his options and think through useful skills to assist him in solving the problem in the future. The following two principles will help you to address the issues in the most effective way.

Principle 92: Wait Until Later

You can say, "Let's both think about this and come back in 10 minutes to discuss it." Then set the timer. That gives the child (and you) time to consider the actions and think about the best way to handle it. With an older child, you may say, "We'll discuss this at 2:00. We both need time to cool off and think." Then you can meet calmly with the child and say, "Let's talk about what happened. What would a better choice have been?"

Because teaching often calls for quick decision-making, we may be tempted to issue an ultimatum we cannot enforce, or that we later feel was not necessary. In order to avoid this, it is good to take time to cool off and think. Telling the child that you need to consider the options or give it some thought not only helps you make a better decision, but it gives the child time to think about what happened. Later, when the child is in a fresh mindset, he will be ready to offer solutions and problem-solve about what can be done more effectively next time.

If a child engaged in behavior that was not safe, we can say, "This is not okay. I can't let you do that. What can I do to help you remember?" This diffuses defensiveness, sets aside power struggles, and puts you and the child into a problem-solving mindset that will result in positive solutions.

We want to help the child develop internal self-regulation, rather than become dependent on us to intervene in his behavior choices. We do not know a child's emotional state or his feelings at the moment he has misbehaved. We cannot assume because he looks or sounds calm that he is calm. We want to wait until later when we are both calm, not distracted, have time to think of better ways to handle the issue, and that we have time to really listen. Then, we can encourage insight about the behavior and build empathy toward others' perspectives and needs.

When we do talk things through, we need to stay sensitive to the child's experiences and ability to understand. With infants, we nurture and model. With toddlers, we guide, demonstrate, and provide support for developing competence. With preschoolers, we support problem-solving processes at higher levels and encourage thinking about how others feel. In early elementary school, we build a sense of responsibility and personal investment in the classroom community. At each level, children need calm assurance and individual support.

● **THINK ABOUT IT!**

Can you remember a time when you did not wait until later and regretted your words or actions? Were you able to repair your relationship with that person? What do you wish you had said or done instead?

_____

_____

_____

Principle 93: Write a Contract

Sit with the child after he has behaved appropriately and the negative emotions have disappeared and write a contract together for future behavior. Be sure to let him have input. Then both parties sign the contract. (This works for older children.)

When children are old enough, it is very useful to give them the opportunity to put their thoughts and feelings in writing. There are many forms that you can use as children are asked to write about what happened to them. One option is to provide "think sheets." The think sheets have three parts: "What happened/What I did/What I will do differently next time?" These questions are very useful and give the child an opportunity to reflect on his behavior so that he will be better prepared in the future to handle the same kind of incident in a more constructive way.

Teachers can help by giving children the opportunity to think through their problems and to plan solutions. After writing a contract, the child and teacher can sign it together. This is a positive conclusion to a problem that has already been solved.

Often children will know that another child has presented past struggles for them and will decide that they should avoid contact in the classroom, lunch line, or playground. Andrew and Collin seemed to have this kind of relationship. When they were not together, each of them was able to obey the rules, listen carefully, get their work done, and engage in activities with a pleasant demeanor. However, they had a hard time negotiating when they were together. Their teacher asked each of them to write down their observations about the problem. This gave them the opportunity to talk together about what was bothering them and to find times when they could work together for a common goal.

If a particular behavior is a persistent problem, brainstorming or holding a class meeting to discuss the situation can be helpful. When we do discuss solutions, our top priority is to remember the Golden Rule Principle and to ask, "How would I want this to be said to me?" We want to approach children with deep respect, knowing they are growing in their understanding and are sensitive to the responses of others.

We can ask children to write (or we can write) their positive choices on the board or on large paper. If we need to revisit the issues, we can whisper privately, "Which of those solutions would have been a better choice?" We want to turn our attention and theirs to the positive solutions.

Addressing Special Issues with Toddlers

Teachers often have questions about guiding behavior with toddlers. Young children require diligent supervision, quick thinking, and creative problem solving to keep issues from repeating. Before patterns get set, review the top 10 principles for guiding toddlers in Figure 8.1. Most behavior can be dealt with through these steps.

The key to successful support of toddlers includes the four Fs: fast, fun, fair, and firm. To keep toddlers safe and involved, all four of these essential ingredients must be present in the teacher's approach.

● **THINK ABOUT IT!**

Name one type of behavior in the classroom that you need to stop. How have you dealt with it in the past?

_____

_____

How would you use the principles you have just learned to intervene now?

_____

_____

Figure 8.1   Top 10 Principles for Toddlers

1. Incompatible Alternative: Give the child something to do that is incompatible with the inappropriate behavior. When the child is sitting/laying on a table: "We sit in the chair at the table so that we can do a puzzle."

2. When–Then/Abuse It–Lose It: "When you wash your hands, then you can play with the toys."

3. Choice: Give the child two choices, both of which are positive and acceptable to you: "Would you like to crawl like a tiger or hop like a rabbit to the diaper changing table?"

4. Establish Routines and Traditions: Toddlers behave better when they know what to expect. Routine helps them to feel competent and secure.

5. Divide and Conquer: Separate children who are reinforcing each other's misbehavior. Take a group of children to another part of the room or a different area when the classroom gets energetic.

6. Follow-Through/Consistency: Don't let the child manipulate you out of using your better judgment. Be firm, but kind.

7. Keep It Simple: Toddlers need simple statements: "Teeth are for eating, not biting." "Gentle hands." "Two feet on the floor." "Walking feet."

8. Nip It in the Bud: Keep your eyes and mind on what is happening. Don't wait until the child is out of control to step in. When you see a child doing something that is dangerous, destructive or embarrassing, take immediate action! Don't let the behavior continue. Use the above principles to switch gears.

9. Sing: Sing what you want the children to do. Get in the habit of making up songs with familiar tunes, such as "If You're Happy and You Know it" and "Jingle Bells," using words that describe what you would like the children to do.

10. Modeling: Toddlers are the masters of imitation. Their eyes are always watching. Make sure you model the behaviors you want to see.

● *Fast* means that toddlers move quickly and situations escalate rapidly. Always be on the lookout to anticipate children's needs so that you can intervene or use an incompatible alternative before the behavior gets out of control. Stay alert and scan the room constantly, always aware of what is going on. On the playground, have teachers spread out, ready to move quickly.

- *Fun* means that toddlers are fun and funny. Be sure to sit with them and listen to the way they see the world. Let them experience your delight in seeing experiences from their perspective. They have short attention spans and need to have enriched stimulation (activities, hands-on materials, music, rhymes, books, puppets) to keep them engaged. Make learning and playing fun. Laugh together frequently and look for funny and fun moments to enjoy.

- *Fair* means that toddlers need adequate materials, so that there are enough to go around and that rules and expectations are clear and consistent. Predictable routines, schedules, and expectations encourage understanding and security.

- *Firm* means that toddlers need limits. Boundaries help toddlers feel safe to explore and be curious. When you set routines for safety, transitions, meals, naps, bathroom activities, and daily plans, be certain that you follow through consistently and support autonomy within safe boundaries.

Making Good Use of the Environment

Sometimes we become so familiar with our surroundings that it is necessary to reevaluate with a critical eye. If children are bumping into each other or having continuing behavior issues during movement or transitions, consider adjusting the existing space. Moving a shelf back one foot can make a big difference. Adjusting the group area by several square feet can solve many behavior issues.

In the same way, we can evaluate how we arrange or seat children. Many teachers let children gather on a carpet for activities. Sometimes this results in a great deal of shifting and nudging. For toddlers and pre-K students, using individual carpet squares can help achieve several positive outcomes. Each child's name is affixed to the carpet piece. This gives the teacher the ability to reorganize (divide and conquer) children day by day, or as the need arises. If two children are distracting each other, the teacher can redistribute the carpet squares in a different order next time. After each activity, the squares are quickly picked up and stored on a shelf.

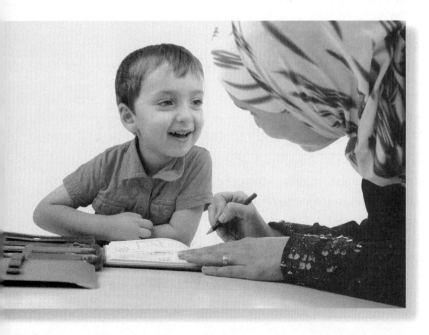

If you prefer to use a large area carpet instead of individual carpet squares, the principle is the same. When you organize children, do so wisely, adapting the seating arrangement to support children's focus. Some children feel more comfortable in chairs, and it is OK to let them choose to use a row of chairs in back. For older children, be sure to consider the best learning needs of each child, and to change seating and study arrangements in thoughtful ways.

Often, when misbehavior occurs, we focus on the child rather than evaluating the environment. This can be true for younger as well as older children. Biting can be stopped in toddler classrooms by changing the environment and the frequency in which adults intervene before children get frustrated. If children have to gain access to materials (toys, trucks, puzzles, etc.) by congregating in one area, this will invite frustration. Consider the following options instead:

- **Divide materials.** Set like materials in baskets around the room. This allows children to separate and gives them space to make choices without obstacles and interference.

- **Divide time segments.** Increase the frequency with which adults intervene and support children's learning and language. Young children need ongoing interaction and support in group contexts. Describe what the child is doing and ask questions. "I see you are putting the smaller blocks on top of the larger ones." "Which one will you choose next?" "How will the monkey come down from the tree?" Frustrations can be avoided when adults are involved and engaging children in meaningful conversation.

- **Divide spaces.** Provide a quiet space where children can be alone and "chill out." Several beanbag chairs grouped together in a corner is as important for first, second, and third graders as it is for preschoolers. When children know they can take a break before they get frustrated and calm themselves down when they feel upset, they are likely to be more responsible for their actions and responses. Use of this spot is encouraged for all children and is a way of supporting respect for children's feelings.

- **Arrange materials.** For children of all ages, arrange materials in order of use to help teach practical strategies. Provide pictures on a sheet of paper that illustrate the order of steps needed. Older children can slide a penny along the order of procedures. Younger children can move a larger plastic marker (small bear, dinosaur, etc.) down the sequence of steps as they complete them. The page can be laminated for repeated use. Using the materials you already have in new ways can help children avoid frustration.

- **Divide groups purposefully.** Rather than leave children in permanent assigned seating, use wisdom in pairing children to support learning and behavior. Vary desk and table arrangements. Adding space between tables or groups of desks can make all the difference in helping children concentrate on learning.

● THINK ABOUT IT!

How can you rearrange children, materials, or the environment to benefit your classroom? What changes will be helpful? You may want to stand in your classroom with a critical eye to determine which changes would have the most impact on behavior and learning.

_____

_____

_____

_____

Staying Objective and Collecting Data

In order to remain objective, we have to understand that our reactions to certain children often depend on factors other than objective analysis. When we step back and assess the situation, we may realize that one child's misbehavior doesn't actually occur as often as we thought it did. This child may simply be frustrating to us, and so we perceive that the behavior happens more frequently than it really does. For that reason, we are tempted to blame him for causing most disruptions in the classroom.

On the other hand, we may not feel another child (whom we like a lot!) does this same behavior very often. Keeping a record may show us that our perception is inaccurate, or reveal that other children are doing the same thing. The behavior may actually be a common problem that we need to address.

Once we see that the behavior is true of many, not just one, we can address it during a class meeting or talk about it as a group. We can review and rehearse the routine as a group to assure a positive outcome. Gathering data helps us quickly analyze the situation to make sure we are responding fairly and supporting the success of all children.

Principle 94: Collect Data

Keep a written record of the frequency of a specific behavior that seems to be continuing. Record the antecedents as well as the consequences. Look for patterns that may give clues as to possible reasons, situations, and/or solutions.

The experiences that precede a specific behavior are the antecedent. Be sure to record the antecedents as well as the results when behavior is working well. What do you notice is different between the two situations? Perhaps something in the environment or in the way an adult responds to this child has made the difference. It is as important to ask, "What is working well—and why?" as much as it is to consider, "What is not working well—and why not?" We may notice a repeated pattern that will help us give more consistent support for the child's success.

As soon as we realize a child's reaction or response has happened several times, we can step in quickly and examine what factors are contributing to it. We want to evaluate any contributing issues right away to see if there is anything we could change that would make a positive difference. We can examine our own actions, the environment, and the actions of others that precede the issue. We want to become thoughtful and purposeful to be sure we are best supporting children's success.

Mr. Howard realized that his toddlers were becoming more aggressive at the beginning of a play period. The next day, he watched carefully to see what happened beforehand. He realized that he had not provided enough of the specific type of trucks that they all wanted to play with. He also realized that the children were congregating in the same corner. By obtaining enough trucks and spacing them out in the room in baskets before playtime, he ensured that every child had equal access. The aggression immediately stopped. Paying attention to the antecedent provided a way for him to adjust the environment to be sure things went more smoothly.

Creating Thoughtful Solutions to Help Children Succeed

Sometimes when we see a child repeating persistent behaviors, we need to stop and assess the situation and see what we can do to make a difference. Sometimes we need to change our own behavior. Other times we can make changes in the environment that will affect a child's response. By watching carefully and keeping a record, we may notice experiences in the child's life that are bothering him or a personal struggle that might be contributing to the problem. We want to look for regular patterns that will help us understand what the child needs. Then we can support him when he needs assistance and become more sensitive to his feelings.

After we have observed carefully, we can sit down with other significant adults in the child's life and talk about ways to work together to address the behavior. Our discoveries can guide the kinds of questions and feedback we give as we support him in making better decisions.

Mrs. Davenport realized that Gavin was often aggressive toward other students when he returned from a weekly resource time outside of her classroom. She knew that she could not change or control what happened somewhere else, so she decided to change how she responded as soon as he returned to her classroom.

Realizing that she had normally been too busy to greet him, she was careful to adapt her approach when he returned. She gave him a touch on the shoulder and said, "I missed you. I am glad you are back. It wasn't the same without you." She did this each time he reentered her room. Within one week, Gavin stopped the aggression. By keeping track of her own responses as well as his, she realized that the outcome could be changed by providing support when Gavin returned to her classroom..

Ms. Draper worried about Jonathan. He had been whining constantly in the classroom and it was a growing concern. She decided to collect data and check the details. She noted how often the behavior happened and watched to see what had been going on before, during, and after the whining.

Ms. Draper was amazed how keeping track helped her to understand the situation better. "First, I realized the behavior wasn't happening as often as I thought. It had seemed he was whining all of the time! I had been worrying about it so much that it seemed like a bigger problem than it really was. When I understood the situation better, I redirected Jonathan's behavior to other activities without drawing attention to it. Much to my surprise, the whining quickly improved. I noticed that I had been responding with attention and sympathy, so I decided to ignore it completely. After that, Jonathan rarely whined."

We must pay attention to the environment and to other people in each situation, so that we can be wise in the ways we encourage and support children. Collecting data can help us see the big picture. As Ms. Draper and Mrs. Davenport did, we may find that there are many possible solutions.

Principle 95: ABC

Learn to think in terms of ABC: antecedent, behavior, and consequences. What was going on before the behavior occurred and what happened afterwards, as a result of the behavior?

● **THINK ABOUT IT!**

Consider children's behaviors in your classroom. What is working well—and why?

_____

_____

_____

What is not working well—and why not?

_____

_____

_____

For the situation you have just described (that is not working well), propose at least two changes that you can make that will help this child (or children) more successfully negotiate a solution.

_____

_____

_____

You can often find patterns in behavior, and accordingly alter your own behavior or the circumstances that led up to the inappropriate behavior. Also, you might need to look at what is gained by the behavior (how the child is benefitting as a result). A child who is overly tired may throw a temper tantrum. In order to get him to stop, he may be given a toy. In the future, he may throw a temper tantrum just to get a toy. Next time, when you realize that children are getting tired, stop and change your focus. Let them take a break to stretch, have a snack, or get a drink of water. By changing the antecedent and/or the consequences, a temper tantrum may be avoided in the future.

Birth to Age 3

- Responsive caregivers should anticipate children's needs and prepare ahead to avoid discomfort and crying. If an infant is fed on a schedule, the bottle should be ready ahead of time, before the baby shows signs of fussing.
- A toddler who is getting energetic can be given a job to do, such as passing out napkins. He is seated last at mealtime (because he is busy passing out napkins), so as to reduce his wait time.

Ages 3 to 8

- A preschooler who is highly interactive or aggressive with a particular peer can be gently guided to play with materials of high interest and encouraged to play with children with whom he more calmly interacts.

- A school-aged child who hasn't been following directions has a planning session with the teacher to walk through the steps he will need for an upcoming project. They can create plans for getting ready, such as working with a peer or following a checklist.

- Children are given the opportunity to "read around the room." This means that they can find a place in the room to read where they feel comfortable and can focus. They may choose to be under a table, under an easel, or on a beanbag, rather than their desk or table.

- Children are given the opportunity to choose a "sitting table" or a "standing table" if there are puzzles or center activities that might otherwise require sitting. Some children can focus a long while if given the option to stand and work.

Rather than become frustrated with the child, we can revisit our plan, reanalyze the factors, review the details with other teachers, and seek a solution that will support each child's physical, social, and cognitive needs. The best course of action is one that takes into consideration every possible option to adapt the environment, materials, lessons, interactions, and use of time to promote positive outcomes.

● **THINK ABOUT IT!**

What are some behaviors that continue to bother you in your classroom that could be remedied by collecting data?

_____

_____

_____

How can you create new routines or ways of approaching the schedule that will be beneficial to behavior in your classroom? How will these changes affect the outcome for the child?

_____

_____

_____

Making Behavior Change Permanent

The strategies in this chapter provide alternatives for supporting children's success that will change the way you approach your role as a teacher. You have options to use, whereas before you may have felt there were roadblocks. You now have skills to implement with children whose past behavior may have seemed impossible to address.

It is not necessary to understand why a child behaves in a certain way. We can never be certain of a child's feelings or motivations. Sometimes teachers ask, "Why did you do that?" However, children themselves are not always aware of the reasons, nor do they yet have the complexity to understand "why." Understanding a child's perspective is helpful for us to better support his overall development and to encourage us to be sensitive to his individual needs. However, the principles in this chapter work to turn behavior around, even if we do not understand the origins or reasons for it. We are able to affect outcomes by choosing effective words and actions, regardless of a child's motivations.

Implementing new strategies will soon become easier for you. Children will be watching you. They will feel the consistency in your expectations and see that you are giving them opportunities to adjust and adapt in new and better ways. As they see you provide more constructive options and more consistent support for their success, they will have more opportunities to develop the lasting skills they need. They will quickly adjust their behavior if you continue to be calm, responsive, and consistent while giving them opportunities to succeed.

Summary

Every behavior challenge represents an opportunity to connect with a child, to evaluate available resources, and to make constructive decisions about what strategies to use. Rather than be reactive, we can be proactive about our plans and responses. We want to provide safety and support each skill needed for success. In each interaction, the 101 principles provide effective alternatives that create positive solutions to common behavior challenges.

Using the Principles in Your Classroom

Make a Plan

Make a list of behaviors that have previously been frustrating to you. Using the principles in the chapter, write the steps you will follow to create a positive outcome for each behavior.

Keep Data

To reflect on your use of the principles, keep a notebook with a record of principles you used. What led up to the situation? How did the situation turn out? How did you feel about it? What did you learn about your own impact on behavior outcomes?

Get Support of Another Person for Your Own Practice

To reflect on your use of the environment, discuss the following questions with your assistant, co-teacher, or colleagues:

- Have I implemented one new principle from this chapter each day?
- Have I practiced the steps to turn behavior around?
- Have I provided alternatives to sitting for young children who need frequent movement breaks?
- Have I created alternatives to sitting for long periods of time for school-aged children?
- Have I developed lessons that are motivating and interesting?

- Have I engaged children in meaningful discussion?
- Have I evaluated the room environment and materials to be sure they support optimal opportunity for children's success?
- Have I reviewed the daily schedule to ensure that it maximizes the use of time and provides flexible and adaptive support for all children to complete projects and lessons?
- Have I reviewed transitions and routines with my co-teachers and other colleagues to be sure we are creating effective and smooth movement from one activity to the next?
- Have I helped all children feel included and valued?

Stay Emotionally Detached

Become reflective about ways that you bring frustration or anger to the classroom. This will help you stay emotionally detached when children need your calm support. If frustration or anger continues to plague you, be sure to talk about it with a trusted friend. Realizing which actions are unhealthy and self-defeating and which are healthy and productive can help you make better choices for yourself. These strategies will help children handle their frustrations in more constructive ways as well.

One of the best ways to stay emotionally detached is to be sure that you understand the ways both adults and children "act out" anger if they don't know how to "talk it out." Figure 8.2 describes the ways we handle anger in productive and non-productive

Figure 8.2 Promoting Healthy Strategies to Handle Anger

Unhealthy		Healthy		Healthiest	
Turn It Inward	**Turn It Outward**	**Non-Productive Outlet**	**Productive Outlet**	**Talk It Out**	**Solve the Problem**
Dislike self Hurt self Stomachaches Headaches Depression Suicide	Hit back Hurt others Lash out Sarcasm Ridicule Embarrass Bully	Kick a box Slam a door Punch a punching bag Throw things Beat on a pillow Knock a hole in the wall	Exercise Paint Scrub or clean Play ball Play with play dough Dance Sing Color Write	Choose: • The right place • The right time • The right person Use I-messages: "When you _____, then _____ [describe what happened]. I feel _____ [describe your feelings]. I wish that _____ [describe what behavior you would like instead]." "When you leave your coat on the floor, someone may trip over it, and I feel frustrated and concerned. I would like for you to hang your coat on the hook in your cubby."	1. Pinpoint the problem 2. Brainstorm solutions 3. Select one solution (vote) 4. Implement the plan 5. Check on progress (revisit the plan at appointed time) 6. Choose another solution Don't stop until the problem is solved—or until you can make your peace with it. Start over, if necessary!

ways, with constructive solutions for identifying, talking out, and solving a problem in healthy ways. You can use this chart for personal reflection or for professional development to promote conversation among colleagues about creating positive outcomes.

Teacher Tips

The following are comments from teachers who have been trained to use the 101 principles in their early care and education settings and elementary classrooms.

We were at the library during storytime when two boys were annoying each other by invading each other's personal space. They took turns putting a foot under each other's chairs and kept putting their hands all over each other. I pulled up a chair, sat between them, and read their book. It redeemed the situation and made it pleasant without me needing to fuss at them. The Divide and Conquer Strategy worked!

Jamal had lost his gym shoes. When I asked him what happened, he became very agitated and was rude in his response. Instead of reprimanding him for speaking to me in this manner and letting myself get upset, I spoke to him very respectfully, calmly, and in a nice tone of voice. After listening, he realized how he was acting and changed his entire disposition. It made a big difference that I stayed emotionally detached.

Jaden got upset and angry when another child took his book. Instead of making a big deal, my assistant offered to take him for a short walk. This resolved the situation. It benefited both children and ended the problem that arose when Jaden didn't want to share. Briefly changing the environment for him helped him let go of his frustration.

I used the Take a Break Principle when one child in my class kept throwing the blocks around. I had tried other 101 principles but finally asked him to sit in the beanbag chair until he was ready to join the group again and use the blocks properly. It worked. He was gone for about three minutes and when he came back, he did not misuse the blocks at all.

During gym games, Terrance became upset while arguing about the rules with another boy. I calmly came over and asked him to take a break from the game and come back when he felt he could participate. About five minutes later, he asked if he could come back. I told him it was his decision. He said he was ready and continued playing. After that, I did not have any more problems with Terrance. It worked so well because he felt respected and he controlled when he could come back.

During recess, a child from another class made a critical comment about the way one of my students was playing a game. I quickly invited my student to play with me. By taking action instead of talking to the other child, the message was clear. The other child apologized to my student, and asked to play the new game with us. Mission accomplished.

I was having a disagreement with my assistant that left us both quite frustrated. I asked her if we could take some time to cool off, reevaluate our position, and consider the other's opinion. We agreed to come back in one hour and resolve our dilemma. It worked great. When we started talking again, we both had a much better disposition and began the conversation with an objective of compromise and respecting the other's view.

I had a difficult time getting Jennifer to turn her homework in on time. She did the work, but for some reason didn't bring it to school. I decided to sit with her and have her brainstorm a solution to the problem. It occurred to me that I always took responsibility for asking about this and that she should choose her own solution. I asked her to make a contract by writing a solution down and signing it. She willingly wrote out a solution and signed it. I read her plan and praised her for taking responsibility for herself. Unbelievable. She started handing in her homework after that.

Research on the Run

Responding to Misbehavior

- The way adults respond to children becomes a foundation for the perceptions children form of themselves and others (Koplow, 2002).

- Early experiences of stress and levels of low emotional connection create detrimental outcomes for a child's ability to be resilient, self-regulated, and adaptive (Siegel, 2003).

- Children are unable to demonstrate healthy ways of resolving conflict unless adults model and demonstrate social conflict skills, provide feedback and validation, and teach skills for social and emotional competence (Warren, Bassett, & Denham, 2008).

Learning Effective Skills

- Teachers themselves are often uncertain how to proactively and successfully redirect behavior. "If a teacher cannot effectively manage children's behavior, she is likely to spend a disproportionate amount of time addressing misbehavior, thereby limiting her opportunities to teach" (Pianta & Hadden, 2008, p. 21).

- Often, little training is provided for behavior and discipline needs in before- and after-school programs (CASEL, 2007; National Scientific Council on the Developing Child, 2004; 2005).

- Even though the research advocating the benefit of positive interactions in early childhood (birth to age 8) is so compelling, teachers, assistants, and others who work with children often lack adequate skills to create positive outcomes and continue to be frustrated with challenging behaviors (Fox & Smith, 2007; Ingersoll & Smith, 2003; Oliver & Reschly, 2007).

- It is critical that training is provided for specific strategies to redirect behavior that are respectful, effective, and assure success (Sawka-Miller & Miller, 2007).

Getting Positive Results Using the Principles in Action

What happened or led up to the interaction?

_____

_____

_____

Which principle did you use?

_____

_____

_____

How did the situation turn out? (How did the child/children respond?)

_____

_____

_____

What did you learn?

_____

_____

_____

What happened or led up to the interaction?

_____

_____

_____

Which principle did you use?

_____

_____

_____

How did the situation turn out? (How did the child/children respond?)

_____

_____

_____

What did you learn?

_____

_____

_____

Guide to the Principles

84. **Nip It in the Bud:** When you see a child doing something that is dangerous, destructive, or embarrassing (to you or to himself), take immediate action. Don't let the behavior continue, hoping that it will go away. It usually gets worse if the child knows you are watching and you are doing nothing about it. Giving a hand signal might be enough. You might also whisper a code word, such as "red light," that always means "Stop right now!" You might have to approach the child, take his hand, and move him to another place in the *least reinforcing way possible.*

85. **Use Actions Instead of Words:** Don't say anything. Instead of responding when a child says something inappropriate or hurtful, let the words hang in the air. Walk away or take his hand and move to another place. Give him a chance to hear what he just said. Very often, he will make an effort to self-correct or apologize.

86. **Divide and Conquer:** Separate children who are reinforcing each other's misbehavior.

87. **Stay Detached Emotionally:** Try to remain objective, with your eye on the goal of self-discipline. Don't let the child "hook" you emotionally—in other words, don't take his behavior personally.

88. **Take a Break:** Tell the child to take a break and think about what he could do differently that would work better or be more constructive. Give him a place to go until he is ready to come back and behave more productively. This could be a place that you have created in your classroom that is comfortable and quiet. A timer is sometimes helpful. The child can determine how long he needs to reflect, refocus, and calm down. The child is in control here. He can decide when he is ready to rejoin the group or try again.

89. **The Timer Says It's Time:** Set a timer to help children make transitions. "When the timer goes off, you will need to put away your books." "In five minutes, we will need to line up for lunch."

It is a good idea to give the child a chance to choose how long he needs to pull himself together: "It's okay to be upset. How long do you need?" Then allow him to remove himself from the group and set the timer. You may offer the child a choice (and set the timer) when it is necessary to encourage cooperation: "Do you want to pick up the blocks/let Susan have the wagon/share the computer in one minute or two?"

90. **Get Support from Another Person:** Ask someone else to help you reinforce the positive behavior.

91. **Change of Environment:** If the children's misbehavior cannot be stopped, move to another room or location or go outside.

92. **Wait Until Later:** You can say, "Let's both think about this and come back in 10 minutes to discuss it." Then set the timer. That gives the child (and you) time to consider the actions and think about the best way to handle it. With an older child, you may say, "We'll discuss this at 2:00. We both need time to cool off and think." Then you can meet calmly with the child and say, "Let's talk about what happened. What would a better choice have been?"

93. **Write a Contract:** Sit with the child after he has behaved appropriately and the negative emotions have disappeared and write a contract together for future behavior. Be sure to let him have input. Then both parties sign the contract. (This works for older children.)

94. **Collect Data:** Keep a written record of the frequency of a specific behavior that seems to be continuing. Record the antecedents as well as the consequences. Look for patterns that may give clues as to possible reasons, situations, and/or solutions.

95. **ABC:** Learn to think in terms of ABC: antecedent, behavior, and consequences. What was going on before the behavior occurred and what happened afterwards, as a result of the behavior?

Study Guide

a. **Goal Setting:** Review the section "Learning When to Act—Instead of Ignore." When must behavior be stopped? What does "least reinforcing way" mean? How does the idea of stopping without talking, looking, or lecturing conflict with what you previously have done or have believed about behavior intervention?

b. **Questioning and Reflection:** Describe a classroom that you would call chaotic. What were the children doing? How was the teacher responding? Now describe a classroom that impressed you with the attentiveness of the children and the effectiveness of the teacher. What were some approaches that the teacher used or modeled that made a difference?

c. **Case Study:** Mrs. Mason has become determined to step in right away instead of letting inappropriate behavior interfere with her new campaign for respect. It is a rainy day and the children have already missed recess time due to a tornado drill. Two of her children are shoving in the hall on the way to lunch. How could she stop them in the least reinforcing way?

d. **Personal Examples/Group Brainstorming:** Describe a behavior in your classroom that has been dangerous, destructive, or embarrassing or was an impediment to learning. (You may describe a behavior you have observed elsewhere, if this does not apply to your classroom.) Provide five constructive solutions to the situation you have described, using Principles 85 (Use Actions Instead of Words), 86 (Divide and Conquer), 87 (Stay Detached Emotionally), 88 (Take a Break), and 89 (The Timer Says It's Time). One member of a group may state a problem behavior, and the others in turn may apply one of the principles and explain how it would be used.

e. **Learners as Experts:** *Issue 1:* How do the top 10 principles for toddlers address the need for fast, fun, fair, and firm positive guidance? *Issue 2:* Consider children's behaviors in your classroom. What is working well, and why? What is not working well? Why isn't it? For the situation that is not working well, propose at least two changes that you can make in the environment that will resolve the issue. See "Making Good Use of the Environment" and "Staying Objective/Collecting Data," on pages 226–228.

f. **Principles in Action:** Using the "Getting Positive Results Using the Principles in Action" sheet, have each participant share one principle they implemented from this chapter. What happened or led up to the interaction? Which principle did you use? How did the situation turn out? (How did the child/children respond?) What did you learn?

g. **Research on the Run:** Review this section. Use Figure 8.2 to consider how you personally resolve conflict. Which of the non-productive and productive strategies have you used? By understanding which actions are unhealthy and self-defeating, you can make plans to become more healthy and productive. How can you teach these healthy conflict resolution skills to the children in your classroom or school? For extended learning, discuss the "Have I" questions on pages 232–233 to evaluate your own responsive practices for optimal learning.

h. **Looking Ahead:** Set the purpose for upcoming study by introducing chapter objectives. Thank you for sharing your personal insight about responsive, positive guidance and for your commitment to making a difference in the lives of children.

References

CASEL. (2007). The benefits of school-based social and emotional learning programs. Retrieved October 28, 2011, from http://casel.org/why-it-matters/benefits-of-sel

Fox, L., & Smith, B. (2007). Promoting social, emotional and behavioral outcomes of young children served under IDEA. Center on the Social and Emotional Foundation for Early Learning Policy Brief. Retrieved October 28, 2011, from www.nectac.org/~pdfs/calls/2007/challenging behavior/2-smith-619policybrief.pdf

Ingersoll, R. M., & Smith, T. M. (2003). The wrong solution to the teacher shortage. *Educational Leadership, 60*(8), 30–33.

Koplow, L. (2002). *Creating schools that heal: Real life solutions.* New York: Teacher's College Press.

National Scientific Council on the Developing Child. (2004). Children's emotional development is built into the architecture of their brains. Working Paper No. 2. Harvard Family Research Project. Retrieved from www.developingchild .harvard.edu

National Scientific Council on the Developing Child. (2005). Excessive stress disrupts the architecture of the brain. Working Paper No. 3. Harvard Family Research Project. Retrieved from www.developingchild.harvard.edu

Oliver, R., & Reschly, D. (2007). *Effective classroom management: Teacher preparation and professional development.* Washington, DC: National Comprehensive Center for Teacher Quality.

Pianta, R., & Hadden, S. (2008, June). What we know about the quality of early education settings: Implications for research on teacher preparation and professional development. *The State Education Standard*, 20–27.

Sawka-Miller, K., &, Miller, D. (2007). The third pillar: Linking positive psychology and school-wide positive behavior support. *School Psychology Forum: Research in Practice, 2*(1), 26–38.

Siegel, D. (2003). *Healing and trauma.* New York: W. W. Norton.

Warren, H., Bassett, H., & Denham, S. (2008, May). Early emotional development, social cognition, and relationships with others. *Zero to Three*, 32–39.

chapter 9

Collaborating with Families

This chapter will help you identify effective strategies to build teamwork and collaboration with families. You will realize how the perspectives of the teacher and parents can be used to build strong relationships. You will empower parents and families to become partners in the support of their child's school success. As you complete the reading and activities, you will be able to enhance mutual trust and build strong connections.

Research shows that a child does better in school when parents are involved. A child's relationship with a teacher also has a strong influence, even if a parent is not available. Likewise, the family can support their child's development in spite of challenges at school. However, when both school and family work together, the child benefits exponentially. You will cultivate greater sensitivity and responsiveness as you realize your influence in strengthening partnerships with families.

Chapter Principles

96: Chill Out

97: Other Shoe

98: Common Sense

99: Partner/Co-Worker

100: Human

101: Bake a Cake

Chapter Objectives

As you explore the text and activities in this chapter, you will be able to:

- Strengthen the framework of caring and trust between school and home
- Identify opportunities to build bridges and understand family perspectives
- Build strong partnerships through meetings and home visits
- Establish productive, happy, and cooperative parent conferences
- Use meaningful strategies, tips, and activities to connect school and home
- Create "parent chats" to build a network of family support

Building Bridges with Families

When parents come to school, they are bringing their most treasured investment—their child. They want to be sure that teachers will take care of, encourage, protect, and nurture their child's gifts, talents, and abilities. The parent and you have a common goal: to help this child become a responsible friend, an ethical person, a purposeful learner, and a motivated citizen. We want this child to find a reason to reach his potential and invest his energy and commitment to a worthwhile cause. Teachers can draw on this common goal to inspire a strong partnership and facilitate positive relationships between school and home.

Up to this point in our study of the 101 principles, we have learned to invest our energy and utilize proactive skills to redirect children's behavior and engage them in meaningful learning. We have seen that it pays off to foster healthy relationships. We have discovered that children who have been taught social–emotional skills become more cooperative; they thrive in the safety of a caring environment and take on the values and skills that are modeled to them. Our focus and understanding are now framed within the context of positive, responsive relationships.

In the same way, we want to approach our interactions with parents within a framework of authentic caring and trust. It is transformational to communicate to parents with respect. Just as we have learned the importance of connecting with children, we want to build bridges with parents in positive ways, so that a strong relationship is formed. Then, when we need to work together to solve a problem, we have already built a strong foundation of trust.

If we widen the scope of our perspective about our relationship with families, we realize that we can become influential in parents' lives as well as in the lives of their children. Parents are the experts on their child. They know their child better than anyone else. Let them hear—in many ways and often—that we trust their judgment and relationship with their child. The Trust Principle (Chapter 5) is as important with families as it is with children. Our interactions can reinforce a parent's confidence. We can influence the way parents see children's abilities and possibilities as well as their own role as facilitators of their children's success.

In addition, our relationship with parents serves as a role model to the child. He sees us working together because we care about him. Our interaction with his parents affects his feelings about school. We must take every opportunity to strengthen a parent's relationship with his or her child and with the school.

Describe several of the unique traits and needs of the families and community where you teach. How does this knowledge help you as a teacher?

_____

_____

_____

Opening Communication

We want to create a genuine warm openness in our communication with parents, inviting them into a shared partnership where our conversations with them feel uplifting, reassuring, and positive. We want our classroom to be a place children love to be and parents want to come. However, communication about children and school involves many dynamics.

A teacher's previous history with parents and beliefs about families can provide a starting point for reflection and insight. As you consider the following scenarios and strategies, think about your previous experience with parents. What concerns would you like to resolve? What positive experiences do you hope to repeat? By becoming more aware of the ingredients of communication, you can maximize your opportunities to create authentic relationships with parents.

A concerned parent came to a teacher and said, "Are you angry with me?" The teacher honestly responded, "No, I am not at all upset. Did I say or do something that made you feel concerned? Is there something you would like to talk with me about? I have a few minutes and am glad to see you. I wanted to tell you what a great contribution Landon made today to our conversation about changing seasons." By engaging the parent in positive conversation, the parent soon realized that everything was OK. The teacher had soothed the situation by creating a positive connection.

To become more aware of the communication environment, ask yourself whether there are social or physical distractions present. If others are nearby or it is noisy, is this the best place and time to respond? To become more sensitive in listening, you can ask, "Have I understood what was intended? How is this person feeling as he talks?" It is also important to be aware of how you come across in your tone of voice and body language. You want to be unbiased in your perceptions. You can ask yourself, "Do I feel comfortable and calm? What is my reaction to this person?" It takes determination and practice to tune in to these issues, so that you can respond with fairness, caring, and respect.

Differences in personality can affect outcomes. A soft-spoken teacher can feel that a parent's strong words are accusatory when he only meant to communicate a concern. The teacher may hear a strong tone of voice and feel she has been criticized. In the same way, a parent may overreact, feeling a teacher "meant something" by a comment or look. Sensitivity and patience will be necessary so that a foundation of trust can be established.

We must stay objective as we choose our responses, so that we can be certain that we are not projecting our feelings onto others. It is important to keep a direct and honest path open to communication. If we are unsure about how we feel, talking to a trusted colleague may help us sort out our perspective. We can gain valuable feedback by discussing our experiences with a friend who can validate our feelings and assist us in clarifying any unresolved issues. Once we gain understanding, we will become better at helping others feel comfortable.

Principle 96: Chill Out

It's no big deal! Don't make a mountain out of a molehill. This, too, will pass.

Before you enter into a conversation with a parent, ask yourself, "What do I want the outcome of this interaction to be? How can I choose my words and actions to help produce a satisfying resolution? Is this issue important? Is a resolution possible? Is this something that I need to take care of, or is this something I can overlook or perhaps use as a stepping stone to something better?" As we look ahead to the end of each interaction, we can become more mindful of the words we choose and the support we provide, realizing that our response will become a guidepost for the tone of the entire conversation.

THINK ABOUT IT!

Describe a situation when you felt that someone else overreacted to you or misinterpreted your motives. How did it make you feel? What was the result? Were you able to create a positive resolution? Is there anything you wish you had said or done differently?

_____

_____

_____

Reflect on your previous experiences with parents. Is there a concern that prompted you to feel uncomfortable in the past? How might you handle that situation in a more productive way in the future?

_____

_____

_____

Knowing and Understanding Families

Visiting a school building can bring back strong memories for parents. If they had positive experiences as children, the trip to a school building is likely to prompt a sense of expectation and excitement. However, if there are conflicting emotions or negative memories about school, these feelings can carry over to present-day interactions. A father said, "Coming to school for the first time with my boy gave me an anxious feeling, like going to the principal's office." Another said, "The school smells like the lunchroom and reminds me of food I never liked." A mother remembered, "One day, I got completely lost in junior high and was mortified. Just driving up to my child's elementary school with the familiar sandstone front made me feel nervous." Understanding that past experiences are linked to present feelings can help teachers develop greater empathy and insight when relating to parents.

With a growing focus on achievement and testing, parents often have concerns about how the teacher views their child's progress. One father commented, "I feel like my child is my report card. If you don't like him, that is a reflection on me as a parent. I want to know he is normal and making good progress." Parents want teachers to see the best in their child. Teachers will be wise to tune in to the way parents see their children and to realize their concerns.

It requires sensitivity to build a parent's confidence. If their child has had previous negative experiences in school, the parent may develop defensiveness. Perhaps he felt the school didn't respond or understand in the past. He may have experienced difficulty with learning himself and worry that his child will repeat that pattern. At the beginning of a new school year, a teacher's initial interactions with this family will have significant impact.

Parents of infants and toddlers want to know that their child is comforted and cared for while they are at work. They want the teacher to be invested in their child's well-being and will look for reassurance. Hearing about a new milestone or vocabulary word can make this parent's day. Supporting the parent as a full partner will pay off in ongoing cooperation and teamwork.

Honoring family differences can require wisdom and patience for many practical reasons. Teachers may work with parents who speak and read languages other than their own, making educational jargon and acronyms confusing. A parent's cultural beliefs may influence the decision not to ask questions because of the desire to be respectful. Sometimes the "parent" is a teenager or a grandparent. The person picking up and dropping off a child may be a nanny or caregiver unrelated to the family. All of these interactions will require sensitivity. It is critical that the teacher understand the unique family and community context of the children.

A teacher can stay aware to try to avoid misunderstandings. Parents may feel judged if their child has misbehaved or be concerned that a teacher or school holds the parent responsible. They may wonder if the teacher actually caused an issue or think the teacher should have taken care of it. Considering potential issues ahead of time will help you become more proactive and thoughtful as you reach out to families.

The best way to understand another person is to try to understand how you would feel in their situation. What might they need? What is their perspective? What would they like to hear and experience that would put them at ease? By using and sharing the positive strategies from the 101 principles, you let families know that you are on their side and are committed to building their child's competence and supporting his success.

Principle 97: Other Shoe

Look at the situation from the family's perspective. How would you feel if the "shoe were on the other foot"? What if you were the parent? What would you want to hear from the teacher about your child? What words and actions would make you feel connected and respected? What would make you feel good about your role as a parent? What would make you want to be on the teacher's team and invest in a constructive solution?

Teachers also can help parents examine a situation from the child's perspective. How would they feel if they were the child? What words and actions would make him

● **THINK ABOUT IT!**

Consider each point of view. What would you suggest the teacher do to resolve the issue?

1. A parent in Mr. Esterline's room made many suggestions about how to accomplish a task that differed from the teaching plans. The parent's suggestions about the curriculum felt like a challenge to his professionalism. What would be the best way for Mr. Esterline to respond?

_____

_____

_____

2. Mrs. Graybiel's parents like to talk to her while they are picking up or dropping off their children. However, a parent felt slighted because Mrs. Graybiel didn't have time to continue a conversation with her. Later, Mrs. Graybiel heard that the parent was upset. What would be the best way for her to respond?

_____

_____

_____

3. Although Mrs. Jackson wants her parents to participate in important activities, one parent became overly involved and wanted to move in directions that felt threatening to the teacher. The parent asked to assist in the classroom two days a week. What would be the best way for Mrs. Jackson to respond?

_____

_____

_____

4. Expectations between home and school may differ. Parents may assist children with eating and toileting at home and feel worried about whether a child is able to do it alone at school. A child in Mrs. Simmon's room had an accident and the parent expressed irritation with the teacher's way of handling it. What would be the best way for Mrs. Simmon to respond?

_____

_____

_____

or her feel connected and respected? What would inspire cooperation? What support will build his competence?

Trying to put ourselves in someone else's shoes helps us develop the practice of reflection. Before we respond or act, we want to think what impact the words or actions will have on the one who will be receiving them.

Making Parent Connections

The most significant way to build trust is to build a parent's perception that interactions with teachers take place when positive things happen. There are many ways to connect positively with parents to mediate prior fears and to reinforce the team effort you hope for. The first step to build this bridge is to realize that every positive interaction is an investment, a building block that will strengthen your relationship with parents.

You make a parent's day when you tell him something nice about his child. It doesn't have to be significant as long as it is genuine and true. "Today, Ben was so kind and shared his book with another child." We all love to hear good things about our children, and we want to get in the habit of telling parents about them. When parents come in, be sure to connect with them. Say, "Let me tell you about Marie. What a sweet thing she did this morning!" You can also write notes and send home "great moments." If you get in the habit of saying a positive thing every time you see a parent, the bridges you build will become stronger and stronger. These connections will sustain you and the parents when later you need to elicit help with a problem that has surfaced.

Birth to Age 3

- Parents are the experts and know their child best. When you ask questions and really listen, you can learn a lot that will help you be a more effective support to the child.

- Compliment parents on the attributes that you admire. "I love the way you smile at Isaiah." "James is so excited to see you. He can't wait to tell you about his day. He is so lucky to have you to listen." These exchanges only take a moment, but they nourish the bond between parent and child. Every parent does something positive that can be encouraged.

- Tell parents how much you appreciate having their child with you each day. Receiving reassurance that the child is safe, secure, and valued is important for every parent.

- Share the child's strengths and accomplishments with the parent or guardian every day. Daily positive parent connections are not optional. They are necessary for trust and teamwork. Together, you are investing in the best interest of the child. When questions or issues arise, the foundation of trust and understanding will already be present.

- Build on family competence and strength. Rather than point out a child's weakness, think about what is the outcome you *want* and encourage the parent in that activity. For a child who might benefit from concentrated learning time with a parent, say, "Here is a special puzzle that Nia enjoyed working on today. She would like you to help her with it tonight. You can bring it back in the morning." (Be sure the puzzle is in a ziplock or other secure bag or container.)

- Language supports emotional competence. Language and literacy activities will pay off in greater emotional understanding for the child. Send home picture books with questions parents can use as they point to the illustrations (e.g., "What kind of animal is this?" or "Where is the bunny hiding?")

- Provide "a word of the week." These can be emotion words like "happy" that are linked to the song "If You're Happy and You Know It." Highlight simple sentences such as, "There you are!" linked to a game like Peek-a-Boo. Send home repetitive songs like "This Old Man," "Five Little Monkeys," and "Wheels on the Bus" as the "song of the week" to encourage parent participation.

- Each week in your parent letter, share a strategy from the 101 principles along with tips and ideas to encourage positive discipline practices.

Ages 3 to 8

- Encourage positive and fun connections at home. Utilize tongue twisters, poems, jump rope rhymes, riddles, and fun vocabulary words (like those in Fancy Nancy books) that engage parents in enriched language interactions with their children. Ask families to contribute their favorites. Children can learn these together at school and show them off at home. Supply a printed copy.

- Send home learning activities that parents can do with children while shopping or driving in a car. Examples include "I Spy" at the grocery store or "Which is a better buy?" for older children who can use a calculator. Families can be a fantastic resource to share educational activities and ideas.

- Encourage healthy activity. Children need to be engaged, energized, and focused. Encourage an exercise of the week, such as walking/running, jumping jacks, or sit-ups. Let parents know that you are going to focus on healthy living and encourage them to join in with the exercise program. You can highlight this focus in your weekly parent letter. (Healthy children who exercise achieve more in school!)

- Encourage healthy eating habits. Children and their families need to eat a balanced diet with fruit and vegetables every day. Let parents know that you will highlight healthy eating choices at school. You can include ideas for healthy meals and snacks in your monthly newsletter.

Let parents know that all of your classroom rules are stated in the positive. Rules should tell what to do, not what not to do. Ask them to turn around any "shall nots" into affirmations. Instead of, "No pushing your sister," rules should state the positive expectation: "Show respect with your body and words." This may seem inconsequential, but the shift in perspective yields exponential benefits. As parents "catch the vision" at home to focus on strength-based affirmation, they will become even stronger supporters of positive guidance approaches in the classroom.

● **THINK ABOUT IT!**

Try making a new "parent connection" the next time you see a child with his caregiver. When you see a child in the grocery store, at a place of worship, or in an elevator, look for a positive trait that you can share with the parent. Get in the habit of complimenting parents on their children. You will find that it gets easier and feels more natural the more you practice. What did you say? How did the child respond when he heard what you said? How did the parent respond?

_____

_____

_____

_____

Connecting Before School Starts

As soon as you are given a new class list, send home a postcard to each child. Make a phone call or leave a message. You can tell the child you are happy he will be coming to your class and that you are looking forward to meeting him. You can suggest that he bring one thing with him that he would like to share with the class. The message will assure the parents that you are looking forward to having their child join you, and will build a bridge with the child as well.

Connect with parents and children by inviting them in before school starts. This will give you an opportunity to meet and greet them, and allow them to become familiar with your classroom, the school, and your expectations. As soon as possible, hold an orientation or parent meeting to give parents an opportunity to connect with you as well as with each other.

When you have the first meeting, invite the parents to sit in a circle. As parents are coming in, give them a questionnaire. You can personalize this to reflect the needs of your school and your own preferences. Ask what kind of work parents do, have them list their hobbies or interests, and ask whether they have an expertise they would be willing to share. Also ask relevant questions about their child: Does he have a nickname? Does he have any allergies? What are some of his favorite activities, heroes, or pets?

At the end of introductions, you can share your Me Bag, a bag containing some of your favorite objects that represent you. This gives parents a connection with you as an individual and helps them realize interests that you may have in common. As they see and learn more about you, they will get a sense of the energy and personality that you will be bringing to their children as well. Getting a parent on your "team" and building trust is critical for the support of the child.

Keep the communication two-way. You can give out written information for expectations, how to volunteer, and how to get in touch with you, as well as answer any other concerns they may have. Keep the meeting brief, so that they will want to come back, remembering that your purpose has been served if they have made important connections with each other and know that you have their child's best interest at heart.

Schools need to be aware of unique needs of families and make accommodations accordingly so that all parents feel welcome. Conferences and events need to be scheduled to meet varying demands and concerns so that all families feel included, important, and involved. It is important to choose a space and room that allows access and comfort to anyone who has special needs. Be sure to ask ahead of time if any special accommodations are needed.

● **THINK ABOUT IT!**

What do you want to be the outcome of the first parent meeting to be? How can you best accomplish that?

_____

_____

_____

Visiting Families at Home

Home visits are part of many early care and education programs as well as many public and private school programs. They provide an important opportunity to strengthen the relationship between school, home, and community. A visit to a student's home can build trust, communicate a positive perception of the school, and create a genuine connection between the teacher and family. The experience allows the teacher to better understand the context of the family so that he can be sensitive and responsive in meeting the child's needs throughout the year.

The home environment is a comfortable place for some parents to share. Other parents do not want to open their home to teachers. They may be embarrassed or feel the teacher is there to judge. Be patient as you schedule times and be flexible to meet at alternative locations, such as the library or a coffee shop, if a parent requests it. Set a time limit that you have communicated ahead of time, so that everyone feels comfortable about the plans for the visit.

The most important aspect of the home visit is making a relationship connection. Your visit lets the family know that the teacher and school are fully engaged in the success of the child and that you respect the strengths of the family. This out-of-school engagement will teach you so much about your students and will show you some of their daily challenges. You will notice the similarities between parents, and how proud they are of their children, as you gain greater understanding of the role of family identity and relationships.

When you visit families, learn all you can about their perspective of their child. Remain sensitive to the family dynamics. If parents speak a different language, siblings are often willing to participate and translate. Ask parents to tell you about the child's likes, dislikes, home life, and family activities. Share what you are going to focus on for the year, and make sure to provide materials as needed. Ask parents about any concerns they have. They may ask questions about eating at school, bringing toys to school, or social skills. The information you gain will be invaluable as you connect with the child.

● **THINK ABOUT IT!**

What events, activities, or efforts does your school encourage to connect with families at home? What can you envision that would enhance your school's efforts to reach out to families and prepare children for school? How can you contribute?

_____

_____

_____

_____

Conquering Parent Conferences

Knowing the sequence of a successful conference will empower you to feel more comfortable and confident about meeting with parents. The secret is to gain input from the parent. You will learn a great deal about how to be more effective with this child by listening carefully to them. Here are the steps to carry out a constructive conference that will build your relationship and engage cooperation at the same time.

1. Start by saying something positive about the child. Keep a file or notebook in which you have previously recorded examples of positive contributions or behavior. Highlight the child's growth as you show and explain examples of what the child has accomplished.

2. Next, encourage parents to talk. "Tell me about your child. Tell me anything you want me to know. You are the best expert on your child. I want to learn from you."

3. If you need to discuss an issue, focus only on the most important one, and only when the parents can realistically be of help. "There is one thing that I need your help with. This is what we have seen at school. What do you do when this happens at home?" If they report that it does not happen at home, respond with, "What would you do if it did happen at home? I know you want to help me and I want to help you. What could we do to work on it together?"

4. Think about the outcome you hope to achieve.

5. Ask for help. "I am going to watch for signs that your child is getting frustrated and see if I can jump in and help him with some other solutions. Can you do the same at home?"

6. Ask to meet again. "Let's meet back together in two weeks." When the time comes, make sure that you call to remind them. "I am expecting to see you tomorrow. Is that still OK with you?" That way, parents know you are committed to working on it, and they are as well.

7. Start and end on a positive issue. In the middle is one thing that we can both be working on. We can alleviate parents' fears by letting them know that we are going to find a positive solution.

8. When you share anecdotal records and other information about academic progress, it will be most beneficial to focus on the positive. If the child needs support in reading, rather than focus on the deficit, you want to engage the parent's commitment to a positive plan. You want them to leave school feeling better and more interested in supporting the child's growth and success.

9. Focus on the most important goal. The most important role of the conference is to build the connection and address one issue. If you have other information, you can give it to them and say, "Here is additional information. If you want to discuss it further, please let me know." Letting a parent know you really care about their child is the most important goal of the conference.

Help parents to create practical, common-sense solutions to support their child's needs. This emphasis can help them stay objective while supporting his success. Encourage them to defuse power struggles by creating a plan with the child that the child feels good about and that he can realistically achieve.

Principle 98: Common Sense

Use common sense. Is this reasonable? Is your child ready for this challenge or lesson? Is what you are requesting or expecting developmentally appropriate? Is he capable of mastering what you ask, or will he become further frustrated or discouraged? Stay flexible to accommodate children's needs and don't expect perfection. Be patient, and always assist children in experiencing success.

We want parents to know that we have faith and trust in them and will work with them to achieve the best outcome for their child. Sharing positive strategies from the 101 principles can provide reassurance and invite shared partnership in addressing issues.

Birth to Age 3

- During conferences, parents of young children may ask questions about routines and developmentally appropriate practices. Some may address the use of pacifiers, eating concerns (when to introduce solid foods, letting a child eat with a spoon), or napping issues (in what way or how many naps are given). A parent may ask your advice. It is okay to say that at the center, children thrive on predictable schedules and that they adjust beautifully when they can count on a system of routines.

- When communicating about infant routines and schedules, be sure to ask the parent to describe how he or she feels the baby best responds at naptime or when eating at home. Many choices that parents make are preferences and reflect cultural and social differences. For example, some parents bring children with them everywhere and let them nap on the way, whereas others stick to strict schedules. Information we gain by listening carefully to parents helps them feel included in daily decisions and respects their expertise with their own child. The shared communication allows the caregiver to take notes on what is most effective with the child.

- Occasionally, questions come up about more immediate concerns, such as a toddler who has bitten another child. The more consistently adults deal with concerns, the better. It's important to deal with issues in positive ways by using incompatible alternatives and modeling. Of course, we must try to anticipate children's needs and arrange the environment accordingly. This is particularly critical before children are able to express themselves using words. Notice when a child bites. Does it happen at a consistent time? Is there something he could be given to do in place of that? If biting has occurred, respond immediately but calmly, and teach alternative behaviors, such as "blowing kisses," "gentle hands," or "bite something else" (such as a teething ring).

- Rather than focus attention on the misbehavior, we want to teach alternatives in gentle but certain ways that show the child constructive options to communicate and get help. It may be counterintuitive to remain calm and quiet, but consistency of response (anticipating needs, providing incompatible alternatives) will yield the most effective and lasting outcome.

Ages 3 to 8

- An enthusiastic teacher remarked, "I am so excited! I am having parent conferences!" This teacher focused the entire conference on children's successes, accomplishments, improvements, and contributions. If there was any room for growth or he needed a parent's additional support, he would say, "I think Kaleen will become an excellent reader. To help her achieve, I would like you to listen to her read for five minutes each night." He had a packet with a colorful book and activity included ready to send home with the parents.

- Another teacher had a second-grade student who was having trouble sitting during times when he really needed to focus. During the parent conference, Mr. Jackson asked the parents if they could think of a time when Tommy needed to sit at home. The mom said, "Dinner time." Together, they made an agreement that the parents would encourage Tommy to sit for 10 minutes while eating dinner and the teacher would encourage Tommy to sit for 10 minutes during writing. Both agreed to use a timer and let Tommy set it for 10 minutes by himself. Mr. Jackson ended the conference by saying, "I understand that Tommy wants to join the chess club. I think practicing sitting during dinner and writing times will help him when the after-school club begins. With a specific short-term goal in mind, I think we will have success. Let's meet back together in two weeks to see how things are going."

These examples illustrate the impact we can have in creating a partnership with parents. The positive regard we bring to families will yield lasting benefits in our day-to-day interactions as well as in the long-term trust and teamwork we build. Children will experience the unified effort and see that we have their best interest in mind.

● THINK ABOUT IT!

Send home a short survey and ask parents their preferred form of communication. Would they like notifications by phone, text, e-mail, or a social communication network? What would encourage parents to read information that is sent home? How will you communicate with parents whose home language is not English?

_____

_____

_____

_____

_____

Reinforcing Family Confidence

A teacher's interactions with families can reinforce confidence and play a key role in increasing parents' cooperation. You can set a positive tone for communication as you help smooth over concerns that come up. Your choices will affect the way a family views their child's potential to achieve success in school.

Recently a teacher asked, "How can I tell parents that their child needs improvement in several areas?" It helps if we try to put ourselves in the parent's shoes. How would we feel if we were told that there was something wrong with our child?

How much better would the result be if we focused on positive traits as a starting point and showed the parent our goals for the child? "Isabelle is developing positive skills as she relates to others. Today, she shared a book with a friend. I would like for you to compliment her every time you see her helping and sharing at home." This positive affirmation can help a parent shift the focus toward supporting the specific skills we want to help the child establish. After we have redirected the parent's focus, then we can elicit his help with our most pressing concerns.

If a parent comes to talk about a problem she is having with her child, it is all right to share your own experiences. However, rather than give specific advice, it would be better to suggest resources, such as books or professional websites you have compiled, or to share the printed 101 principles.

We should be careful to remain professional at all times. Keeping confidentiality and talking only to those who can be a professional resource or support is essential. If a parent asks you about another child or teacher, it is best to respond, "I don't feel comfortable discussing that with you. I would suggest that you take that concern to an administrator or the persons involved." We have to walk a narrow line and remember that we are experts only in what we have been trained to do—teaching.

Principle 99: Partner/Co-Worker

Support your co-worker's decisions and interactions with parents. If you disagree, move away and let him follow through. It helps to check with your co-workers before you talk to a parent about a specific incident, so that you won't be giving different messages. You need to present a unified front.

Sometimes parents hear about an incident that happened at school from their child. The details may be clouded by the child's perception of the situation. It might be as simple as something that happened on the bus or a rule that was discussed in class. Learning how to respond and work with other teachers builds trust and helps parents feel confident about the way you and your colleagues look out for the best interest of their children.

It is important to have frequent contact and clarification with your colleagues and administrators, so that the procedures for safety and communication with families are followed. It is essential that each teacher understand the expectations of the school about the best way to handle family concerns. Taking time to talk through issues as a team before talking to a parent or family will help you answer questions in a more productive way.

● **THINK ABOUT IT!**

What is your school or center policy regarding communication with parents about incidents that happen at school? If you are not currently working in a school, interview a teacher and ask what the policy is at his or her school.

_____

_____

_____

Connecting Throughout the School Year

There are many ways to encourage parents, grandparents, and important role models in the child's life to become more active in a child's education. It helps to match your school needs with male role models and fathers, such as involving them in classroom activities that relate to their interests. It is important to remember that many children grow up in families without a father, but they may have other father figures in their life. Instead of labeling a reception "donuts for dads," for example, present it as a "man in my life" event. Make sure that those who do not have a family member in attendance are supported by others. All families should feel included, important, and involved.

Facilitate connection events that give the principal or director as well as teachers the opportunity to connect with family members. Examples of "social events with a purpose" include Grandparents' Day, board game evenings, reading and poetry events, "Donuts with the Director," "Pastries with the Principal," and movie nights for families. Be imaginative and let children help plan these special events. These can be as simple or elaborate as needed; the purpose is to provide an opportunity for families to experience the school as a vital part of the life of the family and community.

Use positive strategies daily to keep connections strong between teacher, parent, and child.

Birth to Age 3

- Create a short daily sheet to let parents know about the positive experiences a child had that day. Briefly mention what she ate and accomplished and give other simple reminders or requests: "Bring a sippy cup." "On Thursday we are going to the park." You can name this piece of paper "The Daily Dish," "The 411," "The Happy Report" or any other encouraging combination of words. One teacher named hers "Mrs. Pepper's Petunias." Make it cheerful and positive so that families look forward to receiving it.

- Provide activities such as a song or a page to color that a toddler can complete with an older sibling.

- Remember that children who speak English as a second language are likely to get help from siblings at home, so send home "happy sticky notes" with simple directions and a smile to siblings who help out: "Thanks for reading this story to Paulina!"

- Remind parents about pertinent safety issues where necessary. For example, if you are in a climate where there is a need for sun protection, you can remind the parent to apply sunscreen to the child at home. Be sure to clarify any health and safety requirements regularly and in positive ways.

Ages 3 to 8

- Be creative when you send home notes to parents. A ziplock bag clipped inside of a notebook or tucked in a backpack is a great safe (and dry) place to exchange information or small items.

- When children can write, have them create their own to-do list or reminder bullets for what they need to bring to school the following day.

- Create "take home" packs. These can be put inside of fabric drawstring pouches, plastic envelopes, bags, or baggies. Include a book and related materials for a mini project. Let the children report back to the class on what they learned while reading the enclosed book or subject materials. Items enclosed should be complete (not requiring the parent to add anything) and allow the child to work independently as he explores a topic of his interest.

- Be aware of the complications parents can have when there are mutiple children in the family. Refrain from asking or expecting parents to spend extended periods of time assisting children at home. If you send home letters or information, keep information short, appealing, and to the point. If you send home tasks for children to complete, make sure children can accomplish what is required with a minimum of assistance.

● **THINK ABOUT IT!**

If you were a parent, what would make you want to read daily messages from your child's teacher? What would be your preferred method of communication?

_____

_____

_____

_____

Scheduling Parent Chats

A parent chat is a meeting of parents for the purpose of sharing information, listening to an expert, or learning new parenting skills. It can involve just the parents from your own classroom, or your entire school. You may want to consider bringing together parents with children of similar ages. A parent chat takes place at a designated time (e.g., once a year, once a month, twice a semester) for the purpose of connection and skill-building. This is a positive way to reach out to communities and to build a supportive presence for your school or organization.

We want to do everything we can to build a safe connection and network for parents so that they can build relationships with other parents. Meeting with parents can scaffold and provide support for children's healthy development. It can be a resource for parents to talk about common goals and challenges and find other like-minded parents. A parent chat can become a forum where experts from outside the school such as librarians, nurses, or mental health professionals are invited to lead discussions on a particular topic of concern to all parents. This forum gives parents a chance to meet professionals and learn about resources in the community.

Meeting with parents will connect them to the research-based strategies of the 101 principles and help them build strong bonds with their children that will last a lifetime. Parent chats will encourage personal growth for parents and help them become positive role models and coaches for their own and others' children. The meetings give opportunities to connect with others who care about parenting and raising healthy children. Most of all, they will develop a community in which lasting friendships and support can thrive.

Focus each parent chat on a unique topic, such as positive discipline, sleep issues, or sibling relationships. The first parent chat can be an introductory meeting or for a short period of time (two in the spring or one at the beginning of the fall). Advertise the upcoming parent chat on your class website or social communication network, or in a newsletter or flyer. Encourage every adult who participates in the child's life to attend. Grandparents, nannies, and other family members often come together to talk about the children in their lives. Some schools require all parents to come to three parent chats a year.

Invite parents to sit in a circle. Circles create a friendly atmosphere where everyone has an equal chance to see, hear, and feel included. Remember to smile—a positive attitude is contagious. You can start the parent chat by asking each participant to tell one good thing about their child. The goal is to help parents feel good about themselves and encourage them to connect positively with their children. "What is one thing that you want to share about your child and something you love about him or her?" Suggest that they write positive comments about their child on cards and put them under their child's pillow. "I love the way you smile." "I love to be with you."

You can go around the circle and have parents (as well as grandparents and caregivers) tell the names and ages of their children. Ask, "Do you have a struggle you would like some help with?" Some may say "pass" but others might say, "I have trouble keeping my child in bed at night." The leader can ask, "How about the rest of you? Have you had trouble? Have any of you found things that can work?" Parents have found wonderful ways to make bedtime work and are eager to share what they have tried. Parents of older children will want to talk about other issues related to school and home. Each group is unique. Use the printed list of 101 principles and say, "Let's see if we can find principles that will work." Parents become the experts.

Here are starter ideas and directions for your parent chat:

- Have parents name a behavior or time of day that they find frustrating. Choose principles that will be helpful for that situation.

- Choose a topic of interest on which to focus. You may decide to make this a group guided topic or invite an expert from your community to provide a brief presentation and discussion. Some examples include a librarian, pediatrician, dentist, nurse, music teacher, or other professional who is willing to donate the time to your school or organization. Use handouts on the subjects you choose.

- Hold a parent chat entitled "Getting Your Child Ready to Go Back to School." Provide a handout and a list that will help you communicate the unique expectations of your school. A parent chat is a very effective school transition activity for schools and childcare programs.

- Talk to parents about the importance of spending 15 minutes a day alone with each child.

- Bring red paper plates and make hearts. Have parents complete the statement, "I love you because . . . " and write something about their child to take home.

- Have parents make a list of three character traits they value in their child and then go home and share what they have written on the list with him or her.

- Have parents make a list of the qualities they want to see more of in their child. Have them practice becoming more mindful of improving these areas in themselves in order to become more effective role models.

- Make a list of activities parents can schedule with their child. For example, they can plan a bike ride, a walk, or dinner by candlelight.

- Have parents ask their child to make a list of activities that he would like to do one-on-one with a parent.

- Talk about the importance of reconnecting with children at the end of the day. This is a maximum impact moment. Remind them to stay tuned in to the child. Picking up a child from school, arrival at home, and bedtime are all excellent connecting times for parents and children.

- Be sure to provide parents with a copy of the 101 principles to take home at every meeting. (The 101 principles are located in the appendix.)

- Remember to provide a flier with the date and topic of your next parent chat. Encourage families to bring everyone who cares for the child and to invite neighbors and friends if you have the space. This is a wonderful way to connect your school to the community.

Supporting Families in Stress

We have the privilege of influencing the lives of children at a most important period of development. Our interactions can influence the ways parents, grandparents, and families see a child's potential. Staying sensitive and aware of the need for empathy and support can energize us to go the extra mile as we work with children and families.

Parents often come to school needing a positive place to support them in child rearing. Often both parents are working or a single parent or guardian is at work. There may be no extended family nearby for support. Perhaps there is financial stress, unemployment, or underemployment. There are competing interruptions that may prohibit parents from spending time with children, including media, television, and technology. At the same time, parents may feel it is not safe for their children to play outside. In addition, families can put pressure on children to get high grades or become overinvolved in lessons and sports. Children and parents both may skimp on sleep.

With these pressures, parents will appreciate knowing what to expect, and will value finding school to be a place where they can receive information. They will benefit from knowing that the teacher and school are a ready resource and are on their side to support the child and his growth and development.

Principle 100: Human

Remember that children have feelings too, just like we do. It is in everyone's best interest to treat the children in our care as well as or better than those for whom we are not responsible. Because we have had an opportunity to get to know them well, we have an obligation to look out for their best interests.

Often, children confide in us when they are tired and vulnerable as well as when things are going well. If we work with infants and toddlers, we know their cues, needs, and strengths. We have the power to help or hurt, make or break, shape or destroy their perceptions of themselves as well as prepare them for the future that awaits them. In the same way, we want to view the child from the perspective of the family, knowing that the more we can understand their needs and experiences, the better we can provide for the child's health, well-being, and learning at school.

THINK ABOUT IT!

Describe several of the unique traits and needs of the families and community where you teach. How does this knowledge help you as a teacher? Describe a challenging life experience that you have had. What words or actions would have helped you feel supported during that time? How can you be more supportive of the challenges that your children and families experience?

_____

_____

_____

Addressing Early Intervention with Families

There may be children in our classroom who give us concern. These are the ones that worry us, take time away from our focus, have a hard time fitting in, or who other children find to be difficult. These are the children discussed most in the teacher's lounge.

We may wonder or worry if there is something we can do to be more supportive but aren't sure how to best address the issue. We need to be certain we are using positive guidance strategies. Our primary job is to meet every child's needs in the enriched, inclusive environment of our own classrooms.

Before we talk with parents, we need to have a procedure in place that will help us intervene and find strategies to provide the most positive learning opportunities for this child. First of all, we need to be sure we have utilized all of the strategies presented in the 101 principles to ensure responsive practices. Next, we want to foster cooperation as well as opportunities for meaningful learning. The 101 principles help us to focus on children's strengths and help us remember that children grow into the expectations we have for them. We build their sense of competence by our responses, because they form perceptions about themselves by the way they are treated.

If you are still concerned after exploring and utilizing the 101 principles, then it is time to ask for help. You might ask a trusted colleague to observe and give you feedback. Perhaps she has some simple suggestions to make. She might let you know that she feels the cause of an issue may be environmental and could be improved by simply rearranging the room or schedule or providing the child with extra assistance. You may gain insight about ways that you have inadvertently reinforced the behavior. Perhaps there are social, linguistic, cultural, or ethnic perspectives that must be considered. There may be something else going on that you hadn't noticed while you were busy teaching or caring for other children. Gaining wise, professional feedback from another person's perspective is essential.

We need to take advantage of other people whose job it is to help us—our colleagues, director, or specialists at our school or in our community. They also want the best for the children we teach. Ask, "Can you help me think this through? This is a problem I see happening that I would like to solve. I want to give better resources to this child. What can I do to help and be more effective? Do you have any ideas or suggestions?" Asking for feedback and support is essential. We may simply need a fresh perspective to be informative and useful.

When a parent brings up a question or you need to address an issue, remain professional and reassuring. If you are concerned about a serious problem, such as speech, sight, or hearing, you should describe the behavior you see to the parent and recommend talking with a specialist. If the issue is raised during a parent conference, it is okay to say, "I want to encourage you to keep an eye on . . . as I am concerned about . . ." Be very careful not to make a diagnosis or even hint at one. Consider saying, "This is not my area of expertise, but I think we can turn this around more quickly if we get some outside help."

The best approach is to describe the specific issue in calm words. "I have noticed that when Sasha is sitting at the back of the room, she has difficulty seeing the board." "I notice that when Jacquie sits further away, she has some difficulty hearing." Then wait and see what the parent says. It is likely that she or he has noticed the same issues at home. It is often wise to include an administrator or guidance counselor when dealing with delicate issues. These colleagues can add support as well as provide the necessary professionalism that might be required.

We want to be careful to provide early intervention support to families when it is needed. An effective way to make community resources available for all children is to make sure your school or center provides a list of library locations, family service agencies, and early intervention services. Other helpful information includes health system materials, museum and other enrichment opportunities, and other private early childhood initiative resources that provide service extensions and learning experiences for families and caregivers.

We can encourage parents to gain the help and support of pediatric and other early intervention health services and resources, so that we do not inadvertently make the mistake of misidentifying or labeling children rather than providing solutions and supporting their needs (Harry & Klingner, 2006; O'Connor & Fernandez, 2006). It is important to remember that during the early childhood years, any supportive services are meant to supplement, not replace, the regular enriched classroom experience with a warm and caring teacher.

We need to be careful to recognize the fact that many children get referred to special education because a teacher focuses on a child's deficits or on stopping misbehaviors rather than focusing on strengths and supporting positive behaviors. She may not understand cultural differences that are contributing to a child's actions or words. She may begin to focus on what the child cannot do right, rather than on building his skills. We need to be sensitive to the fact that children of color, culturally diverse children, and English language learners are referred to special education services at three to six times the rate of white children. In addition, black students are labeled emotionally disturbed at almost twice the rate of their white peers and are three times as likely to be referred for mental retardation as white students (U.S. Department of Education, 2006). It is the obligation of every teacher to be reflective and thoughtful about using responsive, positive discipline practices, as this will ensure equitable and fair support for all children.

It is critical to meet the needs of every child, so that they can learn without fear of punitive or punishing measures. Children cannot speak for or defend themselves. As early childhood educators, we must advocate for responsive, caring, respectful, and enriched experiences for all children. Children with special needs, like all children, thrive when surrounded with nourishment, creativity, beautiful esthetics, enriched language, and responsive, sensitive relationships with teachers and other children. Our goal is to provide positive learning environments and relationships so that every child can develop and grow. We want to create the most positive opportunity for every child's success.

● **THINK ABOUT IT!**

With colleagues or on your own, make a list of all of the community resources that would be useful to parents and children. Compile a list of websites that you and others have found to be helpful. Contact your local early childhood organization to see if they provide materials that you can share with parents.

_____

_____

_____

_____

Celebrating Families and Children

Make every day a special day by creating celebrations. Thank parents and families for all they do to enrich your life and the lives of the children in your classroom. Thank them for giving you the privilege of teaching their child.

 ## *Principle 101: Bake a Cake*

When all else fails, bake a cake together (and eat it once it cools). It is a great way to stay connected and build happy memories. This principle reminds us that we need to be more mindful to enjoy our times together and to be thankful for each day's blessings. It is also wise to look for opportunities to celebrate our successes and appreciate those who are responsible for providing these memorable experiences for us. The sky is the limit when it comes to showing gratitude and recognition to others in our lives who have helped us along the way.

Turn ordinary moments into special events. Keep a record of children's and family's efforts and contributions to each other. Be on the lookout for good things! Call attention to milestones and accomplishments. Don't wait for a holiday! Have impromptu family appreciation days, and help children send home notes of gratitude to their parents, family members, and others who make their life special. (You can have them write these on paper cupcakes!) Maximize every opportunity to promote an attitude of gratitude. Children and their families will always remember your spirit of gratefulness and celebration.

Summary

Making connections, understanding family perspectives, using positive communication, and gaining family support are essential components of success. Our investment in building partnerships and collaborating with families will pay off now and in the years to come. As we interact throughout the school year, we can strengthen the partnership between school and home.

Using the Principles in Your Classroom

1. Remember to encourage parents to use incompatible alternatives, give choices, whisper, get on the child's eye level, and use the 101 principles. As you share the strategies, parents will appreciate knowing you are in their corner.

2. Build on your relationship with parents. Extend yourself to them by showing interest in their daily lives. Ask about their visits to the park or library. Show interest in their experiences with their child.

3. Send home thank you notes when parents make contributions. For example, if they bring in flowers, cookies, or cocoons or tadpoles for science, be sure to put your appreciation in a short handwritten note.

4. If your school policy allows it, invite parents in as "mystery readers" at least once a week. ("Mystery" means that children don't know who is coming until they are introduced.) From toddlers to third graders, having parents as role models in the classroom will provide a stronger sense of community and leave a lasting impression on children and the role of parents in education. Invite parents to share a book or lead a circle game, song, or activity. When parents are in the classroom, everyone benefits.

Teacher Tips

The following are comments from teachers who have been trained to use the 101 principles in their early care and education settings and elementary classrooms.

Parent chats are a great time to understand the family and share my genuine care about each child. The best part is that parents stay and talk with each other. A strong sense of community is formed. I always ask, "What are your hopes and dreams for your child?" I have learned that everyone cares about the same things.

When I make home visits, I begin to understand parents' daily challenges and differences between my life and theirs. I also notice similarities: how proud parents are of their children as they display pictures and see how much pride the children take in their home and family. It helps me remember the Human Principle and consider how children feel. I realize my own family is so similar to theirs, despite cultural differences.

Home visits help build the relationship I have with families and parents. I gain perspective on the challenges my students face every day. I return to my classroom with a better sense of refreshment and understanding, and a new light to better understand my students. I make every effort to celebrate families. (They have often Baked a Cake for me!)

I have learned how important it is to be on the same page with parents. Once children know that their parents and I are working on the same team, they work hard to please me and their parents. Families are my full partners and co-workers helping their children be successful.

The main challenge I have faced with parents is a language barrier, so I always smile and communicate a calm and friendly manner. Speaking person-to-person is by far the best way to communicate feeling, care, and compassion. I know that values are caught and not taught and that children are watching.

The biggest lesson I have learned is to keep parents "on board" through constant communication. When I need to address an issue, they already know me and trust me. Building trust with families is essential.

I send weekly Great Moments home to parents with positive remarks on their child's behavior. I can see this pay off when they drop off and pick up their child. Their joy at knowing I love their child is evident. I am celebrating their child and sharing successes with them!

One way to connect with busy parents is to ask questions that elicit excitement. Then I take a minute to brag about their child! I call home once a week to share positive experiences and find parents are very receptive.

For many parents in our neighborhood, school represents a place of disappointment, discouragement, and resentment. I feel it is my responsibility to change parents' attitudes about the school environment, to empower them as their child's first and most important teachers, and to make school a place where they can be successful alongside their child. Looking at the situation from the family's perspective (Other Shoe Principle) changes everything.

Research on the Run

Clarifying Perceptions and Understandings of Parental Involvement

- **Challenge your perceptions.** Popular beliefs include the perception that low-income parents do not care as much, are not competent, or do not value education (Abdul-Adil & Farmer, 2006; Seda, 2007).

- **Know that parents want the best for their children.** Ninety-one percent of Hispanic parents think school is allowing their child the opportunity to have a better life (Hwang and Vrongistinos, 2010).

- **Work to build trust.** Parents report they do not have as much trust in their child's teachers or principals as in the past (Fields-Smith, 2005).

- **Establish strong support.** Students who have strong parental support have a stronger attachment to school and have a higher grade point average. Parental involvement influences students' self-esteem and allows parents to have a positive attitude about school (LeCroy & Krysic, 2008).

- **Say positive things about children.** Parents need to hear positive rather than negative feedback about the things their children are doing in school (Zarate, 2008).

- **Support parental competence.** Children who experience positive, warm, affective exchanges with mothers have less conflict with preschool teachers and were linked to later academic success in high school. The qualities responsible included support, encouragement, and responsiveness. As schools work with parents to achieve these interaction qualities, behavior in school will be affected (Gregory & Rimm-Kaufman, 2008).

- **Make academic partners of parents.** Parent support increases academic outcomes in literacy (Arnold, Zeljo, & Doctoroff, 2008).

- **Communicate school expectations clearly.** When learning expectations and school behavior requirements do not match children's ability to self-regulate and pay attention, behavior problems may result (Bulotsky-Shearer, Fernandez, Dominguez, & Rouse, 2011)

- **Share resources.** Share resources about social and emotional competence and prosocial skills with parents (Denham, 2006).

- **Talk about transition to kindergarten.** Only one-quarter of families meeting with a preschool teacher were doing so to discuss transition to kindergarten issues. Up to 68% of parents in this study wanted to know what they could do to help their child be prepared for kindergarten (Mcintyre, Eckert, Fiese, & DiGennaro, 2007).

- **Share the importance of high-quality interactions.** High-quality classrooms are a predictor of school readiness, regardless of family income or ethnicity (Burchinal & Cryer, 2003).

- **Create positive experiences across cultures.** In 2008, 18.3% of Hispanics ages 16 to 24 dropped out, compared to 4.8% of white students (Behnke, Gonzalez, & Cox, 2010).

- **Be culturally relevant.** More than 20% of U.S. children entering kindergarten are of Latino heritage (Fuller, Gasko, & Anguiano, 2010). Approximately five million school-aged children (grades K–12) receive bilingual or English as a second language learners (ESL) services. The U.S. Census Bureau projects that 40% of the student population in 2030 will be English language learners (ELL) students. Most ELL students (80%) speak Spanish, yet only 12.5% of their teachers have received more than eight hours of training (National Center for Education Statistics, 2008).

- **Send materials home.** Many children in early childhood education classrooms do not have access to English books and materials at home; therefore enriched language interactions at school are especially critical (Lindsay, 2010; Neuman & Celano, 2001).

- **Improve communication.** Cultural differences make communication and assessment challenging (Yates, Ostrosky, Cheatham, Fettig, Shaffer, & Milagros Santos, 2008). Teachers must create trust and build needed connections.

- **Focus on the positive.** Every time we bring out the best in someone else, talk about meaningful experiences, and share positive goals, we move away from "problem-saturated conversations" and create more productive, respectful, and satisfying relationships (Beaudoin, 2011).

Realizing the Benefits of Connecting with Parents

Research shows how much better a child will do in school when parents are involved (Barnett, Epstein, Friedman, Boyd, & Hustedt, 2008):

- Children's achievement improves. They make friends more easily and are more successful learners (NCPIE, 2010).

- Children stay in school longer and take more advanced classes (Barnard, 2004).

- Children's motivation in school increases (Hoover-Dempsey, Walker, Sandler, Whetsel, Green, Wilkins, et al., 2005).

Connecting with English Language Learners and Their Families

- In 2004–2005, about 1.5 million or 10.5% of U.S. students were English language learners. About 79% of English language learners are from Spanish-speaking background (Espinoza, 2008).

- Latino children are much more likely to live in poverty (NCCP, 2011).

- Latino children are less likely to enroll in preschool (Malone, 2010).

- Spanish-speaking English language learners account for 61% of the student population. States with the largest Spanish-speaking population are California, Texas, New York, Florida, Illinois, and Arizona. Other states have experienced a 300% increase in English language learners from 1995–2005, including Alabama, Kentucky, Indiana, North Carolina, Tennessee, and Nebraska (Payán & Nettles, 2007).

- By 2050, one-third of all Americans will be of Latino heritage, and the benefits of high-quality preschool are particularly important for children from non-English-speaking families (Fuller & Kim, 2011).

For more information on universal design for learning and disproportionate referral to special education services, please see these websites:

- Indiana Education Policy Center: www.indiana .edu/%7Esafeschl/cod.pdf

- Harvard Graduate School of Education: www .gse.harvard.edu/news_events/features/2001/ speced03022001.html

- National Education Association (NEA): www .nea.org and www.nccrest.org/Exemplars/Dispor portionality_Truth_In_Labeling.pdf

Professional Standards That Address Collaboration with Families

To promote engagement with families, you may explore the following resources:

- *The Head Start Parent, Family, and Community Engagement Framework* (PFCE) was released by the U.S. Department of Health and Human Services Administration for Children and Families Office of Head Start in August 2011. The PFCE Framework was developed in partnership with programs, families, experts, and the National Center on Parent, Family, and Community Engagement for those who work with families in Head Start Programs with children prenatal to age eight (Office of Head Start, 2011).
- The National Association for the Education of Young Children (NAEYC) provides a literature review and introduces a social exchange model of family engagement (Halgunseth & Peterson, 2009).
- NCATE (NAEYC) *Standard 4: Using Developmentally Effective Approaches to Connect with*

Children and Families includes a bibliography of research along with competencies for teachers:

Students prepared in early childhood degree programs understand that teaching and learning with young children is a complex enterprise, and its details vary depending on children's ages, characteristics, and the settings within which teaching and learning occur. They understand and use positive relationships and supportive interactions as the foundation for their work with young children and families. Students know, understand, and use a wide array of developmentally appropriate approaches, instructional strategies, and tools to connect with children and families and positively influence each child's development and learning.

Key Elements of Standard 4

4a: Understanding positive relationships and supportive interactions as the foundation of their work with children

4b: Knowing and understanding effective strategies and tools for early education

4c: Using a broad repertoire of developmentally appropriate teaching/learning approaches

4d: Reflecting on their own practice to promote positive outcomes for each child (Reprinted with permission from the National Association for the Education of Young Children [NAEYC]. Copyright 2009 by NAEYC.)

Getting Positive Results Using the Principles in Action

What happened or led up to the interaction?

_____

_____

_____

Which principle did you use?

_____

_____

_____

How did the situation turn out? (How did the child/children respond?)

_____

_____

_____

What did you learn?

_____

_____

_____

What happened or led up to the interaction?

_____

_____

_____

Which principle did you use?

_____

_____

_____

How did the situation turn out? (How did the child/children respond?)

_____

_____

_____

What did you learn?

_____

_____

_____

Guide to the Principles

96. **Chill Out:** It's no big deal! Don't make a mountain out of a molehill. This, too, will pass.

97. **Other Shoe:** Look at the situation from the family's perspective. How would you feel if the "shoe were on the other foot"? What if you

were the parent? What would you want to hear from the teacher about your child?

98. **Common Sense:** Use common sense. Is this reasonable? Is the child ready for this challenge or lesson? Is what you are requesting or expecting developmentally appropriate? Is he capable of mastering what you ask, or will he become further frustrated or discouraged? Stay flexible to accommodate children's needs and don't expect perfection. Be patient, and always assist children in experiencing success.

99. **Partner/Co-Worker:** Support your co-worker's decisions and interactions with parents. If you disagree, move away and let him follow through. It helps to check with your co-workers before you talk to a parent about a specific incident, so that you won't be giving different messages. You need to present a unified front.

100. **Human:** Remember that children have feelings too, just like we do. It is in everyone's best interest to treat the children in our care as well as or better than those for whom we are not responsible. Because we have had an opportunity to get to know them well, we have an obligation to look out for their best interests.

101. **Bake a Cake:** When all else fails, bake a cake together (and eat it once it cools). It is a great way to stay connected and build happy memories. This principle reminds us that we need to be more mindful to enjoy our times together and to be thankful for each day's blessings. It is also wise to look for opportunities to celebrate our successes and appreciate those who are responsible for providing these memorable experiences for us. The sky is the limit when it comes to showing gratitude and recognition to others in our lives who have helped us along the way.

Study Guide

a. **Goal Setting:** *Issue 1:* Describe several of the unique traits and needs of the families and community where you teach. How does this knowledge help you as a teacher? *Issue 2:* Consider your previous experiences with parents. Is there a concern that makes you want to be more effective in building collaboration and cooperation?

b. **Questioning and Reflection:** What can you envision that would enhance your school's efforts to reach out to families and prepare children for school? How can you contribute?

c. **Case Study:** *Issue 1:* A parent in Mr. Esterline's room felt strongly that a particular task should be accomplished differently than in the lesson plan. The teacher felt that the parent was challenging his professionalism. What would be the best way for Mr. Esterline to respond? *Issue 2:* A parent felt slighted because Ms. Graybiel didn't have time to continue a conversation with her after school. Later, the teacher heard that the parent was upset. What would be the best way for Ms. Graybiel to respond? *Issue 3:* One of

Mrs. Jackson's parents wanted to assist in the classroom two days a week. The teacher felt uncomfortable and threatened. How should she respond?

d. **Personal Examples/Group Brainstorming:** Home visits, family meetings, and parent conferences can provoke anxiety for teachers. Explain your most challenging issue when interacting with families. Next, identify and describe how you will apply at least one positive solution using the principles in this chapter or the strategies for visits, meetings, and conferences. Remember that your goal is to gain input from parents, empower them as experts, and invest energy into positive relational connections.

e. **Learners as Experts:** As you support families in stress and address early intervention, what concerns or issues are important to you? What community resources can you identify that can be active partners in your school's efforts to support families? How can parent chats make a difference in the partnership between home and school?

f. Principles in Action: Using the "Getting Positive Results Using the Principles in Action" sheet, share one principle you implemented from this chapter. What happened or led up to the interaction? Which principle did you use? How did the situation turn out? (How did the child/children respond?) What did you learn?

g. Research on the Run: After reviewing this section, identify at least three perspectives that parents have about their children that they hope teachers will understand. What can you do to become more culturally competent and responsive to families? How are you supporting the needs of English language learners? Name a significant benefit to the child of collaborating with families.

h. Looking Ahead: Set the purpose for upcoming study by introducing chapter objectives. Thank you for sharing your personal insight about responsive, positive guidance and for your commitment to making a difference in the lives of children.

References

Abdul-Adil, J., & Farmer, D. (2006). Inner-city African American parental involvement in elementary schools: Getting beyond urban legends of apathy. *School Psychology Quarterly, 21*(1), 1–12.

Arnold, D., Zeljo, A., & Doctoroff, G. (2008). Parent involvement in preschool: Predictors and the relation of involvement to preliteracy development. *School Psychology Review, 37,* 74–90.

Barnard, W. (2004). Parent involvement in elementary school and educational attainment. *Children and Youth Services Review, 26,* 39–62.

Barnett, W., Epstein, D., Friedman, A., Boyd, J., & Hustedt, J. (2008). *The state of preschool 2008.* New Brunswick, NJ: National Institute for Early Education Research.

Beaudoin, M. (2011). Respect: Where do we start? *Promoting Respectful Schools, 69*(1), 40–44.

Behnke, A., Gonzalez, L., & Cox, R. (2010). Latino students in new arrival states: Factors and services to prevent youth from dropping out. *Hispanic Journal of Behavioral Sciences, 32,* 385–409.

Bulotsky-Shearer, R., Fernandez, V, Dominiguez, E., & Rouse, H. (2011). Behavior problems in learning activities and social interactions in Head Start classrooms and early reading, mathematics and approaches to learning. *School Psychology Review, 40*(1), 19–36. Retrieved from www.naspronline.org/publications/spr/40-1/spr401Bulotsky-Shearer.pdf

Burchinal, M., & Cryer, D. (2003). Diversity, child care quality, and developmental outcomes. *Early Childhood Research Quarterly, 18,* 401–426.

Denham, S. (2006). Social–emotional competence as support for school readiness: What is it and how do we access it? *Early Education and Development, 17,* 57–89.

Espinosa, L. M. (2008). Challenging common myths about young English language learners. FCD Policy Brief Advancing PK-3 No. 8. Retrieved May 14, 2011, from www.fcd-us.org/sites/default/files/MythsOfTeachingELLsEspinosa.pdf

Fields-Smith, C. (2005). African American parents before and after Brown. *Journal of Curriculum and Supervision, 20*(1), 129–135.

Fuller, B., Gasko, J. W., & Anguiano, R. (2010). Lifting pre-K quality: Caring and effective teachers. University of California–Berkeley, Institute of Human Development. Retrieved October 28, 2011, from www.dcf.state.fl.us/initiatives/childcarestandards/documents/Reference_Material/Lifting_Pre-K_Quality-UCB-IHD.pdf

Fuller, B., & Kim, A. (2011). Latino access to preschool stalls after earlier gains. Retrieved from http://ihd.berkeley.edu/Latino%20preschool%20decline%20-%20NOLA-NJLC-Brief-2011-FINAL.pdf

Gregory, A., & Rimm-Kaufman, S. (2008). Child interactions in kindergarten: Predictors of school success in high school. *School Psychology Review, 37*(4), 499–515.

Halguseth, L. C., & Peterson, A. (2009). Family engagement, diverse families, and early childhood education programs: An integrated review of the literature. Retrieved from www.naeyc.org/files/naeyc/file/ecprofessional/EDF_Literature%20Review.pdf

Harry, B., & Klingner, J. (2006). *Why are so many minority students in special education? Understanding race and disability in schools.* New York: Teachers College Press.

Hoover-Dempsey, K., Walker, J., Sandler, H., Whetsel, D., Green, A., Wilkins, A., & Closson, K. (2005). Why do parents become involved? Research findings and implications. *The Elementary School Journal 106*(2), 105–130.

Hwang, Y., & Vrongistinos, K. (2010). Hispanic parents' perceptions of children's education. *Education, 130*(4), 595–602.

LeCroy, C., & Krysic, J. (2008). Predictors of academic achievement and school attachment among Hispanic adolescents. *Children and Schools, 30,* 197–209.

Lindsay, J. (2010, June). Children's access to print material and education-related outcomes: Findings from a meta-analytic review. *Reading Is Fundamental Literature Review.*

Malone, L. (2010, December). Head Start children go to kindergarten. Administration for Children and Families Office of Planning Research and Evaluation Report. Washington, DC: U.S. Department of Health and Human Services.

Mcintyre, L., Eckert, T., Fiese, B., & DiGennaro, F. (2007). Transition to kindergarten: Family experiences and involvement. *Early Childhood Education Journal, 35*(1), 83–88.

National Association for the Education of Young Children. (2011, June). *2010 NAEYC standards for initial & advanced early childhood professional preparation programs.* Retrieved from www.naeyc.org/files/ncate/file/NAEYC%20Initial%20and%20Advanced%20Standards%206_2011-final.pdf

National Center for Children in Poverty. (2011). Who are America's poor children? The official story. Retrieved from www.nccp.org/publications/pdf/text_1001.pdf

National Center for Education Statistics. (2008). Retrieved from http://nces.ed.gov

National Coalition for Parent Involvement in Education. (2010). Building family–school partnerships that work. Retrieved from www.ncpie.org

Neuman, S., & Celano, D. (2001). Access to print in low-income and middle-income communities. *Reading Research Quarterly, 36*(1), 8–26. Retrieved from www.rif.org/documents/us/RIFandLearningPointMeta-FullReport.pdf

O'Connor, C., & Fernandez, S. D. (2006). Race, class, and disproportionality: Reevaluating the relationship between poverty and special education placement. *Education Researcher, 35*(6), 6–11.

Office of Head Start. (2011, August). *The Head Start parent, family, and community engagement framework: Promoting family engagement and school readiness, from prenatal to age 8.* Retrieved from http://eclkc.ohs.acf.hhs.gov/hslc/Head%20Start%20Program/Program%20Design%20and%20Management/Head%20Start%20Requirements/IMs/2011/pfce-framework.pdf

Payán, R., & Nettles, M. (2007). Current state of English-language learners in the U.S. K–12 student population. Retrieved from www.ets.org/Media/Conferences_and_Events/pdf/ELLsympsium/ELL_factsheet.pdf

Seda, C. (2007). Parental involvement unlocks children's educational potential. *Essays in Education, 19,* 150–159.

U.S. Department of Education. (2006). *Twenty-sixth annual report to Congress on the implementation of the Individuals with Disabilities Education Act.* Washington, DC: Author.

Yates, T., Ostrosky, M., Cheatham, G., Fettig, A., Shaffer, L., & Milagros Santos, R. (2008). Research synthesis on screening and assessing social-emotional competence. Center on the Social Emotional Foundations of Early Learning. Retrieved from http://csefel.vanderbilt.edu/documents/rs_screening_assessment.pdf

Zarate, M. (2008). Understanding Latino parental involvement in education. *The Tomoas Rivera Policy Institute,* 7–19.

Creating Positive Change

This chapter will help you consider the many ways that personal and professional changes are achieved. You will explore the factors that motivate action, clarify your vision, and develop steps that will lead to your goals. Finally, you will identify areas of focus that encourage ongoing professional growth and service. You will discover opportunities to connect with others who are committed to positive, relational guidance, and find resources to share with families and others who work with children.

Through your commitment to positive behavior guidance, you have the power to transform children's lives. As a responsive teacher, you can make a significant contribution to your profession. If you hope to make a difference with your life, you are in the right place. The influence you have on the children you teach can change the direction of their lives.

Chapter Objectives

As you explore the text and activities in this chapter, you will be able to:

- Clarify your professional vision for responsive teaching
- Use multiple resources to understand the benefit of positive guidance
- Become an advocate to promote and support positive guidance practices
- Find opportunities to provide leadership to your school and community
- Understand how to use the 101 principles to meet children's developmental needs
- Share the 101 principles and resources with others to empower change

Establishing a Meaningful Purpose

Did you ever try to change a habit? Did you ever make a list of New Year's resolutions? Perhaps you wanted to walk three times a week, drink eight glasses of water a day, or eat more vegetables. Maybe you tried to change something more challenging, like biting your fingernails or complaining. What did you find when you made up your mind to make a positive change? Did it last?

● **THINK ABOUT IT!**

Think of a time that you made a change that lasted. Why were you successful in making the change last?

_____

_____

_____

Think of a time that you made a change that did not last. Why were you not successful in making the change last?

_____

_____

_____

Even when we want to make a change, it can be a challenge to set a goal in motion and make the effort last. We may need a meaningful reason to want to change. Sometimes the reasons are short term. We might have an upcoming business event to attend. We find a renewed interest in a hobby that we used to enjoy. We might get organized because someone will be visiting. But once the reason passes, we find that we slip back into old patterns.

Other times, the reasons we decide to change are more significant. Perhaps we want to develop healthier habits so that we can live longer for someone we love. Perhaps we realize that being kinder will make an important difference in our relationship with someone we care about. Perhaps we have found inspiration in service to others or in making the world a better place. *This is the power of purpose*—the belief that it is worth it to change.

The same kind of motivation affects us at work. Grandparents' Day is coming, so we work hard with the children to create a positive experience. We may organize the classroom for the beginning of the year, but find that over time, the projects we were working on don't get finished. We may make a list of professional journals we want to order, but can't decide which would help us the most. We may become more observant about our physical environment when a visitor or inspection is due, but put off reorganization until the end of the school year.

Most of the time, the reasons that motivate us to change are tangible—we need to meet a deadline or are accountable to someone else.

However, the reasons to use positive guidance are not always tangible and require deeper reflection. Because these principles are built on a philosophy of relational respect, using them requires a genuine commitment to being an authentic role model. Successful guidance requires intentional practice and persistence. We need to keep in mind our goals and remember that what we do today will pay off both now and in the future.

On a professional level, perhaps we want to have time to talk with our colleagues about how to use the 101 principles effectively and share what we have learned, or to observe another teacher's strategies and to ask questions. We want to talk about our ideas and see how we can be more effective in our approaches to teaching and behavior guidance. There are many reasons why we benefit from professional growth. In order to develop excellence in our practice and raise our teaching to a new level, it helps to set specific goals and create a plan to reach them.

● **THINK ABOUT IT!**

What are some of your greatest hopes for yourself as a teacher?

_____

_____

_____

In what kind of experiences with colleagues do you hope to participate?

_____

_____

_____

Is there a new goal—or perhaps a renewed goal—that you would like to achieve?

_____

_____

_____

How will achieving this goal make you a more responsive teacher?

_____

_____

_____

Clarifying the Vision

In our professional practice, we may hear someone speak inspirationally about why our work with young children is so important. We come to understand that our interactions can show young children how to have better relationships with others. The way we interact with and teach young children may change the entire direction of their lives.

Through our investment in their daily experiences, we boost their learning skills and increase their literacy achievement and social competence. Our work with them encourages their empathy, kindness, and integrity. We can help children discover meaningful goals for their own lives. *This is the power of vision*—helping children see that they can use their gifts and talents to make a difference in the world.

We feel our work is important when we realize that our effort and positive engagement can help children make meaningful contributions to society in the future. We can be life changers; our work can make the world a better place for children. This sense of purpose becomes our guiding light. We want to become more informed, because we understand the greater purpose of our work.

At Senator Edward Kennedy's funeral, his son Ted Kennedy, Jr., explained how he had lost his leg to cancer. On a subsequent winter, he learned a life lesson that stayed with him.

> I was trying to get used to my new artificial leg. And the hill was covered with ice and snow. . . . And as I struggled to walk, I slipped and I fell on the ice. And I started to cry and said, "I can't do this." I said, "I'll never be able to climb up that hill." And he lifted me up in his strong, gentle arms and said something I will never forget. He said, "I know you can do it. There is nothing that you can't do. We're going to climb that hill together, even if it takes us all day." Sure enough, he held me around my waist and we slowly made it to the top. . . . [As] I climbed on to his back and we flew down the hill that day, I knew he was right. I knew I was going to be OK. You see, my father taught me that even our most profound losses are survivable, and . . . it is what we do with that loss, our ability to transform it into a positive event, that is one of my father's greatest lessons. (Charles, 2009)

This is the message we need to give to children: that we will be there for them, no matter what they have brought to us, to ensure their safety and success. As teachers, we must bring a full expectation and confidence of success for every

● **THINK ABOUT IT!**

A vision statement describes what you would like to achieve or accomplish as a teacher, advocate, or role model. Write a statement that will explain to someone else what you feel is your purpose in using the 101 principles. Include at least one major goal for yourself and two major goals for children.

_____

_____

_____

What areas of your own practice will you need to strengthen in order to realize the goals in your vision statement?

_____

_____

_____

child. We must hold a strong vision for them and then support them until they have reached the goal.

We will infuse our teaching with energy once we realize that we are serving an important cause: to let children know they can "be somebody" and that we are there to help them succeed. When we make an authentic investment into children as human beings, it changes the picture for them and for ourselves.

Discovering the Power of Relationships

We need to communicate to children and families that our classrooms are a place of safety, where children can step out in confidence to learn, knowing that we will support their success. Rather than opposing children or feeling there is something wrong with their behavior, we need to say, "I know you are having a hard time with this. Let's work together to help you figure this out. Let's see if we can find a way to make this work better for you." This is *the power of a positive relationship.* We need to communicate to children that they can draw on their own strengths and resources and that we will guide them.

We want to look for colleagues who share our vision and compassion for children. Surrounding ourselves with people who bring out the best in us inspires us to continue learning and growing. Together we can be dedicated to making positive changes in teaching practices and using positive guidance strategies.

The philosophy and strategies of the 101 principles draw on the power of positive relationships to transform the interactions, motivations, and experiences of children. Teachers demonstrate how it feels to be respected, trusted, and honored. For children, this interrelationship between trust and safe relationships within the context of the school environment can provide a sense of purpose that is life sustaining.

● **THINK ABOUT IT!**

In your childhood, who was there for you? Who could you count on? Who are some of the people in your life today who continue to support you? Why is this kind of relationship important for children?

_____

_____

_____

Building a Philosophy of Influence

Most of us would say that we need someone who can cheer us on and hold us accountable for achieving our goals. If we are exercising, it helps to have someone who will meet with us to work out. If we are changing our complaints to positive affirmations, it helps to spend time with others who have a positive outlook and cheerful attitude. All of us benefit from someone who supports our growth and encourages us when we need to make good decisions. We can achieve more when we have someone to share the experience and participate with us in the process. This is *the power of influence* that we have in the lives of children and families when we become this kind of guiding support to them.

It takes time to learn to be good at something. The first time we do it, we might feel awkward and wish that we were better at it. So we make adjustments and get better over time. After our first year of teaching, we can see what we did well and what we need to work on. After several years, we realize our strengths and become more confident in our approach. Using these principles will help you understand how your actions and reactions influence your relationships with children, families, and colleagues. Using the activities and reflections will help you consider what is working well and give you many constructive alternatives to encourage you to try new skills and ideas. Implementing these principles, no matter where you are in your teaching career, will help you improve your influence in guiding children's behavior.

● **THINK ABOUT IT!**

Explain an interaction when you used a 101 principle for positive guidance to create a positive outcome for a child. Why do you think your words, actions, or responses were effective?

_____

_____

_____

Holding High Expectations

Once we have set a goal for ourselves, we must be determined to carry out the needed steps to reach the destination we have chosen. We must feel confident about our ability to persist in the face of challenges. *This is the power of high expectations and self-efficacy*—the belief that we have the resources (internal and external) to make the changes needed to reach a goal. In addition, teacher efficacy means that we have high expectations for every child to achieve. Our belief and support exert a strong influence over children's choices and behaviors.

As teachers, we give children confidence that they can learn needed skills. We hold high expectations that all children can become competent in social interactions. This attitude and approach helps us be consistent as we support their growth and development.

In the same way, we want to set new challenges for ourselves so that we continue to grow as professionals. In order to develop skills of excellence, we need to challenge ourselves to stay current with the changing research in our field. Here are some ideas:

- Ask a colleague to be a professional growth partner.
- Join your local, state, and national early childhood education professional development organizations.
- Share a chapter of this book during a parent chat at your school or center.
- Explore at least three research articles related to the needs of children at risk.
- Examine the latest research trends on professional websites.
- Start a book club to explore culturally sensitive and responsive practices.
- Lead a professional development session on positive guidance at your school.
- Participate in an online webinar sponsored by your state or community early childhood education organization.
- Earn a higher degree or take continuing coursework in early childhood education.
- Get involved in your community's "school readiness" initiatives.
- Volunteer at a local community service organization to offer professional development on positive guidance or to lead a parent chat.
- Volunteer at your local library to read with, tutor, or spend time with a child.
- Become an advocate for positive, responsive discipline.

THINK ABOUT IT!

Which of the previous steps will take you closer to the goals that you identified in your vision statement?

_____

_____

_____

Practicing the Power of Persistence

New behaviors need practice. We need to decide on a new skill (incompatible alternative) to put in the place of an old habit; one satisfying enough that we will continue to use it. We need to keep at it until the new behavior becomes a habit. It takes time to find out what works best and to adjust our thinking and actions until we become successful. *This is the power of persistence*—knowing that our efforts will pay off if we keep trying.

It is ironic that adults realize how hard it is to change our own behavior—let alone someone else's—yet we expect children to be able to change their behavior easily. Children appreciate it when we are patient with them. This doesn't mean that we let our high expectations slip. It means that we will continue to tell them and show them that we will always stay by their side to encourage them in their development.

● **THINK ABOUT IT!**

Name three of the 101 principles that you can apply in your own life to help you take positive steps and work toward your goals. How can you use these strategies to empower your own professional growth and persistence?

_____

_____

_____

Ensuring a Legacy of Leadership

These principles create a safety net of respect and dignity for all children. Words and actions are powerful. They leave an impression on each person with whom we interact. *This is the legacy of leadership.* As we gain a heightened sense of self-awareness and become practitioners of self-reflection, we become critically aware of the key role of our own behavior on the way children act and respond. Our ability to recognize and utilize our own role in influencing behavior outcomes is at the heart of each principle.

A watershed moment occurs when we are able to turn the camera away from the child and onto ourselves. It takes practice to assume responsibility for the role we play in relational interactions. However, when we gain effective skills and realize our astounding influence in children's lives, we plug in to a life-empowering framework for our work in child behavior guidance.

The relational framework of the 101 principles is also life-changing for a child when he comes to value our emotional presence and unwavering commitment to his success.

Instead of challenging him when he has been unable to negotiate a social challenge, we assist him in discovering more healthy ways to solve problems. He feels our warm, consistent encouragement and sees that we are going to stick by him to help him figure out a solution. Day by day, we guide and support his emerging skills. These are the social resources that are going to help him become competent in the classroom and in the world.

The 101 principles provide a roadmap to accomplish this theoretical shift into a framework based on the Golden Rule. Respect is foundational, and treating others as we would want to be treated is essential. When this unmovable relational framework is established, children come to trust us and to trust themselves. They are no longer categorized by their deficits, but empowered by their strengths and value.

The 101 principles change us as well. We no longer focus on what we don't want, but take active steps to support what we do want. We step away from blame and take responsibility for the changes we *can* make. We realize that in focusing on the positive, we have developed a new perspective about our work with children and our ability to create positive change for ourselves and for them.

As we set goals for positive change, we recognize that:

- Early childhood classroom experiences provide a critical foundation for children's future success in school and life.

- The essential need of children is to find meaningful connection and relational security with caregivers, teachers, and parents.

- Positive guidance can nurture, protect, and support healthy social–emotional development and relational competence.

- Culture, individual beliefs, and personal experiences influence adults' choices and interactions with children, particularly in the area of discipline.

- Children's behavior can be guided effectively with consistency, honor, and respect without the use of power, coercion, or punishment.

- The practice of self-reflection allows for personal growth and change.

- A positive, responsive relationship can influence a child's lasting vision and perception of himself.

- An authentic relationship with a caring teacher can transform a child's view of his life purpose.

- A teacher can inspire a family's commitment to their child's school and utilize their language, culture, and understanding of their child as a strength.

- Positive school partnerships can create lasting change for children, families, and communities.

● THINK ABOUT IT!

Describe two personal goals that will encourage you to be your best self as you teach and work with children and families.

_____

_____

_____

What will you do to become a leader and advocate for positive guidance?

_____

_____

_____

Meeting Children's Developmental Needs

All children grow and learn. In order to reach their maximum potential, they need adults who are intentional, supportive, affirming, loving, and respectful. The essential social and emotional needs of children remain the same throughout the early childhood years. The following chart will help you meet their need for a consistent, responsive relationship with you in the context of your goals for the positive guidance of young children.

Child's Needs	Need Is Met When	Teacher/Caregiver Strategies	Desired Child Outcomes
Identity Children need a strong sense of identity.	Caregivers provide emotionally responsive interactions as they authentically observe and listen, thereby becoming intimately aware of each child's cues, sounds, signs, and responses.	By **building a caring community**, teachers will help children experience a strong sense of identity.	• Develops sense of humor • Enjoys close proximity of adults and develops bonds and friendships with peers • Asks appropriately for what he wants • Expresses dissatisfaction of unfairness in appropriate ways • Shows pride in classroom traditions and community
Attention Children need attention.	Caregivers give positive attention to the child by guiding, redirecting, teaching, modeling, and reinforcing behaviors that are in the child's best interest while encouraging their exploration of learning.	By **guiding behavior** with positive, responsive strategies, teachers inspire cooperation and build social and emotional competence.	• Able to listen to and be empathetic to others • Develops "I can do it" attitude • Assumes gradual responsibility for own behavior • Able to sacrifice own needs for the higher good of the group as child matures • Shares accomplishments with sense of pleasure
Respect Children need respect for their bodies, belongings, emotional experiences, shared thoughts and words, physical development, and growth (the whole child).	Caregivers provide respect, which is foundational. When the child is respected, he respects himself and others.	By **showing respect**, teachers model and allow children to experience healthy relationships and connect positively to learning.	• Shows respect for others • Can tell others how he feels and what he thinks using words or actions that represent thoughts and emotions • Feels positively about self and shares experiences with teacher, peers, and family • Uses age-appropriate conflict resolution strategies • Demonstrates growing capacity to use materials in the environment purposefully and respectfully

Child's Needs	Need Is Met When	Teacher/Caregiver Strategies	Desired Child Outcomes
Self-Worth Children need a sense of self-worth—feeling they are important and special just by being themselves.	Caregivers respond with nurturing, caring interactions and meet the needs of children consistently as they arise, understanding a child's desire for validation and approval.	By *giving nurturance,* teachers build growth-fostering connections and teach children to understand themselves and honor others.	• Recognizes and expresses own feelings and responds to feelings of others • Shows kindness and affection toward others • Deals with frustration and anger in appropriate ways • Develops healthy awareness and ability to recognize other perspectives • Responds appropriately to social cues • Can calm self when upset or angry (and tell why when developmentally appropriate) • Experiences enjoyment of relationships with others
Empowerment Children need to be empowered to make healthy choices. As they grow, adults gradually turn over responsibility for child's life to the child.	Caregivers have a vision for all that the child can be (his highest possibilities) and equip child with tools, techniques, skills, and opportunities to reach his fullest potential. Adults advocate for the best interests of the child until the child is able to advocate for himself.	By *fostering independence,* teachers strengthen essential skills for children to solve problems and become self-regulated and motivated learners.	• Delights in "doing it myself" • Can ask for help when needed • Shows excitement at personal success and the success of others • Develops self-regulation (the growing ability to direct own plans and create satisfying outcomes) • Grows in self-discipline, learning to negotiate needs • Shows emerging decision-making skills • Gains self-efficacy (belief that he can be successful in reaching a goal) • Develops understanding of how actions affect others • Negotiates new social situations with comfort (and with confidence when developmentally appropriate)
Trust Children need to be able to trust that they can make things happen and that their needs will be met with gentle consistency.	Caregivers respond reliably to the child's needs when they arise with calm reassurance and intentionally use the environment and interactions to provide consistent emotional as well as physical safety.	By *building resilience,* teachers foster the ability for children to negotiate challenges with flexibility and optimism as they advocate for themselves and others.	• Eagerly shares own ideas and contributes to conversation and activities • Develops awareness and cooperation with boundaries and rules • Demonstrates willingness to entrust adults with experiences and feelings • Comforts (soothes) self; bounces back after challenge or difficulty • Enjoys being part of a task or activity • Shows ability to flex with changes and find needed resources, including connection with adults

(continued)

Child's Needs	Need Is Met When	Teacher/Caregiver Strategies	Desired Child Outcomes
Self-Confidence Children need self-confidence—feeling they can successfully navigate their world and create successful outcomes for learning and relationships.	Caregivers see the individual strengths and nurture unique positive qualities of each child by providing ways for him to contribute talent, skill, gifts, and energy to the overall good of the classroom community.	By ***preventing misbehavior*** through empowering competence and building skills, teachers motivate children to take responsibility and make constructive contributions.	• Demonstrates natural curiosity and love of learning • Shows inquisitiveness about environment and world; asks many questions as language allows • Shows natural expressiveness of individual creativity • Eagerly attempts new activities • Gladly participates in group activities • Persists at moderately challenging problems or new tasks and wants to complete task • Feels comfortable and able to respond to change and social requirements
Belonging and Significance Children need to belong and feel significant by making important contributions to the world and finding purpose in caring about the needs of others.	Caregivers create an environment that supports kindness and generosity, and models awareness of individual differences and the needs and concerns of others.	By ***creating solutions to common behavior challenges,*** teachers help children retain a positive sense of themselves as unique and capable; able to create positive and meaningful outcomes.	• Wants to imitate valued adults and to help others in tasks • Shows caring by recognizing and responding to feelings of others • Responds sympathetically to peers in need and offers help • Shares when appropriate to do so • Wants to help and contribute in meaningful classroom activities • Participates cooperatively in age-appropriate group activities • Respects individual differences • Shows unique interests and values engagement in meaningful tasks
Emotional Attachment Children need emotional attachment and connection within the context of healthy relationships.	Caregivers understand how much adult interactions affect each child and therefore provide a sensitive, responsive, authentic relationship; stay emotionally present, physically attentive, and readily accessible to support all areas of growth; collaborate; empower parents; and support partnerships between school and home.	By ***collaborating with families,*** teachers build needed bridges of trust and shared purpose that protect, enable, and promote children's success in school and life.	• Demonstrates sense of security (shows appropriate attachment to caregivers, family, and peers) • Maintains healthy emotional connections • Enjoys natural exploration and self-discovery • Shows empathy and comforts others when appropriate • Identifies and expresses emotions at developmental level • Listens and focuses with growing attention • Recognizes feelings of others and responds positively • Eagerly engages in age-appropriate dialogue and interaction with adults and peers • Shows pride and engagement when family is involved at school

Summary

101 Principles for Positive Guidance with Young Children presents a cohesive philosophy of relational respect that is critical during the formative years. We want children to become passionate about their contributions to the well-being of themselves and others. We want to help them make sense of their world and to trust their ability to make good decisions both in and outside of school. We want them to experience caring and respect that will guide them toward healthy development, positive engagement in school, and a life of integrity in their actions and commitments.

In order to accomplish this, we need to understand the impact of our commitment to ongoing professional growth. Changing the lives of children begins with personal transformation as we recognize how much children depend on our positive guidance and relationship with them. Responsive teaching happens in partnership with commitment to responsive, positive guidance. *101 Principles for Positive Guidance with Young Children* will revitalize your teaching and enhance your influence with children and families as you continue to use the resources to create lasting change.

Using the Principles in Your Classroom

Set new goals and create a clear vision for change. You may do this alone or meet with co-workers, teachers, students, or others who share your common vision. Use these conversation starters to launch your thinking and discussion.

Reflect

- What goals should teachers have?
- What should the classroom look (and feel) like?
- What qualities do children need for success?
- Which chapter or 101 principles will help you to achieve these objectives?

Consider Change

- Identify: Where are you going?
- Ask: What are you doing well?
- Review practices: What is the research foundation?
- Reflect: Where do you need to improve?
- Collaborate: Who do you need to help you?

Commit to an Empowering Vision

- What is your defining vision?
- What goals will create this vision?
- What steps will you take to achieve the goals?

Use This Text as an Ongoing Professional Development Tool

- Create written goals for your own teaching and guidance strategies. Work together with colleagues to create a schoolwide plan for implementing the 101 principles.
- Focus on the skills children need: prosocial skills, emotional competence, enriched language skills, positive discipline interactions, and an environment prepared with many kinds of learning opportunities. Use the developmental needs chart in this chapter to talk with your colleagues about collaborating to meet these needs.
- Accept that change begins with what you can control: responsive, sensitive interactions with children, trusting relationships with parents, and positive expectations.
- Invest all of your energy into creating what you *do* want.
- Become aware of cultural understandings that will help you be a better communicator to families and children. Understand present issues with English and dual language learners, and make your classroom environment inviting and accessible for all students.
- Understand the risk factors of the children you serve and be a strong liaison between families and community resources such as libraries, social service agencies, health services, and non-profit agencies that promote and support educational activities and services for families.
- Start a professional development reading group. There are many outstanding articles available that will fuel discussion between you and your colleagues and keep you informed about the latest policy and practice issues. You may lead this group "round robin," allowing a different teacher or colleague to lead the discussion each time you meet. These materials can also be used to encourage the families with whom you work.

Teacher Tips

The following are comments from teachers who have been trained to use the 101 principles in their early care and education settings and elementary classrooms.

I struggled with management last year. I struggled with my own emotions, with feeling successful, and with understanding how to teach social and emotional skills effectively to my children. I felt as though I failed to help them function independently, to solve their problems wisely, and to build their self-esteem as high as it can go. I went through a lot of reflection on my own practice and examined what it was about my actions that were inhibiting the full success of my classroom management system. I came to truly internalize the idea that positive guidance isn't rewarding negative behaviors; it is redirecting children to more positive and productive uses of their energy. I committed myself to using the 101 principles. I cannot tell you how much this has transformed my classroom. I am so proud of how well my children are doing. More importantly, I am so proud of how proud they feel to be individuals and to be good friends. I just spent the past two hours trying to pass on the lessons about positive guidance to someone else and deepening my commitment to these principles.

Like a stone thrown in a pond, the ripple effect of the 101 principles will continue to benefit the precious children in my care. The principles have validated the importance of my position and the possibilities for the positive influence on the next generation. I am equipped to guide children's behavior in a way that values and respects them. The 101 principles have greatly improved my relationships, interactions, and behaviors with children and parents.

Not only do the 101 principles for positive guidance work with children and other teachers in my center, but they also benefit our parents. The principles have given me a new commitment to ensuring that I promote positive guidance for children. They have helped me personally as an educator and role model to the children who live in a world filled with many uncertainties. Today's child holds the promise of tomorrow: a promise for better teachers, doctors, lawyers, judges, daughters, sons, mothers, and fathers.

The best advice I can give about positive discipline after my first two years of teaching is—patience, patience, patience. Be patient with children and be patient with your positive system. Realize that it takes time (lots of it) for the things you are trying to teach to sink in. Be patient, calm, and level-headed. The children will begin to mirror your calm, collected style.

Every day at our school, each teacher picks a principle that is printed and kept on strips in a bowl in the office. It seems no matter what I face that day, the strategy that I drew for the day seems to make perfect sense. When the children were getting rough on the playground, I started playing "follow the leader" because I had drawn the Incompatible Alternative Principle. The roughhousing stopped right away. Later, the younger children on the playground were going up the slide. I had picked When–Then/Abuse It–Lose It. I said, "When you go down the slide correctly, then you may go again." I would have moved on to "abuse it, lose it" if it was necessary, but it wasn't. In the past, I would have just yelled out the name of the child who was sliding the wrong way. This method has really helped me refocus on my ability to guide behavior, and I love the connections I keep with the children.

I asked the children, "How might we best get from here to there quietly?" Eventually, they all agreed that walking in a straight line was best. That was so great, because they took ownership of their own behavior.

I have totally learned to avoid power struggles. I never say, "Do it now!" I used to! Yet today, the children are quick to step in and step up to responsibility.

As I began using the principles, I was the one who really began to change. I started ignoring all but positive comments made about children in my school. I began modeling the strategies and focusing attention on the character qualities I hoped for. I feel that I was the one who benefitted most by using them. Using the principles helps me stop and think about what I want the outcome to be. This has created positive outcomes daily for my students.

Because of the 101 principles, I have started playing mind math during the transitions to and from locations in school. I never leave my room without at least two or three activities ready. The children love the transitions, and we play "I Spy" and "Count Steps" and every kind of math game. I even whisper addition problems to see if they can add while they are walking and they whisper the answer to me as they enter the library. They are allowed to create their own transition games and share them with the class. I tell them, "We want your mind to grow the most each day." They are proud that they are learning while they are having fun.

I have a boy who always whistles while he works. I really wanted to help him become aware of it. So I asked him if he would teach the others to whistle. I think that was his "sweet spot" because he has stopped whistling while writing now. I just love taking something that could be bothersome and turning it around into a gift for that child.

I began to think about whether I wanted to stay in the field of teaching. I decided to use the 101 principles for one semester and see if I could find a new outlook. I never dreamed that they would change my perspective not only in the school setting, but in my personal life. I used to think things were going wrong, Now I see each day as a challenge. I realize most of what we need to do in a day requires flexibility. All of these strategies help me to move forward from the challenges and create better results for myself.

My principal decided to invite parents to a parent chat. At first, we only had about 15 families come, but it was very positive. The second time, we had 25 come. We let parents ask questions and apply the principles for positive guidance to their own situations. The greatest benefit is that now the parents connect more positively to me because they understand I only use positive guidance in my classroom. This has been an outstanding way for us to connect.

The 101 principles have opened my eyes and refocused my attention to the most important aspect of my work: creating safe, happy children, confident in who they are. The strategies are vital and easily applicable to every area of childcare and development. I feel reenergized in my purpose as a director. I also feel I have the proper training to be able to implement the principles in my center effectively. The 101 principles have been life-changing.

The skills and tools provided by the 101 principles for positive guidance have become a permanent fixture in my life. These tools are more than just methods and philosophies; they are a roadmap to improve the quality of life, self-esteem, and future of every single child that we encounter.

The 101 principles for positive guidance have changed the way I view discipline. They have changed my life, the lives of my children, and their families. The principles help me be a "magical teacher" and positively influence the lives of children every day.

Research on the Run

Supporting Strength-Based Approaches with Children

We want to focus on supporting strength-based competencies for all children—believing each one can be successful when nurtured and taught in a responsive, caring environment. Teachers can provide support for children's social emotional and academic competence.

- Rather than figure out what is wrong with the child or try to "fix him," we want to analyze the entire classroom environment, including interactions and assessments, to see how we can best serve his needs (Nickerson, 2007).

- We want to consider the way that a teacher's interactions and the quality of the environment affects children's behavior and learning (McWayne & Cheung, 2009).

- We want to focus on ways to engage children and help them develop motivation and persistence so that they can be successful in learning (Rouse & Fantuzzo, 2008).

- We want to reflect on our ability to positively influence the lives of children and families (McFarland, Saunders, & Allen, 2009).

- We want to support protective factors such as teacher–child interactions and the quality of instructional support. These are strength-based approaches that let children know they can succeed. We can show how the quality of responsive, positive behaviors support children's growing social, emotional, and learning competencies (Hamre & Pianta, 2005; NASBE, 2006).

- We want to invest in children's success and build common purpose and understanding that can develop within our community (Ackerman, 2008; Barnett, 2010; Wagner and French, 2010).

- We want to be purposeful about providing quality early experiences for all children (Landry, 2005; NASBE, 2006).

- We want to understand that being consistent in positive interactions is the hallmark of a quality classroom (Connell & Prinz, 2002).

- We can make the world a better place for children through the positive relationships we model (Spencer, Jordan, & Sazama, 2004).

Using Positive Guidance Strategies to Increase Quality

Removing punitive practices and replacing them with positive guidance strategies across all educational settings and age levels is an essential avenue that can provide equal opportunity for children of every socioeconomic level and race. All children should have equal access to the high-quality positive and respectful responsive environments that are consistently linked to greater social and academic outcomes.

- Positive discipline and responsive teaching strategies directly affect children's behavior (Bennett, Elliott, & Peters, 2005; Snyder, Cramer, Afrank, & Patterson, 2005).

- Elements of responsive, high-quality teacher–child interactions affect the growth of related skills such as listening, following directions, self-control, planning, and cooperation (McClelland, Acock, & Morrison, 2006).

- Positive relational interactions support children's engagement and are critical to academic and social success and further affect academic skills from kindergarten through sixth grade. Quality interactions are as important in social–emotional development as learning skills (Fantuzzo, Perry, & McDermott, 2004; Gregory, Skiba, & Noguera, 2010).

- Teaching emotional understanding in the preschool classroom decreases behavior problems (Raikes & Thompson, 2006).

- Warm, caring relationships, positive regard and respect, calm and consistent interactions, and low levels of stress are the elements needed to produce these optimum outcomes for children (Ahnert, Pinquart, & Lamb, 2006; Barnett, 2008).

- Language development thrives within the context of safe, responsive relationships, as emotionally warm interactions are connected to positive feelings about learning (Landry, 2005).

- Adult attitudes and experiences have more impact on teaching practice than research-based training (Barkin, Scheindlin, Ip, Richardson, & Finch, 2007; Thijs, Koomen, & van der Leij, 2008).

- Minority students received punitive disciplinary measures two to three times as much as nonminority students at elementary, middle, and high school levels (Serwatka, Deering, & Grant, 1995).

- Children at risk who most need responsive, supportive interactions are least likely to receive them. "Inequitable access to quality does not stop once they reach kindergarten. These same children are more likely to be in our lowest performing elementary schools and experience multiple years of poor-quality learning environments, thus reinforcing rather than overcoming achievement disparities and shortfalls" (Stark, 2009, p. 6).

- "Responsive, reciprocal, respectful relationships with caring adults who have a deep understanding of the unique stages of child development and effective strategies for stimulating active learning are critical. Respectful relationships are essential to building the social and emotional competence of preschool children and readying them for formal schooling, as is engagement in content rich learning that challenges, scaffolds, and extends skills and builds core dispositions and knowledge that will provide a strong foundation for future learning" (Stark, 2009, pp. 6–7).

- "Teacher training in appropriate and culturally competent methods of classroom management is likely then to be the most pressing need in addressing racial disparities in school discipline" (Skiba, Michael, & Nardo, 2000, p. 17).

Websites for Further Exploration

The following websites provide information on issues relating to the well-being of children.

- Annie E. Casey Foundation Kids Count Data Center: http://datacenter.kidscount.org
- Association of Childhood Education International: www.acei.org
- Center on the Developing Child, Harvard University: http://developingchild.harvard.edu
- Childcare and Early Education Research Connections: www.childcareresearch.org
- First Five Years Fund: www.ffyf.org
- Jean Baker Miller Institute (Relational Cultural Theory): www.jbmti.org
- National Association for the Education of Young Children: www.naeyc.org
- National Center for Children in Poverty: www.nccp.org
- National Center for Early Education Research: www.nieer.org
- National Center for Education Statistics: http://nces.ed.gov
- Pew Charitable Trusts www.pewtrusts.org
- United Nations Convention on the Rights of the Child: www.unicef.org/crc
- Zero to Three: www.zerotothree.org

Study Guide

a. **Goal Setting:** What are some of your greatest hopes for yourself as a teacher? In what kinds of experiences with colleagues do you hope to participate? Is there a new goal—or perhaps a renewed goal—that you would like to achieve? How will reaching this goal make you a more responsive teacher? What steps will you take to make your goal a reality?

b. **Questioning and Reflection:** Think of a time when you made a change in your own behavior and the change lasted. What are some of the reasons you were successful? Think of a time that you made a change that did not last. What were some of the reasons you were not successful?

c. **Case Study:** Who are some of the people in your life who inspire you? What is it about their life stories or character that is uplifting and motivational to you? Why is having an inspirational role model important to children?

d. Personal Examples/Group Brainstorming: (1) Explain what you feel is the major purpose of the 101 strategies for positive relational guidance. (2) Review the section "Meeting Children's Developmental Needs." How do you feel about your own life and the way your own needs were/are met in each of these areas? How do you feel about your ability to meet children's needs after learning the 101 principles?

e. Learners as Experts: (1) In what way does this text change your beliefs about discipline? (2) How have the principles most affected your teaching and guidance practices? (3) What principles would you apply to yourself—to increase your motivation to persist toward your professional growth and life goals? (4) How will your commitment to positive responsive guidance affect children's belief in themselves and their ability to accomplish good things in their lives? (5) As you consider the goals of positive change, what have you gained by connecting research to practice? (See page 281.)

f. Principles in Action: Using the "Getting Positive Results Using the Principles in Action" sheet, share one principle you implemented. What happened or led up to the interaction? Which principle did you use? How did the situation turn out? (How did the child/children respond?) What did you learn?

g. Research on the Run: After reviewing this section, explain why strength-based approaches for guidance are critical to children's school success. How do positive interactions and responsive social–emotional support affect behavior? Why do responsive, positive practices have a distinct impact for children at risk? To what extent are you committed to responsive practices and ongoing use of the 101 principles? How will this decision make a lasting difference to you and to the lives of children with whom you work?

h. Looking Ahead: Be sure to take this text with you into the classroom. It will serve as an ongoing resource for study and review. Thank you for sharing your personal insight about responsive, positive guidance and for your commitment to making a difference in the lives of children.

References

Ackerman, D. (2008). Coaching as part of a pilot quality rating scale initiative: Challenges to—and supports for—the change-making process. *Early Childhood Research and Practice, 10*(2), 1–22. Retrieved March 2, 2012, from http://ecrp.uiuc.edu/v10n2/ackerman.html

Ahnert, L., Pinquart, M., & Lamb, M. (2006). Security of children's relationships with non-parental care providers: A meta-analysis. *Child Development, 7*(3), 664–679.

Barnett, S. W. (2008). Preschool education and its lasting effects: Research and policy implications. National Institute for Early Education Research. Retrieved March 2, 2012, from http://nieer.org/resources/research/Preschool LastingEffects.pdf

Barnett, S. W. (2010). State-funded pre-k passes the million-child mark. *Preschool Matters, 6*(1). Retrieved from http://nieer.org/psm/pdf/61.pdf

Barkin, S., Scheindlin, B., Ip, E. H., Richardson, I., & Finch, S. (2007). Determinants of parental discipline practices from a national sample of primary care practices. *Clinical Pediatrics, 36*(1), 64–69.

Bennett, P., Elliott, M., & Peters, D. (2005). Classroom and family effects on children's social and behavioral problems. *The Elementary School Journal, 105*(5), 461–480.

Charles, D. (2009, August 29). Ted Kennedy Jr brings self, others to tears. Retrieved from http://blogs.reuters.com/frontrow/2009/08/29/ted-kennedy-jr-brings-self-others-to-tears

Council of Chief State School Officers. (2009, November). *A quiet crisis: The urgent need to build early childhood systems and quality programs for children birth to age five: A policy statement of the Council of Chief State School Officers.* Retrieved March 2, 2012, from www.ccsso.org/Documents/2009/Policy_Statement_A_Quiet_Crisis_2009.pdf

Connell, C., & Prinz, R. (2002). The impact of childcare and parent-child interactions on school readiness and social skills development for low-income African American children. *Journal of School Psychology, 40*(2), 177–193.

Fantuzzo, J., Perry, M. A., & McDermott, P. (2004). Preschool approaches to learning and their relationship to other relevant classroom competencies for low-income children. *School Psychology Quarterly, 19*(3), 212–230.

Gregory, A., Skiba, R., & Noguera, P. (2010). The achievement gap and the discipline gap: Two sides of the same coin. *Educational Researcher, 39*(1), 59–68.

Hamre, B., & Pianta, R. (2005). Can instructional and emotional support in the first-grade classroom make a difference for children at risk of school failure? *Child Development, 76*(5), 959–967.

Landry, S. (2005). Effective early childhood programs: Turning knowledge into action. University of Texas Health Science Center. Retrieved March 2, 2012, from www.childrens learninginstitute.org/library/publications/documents/Effective-Early_Childhood-Programs.pdf

McClelland, M. M., Acock, A. C., & Morrison, F. J. (2006). The impact of kindergarten learning-related social skills on academic trajectories at the end of elementary school. *Early Childhood Research Quarterly, 21,* 471–490.

McFarland, L., Saunders, R., & Allen, S. (2009). Reflective practice and self-evaluation in learning positive guidance: Experiences of early childhood practicum students. *Early Childhood Education Journal, 36,* 505–511.

McWayne, C., & Cheung, C. (2009). A picture of strength: Preschool competencies mediate the effects of early behavior problems on later academic and social adjustment for Head Start children. *Journal of Applied Developmental Psychology, 30,* 273–285.

National Association of State Boards of Education (NASBE). (2006). *Fulfilling the promise: The report of the NASBE study group in creating high-quality early learning environments.* Alexandria, VA: Author.

Nickerson, A. (2007). The use and importance of strength-based assessment. *School Psychology Forum: Research In Practice, 2*(1), 15–25.

Raikes, A., & Thompson, R. (2006). Family emotional climate, attachment security and young children's emotion knowledge in a high-risk sample. *British Journal of Developmental Psychology, 24,* 89–101.

Rouse, H., & Fantuzzo, J. (2008). Competence motivation in Head Start: An early childhood link to learning. In C. Hudley & A. Gottfried (Eds.), *Academic motivation and the culture of schooling in childhood and adolescence* (pp. 15–35). New York: Oxford.

Schultz, T. (2008, June). Tackling PK–3 assessment & accountability challenges: Guidance from the national early childhood accountability task force. *The State Education Standard,* 4–11.

Serwatka, T. S., Deering, S., & Grant, P. (1995). Disproportionate representation of African Americans in emotionally handicapped classes. *Journal of Black Studies, 25,* 492–506.

Skiba, R., Michael, R., & Nardo, A. (2000, June). The color of discipline: Sources of racial and gender disproportionality in school punishment. Policy Research Report SRS1. Bloomington, Indiana: Indiana University, Indiana Education Policy Center.

Snyder, J., Cramer, D., Afrank, J., & Patterson, G. (2005). The contribution of ineffective discipline and parent hostile attributions about child misbehavior to the development of conduct problems at home and school. *Developmental Psychology, 41,* 1–12.

Spencer, R., Jordan, J., & Sazama, J. (2004). *Empowering children for life: A preliminary report.* Wellesley, MA: Wellesley Centers for Women.

Stark, D. (2009, November). *A quiet crisis: The urgent need to build early childhood systems and quality programs for children birth to age five.* A Policy Statement of the Council of Chief State School Officers. Retrieved March 2, 2012, from www.ccsso.org/Documents/2009/Policy_Statement_A_Quiet_Crisis_2009.pdf

Thijs, J., Koomen, H., & van der Leij, A. (2008). Teacher–child relationships and pedagogical practices: Considering the teacher's perspective. *School Psychology Review, 37*(2), 244–260.

Wagner, B., & French, L. (2010). Motivation, work satisfaction, and teacher change among early childhood teachers. *Journal of Research in Childhood Education, 24,* 152–171.

appendix A

· ·

List of 101 Principles for Positive Guidance in English

Principles in Chapter 1: Building a Caring Community

1. **Connect Before You Correct:** Find multiple ways to connect with a child. Get to know him and show that you care about him before you begin to try to adapt his behavior. Help him discover his strengths, his uniqueness, and his special gifts by calling attention to them.

2. **Time In:** When you are near a child, give him a gentle touch, a thumbs-up, or a high-five. Think about it. Words don't always covey the message you want to give someone. However, touching is different. Children are less likely to seriously misbehave when they sense a love and respect on the part of an adult who matters to them. What you do is as important as what you say. We need to seize every opportunity to show our personal interest and make sure each child has received individual time and focus from us.

3. **Belonging and Significance:** Remember that everyone needs to feel that he belongs and is significant. Help each child feel important by giving him important jobs to do and reminding him that if he doesn't do them, they don't get done! Help him feel important by being responsible.

4. **Love:** Every child needs an adult who cares and wants to spend time with him. Make an effort to show him how special he is to you.

5. **Class Meeting:** Gather children together any time you sense the need to connect or address a particular issue. Starting the day off with a meeting is a good way to show that you care. Give them an opportunity to reflect, listen, empathize, and problem-solve. Focus on two-way communication. Listen more than you talk. Teachers and children will learn from each other.

6. **Make a Sacrifice:** Make sure you have taken care of your personal business (checking your social networking site, e-mail, texting, or grading papers) before school begins so you can give full attention to the children.

7. **Establish Routines and Traditions:** Children behave better when they know what they can count on. Establish traditions they can anticipate and that provide them with fond memories and feelings of belonging and security.

8. **Talk About Children Positively to Others:** Let children overhear you speaking positively about them—bragging about their good qualities, efforts, and actions— to others.

9. **Put It in Writing:** Start a tradition of sending good thoughts in writing. Leave "I care about you" notes in surprising places.

10. **Kiss Your Brain:** When the child is exhibiting behavior that makes you proud and is making great choices, be sure to praise, thank, and draw attention to his great contributions. Tell him to "kiss your brain!" (Children love this!) They will respond by kissing their hand or finger and patting their head. You can model this action as well.

11. **Positive Closure:** At the end of the day, remind your children that they are special and loved. Help them look for something good, both about the day that is finished and the one that lies ahead.

Principles in Chapter 2: Guiding Behavior

12. **Modeling:** Model the behavior you want. Show the child, by example, how to behave. Children are watching us all the time, and they will grow up to be like us—whether we want them to or not.

13. **Make a Big Deal:** Make a big deal over responsible, considerate, appropriate behavior— with eye contact, thanks, praise, thumbs-up, recognition, hugs, special privileges, or incentives (not food).

14. **Incompatible Alternative:** Give the child something to do that is incompatible with the inappropriate behavior. Say, "Let's pretend we are on a secret mission and see if we can walk all the way to the cafeteria without anyone hearing us." "Help me pick out six markers" (when the child is unfocused or annoying). If a child is bothering you by playing with his shoestrings, instead of mentioning it, simply ask him to help you by sorting the papers or crayons by color.

15. **Choice:** Give the child two choices, both of which are positive and acceptable to you. "Would you rather tiptoe or hop over to the carpet? You choose or I'll choose." "We need to clear off our desks. Do you need one minute or two?" (Then set the timer.) The Choice Principle gives the child two incompatible alternatives. The teacher states the desired goal and then gives the child two choices about how it can be accomplished. "We need to put away the toys. Would you rather help with the puzzles or the blocks?"

16. **When–Then/Abuse It–Lose It:** "When you put your books on the shelf, then you may put on your coat." "When you finish putting the play-dough away, then you may choose a partner for the game."

17. **Follow-Through/Consistency:** Don't let the child manipulate you out of using your better judgment. Be firm (but kind)! Trust your intuition. If it doesn't feel right, don't let the child do it. Come up with choices and alternatives that can help every child to focus on more appropriate behavior and positive learning experiences.

18. **Validation:** Acknowledge (validate) the child's wants and feelings. "I know you feel frustrated with your friend and want to keep both books to yourself. I don't blame you. I would feel the same way. However, she needs to have one. Do you want to choose which one, or shall I?"

19. **Extinction:** Ignore minor misbehavior that is not dangerous, destructive, embarrassing, or an impediment to learning. (Pretend that you didn't hear, move away, or focus on something else.)

20. **Take Time to Teach:** Often we expect children to read our minds and know how to do things they have never been taught. Although our expectations may be clear to us, children may not have a clue.

21. **Punt the Plan:** In the middle of something that is not working, move on to something else. De-stress yourself. Be willing to stay flexible and quickly switch directions when you see that children are unable to focus or need a break.

Principles in Chapter 3: Showing Respect

22. **Golden Rule:** Do unto children what you would have them do unto you! Children will (eventually) treat us the way we treat them. It pays to take a deep breath and think twice, so that we will tread gently. Ask yourself, "How would I want someone to do that to me? How would that make me feel?"

23. **Demonstrate Respect:** Treat the child the same way you treat other important people in your life—the way you want him to treat you, as well as others. Ask yourself, "How would I want her to say that to me?" Think before you speak.

24. **Whisper:** Instead of yelling, screaming, or talking in a loud voice, surprise children by lowering your voice to a whisper. It helps you to stay in control, think more clearly, and most often evokes immediate attention.

25. **Privacy:** Always move to a private place to talk when there is a problem. Discuss issues with a child where he feels safe.

26. **Turtle Time:** Encourage child to withdraw into his "turtle shell" to calm himself down, think more clearly, and keep from reacting in a negative or unproductive way.

27. **Owning the Problem:** Decide who owns the problem by asking yourself, "Who is it bugging?" If it is bugging you, then you own the problem and need to take responsibility for solving it, or you can opt to not let it bug you and let it go.

28. **I-Message:** Own your own feelings. "When you make a mess with the paper towels, the floor gets wet, and I feel frustrated. I would like for you to throw your towels away when you are finished washing your hands." I-messages only work within the context of a caring connection.

29. **Apology:** Apologize easily when you goof or "lose it." ("I wish I could erase what I just said." "You must have been scared by my reaction." "I didn't mean to hurt your feelings." "I was wrong." "I'm sorry.") Apologize *for* the child. ("I'm sorry he knocked you down.") But don't make the child apologize—you might be making him lie or think that wrong-doings can be rectified with an apology.

30. **Get on the Child's Eye Level:** When talking with the child, get down on his eye level and look him in the eye while talking softly to him.

31. **Think of the Outcome:** What is your intention? What outcome are you trying to achieve? Are you trying to take care of an issue for the moment, or are you

trying to help the child learn important problem-solving skills? Keep your eye on your goal.

32. **Anticipation:** Think ahead about whether the child is capable of handling the situation. Be realistic and remember to focus on the children's needs, not just your own agenda. Staying proactive will make a difference in avoiding behavior issues.

33. **Don't Put the Cats with the Pigeons:** Don't place temptation in front of the child. Place materials for an upcoming lesson that may be particularly colorful and attractive away from curious eyes and hands. Set materials out of reach until after you have given instructions and are ready to have the children use them. "Don't place candy out in a dish if you don't want children to eat it!"

Principles in Chapter 4: Giving Nurturance

34. **Get Help:** Staying aware of your limits and getting support from others is vitally important. You may want to ask another teacher to cover for you while you focus on, or spend extra positive time with, a child who seems troubled. Be sure to prioritize and ask for help when you need it.

35. **Take Care of Yourself:** Children pick up on our emotions and model our ways of handling our feelings, so we want to do our best to be a good example of healthy and mature behavior.

36. **Nap/Take a Break:** A nap usually puts everything in better perspective. Teachers and parents are often sleep deprived. Make it a goal to go to bed sooner at night, so that you will feel more energetic during the day. At school, when you see children becoming tired or lethargic, take a stretch break, a music break, or a brain break.

37. **Bunny Planet:** Close your eyes and tell the children that you are going to the Bunny Planet (or another imaginary place). Ask them to tell you when they are ready for you to come back, once things are quiet and they are ready to make good choices.

38. **Read a Book:** Sit down and read to the children. Take your attention away from the child who is behaving inappropriately. Read something engaging and helpful to them until you have cooled off and can deal with the situation in a productive manner.

39. **Have Fun Together:** Children love to know that they bring us joy and pleasure. Lighten up and have fun.

40. **Humor:** Make a game out of it. Have fun. Laugh a lot together. ("How would a rabbit brush his teeth?") Enjoy the child's sense of humor.

41. **Jump Start a Belly Laugh:** Surprise children by teaching them to jump start a belly laugh. Grab hands and jump up and down together, saying, "ho, ho, ho" really fast, until you are genuinely laughing. You'll be surprised how good it feels to laugh. Your body and your brain both get a chance to take a break. When you come back to where you were, you will be more relaxed and have better perspective.

42. **Make It Fun:** See if you can turn a chore into a challenge; a job into a game; a "must" into a "want to." Model pleasure in doing hard work.

43. **Give Life to Inanimate Objects:** Tell the child that "the books are calling," or "the trash is saying that it wants to be taken out to the hall." Give your voice a believable "squeaky" tone to make it more dramatic (and fun).

44. **Institute Mailboxes:** Put a mailbox outside your classroom, and attach one to each child's desk or cubby. Write personal notes (suggestions, thanks, etc.) to put inside the child's mailbox. Be sure to have one on your desk for their messages back to you.

Principles in Chapter 5: Fostering Independence

45. **Good Head on Your Shoulders:** Tell a child frequently, "You have a good head on your shoulders. You decide. I trust your judgment." This brings out the best in the child and shows him that eventually he will be in charge of his own life and responsible for his/her own decisions.

46. **Thank You:** Thank the child for doing the right thing—*before* he does it! "Thank you for dropping your paper scraps into the trash can" (before they land on the floor). "Thank you for tucking your pencil in your desk before you line up" (before the pencil is put away). Children want to be helpful and cooperative, and a gentle reminder (with respectful thanks) encourages success.

47. **Trust:** Let the child know—often and in many ways—that you trust his judgment and his ability to make good choices.

48. **Logical Consequences:** Teach the child that behavior has consequences. If he forgets his sweater, he gets cold. If he forgets his boots, he cannot play on the grass. If he throws his lunch on the floor, it is all gone. If he forgets his homework, he needs to finish it during puzzle time.

49. **Third Party:** Tell a story about a particular situation they may encounter and elicit suggestions. For example, "There is a mom who would like her son to take out the trash. Should she (a) ask him to do it, (b) tell him to do it, (c) let him know the trash is full and needs to be taken out, (d) tell him the 'trash is calling,' (e) ask him to help her with the trash, or (f) other? What should the mom do?"

50. **Self-Correction:** Give the child a chance to self-correct. Without talking or lecturing, give him space and time. Tell him you will check back with him later.

51. **Ask the Child:** Ask the child for input. "Do you think this was a good choice?" "What were you trying to accomplish or tell someone with your behavior?" "What could you have done instead that would have worked better?" "What do you think could help you in the future to remember to make a better choice?" "How would you like for things to be different?" "How about drawing a picture of how you feel right now?" Children have wonderful insight into their own behavior and great suggestions for ways to make things better.

52. **Let the Child Be the Teacher:** Let the child assume the role of teacher (or parent). Ask him to teach you a skill.

53. **Values Are Caught, Not Taught:** Expose children to role models who are passionate about their work. Take piano lessons yourself and watch children absorb your love for music. Eat well and exercise, and watch them imitate your example. Don't talk about what you want to do—do it! Invite professionals and parents to your classroom to present their passion about a job or a hobby.

54. **Teach—Don't Reteach:** Teach children the correct procedures and behaviors as soon as you have an opportunity. It is much harder to go back and undo a learned behavior. Personal items on your desk or a remote control are not toys. Keep them high up out of the reach of a toddler. Children need to know your expectations for entering your classroom on the first day of school. Lining up, cleaning up after a snack, and washing hands are not negotiable.

55. **Successive Approximations:** Don't expect perfection. Acknowledge small steps in the right direction.

56. **Prompt and Praise:** Explain the expected behavior in a non-critical way and praise the child as soon as the behavior occurs.

57. **Sing:** Surprise children by singing what you want them to do. Get in the habit of making up songs with familiar tunes (e.g., "The Farmer in the Dell," "Jingle Bells") and using words to describe your expectations. This approach works well with children of all ages.

58. **Allow Imperfection:** Don't demand perfection. With perfection as the goal, we are all losers.

59. **Encouragement:** Give encouragement as often as possible. Help the child see the progress he has made. "You got three spelling words correct. That is better than last week!" "Doesn't it feel good to be able to zip your own zipper?" "You cleaned up your own spill. You must be proud to know that you did that all by yourself."

Principles in Chapter 6: Building Resilience

60. **Availability:** At school and at home, a child wants—and needs—time spent with the undivided focus of an adult. We need to stop what we are doing, make eye contact, and really take time to talk with and listen to a child. Encourage parents to spend 15 minutes a day with their child at home.

61. **Wants and Feelings:** Allow the child to want what he wants and feel what he feels. Don't try to talk him out of or feel guilty for his wants and feelings.

62. **Empowerment:** Encourage children to solve their own problems. Let them know that their choices will determine their future.

63. **Make Up a Story:** Make up a story giving an account of an incident in which the child was at fault, but using another child's name. Ask the child what the character in the story did wrong—and what he should do differently the next time.

64. **Role-Playing:** Have children act out different roles or ask a child to exchange roles with you. Let him tell you what he would do if he were in your place. Have him sit in your chair at circle time and show you how he perceives you. Taking on other roles helps children gain perspective.

65. **Brainstorming:** Help the child brainstorm possible solutions to the dilemma, problem, or predicament.

66. **Stay Healthy:** Remember the importance of taking good care of yourself—physically as well as emotionally. Eat well, sleep well, and get plenty of exercise. You will not only be able to cope better, but you will also become a good role model for the children you teach.

67. **Keep Your Perspective:** Is it really that important? If not, let it go.

68. **Frog Suit:** Teach the child to "put his frog suit on." The imaginary, invisible frog suit protects the child from being hurt by other children's careless or cruel comments.

69. **Help Me Out:** Elicit the child's support by asking him to help you out.

70. **Teach Children to Stand Up to Bullies:** Empower children by role-playing and letting them practice speaking up (loudly, if necessary) to bullies.

71. **Best Friend:** Elicit help from the child's best friend. Ask a friend to see if he can support the child's behavior, emotions, or learning.

 Principles in Chapter 7: Preventing Misbehavior

72. **Pay Attention:** Keep your eyes and mind on what is happening. Don't wait until the child is out of control to step in.

73. **Remember Who the Grown-Ups Are:** Always remember that you are the grown-up and that you are ultimately responsible for the way things turn out. The child does not have your judgment or history of experiences and can't be held responsible for the ultimate outcome.

74. **Keep It Simple:** "We need to be kind to our friends." "Time for a nap." "Remember the rules." "Gentle hands." "Walking feet." Stating things simply keeps us and our listener focused on the real issue and lets us both stay level-headed about what needs to be done.

75. **Blame It on the Rules:** "Our school rule is to wash your hands before eating." It is important to tell children why rules exist, so that they have a framework when they are reminded of a rule. Once the groundwork of understanding is set, "blaming it on the rules" can help the child follow through.

76. **Shrug:** Learn to shrug instead of arguing. The shrug means, "I'm sorry, but that's the way it is—end of discussion."

77. **Preparation:** Let the child know ahead of time what to expect: "We can go outside and play 'Duck, Duck, Goose' for 20 minutes. Then we have to come back and get in our seats quickly and quietly."

78. **Hand Gestures:** Develop hand gestures that signify "Please," "Thank you," "More," "Stop," "Be careful," "Use your words," and "All done."

79. **Cueing:** Give the child a cue to remind him—ahead of time—of the behavior you want him to exhibit.

80. **Switch Gears:** When the unexpected occurs, look for a way to make the most of the situation. For example, if you have a long wait, suggest that each of you close

your eyes and listen for what you can hear, or look around and find something you have never noticed before. Another name for this principle is "The Plan B Principle." When plan A falls through, then let's make plan B more interesting than plan A might have been.

81. **Do the Unexpected:** React in a surprising way. Start doing jumping jacks! Clap a familiar rhythm such as "Jingle Bells" to relieve the tension and get some perspective. It is amazing how much better you can think and then decide on a more rational way to handle the situation when your head is clear.

82. **Thinking:** Take time to think about your options and consider the outcome. Will it be positive? How do you want this to turn out?

83. **Satiation:** If a behavior is not dangerous, destructive, embarrassing, or an impediment to learning, let it continue until the child is tired of doing it.

 Principles in Chapter 8: Creating Solutions to Common Behavior Challenges

84. **Nip It in the Bud:** When you see a child doing something that is dangerous, destructive, or embarrassing (to you or to himself), take immediate action. Don't let the behavior continue, hoping that it will go away. It usually gets worse if the child knows you are watching and you are doing nothing about it. Giving a hand signal might be enough. You might also whisper a code word, such as "red light," that always means "Stop right now!" You might have to approach the child, take his hand, and move him to another place in the *least reinforcing way possible*.

85. **Use Actions Instead of Words:** Don't say anything. Instead of responding when a child says something inappropriate or hurtful, let the words hang in the air. Walk away or take his hand and move to another place. Give him a chance to hear what he just said. Very often, he will make an effort to self-correct or apologize.

86. **Divide and Conquer:** Separate children who are reinforcing each other's misbehavior.

87. **Stay Detached Emotionally:** Try to remain objective, with your eye on the goal of self-discipline. Don't let the child "hook" you emotionally—in other words, don't take his behavior personally.

88. **Take a Break:** Tell the child to take a break and think about what he could do differently that would work better or be more constructive. Give him a place to go until he is ready to come back and behave more productively. This could be a place that you have created in your classroom that is comfortable and quiet. A timer is sometimes helpful. The child can determine how long he needs to reflect, refocus, and calm down. The child is in control here. He can decide when he is ready to rejoin the group or try again.

89. **The Timer Says It's Time:** Set a timer to help children make transitions. "When the timer goes off, you will need to put away your books." "In five minutes, we will need to line up for lunch." It is a good idea to give the child a chance to choose how long he needs to pull himself together: "It's okay to be upset. How

long do you need?" Then allow him to remove himself from the group and set the timer. You may offer the child a choice (and set the timer) when it is necessary to encourage cooperation: "Do you want to pick up the blocks/let Susan have the wagon/share the computer in one minute or two?"

90. **Get Support from Another Person:** Ask someone else to help you reinforce the positive behavior.

91. **Change of Environment:** If the children's misbehavior cannot be stopped, move to another room or location or go outside.

92. **Wait Until Later:** You can say, "Let's both think about this and come back in 10 minutes to discuss it." Then set the timer. That gives the child (and you) time to consider the actions and think about the best way to handle it. With an older child, you may say, "We'll discuss this at 2:00. We both need time to cool off and think." Then you can meet calmly with the child and say, "Let's talk about what happened. What would a better choice have been?"

93. **Write a Contract:** Sit with the child after he has behaved appropriately and the negative emotions have disappeared and write a contract together for future behavior. Be sure to let him have input. Then both parties sign the contract. (This works for older children.)

94. **Collect Data:** Keep a written record of the frequency of a specific behavior that seems to be continuing. Record the antecedents as well as the consequences. Look for patterns that may give clues as to possible reasons, situations, and/or solutions.

95. **ABC:** Learn to think in terms of ABC: antecedent, behavior, and consequences. What was going on before the behavior occurred and what happened afterwards, as a result of the behavior?

Principles in Chapter 9: Collaborating with Families

96. **Chill Out:** It's no big deal! Don't make a mountain out of a molehill. This, too, will pass.

97. **Other Shoe:** Look at the situation from the family's perspective. How would you feel if the "shoe was on the other foot"? What if you were the parent? What would you want to hear from the teacher about your child?

98. **Common Sense:** Use common sense. Is this reasonable? Is the child ready for this challenge or lesson? Is what you are requesting or expecting developmentally appropriate? Is he capable of mastering what you ask, or will he become further frustrated or discouraged? Stay flexible to accommodate children's needs and don't expect perfection. Be patient, and always assist children in experiencing success.

99. **Partner/Co-Worker:** Support your co-worker's decisions and interactions with parents. If you disagree, move away and let him follow through. It helps to check with your co-workers before you talk to a parent about a specific incident, so that you won't be giving different messages. You need to present a unified front.

100. **Human:** Remember that children have feelings too, just like we do. It is in everyone's best interest to treat the children in our care as well as or better than those for whom we are not responsible. Because we have had an opportunity to get to know them well, we have an obligation to look out for their best interests.

101. **Bake a Cake:** When all else fails, bake a cake together (and eat it once it cools). It is a great way to stay connected and build happy memories. This principle reminds us that we need to be more mindful to enjoy our times together and to be thankful for each day's blessings. It is also wise to look for opportunities to celebrate our successes and appreciate those who are responsible for providing these memorable experiences for us. The sky is the limit when it comes to showing gratitude and recognition to others in our lives who have helped us along the way.

appendix B

List of 101 Principles for Positive Guidance in Spanish

 Principles in Chapter 1: Building a Caring Community/
Principios del Capítulo 1: Crear una Comunidad Cariñosa

1. **Connect Before You Correct/Conexión con el Niño Antes de Corrección:** Encuentre diferentes maneras de "conectarse" con el niño. Aprenda información sobre el niño y demuéstrele que usted se preocupa por él antes de tratar de corregir su conducta. Ayúdele a descubrir sus capacidades, lo que lo hace especial, sus habilidades especiales, llamándole atención a estas cualidades.

2. **Time In/Tiempo Personal:** Cuando esté cerca de un niño, tóquelo ligeramente, déle un "bien hecho" con el pulgar o choque los cinco. Piénselo. Las palabras no siempre expresan el mensaje que usted quiere mandarle a alguien. Sin embargo, tocar es diferente. Es menos probable que los niños cometan faltas de conducta graves cuando sienten cariño y respeto por parte de un adulto que es importante para ellos. Lo que usted hace es tan importante como lo que dice. Necesitamos aprovechar cada oportunidad para demostrar nuestros intereses personales y para asegurarnos de que cada niño reciba tiempo personal de parte de nosotros.

3. **Belonging and Significance/Pertenecer y Ser Importante:** Recuerde que todos necesitamos sentir que formamos parte de algo y somos significantes. Ayuda cada niño a sentirse importante, asignándole trabajos importantesy recordándole que si él no lo hace, ¡nadie más lo hará! Ayúdelo a sentirse importante haciéndolo responsable.

4. **Love/Cariño:** Cada niño necesita un adulto quien los quiere y quiere pasar tiempo con él. Haga el esfuerzo para enseñarle lo especial que él es.

5. **Class Meeting/Juntas de Clase:** Las juntas de clase le ofrecen a los niños la oportunidad de refleccionar, escuchar, recalcar, y solucionar problemas. En cualquier momento que sienta la necesidad a dirigirse u afrontar un problema, reúne a los niños para discutir. Comienza el día, concéntrese en comunicación recíproca en lugar de sermoniar al niño. Escuche más que hablar. Maestros y niños aprenden uno del otro constantemente.

6. **Make a Sacrifice/Haga un Sacrificio:** Asegúrese de hacerse cargo de sus asuntos personales (revisar su sitio de red social, correo electrónico, mensajes de texto, o revisar trabajos) antes de la escuela, y déle toda su atencióna los niños.

7. **Establish Routines and Traditions/Establezca Rutinas y Tradiciones:** Los niños se portan mejor cuando saben qué esperar. Establezca tradiciones que ellos puedan anticipar y que les proporcionen recuerdos y sentimientos de seguridad y pertenencia.

8. **Talk About Children Positively to Others/Dígale Cosas Positivas de los Niños a Otros:** Deje que los niños lo escuchen hablando positivamente acerca de ellos—alabando sus cualidades, esfuerzos, y acciones—a otros.

9. **Put It in Writing/Póngalo por Escrito:** Empiece la tradición de mandar pensamientos positivos por escrito. Déjele una nota que diga "me importas" en lugares inesperados.

10. **Kiss Your Brain/Dale un Beso a Tu Cerebro:** Cuando el niño ha demostrado una conducta que a usted le hace sentir orgulloso, y está tomando buenas decisiones, asegúrese de aplaudirselo, agradecerselo, y poner énfasis en sus excelentes contribuciones. Dígale, "dale un beso a tu cerebro!" (¡A los niños les encanta!) Ellos responderán dándose un beso en la palma de su mano o en sus dedos y tocandose la cabeza. usted también puede modelar esta acción para ellos.

11. **Positive Closure/Cierre Positivo:** Al final del día, recuérdele a sus niños que son especiales y que les quiere. Ayúdelos a pensar en algo bueno, acerca del día que ha terminado y del día que tienen por delante.

Principles in Chapter 2: Guiding Behavior/ Principiods del Capítulo 2: Guiar el Comportamiento

12. **Modeling/Modelo a Seguir:** Modele la conducta que quiere. Muéstrele al niño, por ejemplo, cómo comportarse. Los niños nos están observando todo el tiempo, y ellos crecerán a ser cómo nosotros—así lo quiéramos o no.

13. **Make a Big Deal/Estimar Mucho:** Ponga énfasis en responsabilidad, consideración, conducta apropiada—con atención (sus propios ojos), agradecimientos, reconocimientos, aplausos, abrazos, privilegios especiales, estímulos (no comida).

14. **Incompatible Alternative/Alternativa Incompatible:** Dele al niño algo que hacer que sea incompatible con la actitud inapropiada. Dígale, "Vamos a imaginar que estamos en una mision imposible y veamos si podemos caminar hasta la cafeteria sin que nadie nos escuche." "Ayúdame a escoger 6 marcadores" (cuando el niño esté desconcentrado o enfadado). Si el niño lo está molestando porque está jugando con las cintas de sus zapatos, en lugar de decírselo, simplemente pídale que le ayude a ordenar el papel o las crayolas por color.

15. **Choice/Opción:** Dale dos opciones al niño, las dos deben ser positivas y aceptables. "¿Quieres caminar de puntitas o saltar a la carpeta?" "Tú eliges o yo eligiré por ti." "Necesitamos despejar nuestros escritorios. Necesitan uno o dos minutos?" Empiece a contar el tiempo en el reloj automático. El maestro determina el objetivo que quiere lograr y le da al niño dos opciones de como lograrlo. "Necesitamos guardar los juguetes. ¿Quieres ayudar con los rompecabezas o con los bloques?"

16. **When–Then/Abuse It–Lose It/Cuando–Entonces/Si Abusas Lo Pierdes:** "Cuando pongas los libros en el anaquel, entonces podrás ponerte tu abrigo." "Cuando termines de guardar la Plastilina, entonces podrás elegir un compañero para jugar."

17. **Follow-Through/Consistency/Seguimiento/Consistencia:** No deje que el niño lo manipule a actuar de otra manera que no sea la que usted crea correcta. ¡Sea

firme (pero cordial)! Siga sus instintos. Si no parece correcto, no deje que el niño lo haga. Proponga opciones y alternativas que puedan ayudar al niño a concentrarse en conductas más apropiadas y experiencias de aprendizaje positivas.

18. **Validation/Validación:** Reconozca (valore) lo que el niño quiere y sus sentimientos. "Yo sé que estás enojado con tu amigo, y que quieres quedarte con los dos libros. No te culpo. Yo me sentiría igual. Sin embargo, él necesita uno. ¿Quieres elegir cuál le quieres dar, o lo puedo elegir yo?"

19. **Extinction/Extinción:** No dé atención a faltas de conducta menores si no son peligrosas, destructivas, vergüenzas, o que les impidan aprender. (Pretenda que no escuchónada—aléjese—concéntrese en otra cosa.)

20. **Take Time to Teach/Tómese Su Tiempo Enseñando:** Frecuentemente nosotros esperamos que los niños nos lean la mente para aprender cómo hacer cosas que nunca les hemos enseñado. Aunque nuestras expectativas sean claras para nosotros, puede ser que nuestros niños no tengan ni idea de lo que esperamos.

21. **Punt the Plan/Cambie el Plan:** En medio de algo que no está funcionando, prosiga con algo diferente. No se complique la vida. Esté dispuesto a mantenerse flexible y a moverse en una dirección diferente cuando vea que los niños no se pueden concentrar o necesitan un descanso.

Principles in Chapter 3: Showing Respect/ Principios del Capítulo 3: Demostrar Respeto

22. **Golden Rule/La Regla de Oro:** ¡Hágale a los niños lo que usted les pidiría que le hicieran a usted! Los niños (eventualmente) nos tratarán de la manera en que nosotros los tratamos. Vale la pena tomar un respiro profundo y pensar dos veces, para suavemente poder dejar una huella en ellos. Pregúntese a si mismo, "¿Cómo me gustaría que alguien hiciera eso amí?" "¿Cómo me haría sentir?"

23. **Demonstrate Respect/Demuestre Respeto:** Trate al niño de la misma manera en que trata a otra gente importante en su vida—de la misma manera que usted quiera que lo trate, y a los demás. (¿Cómo me gustaria que él me dijera esto?) Piense antes de hablar. ¿Estuvo mal lo que hizo? Y que deberá de hacer diferente para la próxima vez.

24. **Whisper/Susurro:** En lugar de gritar, o de hablar en voz alta, sorprenda al niño usando una voz tan baja como un susurro. Esto le ayudará a mantener el control, pensar más claramente, y por lo regular obtiene atención inmediata.

25. **Privacy/Privacidad:** Siempre vaya a un lugar privado cuando tenga que hablar de algún problema. Discuta problemas con el niño donde él se sienta seguro.

26. **Turtle Time/Hora de la Tortuga:** Estimule al niño a que se meta en su "caparazón de tortuga" para que se calme, para que piense mas claramente, y para evitar una reacción negativa.

27. **Owning the Problem/Adueñese del Problema:** Decida de quien es el problema preguntándose a si mismo, "¿A quién le está molestando?" Si le está molestando a usted, entonces es su problema y es responsable de resolverlo, o puede decidir no dejar que le moleste (y dejarlo pasar), con sutileza de niño.

28. **I-Message/Mensajes-del-Yo:** Aduéñese de sus sentimientos. "Cuando tú haces un desorden con las toallas de papel, el piso se moja, y yo me desespero. Me gustaría que cuando termines de lavarte las manos, cuidadosamente tires las toallas en el bote de basura." Mensajes-del-yo sólo funcionan cuando se usan en un contexto de mutuo respeto.

29. **Apology/Pida Disculpas**: Pida disculpas facilmente cuando cometa un error o "se desespere." ("Ojalá pudiera borrar lo que acabo de decir." "Te has de haber asustado con mi reacción." "No era mi intención lastimar tus sentimientos." "Me equivoqué." "Lo siento.") Pida disculpas por el otro niño. ("Siento mucho que él te haiga tumbado.") Pero no le pida al niño que se disculpe. Lo podría estar haciendo que mienta o que piense que las malicias se pueden arreglar con una disculpa.

30. **Get on the Child's Eye Level/Póngase al Nivel de los Ojos del Niño:** Cuando esté hablando con el niño, póngase al nivel de sus ojos y mírelo a los ojos mientras le habla suavemente.

31. **Think of the Outcome/Piense en el Resultado:** ¿Cuál es su intención? ¿Qué resultados está tratando de obtener? ¿Está tratando de resolver un problema de forma pasajera, o está tratando de enseñarle al niño las habilidades necesarias para resolver problemas? Mantenga su vista fija en su meta.

32. **Anticipation/Anticipación:** Piense antes de tiempo si el niño será capaz de manejar la situación. Sea realista y recuerde concentrarse en las necesidades del niño, no sólo en su ajenda. Manteniendo al niño ocupado en algo productivo le ayudará a evitar problemas de comportamiento.

33. **Don't Put the Cats with the Pigeons/No Pongas los Gatos con las Palomas:** No le ponga tentaciones delante del niño. Colóque los materiales que puedan ser particularmente coloridos y atractivos a los ojos y manos curiosas fuera de su alcanze. "No ponga dulces en un plato al descubierto si no quiere que los niños se los coman!" Ponga los materiales fuera del alcance hasta que usted haya dado las instrucciones y los niños estén listos para usarlos.

Principles in Chapter 4: Giving Nurturance/ Principios del Capítulo 4: Ofrecer Apoyo

34. **Get Help/Pida Ayuda:** Este principio se refiere a la importancia de priorizar y pedir ayuda cuando la necesite. También puede ser que en algún momento tenga que pedirle a otro maestro que lo cubra mientras usted se enfoca o pasar tiempo extra con un niño que parece seriamente confundido. Mantenerse alerta de sus límites y buscar ayuda física de otros es de vital importancia.

35. **Take Care of Yourself/Cuídese:** Los niños perciben nuestras emociones e imitan la manera en que manejamos nuestras emociones. Queremos hacer lo posible para ser el mejor ejemplo para ellos de cómo comportarnos en una manera saludable y madura.

36. **Nap/Take a Break/Siesta/Tómese un Descanso:** Una siesta usualmente pone todo en una mejor perspectiva. ¡Maestros y padres de familia usualmente no duermen las horas necesarias! Póngase como meta irse a dormir mas temprano en la

noche, para que se pueda sentir más lleno de energía durante el día. En la escuela, cuando vea que sus niños se están cansando, tómense un descanso para estirarse, para escuchar música, o denle un descanso a sus cerebros.

37. **Bunny Planet/Planeta de Conejos** (adaptado de Rosemary Wells): Cierre sus ojos y dígale a los niños que se va a ir al planeta de los conejos (o algún otro lugar imaginario). Pídales que le avisen cuando estén listos para que regrese (cuando las cosas estén calmadas y ellos estén listos para tomar buenas decisiones).

38. **Read a Book/Lea un Libro:** Siéntese a leerle un libro al niño. No lo ponga mucha atención al niño que no se está portando de una manera apropiada. Lea algo interesante y útil hasta que se sienta más tranquilo y pueda manejar la situación de una manera productiva.

39. **Have Fun Together/Diviértanse Juntos:** A los niños les encanta saber que nos traen alegría y placer. Alijérese y diviértase.

40. **Humor/Humor:** Busque momentos de humor. A los niños les encanta hacernos y vernos reír. Disfrute del sentido de humor del niño.

41. **Jump Start a Belly Laugh/Comience Carcajadas de Barriga:** Sorprenda a los niños enseñandoles a comenzar carcajadas de barriga. Tómense de las manos y salten de arriba a abajo juntos, diciendo, "ho, ho" rápidamente, hasta que se estén riendo de verdad. Le sorprenderá lo bien que se siente reírse. Le da a su cuerpo y a su cerebro la oportunidad de "tomarse un descanso," y cuando "regresen" a donde estaban, todos estarán mas relajados y tendrán una mejor perspectiva.

42. **Make It Fun/Hágalo Divertido:** Busque la manera de convertir un que hacer en una competencia; un trabajo en un juego; un "tengo que hacer" en un "quiero hacer." Modele placer cuando haga trabajo duro.

43. **Give Life to Inanimate Objects/Dele Vida a Objetos No-Animados:** Dígale al niño que "los libros le están llamando" o que "el basurero está pidiendo que lo saque al pasillo." Dele a su voz un tono "chillante" que lo haga más dramático (y divertido).

44. **Institute Mailboxes/Instituya Buzónes de Correo:** Coloque buzónes afuera del salón, y sujete uno al escritorio de cada uno de los niños. Escriba notas personales (sugerencias, agradecimientos, etc.) y pongalas en los buzónes de los niños. Asegúrese de tener uno en su escritorio en donde ellos puedan depositar sus respuestas.

Principles in Chapter 5: Fostering Independence/ Principios del Capítulo 5: Formentar la Independencia

45. **Good Head on Your Shoulders/Buena Cabeza en Tus Hombros:** Dígale al niño frecuentemente, "Tienes una buena cabeza en tus hombros. Tú decide. Yo confío en que tomarás una buena decisión." Esto sacarálo mejor del niño y le enseñará que eventualmente él estará a cargo de su propia vida y será responsable de sus propias decisiones.

46. **Thank You/Gracias:** Agradézcale a los niños cuando hagan las cosas bien— ¡antes de que lo hagan! "Gracias por tirar tu basura de papel en el basurero" (en cuanto vea que la basura puede terminar en el piso.) "Gracias por guardar tu

lápiz antes de ponerte en fila" (antes de que guarde el lápiz). Los niños quieren ayudar y cooperar, y un suave recordatorio (un agradecimiento con respeto) promoverá su éxito.

47. **Trust/Confianza:** Déjele saber al niño—de diferentes maneras y frecuentemente—que confía en su habilidad de tomar las decisiones correctas.

48. **Logical Consequences/Consecuencias Lógicas:** Enséñele al niño que nuestras acciones tienen consequencias. Si se le olvida su abrigo, le dará frío. Si se le olvidan sus botas, no podrá jugar en el zacate. Si tira su comida en el piso, ya no se la podrá comer. Si se le olvida su tarea, tendrá que terminarla durante el tiempo designado para jugar con los rompecabezas.

49. **Third Party/Terceras Personas:** Cuente la historia de alguna situación en particular que usted esté tratando de resolver y pida sugerencias. Por ejemplo, "Hay una mamá a la que le gustaría que su hijo saque la basura. ¿Crees que ella debe (a) pedirle que lo haga? (b) decirle que lo haga? (c) dejarle saber que el basureroestá lleno y que alguien necesita sacarla? (d) decirle que "la basura lo está llamando"? (e) pedirle que le ayude con la basura?, u (f) otra opción? ¿Qué debe de hacer la mamá?"

50. **Self-Correction/Auto-Corrección:** Déle al niño la oportunidad de auto-corregirse. Déle su espacio y tiempo sin hablar o cermoniarlo. Dígale que luego regresará a ver cómo sigue y qué está haciendo.

51. **Ask the Child/Pregúntele al Niño:** Pídale su opinión al niño. "¿Tú crees que esto fue una buena idea?" "¿Qué estabas tratando de hacer o decir con tu actitud?" "¿Qué podrías haber hecho en lugar de lo que hiciste que hubiera funcionado mejor?" "¿Qué crees que te ayudaría a recordar en el futuro que puedas tomar una mejor decisión?" "¿Cómo te gustaría que las cosas hubieran pasado?" "¿Qué tal si haces un dibujo que demuestre cómo te sientes en este momento?" Los niños tienen una estupenda percepción de su propia conducta y excelentes sugerencias de cómo mejorar las cosas.

52. **Let the Child Be the Teacher/Deje Que el Niño Sea el Maestro:** Permita que el niño tome el papel de maestro (o padre). Pídale que le enseñe una habilidad.

53. **Values Are Caught, Not Taught/Los Valores Se Pegan, No Se Enseñan:** Exponga a los niños a modelos a seguir que son entusiastas en su trabajo. Tome clases de piano usted mismo y observe como los niños absorven su amor por la música. Coma bien y haga ejercicio, y mírelos seguir su ejemplo. No hable de lo que quiere hacer—¡hágalo! Invite a profesionales y a padres de familia a su salón de clases para que les enseñen la pasión que ellos tienen por su trabajo o pasatiempos.

54. **Teach—Don't Re-Teach/Enseñe—No Vuelva a Enseñar:** Enséñele a los niños el procedimiento y la conducata correcta en cuanto se le dé la oportunidad. Es mucho más difícil regresar y corregir una conducta que ya ha sido adoptada. Los materiales de oficina que están en nuestros escritorios no son juguetes. Manténgalos en un lugar alto y fuera del alcanze del niño. Los niños necesitan saber las expectativas que usted tiene antes de entrar en su salón el primer día de clases. Saltar

lugares en la línea, limpiar despés de comer bocadillos, y lavarse las manos no son decisiones que se pueden discutir o eliminar.

55. **Successive Approximations/Aproximaciones al Éxito:** No espere la perfección. Reconozca pasos pequeños en la dirección correcta.

56. **Prompt and Praise/Reconozca y Pronto:** Explíquele al niño la actitud que usted espera de él de una manera tranquila y reconozcasu esfuerzo en cuanto la conducta se presente.

57. **Sing/Cante:** Sorprenda a los niños cantando lo que quiere que hagan. Haga inventar canciones una costumbre (con ritmos familiares, por ejemplo "Campanas de Belén") y use palabras que describan sus expectativas. Este procedimiento funciona con niños de todas las edades.

58. **Allow Imperfection/Permita Imperfecciones:** No demande perfección. Todos somos perdedores cuando tenemos perfección como meta.

59. **Encouragement/Estímulo:** Estimule a los niños lo más que le sea posible. Ayude al niño a ver el progreso que ha hecho. "Deletreaste tres palabras correctamente. ¡Es mejor que la semana pasada!" "¿Se siente bien el poder cerrar el cierre tu mismo verdad?" "Limpiaste tu propio derrame. Estoy seguro de que estás muy orgulloso de saber que lo hiciste tú solo."

Principles in Chapter 6: Building Resilience/ Principios del Capítulo 6: Fortalecer la Resistencia

60. **Availability/Disponibilidad:** En la escuela y la casa, un niño quiere—y necesita— pasar tiempo con un adulto que le preste toda su atención. Cuando hacemos esto, paramos de hacer lo que hacemos, nos miramos a los ojos, y tomamos el tiempo para hablar y escuchar al niño con atención. Anime a los padres a pasar 15 minutos al día con sus hijos en la casa.

61. **Wants and Feelings/Deseos y Sentimientos:** Permítale al niño que desee lo que quiera y que sienta lo que quiera sentir. No trate de convencerlo de algo diferente o de hacerlo sentir culpable por lo que quiere y lo que siente.

62. **Empowerment/Autonomía:** Desarrolle la competencia, habilidades, maestría, e independencia del niño. Anímelo a que resuelva sus propios problemas. Déjele saber que sus decisiones determinarán su futuro.

63. **Make Up a Story/Invente una Historia:** Invente una historia que contarle al niño—usando el nombre de otro niño—pero hablando de un accidente ocurrido de él cual el niño tuvo la culpa. Pregúntele al niño lo que el niño del cuento hizo mal—y lo que debe hacer diferente la próxima vez.

64. **Role-Playing/Actuación:** Pídale al niño que cambie de papeles con usted. Deje que le diga lo que él haría si estuviera en su lugar. Déjelo que se siente en su silla mientras coviven en círculo en la alfombra y que le muestre la manera en que él percibe su forma de ser y de actuar. Permita que los niños experimenten con papeles diferentes para que entiendan perspectivas distintas.

65. **Brainstorming/Lluvia de Ideas:** Junto con el niño, hagan una lista de posibles soluciones al dilema, problema, o apuro.

66. **Stay Healthy/Manténgase Saludable:** Recuerde la importancia de cuidarse—tanto físicamente como mentalmente. Coma bien, duerma bien, y haga bastante ejercicio. No sólo podrá adaptarse mejor, sino que también será un buen ejemplo a seguir para los niños que está educando.

67. **Keep Your Perspective/Mantenga Su Perspectiva:** ¿Es esto de verdad importante? Si no, déjelo pasar.

68. **Frog Suit/Traje de Rana:** Enséñele al niño a ponerse el "traje de rana." El traje de rana proteje al niño de comentarios crueles o descuidados hechos por otros niños, que lo puedan lastimar.

69. **Help Me Out/Ayúdame:** Obtenga la ayuda del niño. Pídale que le ayude.

70. **Teach Children to Stand Up to Bullies/Enséñele a los Niños a Defenderse de los Matones:** Capacite a los niños por medio de desempeñar un papel dramatizado y dejándolos contestar (en un tono fuerte, si es necesario) a niños matones que los molesten.

71. **Best Friend/Mejor Amigo:** Obtenga ayuda del mejor amigo del niño. Pregúntele al amigo si él o ella puede apoyar al niño a mejorar su conducta, emociones, o aprendizaje.

🐞 *Principles in Chapter 7: Preventing Misbehavior/ Principios del Capítulo 7: Prevenir la Mala Conducta*

72. **Pay Attention/Ponga Atención:** Mantenga sus ojos y su mente abierta a lo que está pasando. No espere hasta que el niño esté fuera de control para involucrarse en el asunto.

73. **Remember Who the Grown-Ups Are/Recuerde Quien Es el Adulto:** Siempre recuerde que usted es el adulto y que al final usted es responsable de la manera en que termine la situación. El niño no tiene el conocimiento o historia de experiencias que usted tiene y no es posible que lo haga responsable del resultado final.

74. **Keep It Simple/Haga las Cosas Sencillas:** "Tenemos que ser amables con nuestros amigos." "Es hora de tomar una siesta." "Recuerda las reglas." "Manos gentiles." "Pies caminadores."

75. **Blame It on the Rules/Culpe a las Reglas:** "Las reglas de nuestra escuela dicen que tenemos que lavarnos las manos antes de comer."

76. **Shrug/Encoja los Hombros:** Aprenda a encoger los hombros en lugar de discutir. Encoger los hombros significa, "Lo siento, pero así son las cosas—fin de la discusión."

77. **Preparation/Preparación:** Déjele saber a los niños lo que pueden esperar con tiempo de anticipación. "Podemos salir afuera a jugar un juego de ronda por 20 minutos. Después tendremos que regresar y sentarnos rápidamente y tranquilamente."

78. **Hand Gestures/Gestos con las Manos:** Desarrolle gestos con las manos que signifiquen, "Por favor," "Gracias," "Más," "Alto," "Ten cuidado," "Usa tus palabras," y "No."

79. **Cueing/Pistas:** Déle pistas al niño que le ayuden a recordar—con tiempo de anticipación—la actitud que usted está esperando de él.

80. **Switch Gears/Cambio de Direccion:** Cuando algo inesperado ocurra, busque la manera de sacarle provecho a la situación. Por ejemplo, si tienen que esperar por un largo tiempo, propongales que cierren los ojos y pongan atención a lo que puedan escuchar, o que miren alrededor y encuentren algo que nunca antes habían notado. A este principio también se le llama "El Principio Plan B." Cuando su plan A no funciona, es hora de hacer un plan B más interesante de lo que el plan A hubiera sido.

81. **Do the Unexpected/Haga lo Inesperado:** Reaccione en una manera sorprendente. ¡Empiece a saltar! Aplauda en un ritmo familiar ("Campanas de Belén") para eliminar la tensión y obtener alguna perspectiva. Es extraordinario como, cuando su cabeza está despejada, puede pensar mejor y decidir como manejar la situación de una manera más racional.

82. **Thinking/Piense:** Tómese su tiempo para pensar en las opciones que tiene. Considere el resultado. ¿Será positivo? ¿Cómo quiere que termine esto?

83. **Satiation/Saciedad:** Permita que la conducta continue (si no es peligrosa, destructiva, vergonzosa, o un impedimento para su aprendizaje) hasta que el niño se canse de hacerlo.

Principles in Chapter 8: Creating Solutions to Common Behavior Challenges/Principios del Capítulo 8: Crear Soluciones a Problemas de Comportamiento Comunes

84. **Nip It in the Bud/Atájelo en el Princípio:** Cuando vea a un niño haciendo algo peligroso, destructivo, o vergonzoso (para usted o para él mismo), tome acción inmediata. No deje que la conducta continue, esperando que desaparezca por sí sola. Puede ser que hasta una seña con la mano sea suficiente. También puede susurrar una palabra en código, por ejemplo, "luz roja," que siempre significa "Détente ahora mismo!" Puede acercarse al niño, tomarlo de la mano, y moverlo a otro lugar de la manera menos reforzante posible. Esto significa que aún cuando se acerca al niño o lo mueve, no tiene que hacer contacto de vista o hablar con él.

85. **Use Actions Instead of Words/Use Acciones en Lugar de Palabras:** No diga nada. Cuando el niño diga algo inapropiado o dañino, en lugar de contestar, deje que las palabras "se queden en el aire." Retírese o tómelo de la mano y muévalo a otro lugar. Déle la oportunidad de "escuchar" lo que acaba de decir. Muchas veces, él hará el esfuerzo por "auto-correjirse" o pedir disculpas.

86. **Divide and Conquer/Divida y Conquiste:** Separe a los niños que están reforzando su conducta el uno al otro. Ponga un adulto en medio de los dos niños cuando estén en circulo en la alfombra.

87. **Stay Detached Emotionally/No Haga Enlaces Emocionales:** Mantenga su atención en su objectivo, con su vista en su meta (auto-disciplina) y no deje que el niño

lo "enganche" emocionalmente—en otras palabras, no tome su comportamiento como cosa personal.

88. **Take a Break/Tómese un Descanso:** Deje que el niño se "tome un descanso" y que piense en lo que podría haber hecho diferente que hubiera funcionado mejor o que hubiera sido mas provechoso. Asígnele un lugar a donde él pueda ir hasta que se sienta listo para regresar y comportarse de una manera más productiva. Este puede ser un lugar cómodo y tranquilo que usted ha creado en su casa o en su salón de clases. Un reloj automático puede ayudar. El niño puede determiner cuanto tiempo necesita para reflexionar, reorientarse, y calmarse. El niño tiene el control en esta situación. Él puede decidir cuando se siente listo para regresar al grupo y intentar otra vez.

89. **The Timer Says It's Time/El Reloj Automático Dice Que Ya Es Hora:** Ajuste el reloj automático para hacer la hora de transición más fácil. "Cuando suene el reloj, será hora de que guarden los libros." "Tenemos que formarnos para comer en cinco minutos." El darle la oportunidad al niño de decidir cuanto tiempo necesita para alistarse, es una buena idea: "Es normal que estés irritado. ¿Cuánto tiempo necesitas?" Después, déle permiso de retirarse del grupo y déjelo ajustar el reloj automatico según lo necesite. También puede darle una opción al niño (y ajustar el reloj) cuando es necesario que el niño haga algo que no quiere hacer, "¿Quieres juntar los bloques/darle el carro a Susana/compartir la computadora en un minuto o dos?"

90. **Get Support from Another Person/Obtenga el Apoyo de Otra Persona:** Pídale a alguien que le ayude a reforzar actitudes positivas.

91. **Change of Environment/Cambie el Ambiente:** Si usted no puede parar la mala conducta de los niños, llévelos a otro salón o lugar. (Llévelos para afuera).

92. **Wait Until Later/Déjelo Para Después:** "Hablaremos de esto a las 2:00. Los dos necesitamos tiempo para calmarnos y pensar." Después podemos reunirnos con el niño tranquilamente y decirle, "Vamos a hablar de lo que pasó. ¿Cuál podría haber sido una mejor opción?"

93. **Write a Contract/Haga un Contrato por Escrito:** Siéntese con el niño después de que la emoción negativa haya desaparecido y que se haya comportado apropiadamente, y juntos escriban un contrato de conducta para el futuro. Asegúrese de dejarlo aportar su opinión. Después, firmen el contrato. (Esto funciona con niños mayores.)

94. **Collect Data/Acumule Datos:** Mantenga un registro escrito de la frecuencia de malas conductas. Registre los antecedentes y las consecuencias. Busque patrones de repetición que le puedan dar pistas de posibles razones, situaciones, y/o soluciones.

95. **ABC/ACC:** Aprenda a pensar en terminos ACC (antecedente, comportamiento, y consequencias). ¿Qué estaba pasando antes de que la conducta ocurriera y qué pasó después, como resultado de esa conducta?

Principles in Chapter 9: Collaborating with Families/ Principios del Capítulo 9: Colaborando con las Familias

96. **Chill Out/Relájate:** ¡No es un gran problema! No hagas de un grano de arena una montaña. Esto también pasará.

97. **Other Shoe/El Otro Zapato:** Mire la situación desde el punto de vista de la familia. ¿Como se sentiría usted si "el zapato estuviera en el otro pie?" ¿Que si usted fuera el padre? ¿Qué le gustaría que el maestro le dijera acerca de su hijo?

98. **Common Sense/Sentido Común:** Use su sentido común. ¿Es esto razonable? ¿Está el niño con quien estoy trabajando listo para esta lección o reto? ¿Es lo que estoy pidiendo o esperando apropiado para su edad/desarrollo? ¿Es el niño capaz de hacer lo que le pido, o le causará frustración y desaliento? Mantenga una actitud flexible para adaptarse a las necesidades de los niños, y no espere perfección. Utilice diferentes maneras de explicar los conceptos y procedimientos. Sea paciente y siempre ayude al niño a experimentar lo que es tener éxito.

99. **Partner/Co-Worker/Compañero de Trabajo:** Apoye la manera en que su compañero de trabajo maneja la situación. Si usted no está de acuerdo, retírese y déjelo terminar. También es una buena idea el consultar con su compañero de trabajo antes de hablar con un padre de familia acerca de algún problema en particular. De esta manera evitarán dar mensajes diferentes. Es necesario que se presenten como una unidad.

100. **Human/Humano:** Recuerde que al igual que nosotros, los niños también tienen sentimientos. Es por el bien de todos tratar a los niños en nuestro cuidado tan bien o mejor que como tratamos a los niños de los que no somos responsables. Por el hecho de que hemos tenido la oportunidad de llegar a conocerlos muy bien, tenemos la obligación de velar por su bien.

101. **Bake a Cake/Hagan un Pastel:** Cuando todo lo demás fracase, hagan un pastel juntos (y cómanselo cuando se enfrie). Es una excelente manera de mantenerse conectados y construir felices recuerdos. Este principio nos recuerda que necesitamos tomarnos un tiempo para disfrutar nuestro tiempo juntos y agradecer por las oportunidades que se nos presentan cada día. También es sensato buscar oportunidades para celebrar nuestros logros y agradecerle a las personas que nos han ofrecido estas inolvidables experiencias. No hay límites en cuanto a expresarles gratitud y reconocimiento a las otras personas en nuestras vidas quienes nos han ayudado a lo largo de la vida.